# Natural Language Processing for Prolog Programmers

# Natural Language Processing for Prolog Programmers

*Michael A. Covington*

*Artificial Intelligence Programs*
*The University of Georgia*
*Athens, Georgia*

PRENTICE HALL, Englewood Cliffs, New Jersey 07632

**Library of Congress Cataloging-in-Publication Data**

Covington, Michael A.
   Natural language processing for Prolog programmers /
Michael A. Covington.

     p.  cm.
   Includes bibliographical references and index.
   ISBN 0-13-629213-5
   1. Prolog (Computer program language)  2. Natural language
processing (Computer science)  I. Title.
QA76.73.P76C67  1994
005.13′3—dc20     92-42362
          CIP

Acquisitions editor: *Marcia Horton*
Production editor: *Irwin Zucker*
Prepress buyer: *Linda Behrens*
Manufacturing buyer: *David Dickey*
Supplements editor: *Alice Dworkin*
Copy editor: *Robert Lentz*
Cover design: *Maureen Eide*
Cover illustration: *Melody Covington*
Editorial assistant: *Dolores Mars*

© 1994 by Prentice-Hall, Inc.
A Simon & Schuster Company
Englewood Cliffs, New Jersey 07632

The author and publisher of this book have used their best efforts in preparing this book. These efforts include the development, research, and testing of the theories and programs to determine their effectiveness. The author and publisher make no warranty of any kind, expressed or implied, with regard to these programs or the documentation contained in this book. The author and publisher shall not be liable in any event for incidental or consequential damages in connection with, or arising out of, the furnishing, performance, or use of these programs.

Printed in the United States of America

10  9  8  7  6  5  4  3  2  1

ISBN 0-13-629213-5

Prentice-Hall International (UK) Limited, *London*
Prentice-Hall of Australia Pty. Limited, *Sydney*
Prentice-Hall Canada Inc., *Toronto*
Prentice-Hall Hispanoamericana, S.A., *Mexico*
Prentice-Hall of India Private Limited, *New Delhi*
Prentice-Hall of Japan, Inc., *Tokyo*
Simon & Schuster Asia Pte. Ltd., *Singapore*
Editora Prentice-Hall do Brasil, Ltda., *Rio de Janeiro*

SOLI DEO GLORIA

# Contents

## Appendices

# Preface

Natural language processing (NLP) presents a serious problem to the would-be student: there is no good way to get into it. Most of the literature presumes extensive knowledge of both linguistics and computer programming, but few people have expertise in both fields.

This book is designed to fill the gap. It is meant for computer science students and working programmers who know Prolog reasonably well but have little or no background in linguistics. I wrote it for my own course at the University of Georgia. Others will, I hope, find it suitable for a one-semester undergraduate or graduate course.

Throughout the book, I assume that NLP is an area of applied linguistics. Thus an important goal is to present lots of applicable linguistic theory. I also assume that NLP is distinct from, though related to, knowledge representation. Both of these assumptions contrast with older approaches, in which NLP was viewed primarily as a knowledge-representation problem to which linguistic theory was only marginally relevant.

Judge this book by what it contains, not by what it leaves out. This is first and foremost a book of *techniques*. It must necessarily concentrate on problems for which there are widely accepted solutions that lend themselves to implementation in Prolog. It is not a comprehensive handbook of NLP. Nonetheless, I have covered a wider range of topics than is usual in books on NLP in Prolog.

In a one-semester course it is not necessary to cover the whole book. The core of the material is in Chapters 1, 2, and 3, after which one can proceed to any of the subsequent chapters (except that Chapter 8 depends on Chapter 7). Appendix A presents a review of Prolog that may be needed, in whole or in part, by some classes or some individuals.

As befits an advanced text, many of the exercises are somewhat open-ended. Exercises marked **for discussion** are those where considerable disagreement about the correct answer is possible; **project** denotes exercises requiring extended work.

The computer programs in this book should run under any "Edinburgh-compatible" Prolog implementation. They have been tested under Quintus Prolog, ALS Prolog, Arity Prolog, LPA Prolog (marketed in the United States as Quintus DOS Prolog), and Expert Systems Limited Prolog–2 (which requires ': - `state(token_class,_,dec10).`' added at the beginning of each program). These programs do not run in Turbo Prolog, which is a radically different language, nor in Colmerauer's Prolog II or Prolog III languages.

Many people have helped me refine the material presented here. I am particularly indebted to all the students who have ever taken CS 857 at the University of Georgia, especially Martin Volk and Xilong Chen; to Bob Stearns, Donald Nute, and Richard O'Keefe, who gave me detailed feedback; and to my wife Melody and daughters Cathy and Sharon, who patiently endured lots of busy evenings and weekends. I would also like to thank the reviewers: Stan C. Kwasny, Washington University; Monagur N. Muraldharan, University of Iowa; Gordon Novak, University of Texas-Austin; and Douglas Metzler, University of Pittsburgh.

I am always interested in hearing from readers with questions or suggestions for improving the book. The University of Georgia intends to make the computer programs from this book (but not the answers to exercises) available by anonymous FTP from `ai.uga.edu`; they are, of course, also on a diskette available from Prentice Hall.

*Michael A. Covington*
*Athens, Georgia*
*March 1993*

# Natural Language Processing for Prolog Programmers

# CHAPTER 1

# Natural Language

## 1.1 WHAT IS NLP?

Natural language processing (NLP) is the use of computers to understand human (natural) languages such as English, French, or Japanese. By "understand" we do not mean that the computer has humanlike thoughts, feelings, and knowledge. We mean only that the computer can recognize and use information expressed in a human language. Some practical applications for NLP include the following:

- English as a command language—that is, the use of human languages in place of the artificial languages presently used to give commands to computers.
- Databases and computer help systems that accept questions in English.
- Automatic translation of scientific and technical material and simple business communications from one human language to another.
- Automatic construction of databases from texts of a technical nature, such as equipment trouble reports or medical case reports.

All of these applications already exist in prototype form. Some of them are in commercial use—for example, a computer program regularly translates weather reports from English into French in Canada (Thouin 1982).

These applications are successful because they don't require the computer to know much about the real world. Database programs simply use English to represent information they would otherwise represent in some other form. Translation programs take advantage of the fact that technical texts seldom refer to anything outside a well-defined area of knowledge. It would be much harder to get computers to understand poetry, fiction, or humor, because understanding these kinds of material requires extensive human experience and knowledge of the real world.

Successful NLP, then, depends on putting limits on the need for outside knowledge and human experience. It also depends on two other things.

First, NLP depends on cheap computer power. Here the advent of powerful microcomputers in the 1980s has made a big difference. Previously, NLP was so expensive that people would accept only perfect results, which were never achieved. That situation has changed. Machine translation, for instance, is making a comeback. Imperfect translations may not be worth $1000 a page, but if they can be had for 10 cents a page, people will find plenty of uses for them.

Second, and even more important, NLP depends on exact knowledge of how human languages work—and right now we don't know enough. Until recently, languages were studied almost exclusively for the purpose of teaching them to other human beings. The principles that underlie *all* human languages were (rightly, for the purpose) ignored. The science of linguistics is only a few decades old, and there is still no consensus about some of the most basic facts. This sometimes comes as a shock to computer programmers who expect complete descriptions of human languages to be available off-the-shelf.

This chapter will survey the scientific study of human language, with an emphasis on basic concepts and terminology that will be used in subsequent chapters.

**Exercise 1.1.0.1**

List several reasons why weather reports are especially easy for computers to process.

**Exercise 1.1.0.2**

Give an example of an ordinary English sentence whose meaning is quite unclear in isolation, but perfectly clear when heard in the appropriate context.

**Exercise 1.1.0.3   (for discussion)**

Under what circumstances would you be willing to use an imperfect, machine-generated translation of a foreign-language paper or document? Under what circumstances would it be dangerous to do so?

## 1.2 LANGUAGE FROM A SCIENTIFIC VIEWPOINT

On many points linguists *do* agree. Here are some of the most important.

First, LANGUAGE IS FORM, NOT SUBSTANCE. That is, a language is not a set of utterances or behaviors—it is the underlying system of rules (regularities) that the behaviors follow.

Another way to say this is to distinguish between the speaker's COMPETENCE (the system) and his or her PERFORMANCE (the observable behavior). This distinction recognizes that accidental mispronunciations, interrupted sentences, and the like, are not really instances of the language that the person is speaking; instead, they are deviations from it.

Second, language is ARBITRARY. A language is a set of symbols which people agree to use in specific ways. There is no deep reason why the word for 'chair' should be *chair* in English, *chaise* in French, *Stuhl* in German, and so forth. These words just happen to have these meanings. If you decided you wanted to call a chair a table, this would be "wrong" only in the sense that you would not be cooperating with other speakers of English.

Third, language is DISCRETE (digital), not continuous (analog). That is, languages rely on symbols that are sharply distinct, not positions on a continuum. For example, if you make a sound that is physically between *a* and *e,* speakers of English will hear it as either *a* or *e,* or else they will ask you which sound you meant. They will take it for granted you meant one sound or the other.

Similarly, if you see a color intermediate between red and orange, you can call it *red* or you can call it *orange,* or you can even use both words in some combination, but you cannot normally make up a word whose pronunciation is a physical mixture of the pronunciations *red* and *orange.* You have to choose one or the other.

Fourth, all human languages use DUALITY OF PATTERNING, in which words are strings of sounds, and utterances are strings of words. The words have meaning; the sounds, by themselves, do not. A complex word such as *dogcatcher* can be divided into meaningful units such as *dog, catch,* and *er,* but each of these is a string of smaller units that have no meaning.

Fifth, ALL LANGUAGES ARE ABOUT EQUALLY COMPLICATED, except for size of vocabulary. Primitive cultures do not have simpler languages, nor are ancient languages simpler than modern ones.

Languages change constantly, but each change is a trade-off. Simplifying the sound system may complicate the system of verb forms, or vice versa. Often, a language evolves in a particular direction for thousands of years; for example, the languages descended from Latin have gradually lost the noun-case system. But other languages, such as Finnish, are evolving in the opposite direction; the noun cases of Finnish are getting more complex. There are no simple ways to predict what the languages of the future will be like.

Sixth, EVERYONE SPEAKS HIS OR HER OWN LANGUAGE. My English is not entirely the same as your English, though it is probably very close. Because of the way language is learned, slight differences between individuals, and large differences between societal groups, are inevitable.

This point is worth emphasizing, because some people think that only the most prestigious, educated dialect of a language is "real" and that people who speak other dialects simply can't talk (or even think) very well. The truth is that every variety of a language has definite rules of grammar, but the rules vary from dialect to dialect.

**Exercise 1.2.0.1**

Does tone of voice in English follow the principle of discreteness? Explain and cite evidence for your conclusion.

**Exercise 1.2.0.2**

Suppose someone claims that there is no duality of patterning in the Chinese language because the written symbols stand for whole words. How would you answer this claim?

**Exercise 1.2.0.3**

The sounds of *w* and *wh* have become the same in English as spoken in England and most of the United States; they remain distinct in Scotland and the Deep South.

On the whole, does this change simplify the language or complicate it? In what ways does it make English easier to speak or understand? In what ways does it make it harder? Point out a pair of words that have become harder to distinguish as a result of this sound change.

## 1.3 LANGUAGE AND THE BRAIN

Speaking languages is a distinctively human activity. So is playing checkers. Why, then, is there a science of linguistics but not a science of checkerology?

The answer is that there is good evidence that the human brain is specially structured for language, but not for checkers. When people play checkers they are merely using mental abilities that they also use for many other purposes, but this is not the case with language.

The evidence comes from two main sources. The first is the study of brain injuries. There are specific areas of the brain which, when injured, impair a person's use of language in specific ways. Damage to one area affects the ability to construct sentences; damage to another area affects word recognition; and so forth. To a surprising extent, corresponding parts of the brain have corresponding functions in all individuals. By contrast, there is of course no specific area of the brain devoted to checker-playing, and brain injuries that stop a person from playing checkers while leaving the rest of his or her mental abilities intact are rare or nonexistent.

The second kind of evidence comes from language acquisition. All children learn the language of the people around them, whether or not anyone makes any effort to teach them how to talk. This learning takes place in definite stages and is quite independent of the general intelligence of the child; even mentally retarded children learn exactly the language to which they are exposed, though they learn it more slowly. It appears, then, that acquiring a native language is like learning to walk—it is a matter of activating structures in the brain that are pre-programmed for the purpose, rather than learning information from scratch. Cook (1988, ch. 3) discusses this issue in detail.

**Exercise 1.3.0.1    (for discussion)**

All known languages have duality of patterning (defined in Section 1.2). Does this fact constitute evidence that the brain is pre-programmed for language? Why or why not?

## 1.4 LEVELS OF LINGUISTIC ANALYSIS

The structure of any human language divides up naturally into five levels: PHONOLOGY (sound), MORPHOLOGY (word formation), SYNTAX (sentence structure), SEMANTICS (meaning), and PRAGMATICS (use of language in context). The levels do, of course, interact to some extent. This section will survey the five levels and define many commonly used terms.

### 1.4.1 Phonology

Phonology is the study of how sounds are used in language. Every language has an "alphabet" of sounds that it distinguishes; these are called its PHONEMES, and each phoneme has one or more physical realizations called ALLOPHONES.[1] Consider for example the *t* sounds in the words *top* and *stop*. They are physically different; one of them is accompanied by a puff of air and the other isn't. (Pronounce both words with your hand in front of your mouth to see which is which.) Yet in English these two sounds are allophones of the same phoneme, because the language does not distinguish them. Other languages, such as Hindi, make a distinction between these two sounds.

From the NLP point of view, the main challenge in phonology is that sound waves are continuous but phonemes are discrete. In order to understand speech, a computer must segment the continuous stream of speech into discrete sounds, then classify each sound as a particular phoneme. This is a complicated problem in pattern recognition.

One difficulty is that consecutive sounds overlap. In the word *man,* the *a* and the *n* are almost completely simultaneous. (A pure *a* followed by a pure *n* would sound unnatural.) In the word *bit,* the *b* and the *t* are almost completely silent; they are recognized by their effect on the *i* between them. The influence of adjacent sounds on each other is called COARTICULATION.

Another difficulty is that speech varies from one person to another and even from occasion to occasion with the same speaker. Some New Yorkers pronounce *pat* exactly the way some Texans pronounce *pet.* This is one of the reasons speech-recognition systems have to be 'trained' for the speech of a particular person.

SPEECH SYNTHESIS, the creation of speech by computer, is considerably easier than speech recognition. A synthesizer's most important task is to simulate coarticulation. This is usually done by providing several allophones for each phoneme, each to be used when a different kind of phoneme is adjacent. Recognizable speech has been generated by this method since the 1960s.

The hardest part of speech synthesis is INTONATION (tone of voice). The buzzing, robotlike sound of cheap synthesizers is due to the fact that they have no intonation; the voice always stays at the same pitch. More sophisticated synthesizers try to model realistic intonation. The best synthesized English that I have heard sounded quite lifelike;

---

[1]Halle (1959) showed that classical phonemic theory misses some generalizations, and more modern theories of phonology do not refer to phonemes as such. But the classical phoneme remains a useful working approximation, particularly for speech synthesis.

it sounded like a person who had a cold (because the nasal sounds were not quite perfect) and a slight Swedish accent (because the intonation was not quite right, either). Algorithms are being developed that calculate intonation from sentence structure.

Technologically, computer speech is quite separate from the rest of natural language processing, and this book will not treat it further. [For the basics see Denes and Pinson (1963), which is much more relevant than the date suggests; then, for in-depth technical coverage, see O'Shaughnessy (1987).] Computer speech relies heavily on waveform analysis and pattern recognition, while computational morphology, syntax, semantics, and pragmatics rely on symbolic programming and automated reasoning.

**Exercise 1.4.1.1**

People whose native language is Spanish often have trouble distinguishing the sounds of *b* and *v* in English. What does this tell you about the phonemes of Spanish?

**Exercise 1.4.1.2**

Would a speech synthesizer designed for English be able to speak French or Chinese? Explain.

## 1.4.2 Morphology

Morphology is word formation. Every language has two kinds of word formation processes: INFLECTION, which provides the various forms of any single word (such as singular *man* and plural *men*, present *runs* and past *ran*), and DERIVATION, which creates new words from old ones. For example, the creation of *dogcatcher* from *dog, catch,* and *–er* is a derivational process.

Unfortunately, the distinction between inflection and derivation is often unclear; we don't know precisely what we mean by "different words" versus "different forms of the same word."

One guideline is that only derivation, not inflection, can introduce an unpredictable change of meaning. That is, derivation produces words which are listed separately in a speaker's mental dictionary (LEXICON) and can thus have meanings that are not predictable from their parts.

Consider *dogcatcher.* You may know what *dog* and *catch* mean, but this does not tell you that a *dogcatcher* is a public official rather than, say, a machine or a trained tiger. The word *dogcatcher* means more than just "something that catches dogs." Thus we know that it is created derivationally.

Another guideline is that derived forms are often missing—that is, you have to learn whether or not a derived form actually exists—while inflected forms are almost never missing (nonexistent). Every English verb has a past tense; that's inflection. Some adjectives form nouns ending with *ity* (such as *divine : divinity*); others don't, and there's no way to predict in advance whether any particular adjective will take *ity*; that's derivation.

But the catch is that derivation *can* be almost as regular as inflection. The English suffix *ness* behaves very regularly, forming nouns from practically all adjectives, such as *goodness, badness, blueness,* etc., from *good, bad,* and *blue.* There is nothing unpredictable about the words thus created. Still, we call this process derivational because it creates words of one category (nouns) from words of another category (verbs).

Inflection in English is much simpler than derivation. An English verb typically has only a few forms (such as *catch, catches, caught, catching*), and a noun has only two forms (*dog, dogs*). Most of these are formed by very regular rules, but a few are irregular (we say *caught* rather than *catched*).

Contrast this with Latin, where every verb has hundreds of forms, such as *capio* 'I catch', *capis* 'you catch', *cepi* 'I have caught', *cepisset* 'he might have caught'. Latin also inflects nouns to indicate their position in the sentence; 'dog' is *canis* if it is the subject but *canem* if it is the direct object. Russian, Japanese, Finnish, and many other languages have inflectional systems that are equally complex.

The simplicity of English inflection has led NLP researchers to neglect morphology. If other languages are to be processed effectively, adequate computational models of morphology will have to be developed. We will return to this topic in Chapter 9.

### Exercise 1.4.2.1

Say whether each of the following word formations is inflectional or derivational, and give the reason for your conclusion.

   **(a)** *observed* from *observe*
   **(b)** *observation* from *observe*
   **(c)** *dogs* from *dog*
   **(d)** *high school* from *high* and *school*

### Exercise 1.4.2.2    (for discussion)

Briefly describe the morphology of a foreign language you have studied, and compare it to English.

### 1.4.3 Syntax

Syntax, or sentence construction, is the lowest level at which human language is constantly creative. People seldom create new speech sounds or new words. But everyone who speaks a language is constantly inventing new sentences that he or she has never heard before.

This creativity means that syntax is quite unlike phonology or morphology. A good way to describe the sounds or word-formation processes of a language is to simply make a list of them. But there is no way to make a list of the sentence structures of a language—there are too many. In fact, if there is no limit on sentence length, the number of sentence structures is demonstrably infinite.

Noam Chomsky (1957) was the first to make this point. He introduced GENERATIVE GRAMMAR, which describes sentences by giving rules to construct them rather than by listing the sentences or their structures directly. For example, the rules

$$
\begin{array}{rcl}
sentence & \rightarrow & noun\ phrase + verb\ phrase \\
noun\ phrase & \rightarrow & determiner + noun \\
verb\ phrase & \rightarrow & verb + noun\ phrase \\
determiner & \rightarrow & \text{the} \\
determiner & \rightarrow & \text{a} \\
noun & \rightarrow & \text{dog} \\
noun & \rightarrow & \text{cat} \\
verb & \rightarrow & \text{chased} \\
verb & \rightarrow & \text{saw}
\end{array}
$$

generate a number of sentences, among them this one:

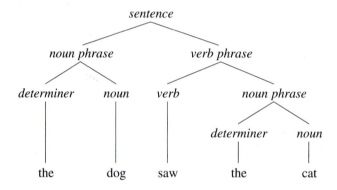

Rules of this type have become standard not only in linguistics, but also in computer science and especially in compiler development. Crucially, a finite set of rules can describe an infinite number of sentences. We will return to this point in Chapters 3 and 4.

Recognition of sentence structure by computer is called PARSING. To parse a sentence the computer must match it up with the rules that generate it. This can be done either TOP-DOWN or BOTTOM-UP. A top-down parser starts by looking for a sentence, then looks at the rules to see what a sentence can consist of. A bottom-up parser starts by looking at the string of words, then looks at the rules to see how the words can be grouped together. The best parsers use a combination of the two approaches (see Chapter 6).

Parsing of English has been studied extensively, and some NLP researchers consider it practically a solved problem. The issue today is what is the *best* way of parsing English, not whether there *is* a way. Parsing of other languages has not been investigated as thoroughly; most present-day parsing techniques rely on fixed word order and do not work well for languages in which word order is highly variable, such as Latin, Russian, or Finnish.

**Exercise 1.4.3.1**

Use the rules above to generate two more sentences, and draw tree diagrams of their structures.

### 1.4.4 Semantics

Semantics, or meaning, is the level at which language makes contact with the real world. As a field of study, semantics has only recently started to mature. For a long time it was unclear how to describe the meanings of natural-language utterances. Suitable tools have now been provided by mathematical logic and set theory, and since 1970 the study of semantics has made great strides.

The distinction between SENSE (meaning) and REFERENCE is basic. In the sentence

*The president said he hated broccoli.*

the word *president* MEANS 'chief executive of the United States' but REFERS to George Bush. Clearly, *president* could refer to someone else—whoever happened to be president at the time. The sense of a word determines what it *can* refer to; anything that we call *president* has to be a chief executive, unless we change the meaning of the word.

There are many different kinds of reference. In a sentence like *The lion is the king of beasts,* the word *lion* refers to a species, not an individual lion. Reference was studied extensively by medieval logicians (who called it *suppositio*), and their classifications are still sometimes used.

Multiple kinds of reference are particularly a problem with plurals. If I say *the students are wearing sweaters* I mean that each student individually is wearing a sweater, but if I say *the students are numerous* I do not mean that each student is numerous—I mean that the *set* of students is large.

Many words are AMBIGUOUS, i.e., they have more than one meaning. Consider *pen* in the sentence *There is ink in the pen* versus *There are pigs in the pen.* Or think of how many things *pipe* can mean—anything from a flute to a piece of plumbing. Some of the meanings of *pipe* are connected in understandable ways, and some are not. The point is that they are distinct, and in a particular context, the hearer must pick out the right sense for the word, a process called WORD-SENSE DISAMBIGUATION. Human beings are very good at this, but good computer techniques have not yet been developed.

Sentences can be ambiguous, too, either because words within them are ambiguous, or because the sentence has more than one possible structure. A famous example is *I saw the boy with the telescope,* in which *with the telescope* modifies either *the boy* or *saw*—it says either which boy I saw, or how I saw him.

SEMANTIC COMPOSITION is the combining of meanings of words to form the meanings of phrases and sentences. Clearly the meaning of *John loves Mary* is a combination, somehow, of the meanings of *John, loves,* and *Mary.* Just as clearly, however, the meanings are not just piled together in a structureless way; if they were, *John loves Mary* would mean the same thing as *Mary loves John,* and it doesn't.

One way to account for semantic composition is to represent meanings as logical formulas. Some examples:

$$loves(john, mary) \qquad \text{'John loves Mary'}$$
$$(\forall x)crow(x) \rightarrow black(x) \qquad \text{'All crows are black'}$$

LAMBDA NOTATION, which we will meet in Chapter 2, provides a way to encode formulas with information missing, thus:

$$(\lambda x)loves(x, mary) \qquad \text{'loves Mary'}$$
$$(\lambda y)(\lambda x)loves(x, y) \qquad \text{'loves'}$$

This gives us representations for the meanings of words and phrases as well as whole sentences. We will explore this more fully in Chapter 7.

IDIOMS are phrases whose meaning is not predictable from the meanings of the parts. A classic example is *kick the bucket,* which means 'die'. The meanings of idioms are said to be NONCOMPOSITIONAL; idioms have to be listed in the lexicon.

**Exercise 1.4.4.1**

Each of the following sentences is ambiguous. Identify two distinct meanings for each sentence, and say whether the ambiguity is caused by ambiguous words, ambiguous structure, or both.

1. *Students may come into the room.*
2. *I need to ask for books in Spanish.*
3. *Flying planes can be dangerous.*
4. *I detest visiting relatives.*

## 1.4.5 Pragmatics

Pragmatics is the use of language in context. The boundary between semantics and pragmatics is uncertain, and different authors use the terms somewhat differently. In general, pragmatics includes aspects of communication that go beyond the literal truth conditions of each sentence.

Suppose, for example, that while lecturing, I look at a student sitting next to the open door of the classroom and ask, *Can you close the door?* If she just answers *Yes* she's missed the point. My question was implicitly a request. Without knowing the pragmatics of English a person (or a computer) would fail to realize this. Whereas syntax and semantics study sentences, pragmatics studies SPEECH ACTS and the situations in which language is used.

An important concept in pragmatics is IMPLICATURE. The implicature of a sentence comprises information that is not part of its meaning, but would nonetheless be inferred by a reasonable hearer. In the example just mentioned, *Can you open the door?* is, by implicature, a polite request, not just a question; if it were only a question there would be little reason for asking it.

Or suppose that I say:

*I have two children.*

If I have only one child, or none, this is false. If I have three children, my statement is true but (in most contexts) MISLEADING, because it leads a reasonable hearer to infer that I have *only* two. False meanings make a sentence false; false implicatures merely make it misleading.

Unlike the meaning of a sentence, the implicature can be cancelled. Consider the dialogue:

*If you have at least two children you're exempt from military service.*

⋮

*On what ground do you claim exemption?*
*I have two children.*

This is both true and appropriate, in context, when spoken by a father of three.

Implicature was first studied by Grice (1975), who identified a number of MAXIMS (principles) which people follow when making statements, such as "Be relevant" and "Make the strongest statement that is true" (avoid misleading understatements; don't say the temperature is "above freezing" if it is in fact 90°).

Another concern of pragmatics is PRESUPPOSITION. The presuppositions of a statement are the things that must be true in order for the statement to be either true or false.[2] For example, both *The present king of France is bald* and *The present king of France is not bald* presuppose that there is indeed a king of France. If there is no such king, these sentences are neither true nor false.

Like implicatures, presuppositions can be CANCELLED. The basic meaning of a sentence, however, cannot be cancelled. I can say *The present king of France is not bald because there is no king of France,* explicitly doing away with the presupposition that such a king exists. Similarly, I can say *I have two children; in fact I have three,* cancelling the implicature that I have *only* two. But if I try to cancel the basic meaning of a sentence, I contradict myself. English does not allow people to say *I have two children; in fact I have only one.*

Pragmatics also includes the study of DISCOURSE (the way sentences connect together to convey information). Discourse structure is especially important when computers generate natural language text. A human being might say, "The employee with the highest salary is Joe Smith, the CEO." A computer retrieving the same information from a database might construct a boring, wordy monologue such as, "The maximum salary is the salary of Smith. The first name of Smith is Joe. The title of Smith is CEO." Obviously this is not satisfactory. An important but largely unexplored question is how to make computers organize discourse the same way people do.

**Exercise 1.4.5.1**

Distinguish between the basic meaning and the implicature of each of the following utterances. Show how each implicature can be cancelled.

**1.** *Parent to child*: It's bedtime.

---

[2]This is one of several rival definitions; the exact nature of presupposition is still an open question.

**2.** Some of the students passed the course.

**3.** It's hot today—the temperature is over 90°.

## 1.5 WHY USE PROLOG?

Of all the programming languages available today, Prolog may be the most suitable for natural language processing. Here are some reasons.

- Large, complex data structures are easy to build and modify. This makes it easy to represent syntactic and semantic structures, lexical entries, and the like.
- The program can examine and modify itself. This allows use of very abstract programming methods.
- Prolog is designed for knowledge representation and is built around a subset of first-order logic; extensions to this logic are relatively easy to implement.
- A search algorithm, depth-first search, is built into Prolog and is easily used in all kinds of parsers. In fact Prolog also has a built-in, ready-to-use parser (see Chapter 3).
- Unification (pattern matching) is built into Prolog and can be used to build data structures step-by-step in such a way that the order of the steps does not matter.

Lisp shares only the first two of these advantages. Conventional languages such as Pascal and C lack all of them. Of course natural language processing *can* be done in any programming language, but some languages are much easier to use than others.

## 1.6 FURTHER READING

Readers who have not studied linguistics would do well to read Fromkin and Rodman (1988) or Akmajian, Demers, Farmer, and Harnish (1990) for general background. Two comprehensive handbooks are *The Cambridge Encyclopedia of Language* (Crystal 1987) for nonspecialists, and *Linguistics: The Cambridge Survey* (Newmeyer 1988) for in-depth coverage.

Newmeyer (1983, 1986) surveys modern linguistic theory. The first of these is an especially good explanation of the goals of theoretical linguistics (and, implicitly, why theoretical linguists do not produce the ready-to-use descriptions that NLP implementors want). The second traces the development of syntactic theory since 1957. For extensive (but far from complete) accounts of the syntax of English see Radford (1988) and Gazdar et al. (1985). On lexical semantics see Palmer (1981); on semantics and logic, Bach (1989); and on pragmatics, Levinson (1983).

The best survey of natural language processing is Allen (1987), which uses Lisp for examples of implementation. Moyne (1985) is also useful. Smith (1991) gives an especially wide-ranging survey of computers and natural language, including not only NLP, but also text statistics, speech synthesis, and related fields. Winograd (1983) gives an accessible but thorough survey of syntax from a computational point of view; the second volume, to deal with semantics, has not yet been published. Obermeier (1989) surveys commercial applications of NLP.

The leading NLP journal is *Computational Linguistics;* relevant papers also appear in *Literary and Linguistic Computing* and especially in the proceedings of the many Association for Computational Linguistics (ACL) and international COLING conferences. Articles about practical natural-language user interfaces for software often appear in the *International Journal of Man–Machine Studies.* Grosz et al. (1986) reprint a number of classic NLP papers, and there are many relevant articles in the *Encyclopedia of Artificial Intelligence* (Shapiro 1987). Gazdar et al. (1987) give a bibliography of more than 1700 NLP books and papers.

On NLP in Prolog see Pereira and Shieber (1987); Gazdar and Mellish (1989, also available in Lisp and Pop-11 editions); and Gal et al. (1991).

# CHAPTER 2

# Templates and Keywords

## 2.1 TEMPLATE MATCHING

### 2.1.1 ELIZA

In 1950, Alan Turing proposed that a machine should be considered intelligent if a human being, communicating with it by teletype, could not distinguish it from another human being. In 1966, Joseph Weizenbaum published a computer program called ELIZA that seemed to pass Turing's test (admittedly with a different kind of conversation than Turing envisioned) but obviously did not contain humanlike intelligence.

ELIZA carried on a dialogue with its user, in English, in the manner of a psychological counselor. Figure 2.1 shows a typical dialogue (from Weizenbaum 1966). ELIZA was so convincing that people willingly told it their troubles and asked Weizenbaum to go away so they could converse in private. Psychiatrists even thought it was a practical way of administering therapy. Weizenbaum was alarmed at this; far from a triumph of artificial intelligence, he considered ELIZA to be evidence of how easy it is to deceive people with computers.

After all, ELIZA did not "understand" much of its input, if "understanding" means responding to the information content. ELIZA merely recognized certain patterns of words and gave appropriate "canned" responses. For example, if the user typed *You are X*, ELIZA could respond *What makes you think I am X*, where *X* is any adjective. Any

```
Men are all alike.
IN WHAT WAY
They're always bugging us about something or other.
CAN YOU THINK OF A SPECIFIC EXAMPLE
Well, my boyfriend made me come here.
YOUR BOYFRIEND MADE YOU COME HERE
He says I'm depressed much of the time.
I AM SORRY TO HEAR YOU ARE DEPRESSED
It's true. I am unhappy.
DO YOU THINK COMING HERE WILL HELP YOU NOT TO BE UNHAPPY
I need some help, that much seems certain.
WHAT WOULD IT MEAN TO YOU IF YOU GOT SOME HELP
Perhaps I could learn to get along with my mother.
TELL ME MORE ABOUT YOUR FAMILY
My mother takes care of me.
WHO ELSE IN YOUR FAMILY TAKES CARE OF YOU
My father.
YOUR FATHER
You are like my father in some ways.
WHAT RESEMBLANCE DO YOU SEE
You are not very aggressive but I think you don't want me to
  notice that.
WHAT MAKES YOU THINK I AM NOT VERY AGGRESSIVE
You don't argue with me.
WHY DO YOU THINK I DON'T ARGUE WITH YOU
You are afraid of me.
DOES IT PLEASE YOU TO BELIEVE I AM AFRAID OF YOU
My father is afraid of everybody.
WHAT ELSE COMES TO MIND WHEN YOU THINK OF YOUR FATHER
Bullies.
DOES THAT HAVE ANYTHING TO DO WITH THE FACT THAT YOUR
  BOYFRIEND MADE YOU COME HERE
```

**Figure 2.1**    A sample session with ELIZA. The machine's responses are in upper case.

sentence containing words like *mother* would get a reply such as *Tell me more about your family.* And a sentence containing nothing that ELIZA recognized would evoke a response such as *Tell me more* or *Go on.*

**Exercise 2.1.1.1**

> If your computer has the Gnu Emacs editor, you can play with a somewhat updated version of ELIZA. Simply get into Emacs and type: *Esc* x doctor *Return.*

## 2.1.2 Other Template Systems

ELIZA was an example of a TEMPLATE SYSTEM or PATTERN-MATCHING SYSTEM, a technology that is still useful today.  (A TEMPLATE is a pattern such as *I am X.*) What

ELIZA proved is that templates are powerful enough for quite realistic natural-language dialogue.

Several other classic AI programs used templates. One of these was SIR (Semantic Information Retrieval) by Bertram Raphael (1968). SIR could do enough logical reasoning to answer questions such as, "Every person has two hands. Every hand has two fingers. Joe is a person. How many fingers does Joe have?"

Another was Bobrow's STUDENT, which could solve high-school-level mathematical problems stated in English. A noteworthy feature of STUDENT is that it used recursive templates. For example, the template *if X then Y* allowed whole sentences in place of *X* and *Y* and would apply whole-sentence templates to them. Bobrow (1968) describes the original system and Norvig (1991) reimplements it in Common Lisp.

SIR, STUDENT, and their kin were developed mainly to study the information content of natural language, not to model the syntax. Nobody claims that templates are a realistic model of the way the human mind processes language. They are, however, a quick way to extract useful information from natural-language input, adequate for many practical user-interface applications. One modern example is HAL, the English-language command interface for the Lotus 1-2-3 spreadsheet program. Though its internal workings have not been made public, HAL shows the rigidity of syntax that is typical of a template system (see Petzold 1987).

## 2.2 DOS COMMANDS IN ENGLISH

### 2.2.1 Recipe for a Template System

In this section we will develop a template system that lets the user type commands to MS-DOS (PC-DOS) in English. The same could be done just as easily for UNIX or another operating system. See Lane (1987) for a different DOS-in-English system written in Turbo Prolog.

Like most template systems, ours will translate English into a formal language, in this case DOS command language. The formal language has two important characteristics:

- It is much less expressive than English; many English words and expressions simply cannot be translated into it.
- The human user knows about these restrictions on expressive power and can restrict the English input accordingly. For example, people know that when talking to DOS, it makes sense to say *Show me the BAT files on drive D* but not *Look on my works, ye mighty, and despair.*

This means that the template system can get away with covering only a tiny part of the English language.

The first step in designing a template system is to write down a lot of sample input sentences with the desired translations, then try to find patterns in them. For example:

| | |
|---|---|
| *What files are on drive B?* | ⇒ `dir b:` |
| *Delete all my files.* | ⇒ `erase *.*` |
| *Run the word processor.* | ⇒ `wp` |

Figure 2.2 shows a larger set.

At this stage you may well decide that DOS command language isn't powerful enough. For example, the user can't say *Erase all files older than 1/29/90* because there is no DOS command corresponding to it; the *erase* command does not check the date of a file. This is a separate issue from natural language processing; we'll leave it behind, but you have been warned. The success of any natural-language-driven software depends on whether the software can do what the user wants, not just whether it understands English.

The next step is to write a set of rules to do the translation. These will be of two types:

- SIMPLIFICATION RULES discard unnecessary words and make equivalent words look alike. For example, *display* might get rewritten as *show,* and *the* might get dropped altogether.

- TRANSLATION RULES actually map a template into the formal language, such as `[show,files,on,disk,X]` ⇒ `['dir',X,':']`.

| | | |
|---|---|---|
| *What is on disk A?* | ⇒ | `dir a:` |
| *What is on the disk in drive A?* | ⇒ | `dir a:` |
| *What files are on disk A?* | ⇒ | `dir a:` |
| *What files are there on the disk in drive A?* | ⇒ | `dir a:` |
| (Likewise for any drive.) | | |
| | | |
| *Are there any EXE files on disk A?* | ⇒ | `dir a:*.exe` |
| *Are there any EXE files on the disk in drive A?* | ⇒ | `dir a:*.exe` |
| *What EXE files are there on disk A?* | ⇒ | `dir a:*.exe` |
| *What EXE files are there on the disk in drive A?* | ⇒ | `dir a:*.exe` |
| (Likewise for *BAT files, COM files,* etc.) | | |
| | | |
| *Copy everything from disk A to disk B.* | ⇒ | `copy a:*.* b:` |
| *Copy everything from (the disk in)* | | |
| *drive A to (the disk in) drive B.* | ⇒ | `copy a:*.* b:` |
| *Copy (all) files from ...(etc.)* | ⇒ | `copy a:*.* b:` |
| | | |
| *Copy all BAT files from ...(etc.)* | ⇒ | `copy a:*.bat b:` |

**Figure 2.2**   Some English sentences and their translations into DOS command language.

Simplification rules (Ø denotes the empty string):

| | | |
|---|---|---|
| *the* | ⇒ | *Ø* |
| *is* | ⇒ | *Ø* |
| *are* | ⇒ | *Ø* |
| *there* | ⇒ | *Ø* |
| *any* | ⇒ | *Ø* |
| *disk in drive* | ⇒ | *drive* |
| *disk in* | ⇒ | *drive* |
| *disk* | ⇒ | *drive* |
| *what files* | ⇒ | *files* |
| *what* | ⇒ | *files* |
| *file* | ⇒ | *files* |
| *everything* | ⇒ | *all files* |
| *every* | ⇒ | *all* |

Translation rules:

| | | |
|---|---|---|
| *Files on drive X?* | ⇒ | `dir X:` |
| *X files on drive Y?* | ⇒ | `dir Y:*.X` |
| *Copy all files from drive X to drive Y.* | ⇒ | `copy X:*.* Y:` |
| *Copy all X files from drive Y to drive Z.* | ⇒ | `copy Y:*.X Z:` |

⋮

**Figure 2.3**  Examples of simplification and translation rules.

The purpose of the simplification rules is to reduce the number of translation rules. There's a trade-off; if you put in too many simplification rules, you may lose distinctions that you later on want to preserve. It's common for some of the simplification rules to get dropped as the system becomes more complete.

Figure 2.3 shows simplification and translation rules to handle the sentences in Figure 2.2. Note that every sentence goes through *all* the simplification rules that match any part of it, and then through *one* translation rule (the one that matches the whole sentence).

What about sentences that the system can't recognize? Some of these will be typing errors and the like. Others will be reasonable sentences that you didn't provide for. The appropriate thing to do is store them on a file so that you can come back and modify the system later to handle them.

**Exercise 2.2.1.1**

In addition to the examples in Figure 2.2, write down at least 20 more English sentences and their translations into MS-DOS command language (or the command language of your computer).

**Exercise 2.2.1.2**

Write a set of simplification and translation rules (in any notation you care to use) to handle those sentences. Notice that if you do this intelligently, your rules will also handle many sentences that you didn't originally think of.

## 2.2.2 Implementing Simplification Rules

Simplification rules use templates for *parts* of sentences. For example, the word *everything* gets simplified to *all files* wherever it occurs, and the phrase *what files* is simplified to *files*.

What we need is a way to match simplification rules to the input list. The match can occur anywhere in the list. Accordingly, the program works through the list, word by word, comparing it to all the templates at every point:

```
[copy,files,from,disk,in,drive,a,to,drive,b]   (No match)
     [files,from,disk,in,drive,a,to,drive,b]   (No match)
           [from,disk,in,drive,a,to,drive,b]   (No match)
                [disk,in,drive,a,to,drive,b]   (Matches 'disk in')
```

The next question is how to store the templates. Here open lists come in handy. It's much easier to match [disk,in,drive,a,to,drive,b] with [disk,in|X] than with [disk,in]. The latter would require a special procedure to compare elements one by one; the former can be done by ordinary Prolog unification. Here, then, are a set of simplification rules expressed as open lists:

```
% sr(T1,T2)
%  Simplification rules.

sr([the|X],X).
sr([is|X],X).
sr([are|X],X).
sr([there|X],X).
sr([any|X],X).
sr([disk,in,drive|X],[drive|X]).
sr([disk,in|X],[drive|X]).
sr([disk|X],[drive|X]).
sr([what,files|X],[files|X]).
sr([what|X],[files|X]).
sr([file|X],[files|X]).
sr([everything|X],[all,files|X]).
sr([every|X],[all|X]).
```

That is: [the|X] simplifies to X; [disk,in|X] simplifies to [drive|X]; and so on.

The order of the simplification rules matters because more than one rule can match the same input. For example, *disk in drive A* matches both

$$disk\ in\ drive \Rightarrow drive$$

and

$$disk \Rightarrow drive.$$

If both rules match, the first one should take precedence; thus it must be tried first. Otherwise the result might be *drive in drive A*.

After one simplification rule works on the string, the result gets fed into the simplification rules again. This makes it possible, for example, to simplify *all files* to *every file* and then change *every file* to *everything*. You can even get loops; a loop will happen if there is a rule that changes *every* to *all* and also a rule that changes *all* to *every*. The complete simplification routine looks like this:

```
% simplify(+List,-Result)
%  Applies simplification rules to List giving Result.

simplify(List,Result) :-             % A simp. rule matches
   sr(List,NewList),                 % so apply it and then
   !,                                % try to further simplify
   simplify(NewList,Result).         % the result

simplify([W|Words],[W|NewWords]) :-  % No simp. rule matches
   simplify(Words,NewWords).         % so advance to next word

simplify([],[]).                     % No more words
```

**Exercise 2.2.2.1**

Using `simplify/2` given above, implement all the simplification rules that you developed in Exercise 2.2.1.2.

## 2.2.3 Implementing Translation Rules

Translation rules are relatively simple because each of them is supposed to match the whole list of words:

```
% tr(?Input,?Result)
%  Translation rules.

tr([quit],[quit]).
tr([files,on,drive,X,'?'],['dir ',X,':']).
tr([X,files,on,drive,Y,'?'],['dir ',Y,':*.',X]).
tr([copy,all,files,from,drive,X,to,drive,Y,'.'],
                          ['copy ',X,':*.* ',Y,':']).
```

The output of a translation rule is a list of atoms which, when converted back into character strings and concatenated, will give the appropriate DOS command. (The first of these rules handles the "quit" command that the user will use to exit from the program.)

The procedure that applies the translation rules will simply find a rule that applies to the input, then execute a cut, or complain if no rule is applicable:

```
% translate(-Input,+Result)
%  Applies a translation rule, or complains
%  if no translation rule matches the input.

translate(Input,Result) :-
   tr(Input,Result),
   !.

translate(_,[]) :-
   write('I do not understand.'),
   nl.
```

**Exercise 2.2.3.1**

Implement all the translation rules that you developed in Exercise 2.2.1.2. Make sure these fit together properly with the simplification rules that you have just implemented.

## 2.2.4 The Rest of the System

Once the translation rules have produced a command, the next step is to pass the command to the operating system. How this is done depends on the exact version of Prolog.

The first step in ALS Prolog (which is typical) is to concatenate the atoms into a character string, so that for example ['dir ','a:'] becomes "dir a:". This is simple; just expand each atom into a list of characters, and append the lists:

```
% make_string(+ListOfAtoms,-String)
%  Concatenates a list of atoms giving a string.
%  Example: ['a','b','c'] gives "abc".

make_string([H|T],Result) :-
   name(H,Hstring),
   make_string(T,Tstring),
   append(Hstring,Tstring,Result).

make_string([],[]).

% append(?List1,?List2,?List3)
%  Appending List1 to List2 gives List3.

append([H|T],L,[H|Rest]) :- append(T,L,Rest).
append([],L,L).
```

The complete procedure to pass a command to DOS is:

```
% pass_to_os(+Command)
%  Accepts a command as a list of atoms, concatenates
%  the atoms, and passes the command to the operating system.

pass_to_os([quit]) :- !.

pass_to_os([]) :- !.

pass_to_os(Command) :-
   make_string(Command,S),system(S).
```

Notice that pass_to_os ignores [quit] (the quit command) and [] (the output of an unrecognized command).[1]

    Finally, we're ready to define the main procedure of the template system. Its purpose is to accept sentences from the user and run them through simplify, translate, and pass_to_os in succession. The main loop uses repeat so that execution will continue even if the processing of any particular command fails. Here, then, is the main procedure:

```
% process_commands
%  Repeatedly accepts commands in English,
%  simplifies and translates them,
%  and passes them to the operating system.

process_commands :-
   repeat,
     write('Command: '),
     read_atomics(Words),     % defined in Appendix B
     simplify(Words,SimplifiedWords),
     translate(SimplifiedWords,Command),
     pass_to_os(Command),
     Command == [quit],
   !.
```

The template system is now complete.

---

[1]The equivalent of make_string(Command,S), system(S) in some other Prologs is:

| | |
|---|---|
| Arity Prolog: | concat(Command,S), shell(S) |
| LPA (MS-DOS): | make_string(Command,S), name(C,S), dos(C) |
| ESL Prolog-2: | make_string(Command,S), list(S,C), command(C,32000,display) |
| Quintus (UNIX): | make_string(Command,S), name(C,S), unix(system(C)) |
| Quintus (VMS): | make_string(Command,S), name(C,S), vms(dcl(C)) |

Consult your manual for further guidance.

### Exercise 2.2.4.1

Find out how your Prolog passes commands to the operating system, and get `pass_to_os` working. Verify that

```
?- pass_to_os([dir]).
```

(or the equivalent) works correctly.

### Exercise 2.2.4.2

Modify `pass_to_os` so that it displays the command on the screen before passing it to the operating system.

### Exercise 2.2.4.3

Using your answers to several previous exercises, build a working, though small, template system that translates English sentences into DOS commands.

### Exercise 2.2.4.4

Modify your DOS-in-English system so that if the user types an unrecognized sentence, this sentence is recorded in a file for you to see. (This will enable you to improve the system later, to accommodate more of the sentences that users actually type.)

[Hint: Consult your Prolog manual to find out how to open a file in append mode (i.e., open an already existing file so that you can write at the end).]

### Exercise 2.2.4.5    (project)

Expand your DOS-in-English system so that it becomes a practical (if still modest) piece of software. Modify it in any ways you can think of that will make it more useful. This is a very open-ended project; depending on how much work you choose to do, it could be anything from a weekend assignment to a Ph.D. thesis.

### Exercise 2.2.4.6    (project)

*ELIZA in Prolog.* Implement a version of ELIZA. To do this, you will have to implement:

- A simplifier that can translate *you* to *me* and *me* to *you* without getting into a loop;
- A matching algorithm more powerful than ordinary Prolog unification, so that a variable can match more than one word in a list (for example, `[X,says,that,Y]` should match *my mother says that airplanes are dangerous*);
- A strategy for identifying the most important word in a sentence (for example, *computer* is more important than *mother,* which is more important than *why*), so that if more than one template matches the input, the template that recognizes the most important word can be chosen;
- A way to give different responses to the same question at different times.

Weizenbaum (1966) gives a complete, though disorganized, set of simplification and translation rules for ELIZA; Norvig (1991) describes how to implement ELIZA in Lisp.

**Exercise 2.2.4.7   (project)**

*English grammar and style checking.* Some commonly misused words and phrases can be recognized by a template system. Examples:

- *comprised of* (standard English is *composed of*);
- *inasmuch as, in point of fact, in the area of* (these are grammatical but should usually be replaced by clearer, more direct wordings such as *because, in fact,* or *in*);
- *very* (much overused; should often be deleted);
- *does not only* (a common mistake in the English of people whose native language is German or Scandinavian).

Write a program that will read English documents (business letters, computer documentation, etc.), and point out words and phrases such as these.

## 2.3 KEYWORD ANALYSIS

### 2.3.1 A Time-Honored Approach

An alternative to template matching is KEYWORD ANALYSIS. Instead of matching the whole sentence to a template, a keyword system looks for specific words in the sentence and responds to each word in a specific way.

One of the first keyword systems was that of Blum (1966). Inspired by ELIZA, Blum wrote a program to accept sentences such as

*Copy 1 file from U1 to U2, binary, 556 bpi.*

and convert them into commands for a program that managed magnetic tapes.

Though he took ELIZA as his model, Blum ended up using quite different techniques. He distinguished three kinds of keywords: requests (*list, copy, backspace,* etc.), "qualifiers" that further described the request, such as *binary* or *blocked,* and "quantifiers" (numbers) such as *5 files* or *556 bpi* (= bits per inch). His program simply collected all the requests, qualifiers, and quantifiers in the input and put them together into a properly formed command, paying very little attention to the word order and completely ignoring unrecognized words.

Keyword analysis has been reinvented several times, with slight variations, and keyword systems have had a long and successful history. Unlike template systems, they are not thrown off by slight variations of wording; unrecognized words are simply skipped. Keyword systems are useful in any situation where the input is known to contain certain kinds of information, and other information, if any, can be ignored.

Two prominent keyword systems today are AICorp's Intellect and Symantec's Q&A; Obermeier (1989) lists many others. Both Q&A and Intellect are database query systems and both work very much like the system to be developed later in this chapter. Wallace (1984) describes a much more elaborate keyword system written in Prolog.

## 2.3.2 Database Querying

In this section we will develop a keyword-analysis program to process database queries that are expressed in English. Before doing this, however, we must say a few things about databases.

**Tables and tuples.**   A RELATIONAL DATABASE consists of one or more TABLES such as the following:

| ID number | Name | Birth date | Title | Salary |
|-----------|------|------------|-------|--------|
| 1001 | Doe, John P. | 1947/01/30 | President | 100000 |
| 1002 | Smith, Mary J. | 1960/09/05 | Programmer | 30000 |
| 1003 | Zimmer, Fred | 1957/03/12 | Sales rep | 45000 |
| ⋮ | ⋮ | ⋮ | ⋮ | ⋮ |

The database is a collection of ROWS or RECORDS (lines), each divided into ATTRIBUTES (FIELDS). Each attribute has a name. One specific field—in this case, the ID number—is the KEY or IDENTIFIER; it is unique to each record and can be used to identify the record.

Formally, each record is a TUPLE (an ordered set of a specific number of items), a table is a set of tuples, and each table expresses a RELATION between the values in its tuples. A true relational database can consist of many tables; a FLAT-FILE DATABASE, which is less powerful, consists of one table only. For more on database theory, see Date (1990).

**Queries.**   The main function of a database is to answer QUERIES (requests for information). Database manipulation has a semantics all its own; regardless of the language used, the meanings of most queries will have the form

*Do action A to all records that pass test T.*

For example, if the query is

*Show me all programmers with salaries over 25000.*

then the action is *display* and the tests are *Title = programmer*, *Salary > 25000*.

Most large databases use STRUCTURED QUERY LANGUAGE (SQL) (pronounced "sequel"). In SQL the query just mentioned would be expressed as:

```
SELECT NAME, SALARY FROM TABLE1
   WHERE SALARY > 25000
   AND TITLE = 'PROGRAMMER'
```

In this chapter, however, we will use a database consisting of Prolog facts and construct queries in Prolog. The techniques are very much the same, and we avoid having to learn another language. Several Prolog implementations include the ability to access SQL databases through Prolog queries.

### 2.3.3 A Database in Prolog

In order to experiment with natural-language access to databases, we need a database. We will construct a simple database in Prolog, but it will be designed to act like a single table rather than to use Prolog in the most effective way. In this respect the Prolog system will act as if it were accessing a large database implemented in some other language.

First, the records themselves:

```
employee(1001,'Doe, John P.',[1947,01,30],'President',100000).
employee(1002,'Smith, Mary J.',[1960,09,05],'Programmer',30000).
employee(1003,'Zimmer, Fred',[1957,3,12],'Sales rep',45000).
```

Next, predicates to retrieve the values of the individual attributes, given the key:

```
full_name(ID,N) :- employee(ID,N,_,_,_).
birth_date(ID,B) :- employee(ID,_,B,_,_).
title(ID,T) :- employee(ID,_,_,T,_).
salary(ID,S) :- employee(ID,_,_,_,S).
```

Finally, predicates to do other things to the records—in this case, merely display them and remove them:

```
display_record(ID) :-
    employee(ID,N,B,T,S),
    write([ID,N,B,T,S]),
    nl.

remove_record(ID) :-
    retract(employee(ID,_,_,_,_)).
```

A fully functional database would also have a way to UPDATE (change) the attributes in each record.

**Exercise 2.3.3.1**

Make up a tiny relational (not flat-file) database and implement it in Prolog clauses. Include at least two tables and give an example of a query that does something useful by accessing both tables. Indicate which attribute is the key in each table.

**Exercise 2.3.3.2**

What is the relationship between first-argument indexing (see Appendix A) and the concept of a key in a database?

### 2.3.4 Building a Keyword System

Keyword systems work well for database querying because each important concept associated with the database has a distinctive name. A keyword system responds only to the words that identify fields, values, comparisons, and the like, and ignores all the other words.

Like a template system, the keyword system can have `simplify` and `translate` stages. However, the `simplify` stage is relatively unimportant and is often unnecessary. Its only function is to make synonymous words look alike. There is no need for `simplify` to drop unnecessary words such as *the*, because `translate` will drop all the words it does not recognize.

The `translate` stage does most of the work. The output of `translate` will be a Prolog query that picks out the appropriate records and performs some action on them. We want to act on all the records that pass the test, so we will attempt as many alternative solutions to the query as possible.

The main procedure will therefore look something like this:

```
% process_queries
%  Accepts database queries from the keyboard and
%  executes all solutions to each query.

process_queries :-
   repeat,
     write('Query: '),
     read_atomics(Words),
     % some systems would have a 'simplify' stage here,
     translate(Words,_,Query),
     write(Query), nl,            % for testing
     do_all_solutions(Query),
     Words == [quit],
   !.

% do_all_solutions(+Query)
%  Makes execution backtrack through all solutions to Query.

do_all_solutions(Query) :-
   call(Query),
   fail.

do_all_solutions(_).
```

The anonymous variable in the arguments of `translate` will be explained later.

**Exercise 2.3.4.1**

In `process_queries`, what should `translate` do with the `quit` command? (Don't just say "it should ignore it"; be more specific.)

**Exercise 2.3.4.2**

When `process_queries` terminates, does it succeed or fail?

## 2.3.5  Constructing a Query

From the keyword system's point of view, there are only five kinds of words:

- ACTIONS such as *display, erase, select,* etc. (we may want to supply *display* as the default action for queries that do not name an action);
- TESTS such as *programmer, president, male, female,* etc., each of which requires a specific value in a specific attribute;
- COMPARISONS such as *greater, over, under,* etc., each of which takes two arguments;
- ARGUMENTS of the comparisons, such as *salary* (which retrieves the value of a field) and *25000* (which is a constant); and
- NOISE WORDS, i.e., unrecognized words which can be skipped.

The string of words must be translated into a Prolog query. This is done by working through it, word by word, and adding something to the query for each meaningful word. Assuming the input list is `[show,programmer,salary,over,25000]`, the process should go roughly as follows:

| Word | Query |
|------|-------|
| *show* | `..., display_record(X)` |
| *programmer* | `title(X,programmer), ... display_record(X)` |
| *salary over 25000* | `title(X,programmer), salary(X,Y), Z=25000, Y>Z, display_record(X)` |

Notice that the action goes at the *end* of the query because we don't want it to be executed until all the tests have been fulfilled. All the other tests, however, come at the beginning, roughly in the order in which the human user gave them. Further, the comparison *salary over 25000* translates into three queries (or in any case two), not just one.

Moreover, the variable X, identifying the record to be retrieved, is shared by all the goals in the query. Otherwise there would be nothing to make them all apply to the same record.

We will put the query together by joining the goals with commas. Recall that if x, y, and z are Prolog queries, then so is `(x,y,z)`. The comma is an infix operator and is right associative so that `(x,y,z)` = `(x,(y,z))`. Prolog executes a query of the form `(a,b)` by executing a and then b.

Knowing this, we can write rules to translate words into queries. Specifically, we can define a predicate with a clause for each word that will translate that word and then call the predicate recursively to translate the rest of the list, thus:

```
translate([show|Words],X,(Queries,display_record(X))) :-
    !,
    translate(Words,X,Queries).

translate([programmer|Words],X,(title(X,programmer),Queries)) :-
    !,
    translate(Words,X,Queries).
```

The first of these puts an action at the end of the compound query; the second puts an ordinary test at the beginning. Together these two rules translate

```
[show,programmer,...]
```

into

```
((title(X,programmer),...),display_record(X)
```

where . . . stands for the rest of the list and its translation, respectively.

Any word for which there is no specific translation should be skipped. Together with the cuts in the previous clauses, the following clause takes care of this:

```
translate([_|Words],X,Query) :- translate(Words,X,Query).
```

Finally, what happens at the end of the list? It would be handy if Prolog had a "null" or "empty" query that could serve as the translation of an empty list. Sure enough, there is such a thing—the built-in predicate `true`, which does nothing, but always succeeds. Thus we can write

```
translate([],_,true).
```

and then `translate` will render `[show,programmer]` (with no subsequent words) as:

```
((title(X,programmer),true),display_record(X))
```

It takes less time to execute the redundant `true` in the query than to perform extra checks and avoid putting it there.

**Exercise 2.3.5.1**

Get `translate` working in the form shown. Add at least three more words to its vocabulary and demonstrate that it works correctly.

**Exercise 2.3.5.2**

Will our keyword system need a special routine to discard punctuation marks?

**Exercise 2.3.5.3**

Modify `translate` so that it prints a warning when a word more than five letters long is ignored. (A more sophisticated system might have a list of hundreds of words that it can safely ignore, and print a warning whenever it ignores a word that is not on this list.)

## 2.3.6 Lambda Abstraction

The alert reader will have noticed two things. First, we haven't tackled comparisons and their arguments yet. Second, the above clauses for `translate` contain a mysterious variable X whose only purpose is to get unified with all the variables in the query, so that they all become the same variable. As you might guess, the task of keeping the variables straight gets complicated when we start dealing with arguments of comparisons.

Accordingly, we're going to pull out one of our most powerful tools: LAMBDA ABSTRACTION.

Lambda abstraction (or LAMBDA CALCULUS) may be the most useful technical tool in all of semantics. It was introduced by the logician Alonzo Church (1941) as a way to turn formulas into properties.

In formal logic, *mortal*(*Socrates*) means *Socrates is mortal,* and *mortal*(*Plato*) means *Plato is mortal.* So how do you say simply *mortal?* According to Church, the property of being mortal is expressed by the formula

$$(\lambda x) mortal(x)$$

where $\lambda$ is the Greek letter lambda, and $(\lambda x)$ means that $x$ in the formula is to be supplied as an argument.

Here's a more familiar example. In ordinary mathematics we "define" a function $f$ by writing a formula such as

$$\text{Let } f(x) = 4x + 2.$$

But this is really a definition, not of $f$, but of $f(x)$; the reader is left to assume that the definitions of $f(y)$, $f(z)$, and $f(a + b + c)$ are analogous, with $y$ or $z$ or $a + b + c$ substituted for $x$. If, instead, we say

$$\text{Let } f = (\lambda x) 4x + 2.$$

lambda abstraction makes it explicit that $x$ is not part of the definition, but merely a stand-in for a value to be supplied from elsewhere.

The programming language Lisp uses lambda expressions regularly; in fact it is built around them. A function definition such as

```
(DEFUN F(X) (+ (* 4 X) 2))
```

was written, in the earliest dialect of Lisp, as:

```
(DEFINE F  (LAMBDA (X) (+ (* 4 X) 2)))
```

That is, the definition of F is a lambda expression that says, "Give me a value—I'll call it X—and I'll multiply it by 4, add 2, and give you the result." Then F is the name of this function, and the lambda expression describes the function.

**Exercise 2.3.6.1**

Assuming that *studies(plato, philosophy)* means 'Plato studies philosophy', use lambda abstraction to write expressions that mean:

1. 'studies philosophy'
2. 'Plato studies'
3. 'studies'

**Exercise 2.3.6.2**

What is the result of supplying the argument 200 to the expression $(\lambda q)q^2 - q + 35$? Distinguish supplying the argument from evaluating the expression.

## 2.3.7 Lambdas in Prolog

Now back to the main story. Because Prolog is built around predicates rather than functions, the need for lambda expressions does not arise immediately, and there is no standard notation for them. Nonetheless, they are easy to construct and use. While we're at it, we're going to extend lambda abstraction beyond its original use, and use lambdas to indicate any part of a formula that is supplied from outside, whether or not our intent is to define a function or a property.

To see the need, recall that we defined *programmer* as `title(X,programmer)`, and *show* as `display_record(X)`. In order to translate a query such as *show all programmers,* we need to put the definitions of *show* and *programmer* together in such a way that the X's in them are the same variable. But this isn't easy. The structures `title(X,programmer)` and `display_record(X)` have different principal functors; they don't unify with each other, and there is no easy way to get the X's in them unified together.

At this point we have two options. We could use '`=..`' to decompose terms into lists and then search for the variables in the lists. Or—more simply—we could keep another copy of the variable in an easily accessible place outside the term.

That's where lambda expressions come in. A lambda expression is merely a two-argument term whose arguments are a variable and a term in which that variable can occur. For example:

```
lambda(X,title(X,programmer))
lambda(X,display_record(X))
```

Notice that `lambda` doesn't mean anything in Prolog; it's just an arbitrary functor that I picked. It's also rather long. To be more concise, let's use the character ^ as an infix operator to hold lambda expressions together. Then we can write

```
X ^ title(X,programmer)
X ^ display_record(X)
```

and say that the first of these defines *programmer* and the second defines *show*. In ordinary lambda notation they would be $(\lambda x)title(x, programmer)$ and $(\lambda x)display(x)$, respectively.

Notice that we don't need an op declaration because ^ is already an infix operator. In arithmetic expressions, it denotes exponentiation; in arguments to setof and bagof, it indicates that certain variables are to take on all possible values. Neither of these uses conflicts with the way we are using it here.

Further, ^ is right-associative so that X^Y^f(X,Y) is legal and means X^(Y^ f(X,Y)).[2] That's exactly how lambda notation deals with multiple arguments: "Give me the first argument—I'll call it *X*—and I'll give you a lambda expression that only wants one more argument."

**Exercise 2.3.7.1**

In Prolog, what is the result of unifying [X^green(X),Y^frog(Y)] with [A^B,A^C]?

**Exercise 2.3.7.2**

Define a predicate supply_argument that will take a lambda expression and an argument, and supply that argument to that lambda expression, like this:

```
?- supply_argument(X^green(X),kermit,Result).
Result = green(kermit)
```

Hint: The correct answer is very short.

**Exercise 2.3.7.3**

What is the result of supplying the argument felix to the lambda expression Y^X^ chases(X,Y)?

### 2.3.8 The Complete System

Armed with lambda notation, we can store the definitions of words separately from the translate predicate itself. That's important because now translate needs only four clauses—for actions, tests, comparisons, skipped words, and the empty list—rather than a clause for each word. The clauses for translate are now:

```
% translate(+Words,-Variable,-Query)
%   Translates Words (a list of atoms) into Query
%   (a compound Prolog query to access the database).
%   Variable serves to identify the records being retrieved.
```

---

[2]In Arity Prolog version 4, you cannot write a functor adjacent to a left parenthesis unless that parenthesis introduces its argument list. So instead of ^( you must write ^ ( within formulas.

```
translate([W|Words],X,(Queries,Q)) :-
   action(W,X^Q),
   !,
   translate(Words,X,Queries).

translate([W|Words],X,(Q,Queries)) :-
   test(W,X^Q),
   !,
   translate(Words,X,Queries).

translate([Arg1,W,Arg2|Words],X,(Q1,Q2,Q3,Queries)) :-
   comparison(W,Y^Z^Q3),
   !,
   argument(Arg1,X^Y^Q1),
   argument(Arg2,X^Z^Q2),
   translate(Words,X,Queries).

translate([_|Words],X,Query) :-     % skip unrecognized word
   translate(Words,X,Query).

translate([],_,true).
```

The definitions of words look like this:

```
action(show,X^display_record(X)).
action(display,X^display_record(X)).
action(delete,X^remove_record(X)).

test(programmer,X^title(X,'Programmer')).
test(salesrep,X^title(X,'Sales rep')).

comparison(over,Y^Z^(Y>Z)).
comparison(under,Y^Z^(Y<Z)).

argument(salary,X^Y^salary(X,Y)).
argument(birthdate,X^Y^birth_date(X,Y)).
argument(N,_^Y^(Y=N)) :- number(N).
```

The last clause lets us use any number as an argument without looking anything up in the database.[3] That is, it provides for numeric constants. Like salary and birth_date, a number has two arguments, one for the person and one for the value, but the first argument is ignored.

**Exercise 2.3.8.1**

> What is the crucial difference between the first two clauses of translate? That is, what is the difference between the way it treats actions and the way it treats tests?

---

[3] In ESL Prolog-2, use numeric(N) instead of number(N).

**Exercise 2.3.8.2**

Put all these bits and pieces together and build a working natural language database query system. Add at least five words to its vocabulary in addition to the words defined in the code shown above.

**Exercise 2.3.8.3    (large project)**

Using techniques from this and the previous chapter, plus anything else that occurs to you, build a natural language query system for a real database.

One possibility is to answer queries about users of a UNIX system. A suitable two-table database is easy to obtain. The file `/etc/passwd` contains the user name and real name of every user (along with a lot of other information that is not useful). The command `last -200 >myfile` will write, on `myfile`, a database about the 200 most recent interactive sessions, showing who logged in when and for how long. By combining these databases you can answer such questions as, "How many times did Jane Smith log in this week?"

To use these files, you will need to write a procedure that reads them line by line using an appropriate tokenizer (see Appendix B), builds a Prolog fact from each line, and asserts that fact into the knowledge base. The database will then consist of Prolog facts and can be queried using the methods developed in this chapter.


## 2.4 TOWARD MORE NATURAL INPUT

### 2.4.1 Ellipsis

Often the queries or commands typed by the user are incomplete, the assumption being that part of the query will be the same as the previous one. For example:

```
user:       What programmers have salaries over 25000?
computer:   (prints a list or table)
user:       Over 30000?
computer:   (prints another list or table)
```

Here *Over 30000?* is an example of ELLIPSIS (omission of repeated words).

Ellipsis is fairly easy to handle in keyword systems. If the new query is incomplete (lacking an action, for instance), retain all parts of the previous query that are not explicitly replaced in the new one.

**Exercise 2.4.1.1**

Modify your keyword system so that if the user does not supply an action, the same action will be used as in the previous query.

### 2.4.2 Anaphora

ANAPHORA is the use of special words (ANAPHORS) to stand for individuals, events, or other things already referred to. Anaphoric pronouns such as *he, she, it,* and *(the) ones* refer to people or things; the anaphoric verb *does/did* refers to actions or states. Adverbs such as *then* and *there* can provide anaphoric reference to times and places.[4]

Anaphora is obviously useful in query systems. Users would like to be able to say things like:

> *Give me a list of sales representatives in Georgia.  List the ones in Florida.  Now list the programmers there.*

To handle anaphora, the system must remember important characteristics of earlier queries and must be able to figure out what the anaphors refer to.  Usually, an anaphor refers to the most recently mentioned thing that it *can* refer to; *she* would refer to the most recently mentioned woman, for instance. In keyword systems, this is usually sufficient. A full account of anaphora will require a much more powerful theory of semantics and pragmatics (see Chapters 8 and 9).

Two other points need to be made. First, noun phrases marked with *the* are much like anaphors. If you say *the boat* you mean either a previously mentioned boat, or a boat that can be uniquely identified from the context.

Second, anaphors usually stand for referents (things referred to), not words or phrases. Occasionally this distinction is important. For example,

> *If any customer has overpaid, display his balance.*

is obviously not the same as:

> *If any customer has overpaid, display any customer's balance.*

Again, consider a discourse such as:

> *Display the first record.*
> *Now display the next record.*
> *Now delete it.*

The last sentence does not mean 'delete the next record'; it means 'delete the record that I just now referred to as "next".'

**Exercise 2.4.2.1**

Modify your keyword system to properly handle the anaphoric phrases *which of them* and *which ones* (each referring to whatever records were retrieved by the previous query). The user should be able to say such things as *Show me all the programmers* and then *Which of them have salary over 25000?* or the like.

---

[4]Some linguists reserve the term ANAPHORA for pronoun reference only.

# CHAPTER 3

# Definite-Clause Grammars

## 3.1 PHRASE STRUCTURE

### 3.1.1 Trees and PS Rules

Templates and keywords ignore the role of CONSTITUENT STRUCTURE in human language. That is, they fail to recognize that a sentence is not just a string of words—the words are grouped into phrases, each of which consists of shorter phrases. This is a serious loss, because many of the important properties of language are organized around constituent structure.

Look for example at Figure 3.1. This tree diagram does two things:

- It groups the words into CONSTITUENTS such as *the dog* and *into the garden.*
- It gives names to the constituents, such as "noun phrase" and "prepositional phrase."

For example, the diagram claims that *into the garden* is a constituent and *a cat into* is not a constituent. This claim appears to be true. You can omit *into the garden,* or replace it with a single word such as *away,* without grossly changing the structure of the rest of the sentence. You can't do this with *a cat into.*

The diagram also claims that *the dog, a cat,* and *the garden* are phrases of the same kind (they are all labeled NP). This, too, appears to be a reasonable claim; these

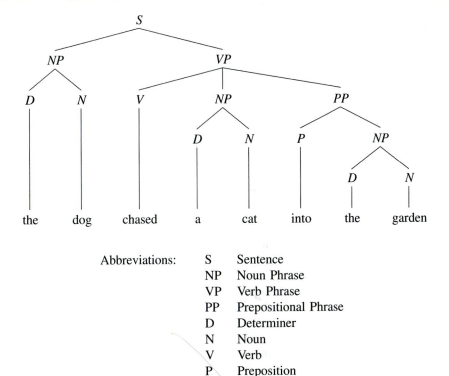

**Figure 3.1**  Constituent structure of a simple sentence.

three phrases have many syntactic and semantic properties in common. Indeed, you get grammatical sentences if you interchange them with each other.

Contrast all of this with a template or keyword system. Neither templates nor keywords break the sentence into constituents in any systematic way, and neither of them has a clear way to say that two sequences of words, found in different places, are constituents of the same type.

The structure shown in Figure 3.1 is sanctioned, or GENERATED, by the following set of PHRASE-STRUCTURE RULES (PS RULES):

$$
\begin{array}{rcl}
S & \rightarrow & NP\ VP \\
NP & \rightarrow & D\ N \\
VP & \rightarrow & V\ NP \\
VP & \rightarrow & V\ NP\ PP \\
PP & \rightarrow & P\ NP \\
D & \rightarrow & \text{the} \\
D & \rightarrow & \text{a} \\
N & \rightarrow & \text{dog} \\
N & \rightarrow & \text{cat}
\end{array}
$$

$$N \rightarrow \text{garden}$$
$$V \rightarrow \text{chased}$$
$$V \rightarrow \text{saw}$$
$$P \rightarrow \text{into}$$

The rules mean: "An S can consist of an NP followed by a VP. An NP can consist of a D followed by an N. A VP can consist of a V followed by an NP" (and so on).

A set of rules such as these is called a GRAMMAR. We say that the grammar GENERATES every sentence whose structure is entirely consistent with the rules. For example, this grammar also generates the sentence *The cat saw the dog* assigning it the structure shown in Figure 3.2. A grammar that generates sentences by means of explicit rules, rather than merely describing them in some other way, is called a GENERATIVE GRAMMAR. Ultimately, we would like to discover all the phrase-structure rules of English (together with any other kinds of rules that might be needed) and build a complete generative grammar of English.

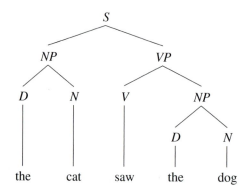

**Figure 3.2** The tree structure of a sentence shows the rules by which it is generated.

**Exercise 3.1.1.1**

Give tree diagrams of three more sentences that are generated by the grammar just given.

## 3.1.2 Phrase-Structure Formalism

Formally, each phrase-structure rule has a NONTERMINAL SYMBOL on the left (such as *S*, *NP*, etc.) and an EXPANSION of this symbol on the right. The expansion consists of a series of symbols which may be either terminal or nonterminal. The TERMINAL SYMBOLS are the words that actually occur in the language, such as *cat* and *saw*.

Commonly, there is more than one rule expanding the same symbol. This means that more than one expansion is permissible. For example, in the grammar just given, *N* can be either *cat* or *dog*.

A symbol can even expand to nothing at all. According to one popular analysis, the structure of *Birds fly* is:

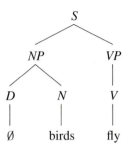

According to this analysis, the sentence begins with a determiner but you can't see it or hear it; it is the NULL (silent) determiner, introduced by the rule

$$D \quad \rightarrow \quad \emptyset$$

Not all linguists accept this analysis, but the formalism provides for it.

Parentheses in a phrase-structure rule denote items that can be left out. For example, the rule

$$VP \quad \rightarrow \quad V \ (NP)$$

is really an abbreviation for two alternative rules:

$$VP \quad \rightarrow \quad V \ NP$$
$$VP \quad \rightarrow \quad V$$

That is, the rule says that a VP consists of a V which may or may not be followed by an NP.

All the phrase-structure rules that we have discussed are CONTEXT-FREE because each of them can apply in any context. For example, the rule $NP \rightarrow D \ N$ asserts that *any* NP can consist of D and N, regardless of where it occurs. The alternative would be CONTEXT-SENSITIVE rules such as "NP expands to D and N, but only when preceded by a preposition." Context-sensitive rules are rarely used in natural-language analysis; they are potentially too complicated and do not lend themselves to a straightforward parsing algorithm.

Some older textbooks refer to generation of a sentence as if it were a process: "Start with an S. Use the first rule to rewrite S as NP VP. Use the second rule to rewrite NP as D N," and so on. This is a misleading way to use the rules because these are certainly not the steps that the human brain goes through when constructing a sentence. (You don't start out by deciding to utter an S, then realize you need an NP and a VP, and then choose your words only at the very last step.) The purpose of the rules is to specify what structures are possible. The rules themselves are not a procedure; rather, many different procedures for creating or analyzing sentences can be built upon them.

**Exercise 3.1.2.1**

Rewrite the rule $VP \rightarrow V \ (NP) \ (PP) \ (PP)$ as a set of rules that do not contain parentheses.

**Exercise 3.1.2.2**

Draw a tree for *The cat saw a problem* as generated by the following grammar:

$$
\begin{array}{rcl}
S & \rightarrow & NP\ Aux\ VP \\
Aux & \rightarrow & \emptyset \\
NP & \rightarrow & Ngroup \\
Ngroup & \rightarrow & D\ N \\
VP & \rightarrow & V\ NP \\
D & \rightarrow & \text{a} \\
D & \rightarrow & \text{the} \\
N & \rightarrow & \text{problem} \\
N & \rightarrow & \text{cat} \\
V & \rightarrow & \text{puzzled} \\
V & \rightarrow & \text{saw}
\end{array}
$$

**Exercise 3.1.2.3**

The grammar in the previous exercise is needlessly complex. Simplify it. After simplification, it should still generate exactly the same sentences and group the words into constituents in the same way. The tree diagrams need not be the same in every detail (in fact if you change the grammar at all, they won't be). Give the tree for *The cat saw a problem* as generated by your simplified grammar.

## 3.1.3 Recursion

Besides being able to describe constituency, phrase-structure rules have another big advantage over templates and keywords: they can be recursive.

Recall that a template system has to match the entire sentence to a pattern. Consider now the four sentences:

*The dog chased the cat.*

*The girl thought the dog chased the cat.*

*The butler said the girl thought the dog chased the cat.*

*The gardener claimed the butler said the girl thought the dog chased the cat.*

Obviously, there's a recursive pattern here: the longer sentences have shorter sentences within them. Specifically, a verb such as *thought, said,* or *claimed* can introduce another complete sentence.

Templates can't describe a recursive structure like this.[1] The best we could do, with templates, would be to have a separate template for each of the sentence structures above. But that's not satisfactory, for two reasons:

- It simply ignores the important fact that all four sentences are examples of the same repetitive pattern.

---

[1]Bobrow's STUDENT could; it was a template system with recursion added. But this is not the way templates are normally used.

- There's no limit to the number of templates that might be needed, because the process can be continued almost without limit, producing longer and longer sentences.

The second of these is the more important. A sentence of this kind could have five verbs, or ten, or maybe even fifteen. It won't have 10,000, but that's because of limits on people's patience and memory capacity, not because of any rule of grammar. This is what linguists mean when they say that a language has a potentially infinite number of different sentence structures.

PS rules solve the problem nicely. Recall that so far, the grammar we are working with is:

$$
\begin{array}{rcl}
S & \rightarrow & NP\ VP \\
NP & \rightarrow & D\ N \\
VP & \rightarrow & V\ NP\ (PP) \\
PP & \rightarrow & P\ NP \\
D & \rightarrow & \text{the} \\
D & \rightarrow & \text{a} \\
N & \rightarrow & \text{dog} \\
N & \rightarrow & \text{cat} \\
N & \rightarrow & \text{garden} \\
V & \rightarrow & \text{chased} \\
V & \rightarrow & \text{saw} \\
P & \rightarrow & \text{into}
\end{array}
$$

To get recursive structures, all we need to do is add a few more rules:

$$
\begin{array}{rcl}
VP & \rightarrow & V\ S \\
N & \rightarrow & \text{gardener} \\
N & \rightarrow & \text{girl} \\
N & \rightarrow & \text{butler} \\
V & \rightarrow & \text{claimed} \\
V & \rightarrow & \text{thought} \\
V & \rightarrow & \text{said}
\end{array}
$$

The crucial change here is that now a VP can contain an S. Because every S contains a VP, this allows there to be sentences within sentences. Now the grammar can generate sentences such as *The butler said the girl thought the dog chased the cat* (Figure 3.3).

**Exercise 3.1.3.1**

How long is the longest sentence that can be generated by the grammar just given?

**Exercise 3.1.3.2**

Give two sentences that are *not* correct English but are generated by the grammar as given so far. Draw trees for these sentences.

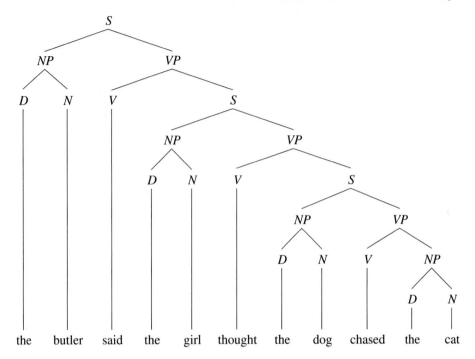

**Figure 3.3**   Recursive PS rules can generate sentences within sentences.

**Exercise 3.1.3.3**

Linguists consider it very important that a generative grammar must not generate ungrammatical sentences (sentences that cannot occur in the language). If it did, it could not be a correct description of the language, nor of any subset of it.

Is this requirement equally important in natural language processing? Explain.

## 3.2 TOP-DOWN PARSING

### 3.2.1 A Parsing Algorithm

To PARSE a sentence is to determine, by an algorithmic process, whether the sentence is generated by a particular grammar, and if so, what structure the grammar assigns to it. (The first few parsers that we build will not give the structure; do not be alarmed. They *find* the structure even though they do not report it.)

There are two major ways to parse:

- A BOTTOM-UP parser looks as the words and tries to combine them into constituents, like this:
  - *The* is a D.
  - *Dog* is an N.
  - D and N together make an NP . . .

- A TOP-DOWN parser starts out looking for a specific constituent, such as S, and uses the rules to figure out what this can consist of:
  - S consists of NP and VP.
  - NP consists of D and N.
  - *The* is a D.
  - *Dog* is an N ...

Both top-down and bottom-up parsers need the ability to BACKTRACK, i.e., try one rule, and if it doesn't work out, back up and try a different one. A parser that backtracks is called a NONDETERMINISTIC parser.

In this chapter we will concentrate on nondeterministic top-down parsing. One way to parse top-down is to give each of the PS rules a procedural interpretation. For example,

- *S → NP VP* means "To parse an S, parse an NP and then a VP."
- *N → dog* means "To parse an N, accept the word *dog* from the input string."

(The input to a parser is always called the INPUT STRING even though in Prolog it is usually a list of atoms, not a string of characters.) This process is often called RECURSIVE DESCENT because each PS rule is made into a procedure, and these procedures can call each other or themselves recursively.

Parsing then becomes a process very much like satisfying Prolog queries. The initial goal is S; some of the rules transform this goal into other goals; and some of the rules satisfy goals by accepting words. Figure 3.4 shows the complete process of parsing *The dog saw the cat*.

In each step the parser either transforms the current goal into a new goal, or satisfies the current goal by accepting a word. Sometimes, although there is no example of it here, the parser backtracks. In all these respects top-down parsing is very much like the way Prolog solves queries. This is not a coincidence; parsing is one of the applications that Alain Colmerauer had in mind when he originally invented Prolog (Colmerauer 1978).

### 3.2.2 Parsing with Prolog Rules

To implement a parser, all we have to do is rewrite the grammar as a set of Prolog clauses. A grammar written in this form is called a DEFINITE-CLAUSE GRAMMAR. "Definite clauses" are merely Prolog rules and facts; definite-clause grammars were introduced to the world by Pereira and Warren (1980), though they were implicit in earlier logic programming research.

In a definite-clause grammar, each PS rule is a clause for a predicate with two arguments, like this:

$$S \quad \rightarrow \quad NP\ VP$$

```
s(L1,L) :- np(L1,L2), vp(L2,L).
```

| Action:              | Goals:   | Input string:        |
|----------------------|----------|----------------------|
| Start with:          | *S*      | *the dog saw the cat* |
| Apply *S → NP VP*    | *NP VP*  | *the dog saw the cat* |
| Apply *NP → D N*     | *D N VP* | *the dog saw the cat* |
| Apply *D → the*      | *the N VP* | *the dog saw the cat* |
| Accept *the*         | *N VP*   | *dog saw the cat*    |
| Apply *N → dog*      | *dog VP* | *dog saw the cat*    |
| Accept *dog*         | *VP*     | *saw the cat*        |
| Apply *VP → V NP*    | *V NP*   | *saw the cat*        |
| Apply *V → saw*      | *saw NP* | *saw the cat*        |
| Accept *saw*         | *NP*     | *the cat*            |
| Apply *NP → D N*     | *D N*    | *the cat*            |
| Apply *D → the*      | *the N*  | *the cat*            |
| Accept *the*         | *N*      | *cat*                |
| Apply *N → cat*      | *cat*    | *cat*                |
| Accept *cat*         | (empty)  | (empty)              |

**Figure 3.4**    Top-down parsing.  Each action changes either the input string or the goal list, or both.

Here:

- L1 is the original input string, such as `[the,dog,saw,the,cat]`;
- L2 is the input string without the initial NP, such as `[saw,the,cat]`; and
- L is the input string without the NP or the VP (in this case, `[]`).[2]

The rule itself could be expressed in English as:

> To parse an S starting with input string L1 and ending with L,
> first parse an NP starting with L1 and ending up with L2,
> then parse a VP starting with L2 and ending up with L.

Or it could be expressed more declaratively as:

> Removing an S from L1 gives L
> if
> removing an NP from L1 gives L2
> and
> removing a VP from L2 gives L.

The rules that introduce terminal symbols (words) take the form

```
n([dog|L],L).
```

---

[2]Alternatively, L1, L2, and L could denote *positions* in the input string: the beginning of the string, the end of the NP, and the end of the VP. But the aforementioned interpretation is more common.

That is, "To parse a noun, remove *dog* from the beginning of the input string." So a complete grammar, in Prolog, looks like this:

```
s(L1,L)   :- np(L1,L2), vp(L2,L).
np(L1,L) :- d(L1,L2), n(L2,L).
vp(L1,L) :- v(L1,L2),  np(L2,L).
d([the|L],L).
d([a|L],L).
n([dog|L],L).
n([cat|L],L).
n([gardener|L],L).
n([policeman|L],L).
n([butler|L],L).
v([chased|L],L).
v([saw|L],L).
```

All of this deserves careful study. Take a moment to convince yourself that a query such as

```
?- s([the,dog,chased,the,cat],[]).
```

really will succeed if and only if, according to the available rules, *the dog chased the cat* is a sentence. Prolog automatically chooses the right rules and backtracks where necessary.

**Exercise 3.2.2.1**

Get this parser working on the computer and use it to parse several sentences.

**Exercise 3.2.2.2**

Is this kind of parsing reversible? That is, what happens if the input string is uninstantiated? Try it and see.

**Exercise 3.2.2.3**

Show how to use this parser to "fill in the blanks" in a template such as [W,X,Y,Z,dog]. That is, give this template to the parser and make the parser generate a five-word sentence that ends with *dog*.

## 3.3 DCG RULES

### 3.3.1 DCG Notation

The conversion of PS rules into Prolog clauses is so simple that it can be done automatically. In fact Prolog includes a facility for doing just this. If you write clauses in DEFINITE-CLAUSE GRAMMAR (DCG) NOTATION, which looks like this,

```
s --> np, vp.
np --> d, n.
n --> [dog].
```

then, upon reading the clauses, `consult` and `reconsult` will convert them automatically into

```
s(L1,L)  :- np(L1,L2), vp(L2,L).
np(L1,L) :- d(L1,L2),  n(L2,L).
n([dog|L],L).
```

or the equivalent.[3] This conversion is done when the clauses are loaded from a file into memory. Once they are in memory, the Prolog system completely forgets that they were ever expressed in DCG notation. That's why, if you type '?- listing.' or '?- listing np/2.' you will see the translated rules, not the rules you wrote.

The DCG translator affects only the clauses with the principal functor '-->'. All other clauses are assumed to be plain Prolog and are left unchanged. Thus your program can contain both DCG rules and plain Prolog clauses.

Here is an example of a grammar in DCG notation:

```
s  --> np, vp.
np --> d,  n.
vp --> v,  np.
d  --> [the];[a].
n  --> [dog];[cat];[gardener];[policeman];[butler].
v  --> [chased];[saw].
```

Every DCG rule takes the form

*nonterminal symbol* --> *expansion*

where *expansion* is any of the following:

- A nonterminal symbol such as np;
- A list of terminal symbols such as [dog] or [each,other];
- A null constituent represented by [];
- A plain Prolog goal enclosed in braces, such as {write('Found NP')};
- A series of any of these expansions joined by commas.

If your Prolog requires all the clauses of a predicate to be contiguous, then the same requirement will apply to DCG rules; for example, you can't have an np rule followed by a vp rule and then another np rule.

---

[3] These translations are used in Arity Prolog and several of the older Prolog implementations. The translations used by Quintus are quite different and are explained in Section 3.3.3.

As in Prolog, the semicolon means 'or.' This is convenient in writing rules such as

```
n --> [dog];[cat];[butler].
```

Apart from this, we avoid using the semicolon because it is potentially confusing. (The vertical bar, '|', is equivalent to the semicolon in Quintus Prolog.)

The translator turns DCG rules into Prolog clauses by adding two extra arguments to every symbol that is not in brackets or braces. These arguments are automatically arranged appropriately for parsing. That's how np in the DCG rule becomes something like np(L1,L2) in the resulting Prolog clause.

Notice that the automatically generated arguments are *not* the same as any variables supplied by the programmer. (They are not named L1, L2, and L; in fact they have no names at all.) A common mistake is to write something like

```
s --> np, { write(L2) }, np.      % WRONG!
```

as if L2 meant something here. It doesn't.

**Exercise 3.3.1.1**

Write $D \rightarrow \emptyset$ as a DCG rule.

**Exercise 3.3.1.2**

What is your Prolog system's translation of each of the following PS rules? (See Section 3.3.3 for an explanation of why some of them may not be what you expect.)

```
s --> np, vp.
n --> [dog].
```

**Exercise 3.3.1.3**

Get the grammar on p. 46 working and use it to parse a few sentences.

**Exercise 3.3.1.4**

What is the difference between the following two rules?

```
n --> [dog].
n --> dog.
```

**Exercise 3.3.1.5**

Here is a devious way of getting access to the input string during parsing:

```
snoop(X,Y,X,Y).
s --> np, snoop(A,B), { write(A), A=B }, vp.
```

That's not a mistake; `snoop` really is written with four arguments in a plain clause, but only two arguments in a DCG clause, because the DCG translator adds arguments. The rest of the grammar is above.

Explain what `snoop` does and why it works. Show how `snoop` could be used to modify the input string during parsing.

### 3.3.2 Loops

Like all left-to-right top-down parsers, DCG-rule parsers go into a loop when they encounter a rule of the form

$$A \quad \rightarrow \quad A\,B$$

—that is, "To parse an A, parse an A and then ..."

The problem, of course, is that this rule calls itself before it has accepted anything from the input string, so there is nothing to keep it from calling itself again and again, ad infinitum. A loop of this kind could be spread over two or more rules, such as:

$$\begin{aligned} A &\rightarrow B \\ B &\rightarrow A\,C \end{aligned}$$

Rules or sets of rules like these are called LEFT-RECURSIVE.

Left-recursion occurs whenever a constituent begins with another constituent of exactly the same kind. Figure 3.5 shows some examples in English. The left-recursive rule

$$NP \quad \rightarrow \quad NP\ Conj\ NP$$

and the left-recursive rule pair

$$\begin{aligned} NP &\rightarrow D\,N \\ D &\rightarrow NP\ Poss \end{aligned}$$

appear to be necessary to describe English sentences correctly.

It has long been known that any left-recursive grammar can be transformed into another grammar that generates the same strings but is not left-recursive. For example,

$$\begin{aligned} NP &\rightarrow NP\ Conj\ NP \\ NP &\rightarrow D\,N \end{aligned}$$

can be changed to:

$$\begin{aligned} NP &\rightarrow NPX\ Conj\ NP \\ NP &\rightarrow NPX \\ NPX &\rightarrow D\,N \end{aligned}$$

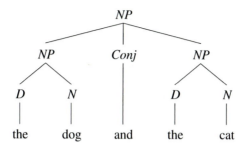

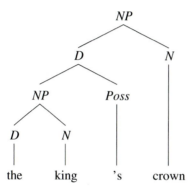

**Figure 3.5**    Two structures in English where a constituent begins with a constituent of the same type. Top-down parsers loop on the rules required for such situations.

Unfortunately, although this generates the right strings, it gives a tree structure that is not entirely right. There is no linguistic evidence that the distinction between NP and NPX actually exists in the language.

Transforming the grammar, then, is not too useful in natural language processing. We prefer to switch to a different parsing algorithm (Chapter 6) or make minor patches in our top-down parsing algorithm to avoid loops while keeping the tree structure correct.

**Exercise 3.3.2.1**

What is the tree structure of *the dog and the cat* according to a grammar containing the rules with NPX just discussed?

**Exercise 3.3.2.2**

Implement the rules

$$NP \rightarrow NP\ Conj\ NP$$
$$NP \rightarrow D\ N$$

in a DCG parser in such a way that no loop occurs. To do this, use `snoop` from the previous section, so that your implementation of *NP → NP Conj NP* will do the following:

**1.** Look ahead, find the conjunction (*and* or *or*) in the input string, and remove it.

**2.** Parse the first NP.

**3.** Parse the second NP.

This is not a theoretically satisfying way to process conjoined noun phrases, but it works.

### 3.3.3 Some Details of Implementation

Two details of implementation remain to be considered. First, in most Prologs the DCG translator is actually a built-in predicate named `expand_term`.[4] Before asserting clauses into memory, `consult` and `reconsult` pass every clause to `expand_term`. If `expand_term` succeeds, its output is used in place of the clause that was passed to it. Otherwise the original clause is used.

This is important because you can invent your own translator (for DCG rules or any other kind of clauses) and implement it by adding clauses to `expand_term`. See your Prolog manual for details.

Second, Quintus Prolog has a special way of translating DCG rules that contain terminal symbols (words). Instead of rendering

```
n --> [dog].
```

as

```
n([dog|L],L).
```

Quintus renders it as

```
n(L1,L) :- 'C'(L1,dog,L).
```

where `'C'` is defined as

```
'C'([X|Y],X,Y).
```

Here `'C'` stands for "connects" and was in fact called `connects` in early Edinburgh implementations.

At first sight the use of `'C'` may seem to be just a waste of time. Why not match the lists directly instead of calling another predicate? The answer, as O'Keefe (1985) explains, is that `'C'` makes a difference when there is an embedded Prolog goal with side effects. Consider for instance the rule

```
p --> [because], { write('Got it!') }, [of].
```

---

[4]In ALS Prolog, expand_term is called builtins:dcg_expand and you have to consult(dcgs) before using it.

This means "To parse a preposition, accept *because,* then write 'Got it!', then accept *of.*" The idea is that the two words *because of* should be treated as a single preposition, and furthermore, perhaps for debugging purposes, we want to see a message when the parser accepts *because.*

In Quintus Prolog, this rule translates to

```
p(L1,L) :- 'C'(L1,because,L2), write('Got it!'), 'C'(L2,of,L).
```

and works as intended. However, in Prologs that use the old-style translation, such as Arity Prolog 4.0, the same rule translates to

```
p([because,of|L],L) :- write('Got it!').
```

which does not give the intended result—it does not write "Got it!" until both *because* and *of* have been accepted. If, instead of `write('Got it!')`, the embedded goal had been a cut, the flow of execution could have ended up substantially different.

ALS Prolog solves the same problem a different way, by translating the rule as:

```
p([because|L1],L) :- write('Got it!'), L1 = [of|L].
```

The ALS translator knows which unifications are supposed to be done after executing the embedded goal, and postpones them appropriately.

**Exercise 3.3.3.1**

What are the results of the queries

```
?- expand_term((s --> np, vp), What).
?- expand_term(green(kermit), What).
```

in your Prolog? (If neither one of them succeeds, find out how to use `expand_term` or its equivalent in the implementation you are using.)

**Exercise 3.3.3.2**

How does your Prolog translate the following rule?

```
p --> {write('Processing because-of')}, [because,of].
```

Explain how you found out. What are the advantages and disadvantages of using this translation?

## 3.4 USING DCG PARSERS

### 3.4.1 Building Syntactic Trees

A practical parser should do more than just say whether or not a sentence is acceptable; it should also report the structure of the sentence. This raises two questions: how to represent tree diagrams in Prolog, and how to get the parser to produce them.

Representing tree diagrams is easy; they correspond to Prolog structures. For example, the tree

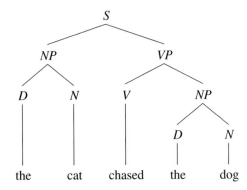

can be represented as the structure:

```
s(np(d(the),n(cat)),vp(v(chased),np(d(the),n(dog))))
```

To produce this representation, the parser will make each rule fill in the part of the structure for which it is responsible. For example, parsing begins with the rule `s --> np, vp`. This rule must therefore contribute the outermost `s(...,...)` in the structure, where the portions represented by ... will be filled in by the np and vp rules, respectively. The np rule in turn will contribute `np(...,...)`, with arguments to be supplied by rules yet lower down.

To implement this process, we'll rely on the fact that DCG notation allows extra arguments on predicates. If, for example, you write

```
s(a,b) --> np(c,d), vp(e,f).
```

the translator will produce:

```
s(a,b,L1,L) :- np(c,d,L1,L2), vp(e,f,L2,L).
```

These extra arguments make a DCG more powerful than an ordinary phrase-structure grammar. (Normally, the extra arguments that you supply are placed before the arguments supplied by the translator, but it's wise to check your implementation.)

In the present case we want the arguments to represent the tree, so the syntactic rules need to look like this:

```
s(s(NP,VP))   --> np(NP), vp(VP).
np(np(D,N))   --> d(D), n(N).
vp(vp(V,NP))  --> v(V), np(NP).
d(d(the))     --> [the].
n(n(dog))     --> [dog].
n(n(cat))     --> [cat].
```

```
v(v(chased)) --> [chased].
v(v(saw))    --> [saw].
```

When the first rule is invoked, its argument is immediately instantiated as `s(NP,VP)`, but the variables `NP` and `VP` are not yet instantiated. The `np` rule then instantiates `NP` to `np(D,N)` so that the whole structure is `s(np(D,N),VP)` but D, N, and VP do not yet have values. The structure will be completely instantiated when parsing is complete. Moreover, if execution backtracks out of a rule, the instantiations established by that rule are undone, just as in ordinary Prolog.

The key idea here is that unification and instantiation give you a way to *work with information that you do not yet have*—just build a partly instantiated structure and instantiate the details later. This technique gives Prolog much of its power.

**Exercise 3.4.1.1**

Get this parser working, then extend it by adding all the rules developed in Section 3.1.3. Show that it generates a correct parse tree for *The butler claimed the dog chased the cat into the garden.*

**Exercise 3.4.1.2**

Construct a parser that outputs structural information, not by instantiating arguments, but by performing a `write` at the beginning and end of each rule, like this:

```
s --> { write('Beginning S...') }, np, vp,
            { write('Finished S.') }.
```

This parser will indicate the structure of *The dog chased the cat* by outputting messages like "Starting S ... Starting NP ... Determiner ... Noun ... End of NP ... Starting VP ..." and so on.

**Exercise 3.4.1.3**

What is fundamentally wrong with the technique used in the previous exercise? Why is its output not always an accurate description of the tree?

**Exercise 3.4.1.4    (project)**

Write a Prolog program that reads a file of DCG rules without arguments and automatically converts them into rules that build a syntactic tree, writing the translation on another file. For example,

```
s --> np, vp.
```

should be translated into

```
s(s(V1,V2)) --> np(V1), vp(V2).
```

To keep it simple, you need not handle rules that use semicolons or curly braces.

**Exercise 3.4.1.5**

Write a predicate called `display_tree_as_outline` that will output a tree structure such as `s(np(d(the),n(birds)),vp(v(fly)))` in an indented outlinelike format, like this:

```
s
 np
  d
   the
  n
   birds
 vp
  v
   fly
```

thus making it easier to see the tree structure. (This is closely related to the "depth" exercises in Appendix A.)

**Exercise 3.4.1.6   (project)**

Write a predicate called `display_tree` that will output a tree structure such as `s(np(d(the),n(birds)),vp(v(fly)))` as an actual tree made of ASCII characters, such as:

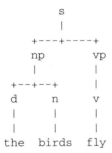

or the like. This project is not easy, but the result is well worth having.

## 3.4.2 Agreement

Another use of arguments is to enforce AGREEMENT. In English, the verb and its subject have to agree in number; that is, they are either both singular or both plural. Most nouns take *-s* in the plural; most third-person verbs take *-s* in the singular, like this:

| | |
|---|---|
| *The dog chases the cats.* | (Singular subject, singular verb) |
| *The dogs chase the cats.* | (Plural subject, plural verb) |
| *\*The dog chase the cats.* | (Singular subject, plural verb) |
| *\*The dogs chases the cats.* | (Plural subject, singular verb) |

(Here as elsewhere, asterisks indicate ungrammatical examples.) Notice that the object (the noun after the verb) is not involved in agreement; you can say either *cat* or *cats* in any of the sentences above.

To make DCG rules account for agreement, we need to attach arguments to the NP and VP to indicate whether each of them is singular or plural:

```
n(singular) --> [dog];[cat];[mouse].
n(plural)   --> [dogs];[cats];[mice].

v(singular) --> [chases];[sees].
v(plural)   --> [chase];[see].
```

The point is that an NP has the same number (singular or plural) as its HEAD NOUN, and a VP has the same number as its HEAD VERB. These rules ensure that this is so:

```
np(Number) --> d, n(Number).
vp(Number) --> v(Number), np(_).
```

The sentence consists of an NP and a VP whose numbers match:

```
s --> np(Number), vp(Number).
```

A parser using these rules will accept only sentences in which the subject and verb agree in number.

### Exercise 3.4.2.1

Get a parser working that uses these rules, and verify that it works as intended. Specifically, it should accept *The dogs chase the cats* but not *\*The dog chase the cats.*

### Exercise 3.4.2.2

Why couldn't the VP rule be written as follows?

```
vp(Number) --> v(Number), np.
```

### Exercise 3.4.2.3

Extend your parser so that it distinguishes between singular and plural determiners. For example, *a* and *an* are used only with singulars; *two* is used only with plurals; and *the* is used with both singulars and plurals. Your parser should reject *\*a dogs, \*two dog,* and the like.

### Exercise 3.4.2.4

Extend your parser so that it distinguishes between count and mass nouns. Give each noun two features, Number (with values singular and plural) and Class (count or mass).

A count noun has a singular and a plural (*dog, dogs*). A mass noun, such as *water* or *stuff*, has no plural, and usually refers to an indefinite amount of a substance.

The difference is important because different types of nouns take different determiners. Some examples:

| TYPE OF NOUN | EXAMPLE | SUITABLE DETERMINERS |
|---|---|---|
| singular count | *dog, theory* | a(n), the, one, every |
| plural count | *dogs, theories* | Ø, the, two, all |
| singular mass | *water, stuff* | Ø, the, all |
| plural mass | (does not exist) | |

Your parser should accept *a dog, the theory, two dogs,* etc., but reject *a dogs, *one theories, *every stuff, *two water,* and the like.

### 3.4.3 Case Marking

Some English pronouns are marked for CASE. This means that the pronoun has a different form before the verb than after it. For example:

*He sees him.*     **Him sees he.*
*She sees her.*    **Her sees she.*
*They see them.*   **Them see they.*

The forms that come before the verb, *he, she,* and *they,* are called NOMINATIVE, and the forms that come after the verb, *him, her,* and *them* are called ACCUSATIVE.[5]

"Before the verb" and "after the verb" is not a very good way of describing where these forms occur. Instead, we can say, much more precisely and accurately, that:

$$S \rightarrow NP\ VP \quad \text{introduces a nominative, and}$$

$$VP \rightarrow V\ NP \quad \text{introduces an accusative.}$$

To account for this with DCG rules, we'll add a second argument for case, alongside the argument for number. The rules for the pronouns will then be:

```
pronoun(singular,nominative)  --> [he]; [she].
pronoun(singular,accusative)  --> [him];[her].
pronoun(plural,nominative)    --> [they].
pronoun(plural,accusative)    --> [them].
```

and we need to change the NP rules:

```
np(Number,Case)  -->  pronoun(Number,Case).
np(Number,_)     -->  d, n(Number).
```

---

[5]*Her* is also a possessive determiner corresponding to *his, your, my,* etc. Don't let this confuse you.

The second of these says that nouns are not marked for case. Because there is no case marking on determiners, nouns, or verbs, the D, N, and V rules can be exactly the same as in the previous section. But we need to change the S rule and the VP rule:

```
s   -->   np(Number,nominative), vp(Number).

vp(Number) --> v(Number), np(_,accusative).
```

Now the parser accounts for case marking of pronouns.

**Exercise 3.4.3.1**

Incorporate these changes into the rules from the previous section, and verify that it accepts *He sees them* and *They see her* but not *\*Them see he* or *\*They see they*.

**Exercise 3.4.3.2**

Should the rule *PP → P NP* specify a nominative or an accusative NP? Cite examples from English to justify your conclusion, then add this rule to your parser, with appropriate case marking.

### 3.4.4 Subcategorization

The structure of the English VP depends on the particular verb. Different verbs require different things after them. For example:

| VERB | COMPLEMENT | EXAMPLE |
|---|---|---|
| sleep, bark | None | *(The cat) slept.* |
| chase, see | One NP | *(The dog) chased <u>the cat</u>.* |
| give, sell | Two NPs | *(Max) sold <u>Bill</u> <u>his car</u>.* |
| say, claim | Sentence | *(Max) claimed <u>the cat barked</u>.* |

If these requirements are not met, the sentence is ungrammatical; you can't say *The dog chased* or *John said the cat* unless the missing part can be clearly understood from the context.

This means we can't really account for the VP with a single rule of the form *VP → V (NP) (NP) (S)*. Instead we need at least four rules,

$$
\begin{array}{rcl}
VP & \to & V \\
VP & \to & V\ NP \\
VP & \to & V\ NP\ NP \\
VP & \to & V\ S
\end{array}
$$

plus a way of associating the right rule with each verb.

One possibility is to eliminate the concept of "verb" from the grammar, and instead, use four different categories (call them V1, V2, V3, and V4). The VP rules would then be:

$$VP \; \rightarrow \; V1$$
$$VP \; \rightarrow \; V2\ NP$$
$$VP \; \rightarrow \; V3\ NP\ NP$$
$$VP \; \rightarrow \; V4\ S$$

and the lexicon would say that *bark* is a V1, *chase* is a V2, and so on.

Notice that if we do this, we are claiming that there is no relationship at all between V1, V2, V3, and V4; no more than between N and P. We will be claiming that *bark, chase, sell,* and *say* are four totally different kinds of words. There will be no way to write a rule that applies equally to all four of them.

That isn't satisfactory. There are two good reasons to put all four kinds of verbs into a single category called V:

- Only V's are marked for tense and number and can serve as the head of a VP.
- Morphologically, all four kinds of V's are alike (they take *-s* in the third person singular, *-ed* in the past, and so on). The morphological part of the parser, which we haven't implemented yet, *should not* distinguish between different kinds of V's.

What we need is a way to have things both ways: treat the various kinds of V's alike and treat them differently. That is, we need a category V, divided into SUBCATEGORIES.

One way to do this is—you guessed it—to add an argument to the V. Then rules that care about this feature can specify its value, and rules that don't care about it can put an anonymous variable in place of it. Here goes:

```
vp --> v(1).
vp --> v(2), np.
vp --> v(3), np, np.
vp --> v(4), s.


v(1) --> [barked];[slept].
v(2) --> [chased];[saw].
v(3) --> [gave];[sold].
v(4) --> [said];[thought].
```

(To keep the example from becoming too complicated, we've dropped the agreement features. A real parser would, of course, keep them.) Now v(1) means a verb of class 1, v(2) means a verb of class 2, etc., and v(_) means a verb of any class. It turns out that v(_) does not occur in any syntactic rules, but only in the morphological part of the grammar.

**Exercise 3.4.4.1**

Construct a complete, working parser that implements subcategorization of verbs. Make it accept the sentences

*The cat slept.*

*The dog chased the cat.*

*The girl gave the dog a bone.*

*The boy said the dog chased the cat.*

but reject sentences in which verbs have the wrong kinds of complements, such as:

*The cat slept the dog.

*The dog chased.

*The girl gave the dog chased the cat.

*The boy said the cat.

## 3.4.5 Undoing Syntactic Movements

You can even use arguments to pick up a word from one position and put it down somewhere else. This surprising ability turns out to be needed when parsing English questions.

Consider a complicated sentence such as:

*Max said Bill thought Joe believed Fido barked.*

This sentence contains four NPs, *Max, Bill, Joe,* and *Fido,* and we can ask a question by substituting *who* for any of them:[6]

*Who said Bill thought Joe believed Fido barked? (Max.)*

*Who did Max say ⊔ thought Joe believed Fido barked? (Bill.)*

*Who did Max say Bill thought ⊔ believed Fido barked? (Joe.)*

*Who did Max say Bill thought Joe believed ⊔ barked? (Fido.)*

The first sentence simply puts *who* in place of *Max.* In each of the others:

- Exactly one NP is missing from somewhere in the sentence (it is denoted by '⊔').
- *Who did* has been added at the beginning.
- The sentence means exactly what it would have meant if *who* had appeared in place of the missing NP.

We would like the parser to move *who* back into the NP position with which it is associated. To do this, we will use arguments to implement a HOLDING LIST on which

---

[6]Like most native speakers, we will ignore the difference between *who* (old nominative) and *whom* (old accusative). For speakers who still distinguish them, the difference between *who* and *whom* is exactly the same as the difference between *he* and *him.*

*who* can be stored. A rule that finds a sentence-initial *who* will put it on the holding list, and a rule later on that needs an NP but can't find one will use the stored occurrence of *who*.[7]

To implement a holding list, each rule needs two arguments, one for input and one for output—that is, one to receive the holding list and one to output the (possibly changed) holding list to the next rule.

Only two rules need special treatment here. In addition to the normal rule $S \rightarrow NP\ VP$, we need a rule to parse sentences that begin with *who*:

```
s(In,Out) --> [who,did], np([who|In],Out1), vp(Out1,Out).
```

That is: In is the input received by the whole sentence (probably an empty list). This rule accepts the words *who did,* then passes [who|In] as input to the NP. The output of the NP is Out1, which gets passed as input to the VP. Finally, the output of the VP is Out, which is also the output of the whole sentence.

Then, in order to allow NPs to be missing, we need an NP rule that accepts no words, but instead uses the *who* that it received in its input:

```
np([who|Out],Out) --> [].
```

That is: One way to parse an NP is to accept *who* from the holding list rather than from the input string.

The remaining rules do not modify the holding list; they just pass it along unchanged from each step to the next. Rules for small constituents that cannot contain an NP do not need arguments, which is why v has no arguments here.

```
s(In,Out) --> np(In,Out1), vp(Out1,Out).

np(X,X) --> [max];[joe];[bill];[fido].
          % Proper names are complete NPs

vp(X,X) --> v.
vp(In,Out) --> v, np(In,Out).
vp(In,Out) --> v, s(In,Out).

v --> [saw];[said];[thought];[believed];[barked].
v --> [see];[say]; [think];  [believe]; [bark].
```

---

[7]In a *who*-question, this list will never have more than one member. The ability to stack more than one *who(m)* is needed for parsing nested relative clauses. For example:

*The boy whom₁ the girl whom₂ we saw ⊔₂ liked ⊔₁ ......*

Holding lists go back to the work of Woods (1970), if not earlier, and are discussed in detail by Wanner and Maratsos (1978).

To parse a sentence, you must give the initial and final values of the holding list—namely [] and []—as extra arguments of s in the query, like this:

```
?- s([],[],[who,did,max,see],[]).
yes
```

Holding lists are the basis of the "extraposition grammars" of Pereira (1981), who develops a useful extension of DCG notation for them. Their counterpart in unification-based grammar is "slash features" (Gazdar, Klein, Pullum, and Sag 1985).

**Exercise 3.4.5.1**

Take the parser just given, get it working, and show that it parses

*Who did Max say thought Joe believed Fido barked?*
*Who did Max say Bill thought believed Fido barked?*
*Who did Max say Bill thought Joe believed barked?*

but does not accept *Who did Max say Joe saw Fido?* or the like.

**Exercise 3.4.5.2**

Modify this parser so that, using another argument, it generates a tree structure. However, the tree should not show the actual order of the words; instead, it should show *who* in the position of the missing NP. For example, the tree for *Who did Bill think said Fido barked?* should be:

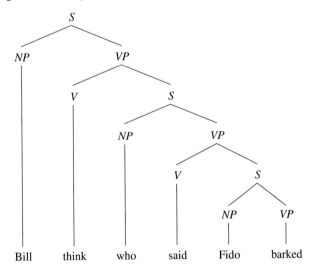

## 3.4.6 Separating Lexicon from PS Rules

It is often convenient to separate the descriptions of individual words (the LEXICON) from the PS rules. This is easy to do. Just write something like:

```
n --> [X], { noun(X) }.

noun(dog).
noun(cat).
noun(gardener).
    :
    :
```

There are two advantages to doing this. First, because of indexing, it is much faster to search through the facts

```
noun(dog).
noun(cat).
```

(etc.) than through rules of the form

```
n --> [dog].
n --> [cat].
```

Second, and more importantly, words can be defined by rules as well as by facts. Here is a LEXICAL RULE that creates a noun ending in *-ness* from every adjective:

```
% noun(+N)
%  Strips the suffix "ness" from N and
%  looks for a corresponding adjective.

noun(N) :-
    name(N,Nchars),
    append(Achars,"ness",Nchars),
    name(A,Achars),
    adjective(A).

% adjective(?A)
%  Lexicon of adjectives

adjective(flat).
adjective(green).
adjective(blue).
```

(Recall that append is not built in.)

This rule is not exactly right—it doesn't change *y* to *i* when forming words such as *ugliness*—but it's a start. The calls to name and append are time-consuming but unavoidable. In a complete working system, it might be better to modify the tokenizer so that some morphological analysis is done before the words are converted into atoms.

**Exercise 3.4.6.1**

Modify this lexical rule so that it changes final *y* to *i* before *-ness.* That is, the rule should produce correct spellings of words like *ugliness* and *sliminess.* Include a way to deal with exceptions such as *dryness* (not *\*driness*). Demonstrate that your implementation can correctly answer queries such as:

```
?- n([ugliness],[]).
```

using the rule `adjective(ugly)` plus the lexical rule.

**Exercise 3.4.6.2**

The lexical rule given so far expects the noun to be instantiated. That is, a query like `noun(flatness)` will succeed but `noun(X)` (with X uninstantiated) will fail. This means that the rule, as shown, is of no use in generating sentences. Rewrite it so that it will work with uninstantiated as well as instantiated arguments.

## 3.5 BUILDING SEMANTIC REPRESENTATIONS

### 3.5.1 Semantic Composition

Syntactic structure is not the only kind of output that a parser can produce. For natural language understanding we also need a semantic representation—that is, a representation of meaning. DCG parsers can produce semantic representations too.

To demonstrate this, we'll work with a tiny subset of English in which the only noun phrases are proper names (Fido, Felix), thereby postponing some complicated questions about the semantics of NPs. The syntax that we will use is as follows:

$$
\begin{array}{rcl}
S & \rightarrow & NP\ VP \\
NP & \rightarrow & \text{Fido} \\
NP & \rightarrow & \text{Felix} \\
VP & \rightarrow & V\ (NP) \\
V & \rightarrow & \text{chased} \\
V & \rightarrow & \text{slept}
\end{array}
$$

We will represent the meanings of sentences in first-order predicate logic, so that *Fido chased Felix* will be *chased(fido, felix)* and *Felix slept* will be *slept(felix)*.

What about the meanings of individual words? Proper nouns are no problem, since they are logical individuals:

$$
\begin{array}{rcl}
Fido & = & fido \\
Felix & = & felix
\end{array}
$$

To represent verbs, we will use lambda expressions, just as we did with keyword systems in Chapter 2. Recall that a lambda expression is simply a formula with an argument missing. Thus if

$$Felix \; slept = slept\,(felix)$$

then

$$slept = (\lambda x)\,slept(x)$$

where $\lambda x$ indicates that the value of $x$ is to be supplied from elsewhere.

So far, so good, but the verb *chased* needs two arguments, a subject and an object. We will represent it with one lambda expression inside another:

$$chased = (\lambda y)(\lambda x)chased\,(x,y)$$

This means, in effect, "Give me a value for $y$, such as *felix*, and I'll give you another lambda expression that needs only a value for $x$, such as $(\lambda x)chases\,(x, felix)$."

The next task is to combine the meanings of the individual words and thereby obtain the meanings of constituents. The parser will do this by supplying arguments to lambda expressions. For example, *fido* combines with $(\lambda x)slept\,(x)$ to give $slept\,(fido)$. Figure 3.6 shows how this works. Meaning seems to flow upward through the tree, as the meanings of smaller constituents get combined to give the meanings of larger constituents and ultimately of the whole S. But how can meaning flow upward when parsing proceeds top-down? The same way structures were built top-down, even though the actual information in them was only acquired at the bottommost (and therefore last) level. The parser will work with partly instantiated structures and instantiate the details when they finally become available.

Now for the implementation. Each predicate will have an argument for the semantic representation. We will represent lambda expressions in Prolog with the operator ^, just as in Chapter 2, so the rules for specific words will be:

```
np(fido)     --> [fido].
np(felix)    --> [felix].

v(X^slept(X))          --> [slept].
v(Y^(X^chased(X,Y)))   --> [chased].
```

Then it is simple to write phrase-structure rules that combine their arguments in the desired ways:

```
s(Pred) --> np(Subj), vp(Subj^Pred).

vp(Subj^Pred) --> v(Subj^Pred).
vp(Subj^Pred) --> v(Obj^(Subj^Pred)), np(Obj).
```

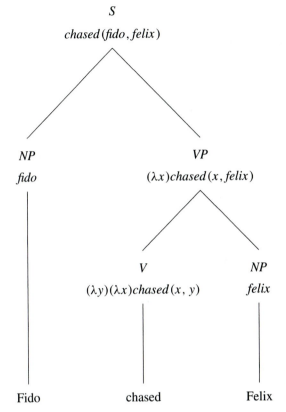

*S*

*chased (fido , felix )*

*NP*

*fido*

*VP*

*(λx)chased (x , felix )*

*V*

*(λy)(λx)chased (x, y)*

*NP*

*felix*

Fido                              chased                    Felix

**Figure 3.6**   Semantic representations are built by combining the meanings of the individual constituents.

The parser will then accept queries such as:

```
?- s(Semantics,[fido,chased,felix],[]).
Semantics = chased(fido,felix)

?- s(Semantics,[felix,slept],[]).
Semantics = slept(felix)
```

Notice that the semantics also goes part of the way toward ensuring that *chased* has an object and *slept* does not. Unlike the original phrase-structure grammar, the parser does not accept *\*Fido slept Felix,* and although it accepts *\*Fido chased,* it produces a partly uninstantiated semantic representation that could easily be rejected by some other part of a natural language processing system.

This is a demonstration of SEMANTIC COMPOSITION, building the semantic representation of each constituent from those of its subconstituents. The technique shown here barely scratches the surface. We will return to semantic representations in Chapter 7, but first, there are many syntactic issues to be addressed.

**Exercise 3.5.1.1**

According to this grammar, what is the semantic representation of *\*Fido chased?*

**Exercise 3.5.1.2**

Get the parser working and add the words *saw, barked, Max,* and *Mary.* Generate semantic representations for *Fido barked* and *Mary saw Max.*

**Exercise 3.5.1.3**

Modify the parser described above so that it builds both syntactic and semantic representations. (Use one argument for each.)

## 3.5.2 Semantic Grammars

A SEMANTIC GRAMMAR is something intermediate between a keyword or template system and a phrase-structure grammar. Semantic grammars use phrase-structure rules, but words are classified by their function in a particular situation (such as computer commands or database queries) rather than general syntactic principles. Representations of meaning are built by any of several techniques, including the method described in the previous section.

Figure 3.7 shows some analyses of sentences that might be assigned by semantic grammars in various situations. There are no "right" or "wrong" analyses; the goal is

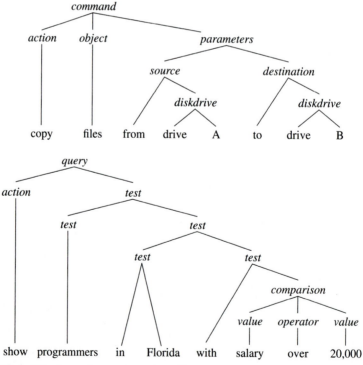

**Figure 3.7**  Semantic grammars assign arbitrary analyses to fit the purposes of a particular computer program.

purely to build something that works for a specific purpose. Parsing is often preceded by simplification just as in a template or keyword system.

**Exercise 3.5.2.1**

Reimplement your keyword system from Chapter 2 as a semantic grammar.

## 3.6 OFFBEAT USES FOR DCG RULES

Some people use DCG rules not just for parsing, but also to define almost any predicate that works through a list item by item. I do not advocate this practice, but you should be aware of it. Here is a predicate that counts the elements in a list:

```
count_off(N) --> [_], count_off(M), { N is M+1 }.
count_off(0) --> [].
```

More precisely, this predicate accepts a specified number of elements from the beginning of the list, thus:

```
?- count_off(N,[a,b,c],[]).
N = 3

?- count_off(N,[a,b,c,d,e,f],[e,f]).
N = 4

?- count_off(2,[a,b,c,d,e],What).
What = [c,d,e]
```

Since this predicate has nothing to do with parsing, the use of DCG notation tends to obscure rather than clarify how it works, and `count_off` would be better off written in plain Prolog:

```
count_off(N,[_|Rest],Tail) :- count_off(M,Rest,Tail), N is M+1.
count_off(0,Tail,Tail).
```

(Note that `count_off(0) --> []` doesn't mean "do this at the end of the list"; it means "do this without accepting anything from the list," although in fact it is the only rule that can apply when the list is empty.)

**Exercise 3.6.0.1**

Use DCG rules to implement a predicate that accepts a list of numbers and computes their sum.

**Exercise 3.6.0.2**

> Is 'dog `-->` "dog".' a legal DCG rule? If so, what does it mean and how might you use it?

**Exercise 3.6.0.3   (project)**

> Write a program that breaks a string of characters into words by using DCG rules. That is, it should convert `"this is it"` to `[this,is,it]` or the like.
>
> This is a reasonable thing to do, because breaking a string into words is a kind of parsing. The phrase-structure rules might include the following, or something similar:

$$
\begin{array}{rcl}
\textit{Token} & \rightarrow & \textit{Special-character} \\
\textit{Token} & \rightarrow & \textit{Alphanumerics} \\
\textit{Alphanumerics} & \rightarrow & \textit{Alphanumeric–character Alphanumerics} \\
\textit{Alphanumerics} & \rightarrow & \varnothing \\
\textit{Alphanumeric-character} & \rightarrow & \textit{a} \\
\textit{Alphanumeric-character} & \rightarrow & \textit{b} \\
\textit{Alphanumeric-character} & \rightarrow & \textit{c} \\
& \vdots &
\end{array}
$$

> For detailed advice see Appendix B.

## 3.7 EXCURSUS: TRANSITION-NETWORK PARSERS

DCG parsers are equivalent in power to an older parsing technique called AUGMENTED TRANSITION NETWORKS (ATNs). This section will briefly review ATNs as well as the simpler transition networks from which they are derived. There is little point in implementing an ATN in Prolog, since DCGs do the same job better, but it is useful to know how ATNs and DCGs correspond.

### 3.7.1 States and Transitions

A TRANSITION NETWORK is a parser that has a number of distinct STATES and proceeds from state to state in a manner controlled by the input string.

Figure 3.8 shows a transition network that parses *the dog, the big dog, the cat,* and nothing else. Circles represent states and arcs represent transitions. A small arrow shows where to start, and a double circle indicates a state in which parsing can stop.

To parse a sentence, the parser must get from the initial state to a state in which it can stop. This is done by following the arcs and accepting, from the input string, the words that are on the arc labels. An unlabeled arc is called a JUMP ARC and allows a state transition without accepting any input. So the process by which this network parses *the dog* is:

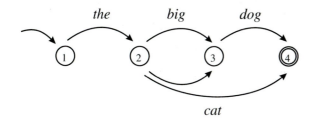

**Figure 3.8**  A finite-state transition network.

Start in state 1.

Go to state 2 accepting *the*.

Go to state 3 via the jump arc.

Go to state 4 accepting *dog*.

Stop.

Because it has a finite number of states, this is a FINITE-STATE TRANSITION NETWORK (FSTN) or FINITE AUTOMATON.

A transition network is DETERMINISTIC if it cannot backtrack, and NONDETERMINISTIC if it can.  More formally, a network is deterministic if, at every step, the choice of arcs is uniquely determined by the next word in the input string.  In natural language processing, we work with networks in which nondeterminism is allowed, and we will assume that they are implemented in such a way that backtracking is possible.

A FINITE-STATE TRANSDUCER is an FSTN in which each of the transitions can produce output as well as accepting input.  Figure 3.9 shows a finite-state transducer that can translate *the big dog* and *the cat* (but almost nothing else) into Spanish.  The arc label *the:el* means "input *the* and output *el*," and likewise for the other labels.  Thus, this network translates *the dog* to *el perro*; *the big dog* to *el gran perro;* and *the cat* to *el gato*.  By reversing the roles of the input and output, we could just as easily get it to translate Spanish into English.

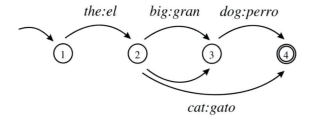

**Figure 3.9**  A finite-state transducer that translates English phrases into Spanish.

A finite-state transition network can contain CYCLES; that is, an arc can loop back to the state that it started in, or even to an earlier state.  This enables the network to accept arbitrarily long strings.  Figure 3.10 shows a network that accepts *the dog*

*the big dog*

*the big big dog*

*the big big big dog*    (etc.).

Although the number of states is finite, the number of words in the input string of this network is not bounded.

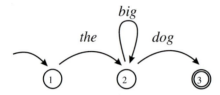

**Figure 3.10**   This finite-state transition network can accept arbitrarily long strings.

Finite-state transition networks are easy to implement in conventional programming languages, but they are clearly not adequate for human language; they provide no way to recognize constituent structure. Nonetheless, they have their uses in implementing templatelike systems (Chapter 2) and in analyzing morphology (Chapter 9).

**Exercise 3.7.1.1**

List the steps that the network in Figure 3.8 goes through when parsing *the cat.*

**Exercise 3.7.1.2**

Does the network in Figure 3.8 parse *the big cat*? Explain.

**Exercise 3.7.1.3**

Does the network in Figure 3.8 accept *the big* (with no words following)? Explain.

**Exercise 3.7.1.4**

Are the networks in Figures 3.8 and 3.10 deterministic?

**Exercise 3.7.1.5**

List the steps that the transducer in Figure 3.9 goes through when translating *the dog* into Spanish.

**Exercise 3.7.1.6**

Can the network in Figure 3.10 accept an infinitely long string? What is the difference between accepting an infinitely long string, and accepting arbitrarily long strings?

### 3.7.2 Recursive Transition Networks

A RECURSIVE TRANSITION NETWORK (RTN) is one in which a state transition can either accept a word, or execute (call) another entire network. In particular, a network can call itself, either directly or indirectly (for example, S can call VP and VP can call S). This makes it possible to parse sentences within sentences. It also means that the number of states available to the parser is no longer finite, because any number of recursive invocations of the same network could be in use at the same time.

Figure 3.11 shows an RTN that parses sentences such as *The gardener said the butler thought the dog barked* (compare Section 3.1.3 above). By using recursion, this network parses an S within an S. Here the lexicon is shown separate from the transition network. This is standard practice, but the lexicon could, of course, be rendered as a transition network if we wanted to do so.

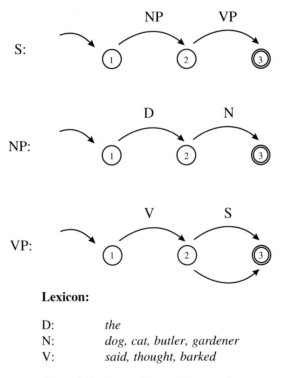

**Figure 3.11**   A recursive transition network.

RTNs are essentially equivalent to phrase-structure rules or DCG rules without arguments. There is, however, a minor difference. RTNs can contain cycles that allow unlimited repetition (Fig. 3.12); DCG rules and ordinary PS rules cannot. This is not a serious problem, because any network containing a cycle can be replaced by a *set* of PS rules that use recursion. For example, the network in Figure 3.12 can be replaced by the rules

$$NP \rightarrow D\ N^1$$
$$N^1 \rightarrow Adj\ N^1$$
$$N^1 \rightarrow N$$

which, of course, go into DCG straightforwardly.

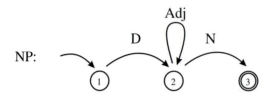

**Figure 3.12**  A cycle in an RTN.

These three rules generate the same sequences as the original network (D N, D Adj N, D Adj Adj N, etc.), but the tree structure is not the same. The rules introduce $N^1$ constituents which the original network does not. Fortunately, there are linguistic reasons for thinking that these $N^1$ constituents are real, and thus that the cycle in the network is not really appropriate for describing the structure of English.

**Exercise 3.7.2.1**

List the steps that the RTN in Figure 3.11 goes through when parsing each of these sentences:

*The dog barked.*

*The butler said the gardener thought the dog barked.*

**Exercise 3.7.2.2**

Construct a definite-clause grammar that is equivalent to the RTN in Figure 3.11.

**Exercise 3.7.2.3**

List the steps that the network in Figure 3.12 goes through when parsing *the big big big dog* (assuming an appropriate lexicon).

**Exercise 3.7.2.4**

Diagram the tree structure of *the big big big dog* using the PS rules given in this section.

### 3.7.3 Augmented Transition Networks (ATNs)

We saw earlier that the real power of DCGs comes from the ability to have arguments on the nodes. The equivalent of a DCG with arguments is an AUGMENTED TRANSITION NETWORK (ATN), which is like an RTN except that:

- Each subnetwork can have REGISTERS (memory locations) in which information can be stored.
- Each arc can have actions associated with it. These actions include storing, retrieving, and testing register values, and adding items to, or retrieving items from, a holding list.

- Data can be transferred between the registers of a subnetwork and the registers of the network from which it was called. For example, register values associated with a noun can be copied into the registers of the NP in which the noun occurs.

There are several different notations for ATNs, with different abstract instruction sets, and, compared to DCGs, all of them are cumbersome. Woods (1970) and Bates (1978) expound ATNs in detail. Pereira and Warren (1980) show that all ATNs can be translated into DCGs, and that, in general, the DCGs are more concise, more readable, and potentially faster to execute.

Figure 3.13 shows a simple ATN that enforces subject-verb agreement. Here are the steps that it goes through when parsing *The dog sees the cats* (ignoring backtracking):

Start in state 1 of S network.
Call NP network.
  Start in state 1 of NP network.
  Accept D (*the*).
  Proceed to state 2 of NP network.
  Accept N (*dog,* NUM=SINGULAR).
  Set register NUM of NP = SINGULAR.
  Proceed to state 3 of NP network and exit.
Set register NUM of S = SINGULAR.
Proceed to state 2 of S network.
Call VP network.
  Start in state 1 of VP network.
  Accept V (*sees,* NUM=SINGULAR).

  Set register NUM of VP = SINGULAR.
  Proceed to state 2 of VP network.
  Call NP network.
    Start in state 1 of NP network.
    Accept D (*the*).
    Proceed to state 2 of NP network.
    Accept N (*cats,* NUM=PLURAL).
    Set register NUM of this NP = PLURAL.
    Proceed to state 3 of NP network and exit.
  Proceed to state 3 of VP network and exit.
Test that NUM of S = NUM of VP
  (the test succeeds; both have the value SINGULAR).
Proceed to state 3 of S network and exit.

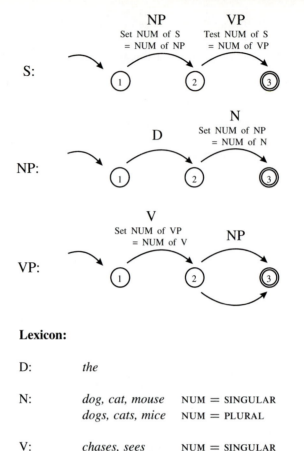

**Lexicon:**

D:          *the*

N:          *dog, cat, mouse*     NUM = SINGULAR
            *dogs, cats, mice*    NUM = PLURAL

V:          *chases, sees*        NUM = SINGULAR
            *chase, see*          NUM = PLURAL

**Figure 3.13**   An augmented transition network that enforces subject-verb agreement.

Figure 3.14 shows an ATN that parses questions such as *Who did the gardener think chased the cat?* using a holding list.

A striking difference between ATNs and DCGs is that ATNs lack the concept of unification. Thus, in place of simply trying to instantiate variables, ATNs have to perform lots of separate assignments and comparisons. In Chapter 5 we will explore the usefulness of unification in grammatical analysis.

**Exercise 3.7.3.1**

Is the network in Figure 3.13 deterministic? Explain.

**Exercise 3.7.3.2**

Construct DCGs equivalent to the networks in Figures 3.13 and 3.14.

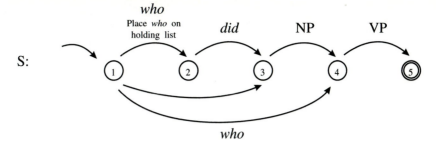

S:

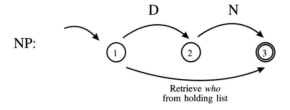

NP:

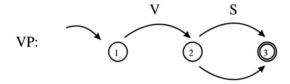

VP:

**Lexicon:**

D:        *the*
N:        *dog, cat, butler, gardener*
V:        *say, said, think, thought, bark, barked*

**Figure 3.14**    An augmented transition network that parses *wh*-questions.

### Exercise 3.7.3.3

List the steps that the network in Figure 3.14 goes through when parsing the sentence *Who did the butler say thought the dog barked?*

# CHAPTER 4

# English Phrase Structure

## 4.1 PHRASE STRUCTURE

The main purpose of this chapter is to develop a rough-and-ready set of phrase-structure rules for parsing some of the major structures of English, and, perhaps more importantly, to illustrate *how* a set of rules is developed.

Developing a formal grammar is a lot like writing a computer program; there are many points at which you can do any of several things as long as you follow up the consequences of your decision consistently. There are many other places at which one choice is probably better than another, but it will take a lot of research to find out which is better, and the difference may never show up during the lifetime of one project.

The rules developed here are not complete, for two reasons. First, if we tried to cover all the PS rules of English, this chapter would be hundreds of pages long. Second, there are structures that cannot be parsed with phrase-structure rules alone; we will look at some of them and develop appropriate parsing mechanisms in the next chapter.

The rules in this chapter incorporate many of the ideas of Radford (1988), Jackendoff (1977), and Gazdar, Klein, Pullum, and Sag (1985) but do not adhere strictly to any theory. In particular, for convenience I ignore the distinction between adjuncts and complements, although I think it is valid; see Radford for a clear and detailed presentation. Students who have been trained in transformational grammar should note that here—as almost always when parsing—we are analyzing *surface* structure and not attempting to capture deep generalizations.

### 4.1.1 Trees Revisited

Before developing PS rules we must look more deeply into their significance. Consider a syntactic tree like the one shown in Figure 4.1. The points where lines begin or end

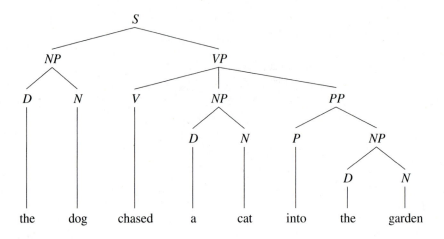

**Figure 4.1**   A syntactic tree.

in a syntactic tree are called NODES. Normally, nodes bear LABELS such as S, NP, VP, NP, or *dog*.

If two nodes are connected by a line, the upper node IMMEDIATELY DOMINATES the lower one. More generally, one node DOMINATES another if you can get from the first node to the second by following lines downward. For example, the first NP node dominates D, N, *the,* and *dog*.

Two nodes are said to be SISTERS if they are immediately dominated by the same node. For example, D and N are sisters in the tree above. Their MOTHER is NP; that is, they are DAUGHTERS of NP.

The words at the bottom of the tree diagram are the TERMINAL NODES. A CONSTITUENT consists of all the terminal nodes dominated (immediately or indirectly) by a particular nonterminal node.

A tree is equivalent to a LABELED BRACKETING of words into groups. For example, the tree shown at the top of page 79 could be written as

$$[_S \ [_{NP} \ [_D \ a \ _D] \ [_N \ dog \ _N] \ _{NP}] \ [_{VP} \ [_V \ barked \ _V] \ _{VP}] \ _S]$$

Without loss of information, the labels could be omitted on either the opening or closing brackets (not both). Labeled bracketings are often used to indicate part of the structure

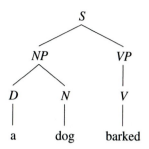

of an example sentence, as in:

*We thought* [<sub>S</sub> *it was raining* ].

**Exercise 4.1.1.1**

In Figure 4.1, which nodes are dominated by VP? Which are immediately dominated by VP?

**Exercise 4.1.1.2**

In Figure 4.1, identify the sisters of PP and the daughters of PP.

**Exercise 4.1.1.3**

Express Figure 4.1 as a labeled bracketing.

**Exercise 4.1.1.4**

Express [<sub>A</sub> [<sub>B</sub> [<sub>C</sub> *xxx yyy* ] ] [<sub>D</sub> *zzz* ] ] as a tree diagram.

## 4.1.2 Constituents and Categories

A tree gives two kinds of information about the sentence: it divides it into CONSTITUENTS (phrases) and classifies these constituents into CATEGORIES such as NP, VP, and the like. For example,

- *the* is a constituent of type D;
- *dog* is a constituent of type N;
- *the dog, a cat,* and *the garden* are constituents of type NP;
- *chased a cat into the garden* is a constituent of type VP;
- *the dog chased a cat into the garden* is a constituent of type S.

How do we know this is the right way to group the words in this sentence—that, for example, *into the garden* really is a constituent and *a cat into* is not? Although none of them is infallible, there are several standard tests for constituency:

- Any string of words that can be MOVED AS A UNIT is probably a constituent. Instead of *The dog chased a cat into the garden* you can say *Into the garden the dog chased a cat.* This argues strongly that *into the garden* is a constituent.

- Any string of words that can be DELETED is probably a constituent. Again, you can leave out *into the garden* without changing the grammatical or semantic relations in the rest of the sentence. This, too, argues that *into the garden* is a constituent.

- Usually, the MEANING of a constituent is, in some sense, a unit. It makes sense to ask what *into the garden* means; it makes much less sense to ask what *a cat into* means.

The strongest argument for the correctness of any phrase-structure tree, however, is the fact that it is generated by a coherent system of rules that also accounts for many other facts about English syntax.

The claims that a tree makes about categories are also important. For example, by labeling *the cat, the dog,* and *the garden* all with the label NP, this tree makes the claim that they are syntactically alike—they can all occur in the same positions. And indeed *a cat chased the dog into the garden,* or even *the garden chased a cat into the dog,* is a grammatical (if somewhat odd) sentence of English.

**Exercise 4.1.2.1**

List all the constituents that are identified by Figure 4.1.

**Exercise 4.1.2.2**

Cite at least two kinds of evidence that *a cat* is a constituent in the sentence *The dog chased a cat into the garden.*

**Exercise 4.1.2.3**

Cite evidence that, in *The dog chased a cat into the garden, the* and *a* belong to the same category.

## 4.1.3 Structural Ambiguity

Many sentences are AMBIGUOUS, i.e., the same sentence can mean two or more different things. Usually the ambiguity is LEXICAL—that is, a word or idiomatic phrase within the sentence can have more than one meaning. For example, *glasses* can mean either spectacles or drinking-glasses.

But some ambiguities are STRUCTURAL; they result from the existence of more than one tree structure for the same string of words. Figure 4.2 shows a striking example: *I saw the boy with the telescope* can mean either that the boy had the telescope, or that I did the seeing with the telescope, and sure enough, the rules of English allow two tree structures, one with each meaning. In one tree, *with the telescope* modifies *boy* (and thus *the boy with the telescope* is a constituent); in the other, *with the telescope* modifies *saw.*

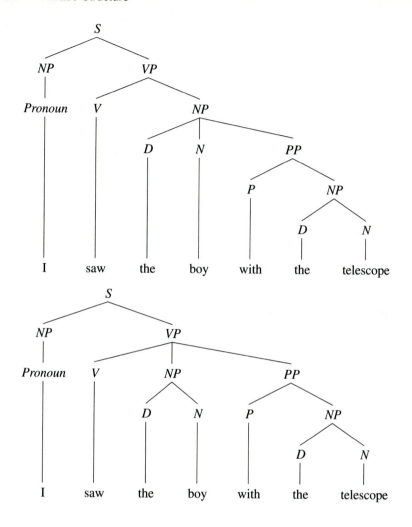

**Figure 4.2**   The two meanings of this sentence correspond to two tree structures.

### Exercise 4.1.3.1

Give the two meanings of each of the following sentences, and state whether the ambiguity is structural, lexical, or both. Explain how you know.

*By 1960 the Soviet Union had several satellites.*
*The painter put on another coat.*
*The judge threw the book at him.*
*Visiting relatives can be tiresome.*
*We like flying planes.*

## 4.2 TRADITIONAL GRAMMAR

### 4.2.1 Parts of Speech

Many of the terms and concepts used in phrase-structure grammar come from a centuries-old tradition. The classification of words into "parts of speech" (nouns, verbs, adjectives, etc.) goes back to classical antiquity (Robins 1967) and was originally developed for Greek and Latin. It works reasonably well for English if some adjustments are made. This section will review traditional grammatical concepts briefly.

Table 4.1 illustrates the traditional parts of speech in English. The classification shown is neither complete nor entirely self-consistent. It is given mainly to illustrate the traditional terminology.

The first thing to note is that these categories are syntactic, not semantic. They are supposed to explain where each word can occur in the sentence; they are not a classification of word meanings. This is important because schoolbooks often say that "a noun denotes a person, place, or thing," "a verb denotes an action or event," and so forth. Such assertions are demonstrably false. Surely a sunset or a burglary is an event, but *sunset* and *burglary* are nouns, not verbs.

This does not mean that meaning is of no help in classifying words. Nouns *do* tend to refer to people, places, and concrete objects, and verbs *do* tend to refer to events, actions, or states. It's just that this tendency is not absolute. It would be odd if *mountain* were a verb or if *kick* were not a verb.[1]

Even when words of different categories refer to the same thing, the meaning is packaged differently. The noun *burglary* and the verb *burglarize* denote the same kind of event, but there is a difference. The verb is marked for tense (past or present) and requires a subject and object; the noun does not. The noun, on the other hand, requires a determiner and can be made plural to denote more than one event of the same kind. In the Middle Ages, these differences in "packaging" were called *modes of signifying* (Covington 1984).

**Exercise 4.2.1.1**

Using traditional terminology, give the category of each word in each of the following sentences:

*Syntax and semantics are my favorite subjects.*
*We found him easily when he was ready.*
*I feel sick.*

**Exercise 4.2.1.2**

A few grammar handbooks say that the sentence *Hopefully, we'll succeed* either is ungrammatical, or means 'We will succeed in a hopeful manner' (not 'We hope we'll succeed' as the speaker intends). Based on what Table 4.1 tells you about adverbs, critique this claim.

---

[1]But *mountain* is a verb in Nootka, a Native American language in which almost every word has both noun and verb forms. English, like most European languages, tends to make other categories into nouns; we have nouns derived from verbs (*destroy → destruction*), adjectives (*red → redness*), and even particles (*out → outing*).

**TABLE 4.1**   TRADITIONAL SYNTACTIC CATEGORIES (PARTS OF SPEECH)

**Nouns**
   **Proper** (name): *Joe, Frankenstein, America*
   **Common** (ordinary)
      **Count** (distinguishes singular from plural): *dog/dogs, theory/theories*
      **Mass (Noncount)** (no plural): *water, air, stuff, superiority*
   **Gerund of verb:** *singing, painting* (as in <u>*painting is fun*</u>)

**Pronouns**
   **Personal:** *he/him, she/her, it, we/us, you, they/them*
   **Reflexive:** *himself, herself, itself, ourselves . . .*
   **Demonstrative (Deictic):** *this, that* (as in <u>*This*</u> *is it*)
   **Indefinite:** *someone, everybody, nobody, something . . .*

**Determiners**
   **Articles:** *the, a (an)*
   **Demonstrative (Deictic):** *this, that* (example: <u>*this*</u> *house*)
   **Quantifiers:** *every, all, some, three*
   **Possessive pronouns:** *my, your, his, her, their*

**Adjectives**
   **Positive:** *big, good, exceptional*
   **Comparative:** *bigger, better*
   **Superlative:** *biggest, best*
   **Participle of verb:** *distracted, singing* (as in *a* <u>*singing*</u> *cowboy*)

**Verbs**
   **Intransitive** (taking no object): *sleep, yell, bark*
   **Transitive** (taking one object): *kick, emulate, destroy, read*
   **Ditransitive** (taking two objects): *give* (as in *give Joe the book*)
   **Copula** (verb of being): *be, am, is, are, was, were*
   **Modals** (preceding another verb): *may, might, can, could, will, would . . .*
   **Auxiliaries** (preceding the verb, can follow a modal): *be, is, are, has*

**Adverbs**
   **Modifying a verb:** *quickly, slowly, today, here*
   **Modifying an adjective or adverb:** *very, extremely, slightly*
   **Modifying the whole sentence:** *hopefully, unfortunately*

**Prepositions**
   **With objects:** *in, before, after, below . . .* (example: <u>*in*</u> *the house*)
   **Without objects (Particles):** *up, down, in, out* (example: *Look it* <u>*up*</u>)

**Conjunctions**
   **Coordinating** (joining constituents of same type)
      **Simple:** *and, or*
      **Correlating:** *both . . . and, either . . . or, neither . . . nor*
   **Subordinating** (joining embedded sentence to main sentence):
      *before, after, although, because, when, whenever*

**Interjections:** *no! yes! oh! ouch! wham! bang! alas!*

### 4.2.2 Grammatical Relations

Traditional grammar analyzes sentences, not by drawing constituency trees, but by identifying relationships that connect one word to another. For example, in *The dog chased
the cat into the garden,* a traditional grammarian would say that:

> *dog* is the SUBJECT of *chased;*
>
> *cat* is the (DIRECT) OBJECT of *chased;*
>
> *into the garden* MODIFIES (describes) *chased;*
>
> *garden* is the object of the preposition *into;* and
>
> the three occurrences of *the* modify *dog, cat,* and *garden* respectively;

Table 4.2 lists the traditional names for grammatical relations. As you can see, there is
often some uncertainty whether a grammatical relation belongs to a word or to a whole
phrase; some people say the object of *chased* is *cat* and others say it is *the cat.* In
traditional grammar this uncertainty was never entirely cleared up.

---

**TABLE 4.2**   GRAMMATICAL RELATIONS IN TRADITIONAL
GRAMMAR

---

**Subject:** Noun phrase required to precede a verb.
  Examples: *Birds fly. All the students are listening.*
  **Clause** (embedded sentence) as subject: *That he succeeded is amazing.*

**Predicate:** The entire verb phrase.
  Examples: *Birds fly. All the students are playing soccer.*

**Object:** Noun phrase required to follow a verb or preposition.
  Object of preposition: *in the house*
  Object of verb: *John loves Mary. Asimov wrote two hundred books.*
  **Indirect** (first) object of two-object verb: *John gave Bill the answers.*
  **Direct** (second) object of two-object verb: *John gave Bill the answers.*

**Complement:** Something other than an NP required after a verb.
  Adjective as complement: *He looked silly.*
  **Clause** (embedded sentence) as complement: *We thought he was crazy.*

**Modifier:** Any word or phrase that describes another.
  Adjective modifying noun: *big dogs*
  Adverb modifying verb: *barks loudly*
  Clause modifying sentence: *When they sang, we laughed.*

---

Grammatical relations can be defined in terms of phrase structure. For example,
an object is an NP immediately dominated by VP or PP; a subject is an NP immediately
dominated by S; and so forth (Chomsky 1965).

**Exercise 4.2.2.1**

Using Table 4.2 as a guide, identify as many grammatical relations as possible in the following sentences:

*Three snails crept into the garden.*

*The slimy creatures gave us a sudden surprise.*

*When we saw them, we jumped.*

## 4.3 THE NOUN PHRASE AND ITS MODIFIERS

### 4.3.1 Simple NPs

In constructing a set of phrase-structure rules we will begin with the NP. To a first approximation, the NP rule looks something like this:

$$NP \quad \rightarrow \quad D \ (Adj) \ N \ (PP)$$

This accounts for NPs such as:

*the dog*

*the gray cat*

*the dog in the garden*

*the young boy with the telescope*

The determiner can be null, as in our well-worn example [$_{NP}$ *Birds* ] *fly.* This is accounted for by the rule

$$D \quad \rightarrow \quad \emptyset$$

alongside $D \rightarrow$ *the* and the like.

Most determiners are single words (*the, a, some, every, five,* and the like). For now, we'll ignore NPs in which an article and a quantifier occur together (e.g., [$_D$ *the two* ] *boys*), as well as the internal grammar of numbers such as *three thousand four hundred twenty-two* and complex quantifiers such as *more than three.* For interesting analyses of phrases such as these, see Jackendoff (1977).

In Chapter 3 we saw that a determiner can consist of a complete NP followed by possessive *'s,* as in [$_{NP}$ *the junkman* ]*'s daughter.* The NP can be of almost any type, but there seems to be a requirement that it end in a noun; you can say *the queen of England's crown* but not *\*the boy who ran quickly's prize.* We can assume that this requirement is a matter of morphology (the *'s* ending only goes on nouns) and thus that the PS rules need not account for it.

Pronouns and proper names do not take determiners, nor do they normally take adjectives or prepositional phrases. To account for pronouns and proper names, we introduce two more PS rules:

$$NP \rightarrow Pronoun$$
$$NP \rightarrow Name$$

along with the appropriate lexical entries such as:

$$Pronoun \rightarrow I, me, you, he, him, she, they \ldots$$
$$Name \rightarrow Joe, Bill, Jack, Mary, Fido, Felix \ldots$$

**Exercise 4.3.1.1**

Construct a parser that implements all the PS rules discussed in this section, except for possessives. Use it to parse the noun phrases *birds, the dog, the gray cat, the dog in the garden,* and *the young boy with the telescope.*

This parser must construct a parse tree as a Prolog structure. Your instructor will test it with queries such as:

```
?- np(Structure,[the,gray,cat],[]).
Structure = np(d(the),adj(gray),n(cat))
```

Remember that there is nothing in DCG notation that corresponds to the parentheses indicating optionality in a PS rule. You will have to work out, and implement, all the alternative rules in full.[2]

In most of the subsequent exercises in this chapter you will add rules to this parser. It will ultimately contain over 100 DCG rules.

**Debugging a parser:** If your parser fails to accept a phrase, first check that your rules include all the necessary vocabulary. For example, if

```
?- np(Str,[the,young,boy,with,the,telescope],[]).
```

fails, check that *the, young, boy, with,* and *telescope* are in your DCG rules.

Next try to parse parts of the phrase. For example, try

```
?- np(Str,[the,young,boy],[]).
```

(which, according to the grammar, should also be a noun phrase) and

```
?- pp(Str,[with,the,telescope],[]).
```

This will help you localize the rules that you have written incorrectly.

---

[2]Sometimes you can render *VP → V (NP)* into DCG as 'vp --> v, (np ; []).' where (np ; [])
means 'accept an NP or a null constituent.' But if you use this trick while building tree structure in the way described here, your trees will be littered with unmotivated null constituents.

Once the parse succeeds, you're not through; you must verify that it gives the right structure, and that if more than one parse is possible, all the structures are consistent with the grammar.

### 4.3.2 Multiple Adjective Positions

A noun can take an indefinite number of adjectives in front of it, as long as the meanings add up to something coherent. For example:

> *the big dog*
> *the big green dog*
> *the big hairy green dog*
> *the big fat hairy green dog*
> *the big noisy fat hairy green dog*

This, then, calls for a recursive rule. But the complete NP is not recursive; the other parts of the NP (particularly the determiner) are never multiple.

The solution is to introduce another level of constituent structure between N and NP. Jackendoff calls it N̄, N′, or $N^1$; in Prolog we'll call it n1. Then in place of

$$NP \quad \rightarrow \quad D\ (Adj)\ N\ (PP)$$

we can write:

$$
\begin{aligned}
NP &\rightarrow D\ N^1\ (PP) \\
N^1 &\rightarrow Adj\ N^1 \\
N^1 &\rightarrow N
\end{aligned}
$$

and get structures like the one in Figure 4.3.

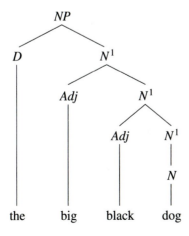

**Figure 4.3**    Recursion on the $N^1$ constituent allows NPs to have multiple adjectives.

**Exercise 4.3.2.1**

Revise your parser to allow multiple adjectives and parse *the big black noisy dog.* It should still parse *the gray cat* and all the other examples from before, but now it should give structures that include $N^1$.

### 4.3.3 Adjective Phrases

An adjective is not always a single word—sometimes it is a phrase, such as *very big.* The $N^1$ rule introduces adjective *phrases,* not just adjectives:

*the very big dog*
*the very big, surprisingly fat dog*
*the very big, slightly underfed, annoyingly messy dog*

So we need to change the first $N^1$ rule to

$$N^1 \quad \rightarrow \quad AdjP\ N^1$$

and define adjective phrase (AdjP) as:

$$AdjP \quad \rightarrow \quad (Degree)\ Adj$$

where *Degree* → *very, slightly, extremely*, etc.

Longer AdjPs come after the noun, not before it, and AdjPs that follow the noun can include prepositional phrases and other complements after the adjective:

*a dog* [$_{AdjP}$ *similar to the first one* ]

We will not account for these here.

**Exercise 4.3.3.1**

Modify your parser to incorporate the rules just introduced, and to parse the examples given (*the very big dog,* etc.). It should still parse all the examples from previous exercises, but now the structures should include AdjP where applicable.

### 4.3.4 Sentences within NPs

An NP such as *the fact that birds fly* has an S within it, preceded by the COMPLEMENTIZER *that.* So we need to modify the NP rule again, and also define a new constituent $S^1$ (more commonly called $\bar{S}$, pronounced "S-bar"):

$$
\begin{aligned}
NP &\rightarrow D\ N^1\ (PP)\ (S^1) \\
S^1 &\rightarrow Comp\ S \\
Comp &\rightarrow that
\end{aligned}
$$

We also need to add the familiar rules:

$$S \quad \rightarrow \quad NP \ VP$$
$$VP \quad \rightarrow \quad V \ (NP)$$

This will account for structures such as those in Figure 4.4.

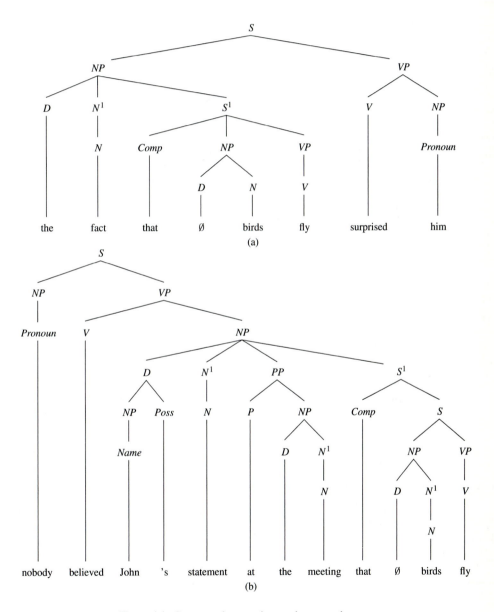

**Figure 4.4**   Sentences that contain complex noun phrases.

**Exercise 4.3.4.1**

Modify your parser to parse the sentences:

*The fact that birds fly surprised him.*

*The students challenged the quite unexpected statement at the conference that birds fly.*

Why do you get two parses for the second sentence? Is it genuinely ambiguous or is the grammar overgenerating?

## 4.4 THE VERB PHRASE

### 4.4.1 Verbs and Their Complements

Verbs take many kinds of complements after them. For example:

| Verb | Type of complement(s) | Example |
|------|----------------------|---------|
| slept | None | *John slept.* |
| chased | NP | *The dog chased the cat.* |
| gave | NP + NP | *John gave us the information.* |
| gave | NP + [PP *to* ... ] | *John gave the information to us.* |
| said | $S^1$ | *John said (that) birds fly.* |
| seemed | AdjP | *John seemed very old.* |
| wanted | *to* VP | *John wanted to leave.* |

In Chapter 3 we looked briefly at the problem of SUBCATEGORIZATION, i.e., ensuring that a verb is not used with the wrong kind of complement. For now, we will ignore subcategorization and simply assume that the input to the parser is grammatical.

To a first approximation, then, we need at least the following rules for VP:

$$VP \quad \rightarrow \quad V (NP) (PP) (NP) (PP) (S^1)$$
$$VP \quad \rightarrow \quad V AdjP$$
$$VP \quad \rightarrow \quad V \text{ to } VP$$

and we need to introduce a null complementizer:

$$Comp \quad \rightarrow \quad \emptyset$$

This accounts for the structures in Figure 4.5, among others. But the first VP rule is far from satisfying, and we will return to subcategorization in Chapter 5.

**Exercise 4.4.1.1**

Based on the PS rules introduced on this section, draw tree diagrams for the following sentences:

*Birds flew into the garden.*

*Max announced at the meeting that the birds looked silly.*

*The birds wanted to leave.*

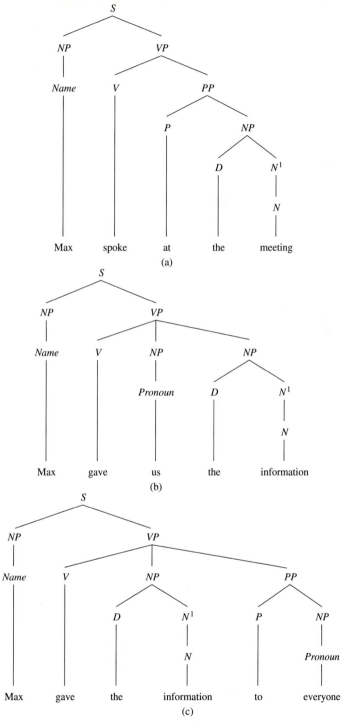

**Figure 4.5** Verbs with various kinds of complements. (Continues on page 92.)

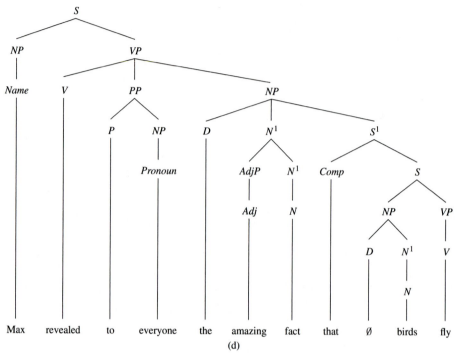

(d)

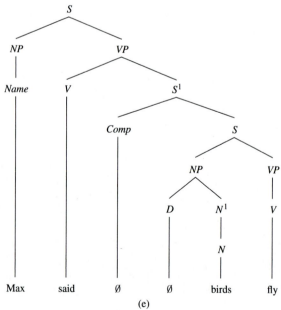

(e)

**Figure 4.5 cont.** (Continues on page 93.)

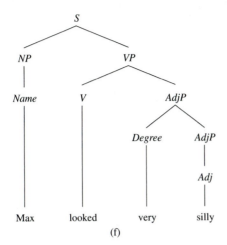

(f)                                        **Figure 4.5    cont.**

**Exercise 4.4.1.2**

Extend your parser to parse the sentences in Figure 4.5 and the sentences in the previous exercise. You need not include all expansions of the VP rule, as long as you include enough to parse the sentences here, and you are prepared to add more as needed later on.

## 4.4.2 Particles

A PARTICLE is a preposition without an object. Particles occur only with specific verbs which require them, such as *look up* or *throw out*. The same verbs also occur without the particles, with somewhat different meanings.

When present, the particle occurs in either of two positions, as shown in Figure 4.6 on page 94. Note that *Joe looked up the tower* is ambiguous (he either looked up the tower in a book, or looked upward along the tower), and that this ambiguity is structural; Figure 4.7 on pages 94 and 95 shows the two structures.

**Exercise 4.4.2.1**

Extend your parser to handle particles and to parse the sentences in Figures 4.6 and 4.7, giving both structures for *Joe looked up the tower*. You need not provide for all the combinations of particles with other parts of the VP; just add enough VP rules to parse the sentences needed for this exercise.

## 4.4.3 The Copula

The COPULA, or verb of being (*is, are,* etc.), takes an NP or AdjP as complement, as shown in Figure 4.8 on page 95.

**Exercise 4.4.3.1**

Extend your parser to parse the sentences in Figure 4.8.

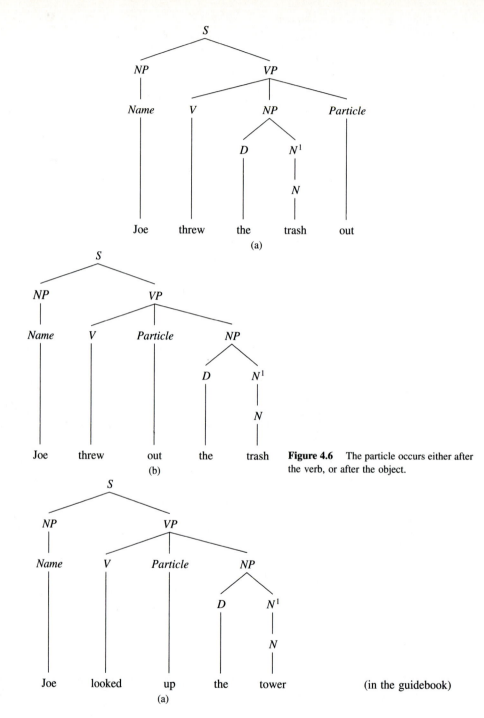

(a)

(b)

**Figure 4.6** The particle occurs either after the verb, or after the object.

(in the guidebook)

(a)

**Figure 4.7** *Up* can be either an ordinary preposition or a particle. (Continues on page 95.)

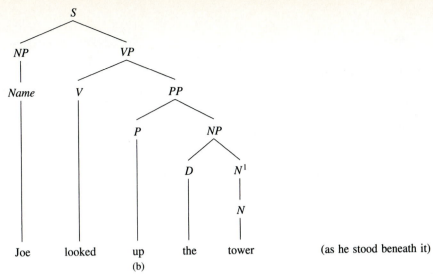

(as he stood beneath it)

(b)

**Figure 4.7    cont.**

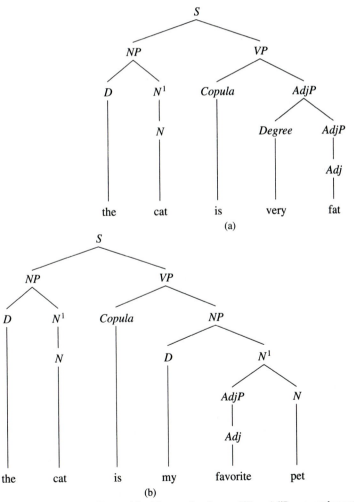

(a)

(b)

**Figure 4.8**   The copula takes an NP or AdjP as complement.

## 4.5 OTHER STRUCTURES

### 4.5.1 Conjunctions

Most occurrences of coordinating conjunctions such as *and* and *or* seem to be governed by a rule

$$X \quad \rightarrow \quad X \; Conj \; X$$

where X is any kind of constituent whatever. That is, any two constituents of the same kind can be joined by a conjunction to make a larger constituent. Figure 4.9 shows some examples.

The rule $X \rightarrow X \; Conj \; X$ cannot be expressed directly in DCG notation; instead it must be replaced by a set of rules

$$NP \quad \rightarrow \quad NP \; Conj \; NP$$
$$AdjP \quad \rightarrow \quad AdjP \; Conj \; AdjP$$

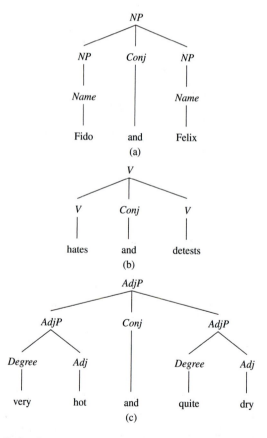

**Figure 4.9**   Conjunctions such as *and* take two constituents of the same kind and make them into a larger constituent.

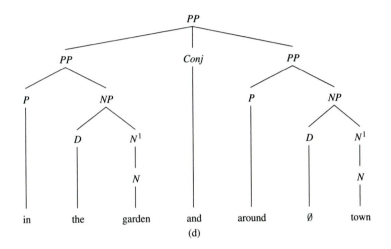

(d)

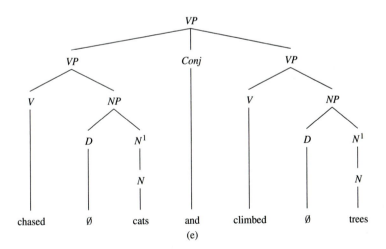

(e)

**Figure 4.9    cont.**

$$PP \rightarrow PP \; Conj \; PP$$
$$VP \rightarrow VP \; Conj \; VP$$
$$V \rightarrow V \; Conj \; V$$

and so on. But even these rules aren't DCG parsable; they cause loops, as noted in Chapter 3, where a trick for handling them was suggested.

Challenging as this is, it is still not the whole story about conjunctions. Hudson (1988) points out that in a sentence like

*John drank* [$_?$ *coffee at breakfast* ] *and* [$_?$ *tea at lunch* ].

the conjoined elements, *coffee at breakfast* and *tea at lunch,* are not constituents (Hudson 1988). Apparently, this sentence arises through a process of ELLIPSIS (omission of understood material) from the complete sentence

[$_S$ *John drank coffee at breakfast* ] *and* [$_S$ *John drank tea at lunch* ].

or at least the properly conjoined VP

*John* [$_{VP}$ *drank coffee at breakfast* ] *and* [$_{VP}$ *drank tea at lunch* ].

There is no standard approach to parsing ellipsis phenomena such as these, but you should be aware of them.

### Exercise 4.5.1.1

Draw a tree for *John drank coffee at breakfast and drank tea at lunch.* Now try to do the same thing with the second occurrence of *drank* omitted. What goes wrong?

### Exercise 4.5.1.2

Why doesn't a loop arise when parsing correlating (discontinuous) conjunctions such as *both . . . and* and *either . . . or*?

### Exercise 4.5.1.3

Add rules to your parser to parse the following sentences:

*It is both very warm and quite dry.*
*John drank both coffee and tea.*

Do not attempt to handle any conjunctions other than *both . . . and.*

## 4.5.2 Sentential PPs

Traditional grammar recognizes numerous SUBORDINATING CONJUNCTIONS, such as *before, after, when, whenever,* and *because,* which allow a whole sentence to modify (describe) some part of another sentence. Examples:

> *I saw him after* [s *he left* ].
> *The discussion after* [s *he left* ] *was surprising.*

Here *after he left* modifies *saw* and *discussion* respectively.

Emonds (1976:172–176) and Radford (1988:134–137) argue convincingly that these "subordinating conjunctions" are not conjunctions at all, but rather *prepositions* of a special kind that take S rather than NP after them. Figure 4.10 shows the kind of structures that this entails.[3]

There are two main reasons to view "subordinating conjunctions" as prepositions. First, some of them *are* prepositions (of the kind we are already familiar with) and can equally well take an NP instead of an S. Examples:

> *The discussion*  $\left\{ \begin{array}{l} after \ [_S \ he \ left \ ] \\ after \ [_{NP} \ the \ meeting \ ] \end{array} \right\}$  *was interesting.*

> *I saw him*  $\left\{ \begin{array}{l} before \ [_S \ he \ left \ ] \\ before \ [_{NP} \ the \ meeting \ ] \end{array} \right\}$ .

Second, sentential PPs occur in the same positions as ordinary noun-phrase-containing PPs. We have just seen them at the ends of NPs and VPs. Both kinds of PPs also occur at the beginning of the sentence:

> $\left\{ \begin{array}{l} After \ he \ left \\ After \ the \ meeting \end{array} \right\}$  *the discussion continued.*

This means that our familiar rule $S \rightarrow NP \ VP$ must be rewritten as:

$$S \quad \rightarrow \quad (PP) \ NP \ VP$$

and the rules for PP become:

$$PP \quad \rightarrow \quad P \ NP$$
$$PP \quad \rightarrow \quad P \ S$$

There is now a subcategorization problem with P because some Ps take only NP; some, such as *whenever,* take only S; and some take either NP or S. For the moment, we will ignore this.

---

[3]For theoretical reasons the object of P may turn out to be not S but S̄ with the null complementizer. In parsing, this makes no difference.

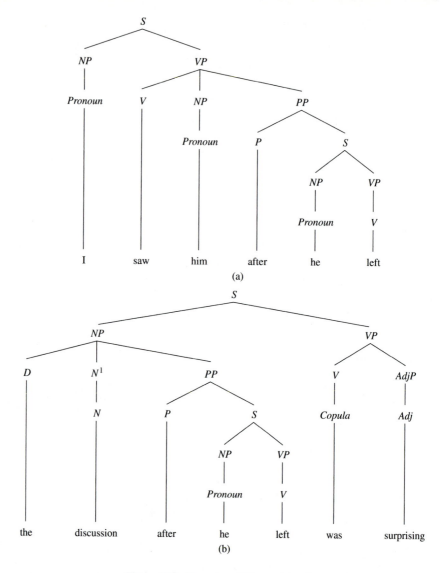

**Figure 4.10**  Examples of PP containing S.

### Exercise 4.5.2.1

The sentence *I heard about the discussion after the meeting* is structurally ambiguous; *after the meeting* modifies either *discussion* or *heard.* Draw trees for its two structures.

### Exercise 4.5.2.2

Extend your parser to handle the sentences in Figure 4.10, as well as:

$$After \begin{Bmatrix} he\ left \\ the\ meeting \end{Bmatrix} the\ discussion\ was\ surprising.$$

Do not attempt to account for subcategorization of prepositions.

## 4.6 WHERE PS RULES FAIL

### 4.6.1 Adverbs and ID/LP Formalism

Like adjectives, adverbs take degree specifiers in front of them. The rule that accounts for this is

$$AdvP \quad \rightarrow \quad (Degree)\ Adv$$

and the resulting structures include

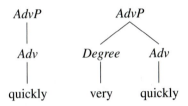

and the like.

The odd thing about AdvPs in English is the variety of positions in which they occur. For example:

*Quickly he chased him into the garden.*
*He quickly chased him into the garden.*
*He chased him quickly into the garden.*
*He chased him into the garden quickly.*

There is good evidence that the first two of these adverb positions hang from S and the latter two hang from VP, so that the structures are as shown in Figure 4.11.

This means that our S and VP rules need to be interspersed with optional AdvPs. Here is a stab at reformulating these rules:

$$S \quad \rightarrow \quad (AdvP)\ (PP)\ NP\ (AdvP)\ VP$$
$$VP \quad \rightarrow \quad V\ (NP)\ (AdvP)\ (PP)\ (NP)\ (AdvP)\ (PP)\ (S^1) \quad \text{(highly dubious!)}$$

This is unsatisfying; the VP rule, in particular, is a real mess. Even though we've left out particles, the VP rule has seven optional elements and is therefore apparently the equivalent of 128 different DCG rules! In reality it's not quite that complex, because some of the options are equivalent to each other; for instance, if you choose $VP \rightarrow V\ NP$,

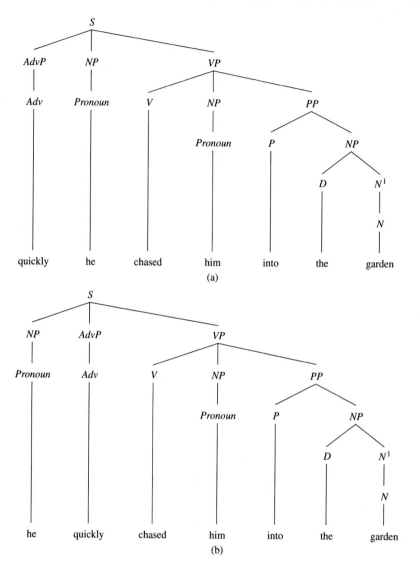

**Figure 4.11** Adverbs occur in many different positions in the English sentence.

it doesn't matter whether you choose the first NP or the second. Still, the whole thing is unwieldy.

What we would really like to say is that adverbs are a fundamentally different kind of thing than nouns or verbs. Instead of occupying fixed positions, AdvPs can go *anywhere* as long as they hang from an S or VP node and do not interrupt another constituent. That is, instead of having *many different* positions, the AdvP has an *unspecified* or "free" position.

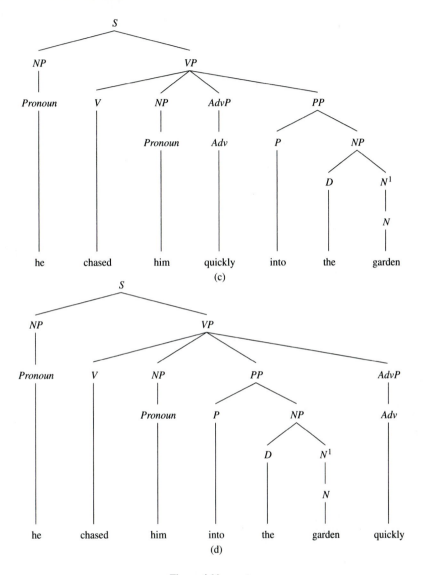

**Figure 4.11    cont.**

But this is something that PS rules can't express. Phenomena like adverb placement led Gazdar, Klein, Pullum, and Sag (1985) and many others to replace PS rules with ID/LP RULES. In ID/LP formalism, a rule such as

$$VP \quad \rightarrow \quad V, NP, PP, AdvP$$

says only that VP immediately dominates V, NP, PP, and AdvP; that's why it's called an ID (IMMEDIATE DOMINANCE) rule. It doesn't say in what order the V, NP, PP, and AdvP occur. The order is established by one or more LP (LINEAR PRECEDENCE) rules such as:

$$V < NP$$
$$V < PP$$
$$NP < S^1$$

which say that V precedes NP, V precedes PP, NP precedes $S^1$, and so on (when they hang from the same node). This is only a partial specification of the ordering. Constituents can occur anywhere as long as they don't violate any LP rules. So if no position is specified for AdvP, AdvP can occur anywhere. ID/LP parsers have been developed (Kilbury 1984, Shieber 1984, Barton 1985, Leiss 1990).

**Exercise 4.6.1.1**

Extend your parser to handle all the sentences in Figure 4.11, plus the same sentences with *very quickly* in place of *quickly*. You need not add rules for expansions of VP that do not occur in these sentences.

**Exercise 4.6.1.2**

Convert the ID/LP rules

$$V \quad \to \quad V, NP, PP, AdvP$$
$$V < NP$$
$$V < PP$$
$$NP < PP$$

into the complete set of equivalent PS rules.

## 4.6.2 Postposing of Long Constituents

There is a general tendency in English for long constituents to be POSTPOSED (placed at the very end of the sentence). This is obviously a practical thing to do; it lets the hearer parse as many constituents as possible, thereby obtaining context, before tackling the longest one.

Here's an example. One reason our VP rule is so complicated is that we must parse both

*Max* [VP *revealed* [NP *the fact* ] [PP *at the meeting* ] ].

and

*Max* [VP *revealed* [PP *at the meeting* ] [NP *the amazing fact that birds fly* ] ].

That is, we have both $VP \rightarrow V\ NP\ PP$ and $VP \rightarrow V\ PP\ NP$. The NP comes at the end if it is exceptionally long.

If we could explain in some other way why the long NP comes at the end of the sentence, we could simplify the VP rule. And indeed this seems like something we could do in ID/LP formalism: specify "the longest daughter of VP comes last" and let this take precedence over the other LP rules. So far, so good.

But there are cases where constituents are actually broken up in order to put a long constituent last. In transformational grammar this is called EXTRAPOSITION FROM NP (Radford 1988:448–456). Some examples:

> *A new book* came out *about the anatomy of dinosaurs.*
> *A problem* arose *that nobody expected.*
> John called *people* up *who were from Boston.*

Here *about the anatomy of dinosaurs* clearly modifies *book,* not *came out,* and the situation is analogous in the other two sentences.

The structures that we would like to assign these sentences are shown in Figure 4.12. The trouble is, these structures aren't trees. They contain DISCONTINUOUS CONSTITUENTS that cannot be generated by PS rules.

The standard analysis of these sentences is to say that the PS rules generate them with the constituents unbroken, and another kind of rule, called a TRANSFORMATION, then moves a constituent to the end. On this analysis, the DEEP (untransformed) structure of

> *A problem* arose *that I hadn't foreseen.*

is

> [NP *A problem that I hadn't foreseen* ] *arose.*

and the postposing of *that I hadn't foreseen* is a separate process.

To parse sentences with extraposed constituents, the parser will have to be ready, after parsing what appears to be a whole sentence, to pick up an additional constituent at the end and insert it in the proper place. The extraposition grammars of Pereira (1981) were designed partly to solve this problem. Extraposed constituents can also be handled by using features to pass information from one node to another as we did with *wh*-questions in Chapter 3.

**Exercise 4.6.2.1**

Suggest, in some detail, a way of parsing the sentences discussed in this section. You need not actually implement it.

## 4.6.3 Unbounded Movements

We saw in Chapter 3 that, in questions, the word *who* always appears at the beginning of the sentence, and exactly one NP is missing later on. It is exactly as if [NP *who* ] had

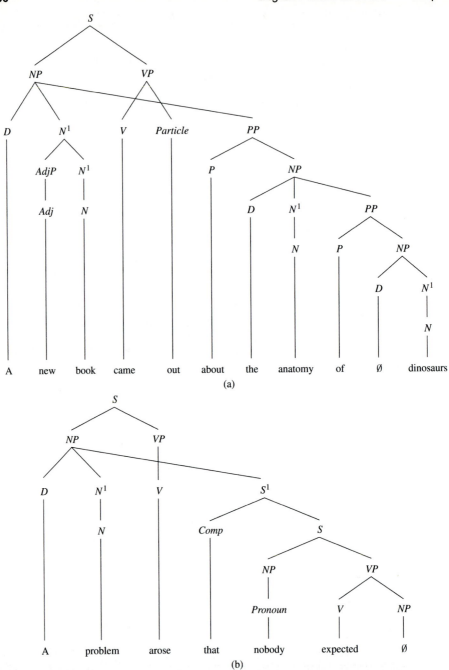

**Figure 4.12** Long constituents are postposed, often breaking up the larger constituents in which they belong.

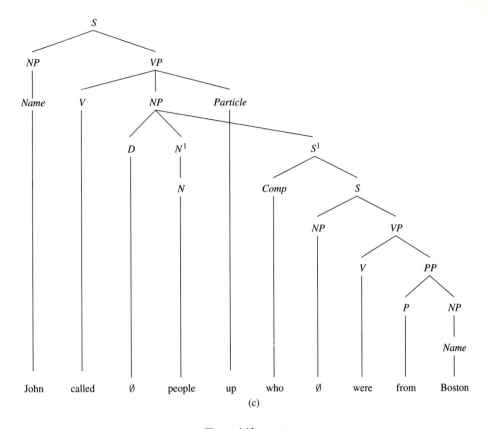

**Figure 4.12   cont.**

been moved from its original site to the beginning. Examples:

> *Who* said Bill thought Joe believed Fido barked? *(Max.)*
> *Who* did Max say ␣ thought Joe believed Fido barked? *(Bill.)*
> *Who* did Max say Bill thought ␣ believed Fido barked? *(Joe.)*
> *Who* did Max say Bill thought Joe believed ␣ barked? *(Fido.)*

Here ␣ represents the missing NP.

This phenomenon, called *wh*-movement, occurs not only in questions, but also in exclamations such as

> *What a noise* Max said Fido made ␣!

and in relative clauses (sentences modifying NPs) as in:

> *the boy who(m)* Fido chased ␣ into the garden

*Wh*-movements can be nested, as in this double relative clause:

> the boy who(m) the girl who(m) we saw ␣ liked ␣

But they cannot cross over each other; at any point, the parser can assume that the most recent *wh*-word will definitely correspond to the next missing NP.

    *Wh*-movement is an UNBOUNDED movement. This means that there can be any amount of structure between the original position of the moved word or phrase and the place it ends up. Thus PS rules cannot account for it. In Chapter 3 we parsed *wh*-questions with the aid of features; this is a standard approach (cf. the 'slash features' of Gazdar, Klein, Pullum, and Sag 1985).

    Some structures are ISLANDS, which means that even unbounded movements cannot move material out of them. Conjoined structures of all types are islands. For example, even though

> *You saw Max and who(m)?*

is grammatical (in a suitable context), it is not possible to perform *wh*-movement and get

> *\*Who did you see Max and ␣?*

because *Max and who(m)* is an island. Islands were discovered by Ross (1967).

**Exercise 4.6.3.1**

> Look back at the feature-based parser for *wh*-questions that we built in Chapter 3. Describe a way to add the rule
>
> $$NP \quad \rightarrow \quad \text{both } NP \text{ and } NP$$
>
> to this parser in such a way that [NP both NP and NP ] will be treated as an island.

## 4.6.4 Transformational Grammar

Rules that rearrange the structure of a tree are called TRANSFORMATIONS. They were introduced by Chomsky (1957), who experimented with PS rules and found them inadequate. Chomsky was the founder of modern generative grammar, and his introductory account of it is still worth reading.

    Once transformations were introduced, linguists used them to account for all sorts of grammatical regularities, including:

- Agreement (Chapter 3) and case marking (Chapter 5), now handled with features.
- The relation between active and passive sentences such as:

*The dog eats the food.*
*The food is eaten by the dog.*

Nowadays these are accounted for by lexical rules (Chapter 9) which create, from every verb such as *eat,* an adjective such as *eaten* with the appropriate meaning.

- Various alternative word orders, such as *That he succeeded surprised me* versus *It surprised me that he succeeded,* which are now treated as alternatives in the PS rules.

Transformational grammar does not lend itself to parsing. The reason is that every transformation is a tree-to-tree mapping and thus cannot be undone without knowing the tree structure. So the parser has to determine the tree structure before undoing any transformations. And if transformations are necessary to account for tree structure, this is impossible.

In practice, transformational parsers rely on a COVERING GRAMMAR, a set of PS rules that account for the structures *after* the transformations have applied. But if the sentence can be parsed with the covering grammar, then there is usually no need to undo the transformations—the parser can proceed with other kinds of analysis immediately. Because of this, transformational grammar is seldom used in natural language processing.

Since the 1970s, the trend has been to replace transformations with more specialized mechanisms, such as features. Emonds (1976) gives a good summary of transformational grammar as it was in its heyday. In Chomsky's current theory, transformations remain as a means of accounting for certain movements, but they are defined in terms of more abstract principles, particularly GOVERNMENT (case assignment, Chapter 5) and BINDING (an abstract relation between specific positions in the sentence, such as the missing NP position and the moved *wh*-word). For an introduction to government and binding theory, see Sells (1985).

**Exercise 4.6.4.1**

Implement, with DCG rules, a covering grammar for a grammar that contains the rules

$$
\begin{array}{rcl}
S & \rightarrow & NP\ VP \\
NP & \rightarrow & D\ N \\
VP & \rightarrow & V\ (NP)\ (PP) \\
PP & \rightarrow & P\ NP \\
D & \rightarrow & \text{the} \\
N & \rightarrow & \text{dog, cat, garden} \\
V & \rightarrow & \text{slept, barked} \\
P & \rightarrow & \text{in}
\end{array}
$$

plus a transformation that optionally moves PP to the beginning of the sentence (as in *In the garden the dog barked*). Note that a covering grammar does not *undo* the transformation; it merely parses a structure in which the transformation may have applied.

## 4.7 FURTHER READING

There is no place you can go to look up "the rules of English" for computer implementation, because linguists do not yet agree on what form these rules should take. One of the most comprehensive modern generative grammars is that of Gazdar, Klein, Pullum, and Sag (1985); the classic study of phrase structure is Jackendoff (1977); and the best introductory textbook, for our purposes, is probably Radford (1988). The classic handbook by Stockwell, Schachter, and Partee (1973) relies so heavily on transformations that it does not lend itself well to parser implementation.

The best way to extend a parser is to feed it some actual text and see where it breaks down, then add rules as needed. For guidance on how to analyze particular syntactic phenomena, see Matthews (1981) on the nature of syntactic structure, and Huddleston (1988), and Quirk et al. (1973, 1985) for detailed descriptions of English. These are DESCRIPTIVE handbooks of grammar; they contrast sharply with PRESCRIPTIVE handbooks designed for teaching English to foreigners or teaching native speakers to write more clearly. Prescriptive handbooks are almost useless to the parser builder.

Among dictionaries, Hornby (1989) is especially useful because it specifies the kinds of complements required by each verb or noun.

# CHAPTER 5

# Unification-Based Grammar

## 5.1 A UNIFICATION-BASED FORMALISM

### 5.1.1 The Problem

In Chapter 3, we added FEATURES (arguments) to the nodes in a phrase-structure grammar in order to do a lot of different things. We used features to account for agreement and case marking, build syntactic trees and semantic representations, and even undo movements.

But we never put all these techniques together into a single grammar. Nor did we examine the role of features in contemporary linguistic theory. In this chapter we will do those things. In the process, we will develop an extension to Prolog that will make it much easier to use features in a grammar.

### 5.1.2 What is UBG?

A UNIFICATION-BASED GRAMMAR is any grammar that:

- encodes information in features and their values;
- gives values to features only through unification, and not through any other kind of computation.

By this criterion the grammars that used features in Chapter 3 were unification-based. So are many of the grammars used in present-day theoretical linguistics. It's time to look at features from a theoretical viewpoint.

Recall, for example, three rules from Chapter 3:

```
s --> np(Number,nominative), vp(Number).
vp(Number) --> v(Number), np(_,accusative).
np(Number,Case) --> pronoun(Number,Case).
```

In unification-based grammar, the same rules are written:

$$S \quad \rightarrow \quad \begin{array}{c} NP \\ \left[ \begin{array}{l} num:\ X \\ case:\ nom \end{array} \right] \end{array} \quad \begin{array}{c} VP \\ \left[\ num:\ X\ \right] \end{array}$$

$$\begin{array}{c} VP \\ \left[\ num:\ X\ \right] \end{array} \quad \rightarrow \quad \begin{array}{c} V \\ \left[\ num:\ X\ \right] \end{array} \quad \begin{array}{c} NP \\ \left[\ case:\ acc\ \right] \end{array}$$

$$\begin{array}{c} NP \\ \left[ \begin{array}{l} num:\ X \\ case:\ C \end{array} \right] \end{array} \quad \rightarrow \quad \begin{array}{c} Pronoun \\ \left[ \begin{array}{l} num:\ X \\ case:\ C \end{array} \right] \end{array}$$

Here every node except S has a FEATURE STRUCTURE, i.e., a set of features and values. The fact that S has no features is purely accidental; a more complete grammar would assign features to the S node as well.

Fig. 5.1 shows a syntactic tree annotated with features. Whenever a PS rule applies, the feature structures in the rule have to unify with the corresponding feature structures in the tree. For example, the first rule requires the NP and VP to have the same number and requires the NP to have *case: nom*.

Unification-based grammar is a relatively new development. Features are not; they go back to traditional grammar and are used freely by Chomsky (1965) and others. But unification did not appear on the linguistic scene until the 1980s.

Further, UBG is not, in itself, a theory of grammar. Rather, it is a framework on which some (not all) theories of grammar are based, just as vector arithmetic is a framework for many theories in physics. Some theories of grammar that use various kinds of UBG are Functional Unification Grammar (FUG, Kay 1985, stemming from work in the late 1970s), Lexical-Functional Grammar (LFG, Bresnan 1982), and Generalized Phrase Structure Grammar (GPSG, Gazdar, Klein, Pullum and Sag 1985).

In this chapter we will develop a UBG formalism similar to that of Shieber (1985), but somewhat adapted to bring it closer to Prolog. We will then implement UBG in Prolog and use it to analyze a variety of phenomena in English.

### 5.1.3 How Features Behave

Features get where they are through several different processes, and although we are going to handle all of these processes through unification, we should start by distinguishing them and giving them names.

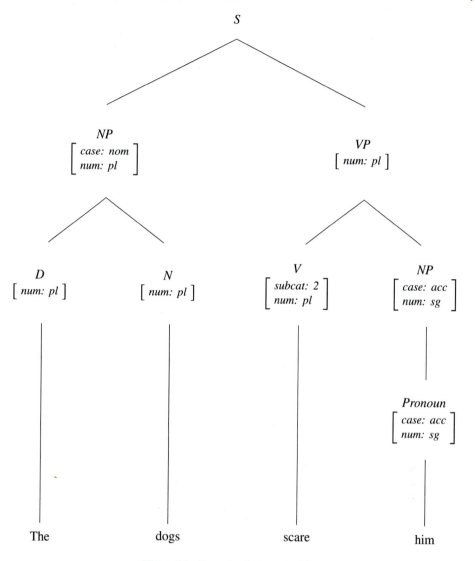

**Figure 5.1**   Example of a tree containing features.

Some features are properties of each word as listed in the dictionary. That is, the LEXICAL ENTRY of a word supplies many of its features. Provisionally, we can think of a lexical entry as a simple PS rule such as:

$$
\begin{bmatrix} \textit{Pronoun} \\ \textit{num: pl} \\ \textit{case: acc} \end{bmatrix} \quad \rightarrow \quad \text{them}
$$

This says that *them* is a pronoun with plural number and accusative case. We'll explore lexical entries further in Chapter 9.

Some features are put in place by AGREEMENT RULES—rules that require a feature on one node to match a feature on another. For example, a plural noun requires a plural determiner (you can't say *one dogs*), and a singular noun requires a singular determiner. More concisely, the noun and the determiner AGREE IN NUMBER. Here is a rule that makes them do so:

$$
\begin{array}{ccc}
NP & & D \qquad\qquad N \\
[\ num:\ X\ ] & \rightarrow & [\ num:\ X\ ] \quad [\ num:\ X\ ]
\end{array}
$$

This is, of course, just the PS rule $NP \rightarrow D\ NP$ with features added. Here the $X$ in the feature structures is a variable, and this rule requires it to have the same value in the three places where it occurs.

Some features get into the tree by ASSIGNMENT; that is, the grammar requires them to have particular values. For example, the direct object of the verb has to have accusative case, so that *I see him* is grammatical and *\*I see he* is not. Here is a rule that assigns accusative case to the object:

$$
VP \quad \rightarrow \quad V \quad
\begin{array}{c}
NP \\
[\ case:\ acc\ ]
\end{array}
$$

This is just $VP \rightarrow V\ NP$ with *case: acc* added in the right place.

Finally, some features get into place by PERCOLATION. That is, some of the features on a phrase are copies of the features of the main word in the phrase. For example, if the main verb in a VP is plural, then the VP itself is plural. The plural feature "percolates up" from the V to the VP. Here is the VP rule just given, but with percolation of the *num* feature added:

$$
\begin{array}{ccc}
VP & & V \qquad\qquad NP \\
[\ num:\ X\ ] & \rightarrow & [\ num:\ X\ ] \quad [\ case:\ acc\ ]
\end{array}
$$

Notice that the VP gets its number from the verb, not from the object.

**Exercise 5.1.3.1**

> For each of the features in Figure 5.1, indicate whether the occurrence of the feature is best explained as coming from the lexical entry or from assignment, agreement, or percolation. Give justification for your claims.

### 5.1.4 Features and PS Rules

Before the 1980s, generative grammars treated agreement, percolation, and the like as processes performed by transformational rules. That is, the PS rules would generate the tree and then the transformations would copy features from place to place. Today, however, the leading view is that all features can be accounted for by just one operation—UNIFICATION—which applies along with each PS rule.

Recall that the purpose of each PS rule is to legitimize a particular part of the tree. For example, the rule

$$NP \quad \rightarrow \quad D\ N$$

legitimizes the structure:

A grammar generates a tree if and only if every part of the tree is legitimized by some rule.

The features on each node in the tree have to be unified with the features on the corresponding node in the rule. For example, the rule

$$
\begin{array}{ccc}
NP & & D \qquad\qquad N \\
\left[\ num\text{: } X\ \right] & \rightarrow & \left[\ num\text{: } X\ \right] \quad \left[\ num\text{: } X\ \right]
\end{array}
$$

requires the structure [*num: X*] to be unified with the feature structures of the NP, D, and N. Thus it ensures that the NP, D, and N have matching *num* features, and thereby accomplishes both agreement and percolation. The actual value of the *num* feature, singular or plural, is supplied in this case by one or more lexical entries. It could also have been supplied by some other rule assigning a *num* value to the whole NP.

**Exercise 5.1.4.1**

Using the NP rule just given, plus the lexical entries

$$D \quad \rightarrow \quad \text{the}$$

$$
\begin{array}{c}
N \\
\left[\ num\text{: } pl\ \right]
\end{array}
\quad \rightarrow \quad \text{dogs}
$$

draw the complete tree for [$_{NP}$ *the dogs* ].

## 5.1.5 Feature-Structure Unification

The features in a feature structure are identified only by name, not by position. Thus

$$
\begin{bmatrix}
person\text{: } 2 \\
number\text{: } plural
\end{bmatrix}
\quad \text{and} \quad
\begin{bmatrix}
number\text{: } plural \\
person\text{: } 2
\end{bmatrix}
$$

are the same feature structure.

Two structures can be UNIFIED if they can be combined without contradiction. For example,

$$
\begin{bmatrix}
a\text{: } b \\
c\text{: } d
\end{bmatrix}
\quad \text{and} \quad
\begin{bmatrix}
a\text{: } b \\
e\text{: } f
\end{bmatrix}
\quad \text{unify to give} \quad
\begin{bmatrix}
a\text{: } b \\
c\text{: } d \\
e\text{: } f
\end{bmatrix}.
$$

This is much like Prolog unification; the main difference is that uninstantiated features are simply left out. Thus there is no need for an "anonymous variable." Variables with names, however, work the same way as in Prolog. For example,

$$\begin{bmatrix} a{:}\ b \\ c{:}\ d \end{bmatrix} \quad \text{and} \quad \begin{bmatrix} a{:}\ X \\ e{:}\ X \end{bmatrix} \quad \text{unify to give} \quad \begin{bmatrix} a{:}\ b \\ c{:}\ d \\ e{:}\ b \end{bmatrix}.$$

The second feature structure doesn't give values for $a$ and $e$, but it imposes a requirement that the values of $a$ and $e$ must be the same. This is a lot like what happens if you unify `f(b,d,_)` with `f(X,_,X)` in Prolog. As in Prolog, we will stipulate that

> *like-named variables are the same if and only if they occur in the same structure or the same rule.*

Feature-structure unification can, of course, fail. In such a case the grammar rule requiring the unification also fails, i.e., cannot apply. For example, the feature structures

$$\begin{bmatrix} a{:}\ b \\ c{:}\ d \end{bmatrix} \quad \text{and} \quad \begin{bmatrix} a{:}\ d \\ e{:}\ f \end{bmatrix} \quad \text{do not unify}$$

(the unification fails) because $a$ cannot have the values $b$ and $d$ simultaneously in the same feature structure.

A big advantage of unification—one that we've already exploited in Prolog—is that it's ORDER-INDEPENDENT. If you unify a set of feature structures, you'll get the same result no matter what order you unify them in. This means that it is often possible to use a single unification-based grammar with many different parsing algorithms. It doesn't matter which unifications get done first, as long as all the prescribed unifications are eventually performed. This gives great freedom to the programmer who is designing a parser.

The order-independence of unification also eliminates a vacuous question that arose in transformational grammar. Consider subject-verb agreement, for example. Does the number feature get copied from the subject onto the verb, or from the verb onto the subject? Obviously, it makes no difference. Yet a transformational grammar has to make the copying go in one particular direction; a unification-based grammar merely says that the number features of the subject and of the verb are equal.

**Exercise 5.1.5.1**

Unify the following feature structures, or indicate why the unification fails.

1. $\begin{bmatrix} number{:}\ sg \\ case{:}\ acc \end{bmatrix}$ and $\begin{bmatrix} number{:}\ sg \\ person{:}\ 3 \end{bmatrix}$

2. $\begin{bmatrix} number{:}\ N \\ case{:}\ nom \end{bmatrix}$ and $\begin{bmatrix} case{:}\ nom \\ person{:}\ 3 \\ number{:}\ pl \end{bmatrix}$

**3.** $\begin{bmatrix} case: C \\ person: P \\ number: sg \end{bmatrix}$ and $\begin{bmatrix} person: 3 \\ number: pl \\ case: acc \end{bmatrix}$

**4.** $\begin{bmatrix} a: b \\ c: Y \\ e: X \end{bmatrix}$ and $\begin{bmatrix} a: Y \\ c: X \\ e: X \end{bmatrix}$

**5.** $\begin{bmatrix} a: b \\ c: Y \\ e: f \end{bmatrix}$ and $\begin{bmatrix} a: Y \\ c: d \\ e: X \end{bmatrix}$

**Exercise 5.1.5.2**

Here are three feature structures:

$\begin{bmatrix} a: b \\ c: X \\ d: X \end{bmatrix}$     $\begin{bmatrix} c: Y \\ e: Y \end{bmatrix}$     $\begin{bmatrix} a: Z \\ e: Z \end{bmatrix}$

Unify the first (leftmost) structure with the second and show the result; then unify that with the third. Then do the same thing again, taking the structures in the opposite order (right to left).

## 5.2 A SAMPLE GRAMMAR

### 5.2.1 Overview

Now it's time to build a real, working unification-based grammar (working in the sense that the rules will fit together properly and generate sentences; we won't put it on the computer just yet). This grammar will be based on the PS rules:

$$
\begin{array}{rcl}
S & \rightarrow & NP\ VP \\
VP & \rightarrow & V\ (NP) \\
NP & \rightarrow & Pronoun \\
NP & \rightarrow & D\ N \\
Pronoun & \rightarrow & \text{he, him, it, they, them} \\
D & \rightarrow & \text{the, a, two} \\
N & \rightarrow & \text{dog, dogs, cat, cats} \\
V & \rightarrow & \text{bark, barks, scare, scares}
\end{array}
$$

To this we will add features to enforce five constraints:

- Number agreement of subject and verb;
- Number agreement of determiner and noun;

- Assignment of nominative case to subject;
- Assignment of accusative case to object;
- Subcategorization to distinguish verbs that do and do not take objects.

**Exercise 5.2.1.1**

Show why each of the five constraints just mentioned is needed. That is, for each constraint, give a sentence (with tree) that is generated by the PS rules but is ungrammatical because it violates the constraint.

### 5.2.2 Lexical Entries

First, the lexical entries. The pronouns are simple:

$$
\begin{matrix}
Pronoun \\
\begin{bmatrix} case:\ nom \\ num:\ sg \end{bmatrix}
\end{matrix}
\quad \rightarrow \quad he
$$

$$
\begin{matrix}
Pronoun \\
\begin{bmatrix} case:\ acc \\ num:\ sg \end{bmatrix}
\end{matrix}
\quad \rightarrow \quad him
$$

$$
\begin{matrix}
Pronoun \\
\begin{bmatrix} num:\ sg \end{bmatrix}
\end{matrix}
\quad \rightarrow \quad it
$$

$$
\begin{matrix}
Pronoun \\
\begin{bmatrix} case:\ nom \\ num:\ pl \end{bmatrix}
\end{matrix}
\quad \rightarrow \quad they
$$

$$
\begin{matrix}
Pronoun \\
\begin{bmatrix} case:\ acc \\ num:\ pl \end{bmatrix}
\end{matrix}
\quad \rightarrow \quad them
$$

Notice that *it* has the same form in both nominative and accusative (you can say both *it scares him* and *he scares it*); we capture this fact by simply leaving out its *case* feature.

Now for the nouns. Ideally, we'd like to have a rule that adds *-s* to the singular form of each noun to make the plural. That will have to wait until Chapter 9; in the meantime we will simply list both the singular and the plural form of each noun:

$$
\begin{matrix}
N \\
\begin{bmatrix} num:\ sg \end{bmatrix}
\end{matrix}
\quad \rightarrow \quad dog
$$

$$
\begin{matrix}
N \\
\begin{bmatrix} num:\ pl \end{bmatrix}
\end{matrix}
\quad \rightarrow \quad dogs
$$

$$\begin{bmatrix} N \\ num:\ sg \end{bmatrix} \quad \rightarrow \quad cat$$

$$\begin{bmatrix} N \\ num:\ pl \end{bmatrix} \quad \rightarrow \quad cats$$

Notice that nouns are not marked for case.

Determiners agree with nouns in number; that is, some determiners are singular and some are plural.

$$\begin{bmatrix} D \\ num:\ sg \end{bmatrix} \quad \rightarrow \quad a$$

$$\begin{bmatrix} D \\ num:\ pl \end{bmatrix} \quad \rightarrow \quad two$$

*The* goes with both singulars and plurals, so we leave its number feature unmarked:

$$D \quad \rightarrow \quad the$$

Next, the verbs. We use a feature called *subcat*(egorization) to distinguish verbs that take an object, such as *scare,* from verbs that don't. Like nouns, verbs are marked for number, but this time the *-s* is *absent* in the plural. We ignore person agreement (*I scare, you scare* vs. *he scares*).

$$\begin{bmatrix} V \\ num:\ sg \\ subcat:\ 1 \end{bmatrix} \quad \rightarrow \quad barks$$

$$\begin{bmatrix} V \\ num:\ pl \\ subcat:\ 1 \end{bmatrix} \quad \rightarrow \quad bark$$

$$\begin{bmatrix} V \\ num:\ sg \\ subcat:\ 2 \end{bmatrix} \quad \rightarrow \quad scares$$

$$\begin{bmatrix} V \\ num:\ pl \\ subcat:\ 2 \end{bmatrix} \quad \rightarrow \quad scare$$

**Exercise 5.2.2.1**

Write lexical entries (in the same form as those above) for *she, elephant, every, all, chase,* and *chases.*

### 5.2.3 Phrase-Structure Rules

The phrase-structure rules are simple. Consider first the rule:

$$\begin{bmatrix} NP \\ num:\ X \end{bmatrix} \quad \rightarrow \quad \begin{bmatrix} D \\ num:\ X \end{bmatrix} \quad \begin{bmatrix} N \\ num:\ X \end{bmatrix}$$

This accomplishes number agreement of D and N, as well as percolation of the number feature of the N up to the NP. (Or down from the NP to the N, depending on your point of view; in UBG it doesn't matter.)

The pronoun rule is even simpler, except that it has to percolate case as well as number:

$$
\begin{array}{cc}
NP & Pronoun \\
\begin{bmatrix} case:\ C \\ num:\ X \end{bmatrix} \quad \rightarrow & \begin{bmatrix} case:\ C \\ num:\ X \end{bmatrix}
\end{array}
$$

There are two VP rules and the *subcat* feature determines which one any particular verb takes:

$$
\begin{array}{ccc}
VP & & V \\
\begin{bmatrix} num:\ X \end{bmatrix} \quad \rightarrow & \begin{bmatrix} subcat:\ 1 \\ num:\ X \end{bmatrix} & \qquad \text{(for verbs without objects);}
\end{array}
$$

$$
\begin{array}{cccc}
VP & & V & NP \\
\begin{bmatrix} num:\ X \end{bmatrix} \quad \rightarrow & \begin{bmatrix} subcat:\ 2 \\ num:\ X \end{bmatrix} & \begin{bmatrix} case:\ acc \end{bmatrix} & \qquad \text{(for verbs with objects).}
\end{array}
$$

The second rule assigns accusative case to the object.

Finally, the S rule assigns nominative case to the subject and enforces subject-verb number agreement:

$$
\begin{array}{ccc}
& NP & VP \\
S \quad \rightarrow & \begin{bmatrix} case:\ nom \\ num:\ X \end{bmatrix} & \begin{bmatrix} num:\ X \end{bmatrix}
\end{array}
$$

In this grammar, the S node itself has no features. As mentioned earlier, this is purely accidental; a more complete grammar would give features to the S, but in this grammar there happen to be none.

**Exercise 5.2.3.1**

Add feature information to the rule $PP \rightarrow P\ NP$ so that, in combination with appropriate lexical entries, it will generate

$$[_{PP}\ for\ him\ ]$$
$$[_{PP}\ for\ them\ ]$$

but not

$$[_{PP}\ for\ he\ ]$$
$$[_{PP}\ for\ they\ ]$$

Write your rule in a form suitable to be added to the grammar we are developing.

### 5.2.4 How the Rules Fit Together

Unification-based rules work equally well when applied bottom-up, top-down, or in any other order. To work out by hand how the rules generate a particular sentence, it is probably easiest to proceed bottom-up.

   Consider the sentence *Two dogs bark.* Does our grammar generate it? To find out, first look at the lexical entries for the three words, and fill in the part of the tree that they supply:

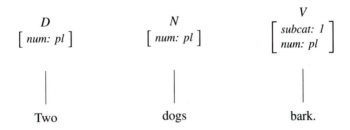

Next, group D and N together into an NP. Note that the *NP → D N* rule requires NP, D, and N to have the same *num* feature. So far, no problem:

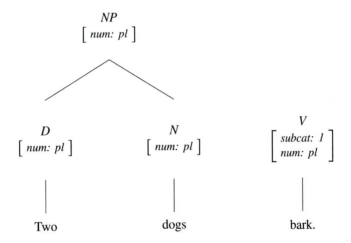

Now we need a VP. The verb has *subcat: 1.* Only one of the two VP rules matches a verb with this feature, namely the rule *VP → V*, which percolates the *num* feature up from V to VP:

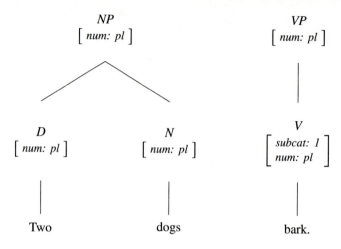

Finally, $S \rightarrow NP\ VP$ requires the NP and VP to agree in number (which they do), and assigns *case: nom* to the NP (which has no visible effect because nouns are not marked for case). Here is the complete structure:

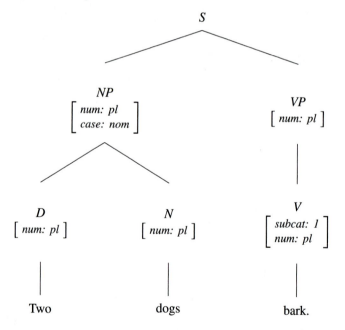

Voilà—the rules generate the sentence.

    It makes equal sense to work top-down, starting with $S \rightarrow NP\ VP$, except that the process involves more suspense because there are lots of variables that don't get instantiated until the last moment. For example, applying the rules $S \rightarrow NP\ VP$, then $NP \rightarrow D\ N$, and then $VP \rightarrow V$, you get

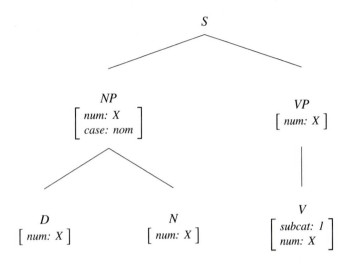

and when you get to the lexical entries, $X$ finally gets instantiated as *sg* or *pl*.

This illustrates a key advantage of unification-based grammar. You don't have to know the values of the variables in order to manipulate them. As long as the right variables are made equal to each other, and the variables eventually get instantiated, everything comes out correct.

**Exercise 5.2.4.1**

By working bottom-up, determine whether the grammar generates each of the following sentences. Show your steps. If the sentence turns out not to be generated, show precisely where the unification fails.

    **1.** *The dogs scare him.*

    **2.** *It barks him.*

    **3.** *The cats bark.*

**Exercise 5.2.4.2**

By working top-down from $S \rightarrow NP\ VP$, show why the grammar does not generate each of the following sentences. That is, show your steps, and point out the feature conflict when it occurs.

    **1.** *It scares he.*

    **2.** *It scare him.*

## 5.3 FORMAL PROPERTIES OF FEATURE STRUCTURES

### 5.3.1 Features and Values

A feature structure is a set of FEATURES (ATTRIBUTES) and VALUES. It contains at most one value for each feature. For example,

$$\begin{bmatrix} a{:}\ b \\ c{:}\ d \end{bmatrix}$$

contains the value $b$ for the feature $a$, the value $d$ for the feature $c$, and no value for the feature $e$. But

$$\begin{bmatrix} a{:}\ b \\ a{:}\ c \end{bmatrix} \qquad \text{(wrong!)}$$

is not a feature structure, because it does not give a unique value for $a$.

A feature is simply a name; no more, no less. A value can be either an atomic symbol (like a Prolog atom or number), or another feature structure. Some examples:

$$\begin{bmatrix} a{:}\ b \\ c{:} \begin{bmatrix} d{:}\ e \\ f{:}\ g \\ h{:} \begin{bmatrix} i{:}\ j \\ k{:}\ l \end{bmatrix} \end{bmatrix} \end{bmatrix} \qquad \begin{bmatrix} semantics{:} \begin{bmatrix} pred{:}\ chases \\ tense{:}\ present \end{bmatrix} \\ syntax{:} \begin{bmatrix} person{:}\ 3 \\ number{:}\ sg \end{bmatrix} \end{bmatrix}$$

Nested feature structures like these allow features to be grouped together. For example, it is often convenient to group all the features that percolate into a structure called *agr*(eement).[1] Then instead of

$$\begin{array}{c} Pronoun \\ \begin{bmatrix} pers{:}\ 3 \\ num{:}\ sg \\ case{:}\ acc \end{bmatrix} \end{array} \quad \rightarrow \quad him$$

we would write:

$$\begin{array}{c} Pronoun \\ \begin{bmatrix} agr{:} \begin{bmatrix} pers{:}\ 3 \\ num{:}\ sg \\ case{:}\ acc \end{bmatrix} \end{bmatrix} \end{array} \quad \rightarrow \quad him$$

(The pronoun will also have other features that are not in the *agr* group; we just haven't seen them yet.) Then—here's the simplification—it becomes possible to percolate *pers*, *num*, and *case* all at once by just percolating *agr*, like this:

$$\begin{array}{c} NP \\ \begin{bmatrix} agr{:}\ X \end{bmatrix} \end{array} \quad \rightarrow \quad \begin{array}{c} Pronoun \\ \begin{bmatrix} agr{:}\ X \end{bmatrix} \end{array}$$

Here is a full description of feature structure unification as we now know it:

---

[1]It is not entirely clear whether *case* belongs in the *agr* group. For now, it's convenient to put it there. In English, case percolates but is not involved in agreement.

- To unify two feature structures, unify the values of all the features.
- If a feature occurs in one structure and not in the other, simply put it into the resulting unified structure.
- If a feature occurs in both structures, unify its values:
  - To unify values that are atomic symbols, check that they are equal; otherwise the unification fails.
  - To unify a variable with anything else, simply make it equal to that thing.
  - To unify values that are feature structures, apply this whole process recursively.

Here are a couple of examples:

$$
\begin{bmatrix} a\colon b \\ c\colon X \end{bmatrix} \text{ and } \begin{bmatrix} c\colon \begin{bmatrix} d\colon e \\ f\colon g \end{bmatrix} \\ h\colon i \end{bmatrix} \text{ unify to give } \begin{bmatrix} a\colon b \\ c\colon \begin{bmatrix} d\colon e \\ f\colon g \end{bmatrix} \\ h\colon i \end{bmatrix}
$$

$$
\begin{bmatrix} a\colon p \\ c\colon X \end{bmatrix} \text{ and } \begin{bmatrix} a\colon Y \\ b\colon q \\ c\colon \begin{bmatrix} d\colon Y \\ e\colon f \end{bmatrix} \end{bmatrix} \text{ unify to give } \begin{bmatrix} a\colon p \\ b\colon q \\ c\colon \begin{bmatrix} d\colon p \\ e\colon f \end{bmatrix} \end{bmatrix}
$$

Without changing the computational power of the formalism, we can in fact allow values to be Prolog terms of any type. This is so because any Prolog term can be translated into a feature structure. For example, f(a,b) could become

$$
\begin{bmatrix} functor\colon f \\ arg1\colon a \\ arg2\colon b \end{bmatrix}
$$

and the list [a,b,c] could be rendered as:

$$
\begin{bmatrix} first\colon a \\ rest\colon \begin{bmatrix} first\colon b \\ rest\colon \begin{bmatrix} first\colon c \\ rest\colon nil \end{bmatrix} \end{bmatrix} \end{bmatrix}
$$

So we will frequently use Prolog terms as a substitute for feature structures, wherever this is more convenient. Naturally, we presume that Prolog terms unify by ordinary Prolog unification.

**Exercise 5.3.1.1**

Unify each of the following pairs of feature structures, or indicate why the unification fails:

$$
\textbf{1.} \begin{bmatrix} a\colon \begin{bmatrix} b\colon c \end{bmatrix} \\ d\colon e \end{bmatrix} \text{ and } \begin{bmatrix} a\colon \begin{bmatrix} f\colon g \end{bmatrix} \\ d\colon X \end{bmatrix}
$$

2. $\left[\, a\colon\, \left[\, b\colon\, c\,\right]\,\right]$   and   $\begin{bmatrix} a\colon X \\ d\colon X \end{bmatrix}$

3. $\begin{bmatrix} a\colon \left[\, b\colon\, c\,\right] \\ d\colon e \end{bmatrix}$   and   $\begin{bmatrix} a\colon \left[\, b\colon X\,\right] \\ d\colon X \end{bmatrix}$

4. $\begin{bmatrix} syntax\colon \begin{bmatrix} category\colon noun \\ number\colon plural \end{bmatrix} \\ semantics\colon \left[\, pred\colon dog\,\right] \end{bmatrix}$   and   $\begin{bmatrix} syntax\colon \left[\, number\colon X\,\right] \\ semantics\colon \left[\, number\colon X\,\right] \end{bmatrix}$

### 5.3.2 Re-entrancy

Feature structures are RE-ENTRANT. Fortunately, this is a property we are familiar with from Prolog. What it means is that if two features have the same value, their values are *the same object,* not merely two objects that look alike.

To take a Prolog example, unify `f(X,X)` with `f(a(b),_)`. The result is `f(a(b),a(b))`. But the important thing is that the result doesn't contain two `a(b)`'s; it contains two pointers to the *same* `a(b)`. That is, its tree structure is something like

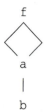

rather than:

```
         f
        / \
       a   a
       |   |
       b   b
```

Feature structures work the same way. If you unify

$$\begin{bmatrix} p\colon X \\ q\colon X \end{bmatrix} \quad \text{and} \quad \left[\, p\colon \left[\, a\colon b\,\right]\,\right]$$

then you get a structure where *p* and *q* have the *same* value, not just two identical-looking values. We will often write this as

$$\begin{bmatrix} p: \begin{bmatrix} a{:}b \end{bmatrix} \\ q: \begin{bmatrix} a{:}b \end{bmatrix} \end{bmatrix}$$

but if we do so, something important is lost. To make it perfectly clear that the two instances of [a:b] are really one structure, we can give it an identifying number and write it only once, thus:

$$\begin{bmatrix} p: \boxed{1} \begin{bmatrix} a{:}\ b \end{bmatrix} \\ q: \boxed{1} \end{bmatrix}$$

Here the first $\boxed{1}$ serves as a label for the structure [a: b]. By writing $\boxed{1}$ a second time, we indicate that the same structure is also the value of another feature.

We will use this notation when it is absolutely necessary to show that a structure is re-entrant. For the most part, however, re-entrancy will be easy to understand from context, especially if you are familiar with Prolog.

Here is a case where the notation with boxed numbers is helpful. Suppose we're grouping agreement features into a structure called *agr* as proposed a couple of sections back, and now we want to construct an *S → NP VP* rule such that:

- the NP and VP share all their *agr* features, i.e., agree in person, number, and whatever else is relevant; and
- the NP has the *agr* feature *case: nom.*

In effect, we want to combine the two rules

$$S \quad \rightarrow \quad \underset{\begin{bmatrix} agr{:}\ X \end{bmatrix}}{NP} \quad \underset{\begin{bmatrix} agr{:}\ X \end{bmatrix}}{VP}$$

$$S \quad \rightarrow \quad \underset{\begin{bmatrix} agr{:}\ \begin{bmatrix} case{:}\ nom \end{bmatrix} \end{bmatrix}}{NP} \quad VP$$

into one. The trouble is that if we give the NP a feature written as *agr: X*, as in the first rule, there's no good way to refer to something within *agr*, as is necessary in the second.

Boxed numbers come to the rescue. We can simply write:

$$S \quad \rightarrow \quad \underset{\begin{bmatrix} agr{:}\ \boxed{1} \begin{bmatrix} case{:}\ nom \end{bmatrix} \end{bmatrix}}{NP} \quad \underset{\begin{bmatrix} agr{:}\ \boxed{1} \end{bmatrix}}{VP}$$

This means: The *agr* features of the NP and of the VP are to be unified with each other, becoming a single structure known as $\boxed{1}$. In addition, $\boxed{1}$ must unify with [*case: nom*]. This has the side effect of giving *case: nom* to the VP, which is harmless because verbs are not marked for case (though it does suggest a reason for not putting *case* in the *agr* group).

**Exercise 5.3.2.1**

Unify the following pairs of feature structures. Use boxed numbers to indicate all re-entrancy. For example,

$$\begin{bmatrix} a{:}\ X \\ b{:}\ X \end{bmatrix} \quad \text{and} \quad \begin{bmatrix} a{:}\ \begin{bmatrix} b{:}\ c \end{bmatrix} \end{bmatrix} \quad \text{unify giving} \quad \begin{bmatrix} a{:}\ \boxed{1}\begin{bmatrix} b{:}\ c \end{bmatrix} \\ b{:}\ \boxed{1} \end{bmatrix}.$$

**1.** $\begin{bmatrix} a{:}\ X \\ b{:}\ X \\ c{:}\ X \end{bmatrix}$　　and　　$\begin{bmatrix} a{:}\ \begin{bmatrix} p{:}\ q \end{bmatrix} \end{bmatrix}$

**2.** $\begin{bmatrix} a{:}\ X \\ b{:}\ Y \\ c{:}\ X \end{bmatrix}$　　and　　$\begin{bmatrix} a{:}\ \begin{bmatrix} p{:}\ Y \end{bmatrix} \\ \\ b{:}\ \begin{bmatrix} e{:}\ f \end{bmatrix} \end{bmatrix}$

## 5.3.3 Functions, Paths, and Equational Style

A PATH is a description of where to find something in a nested feature structure. For example, in the structure

$$\begin{bmatrix} p{:}\ \begin{bmatrix} a{:}\ b \\ c{:}\ \begin{bmatrix} d{:}\ e \\ f{:}\ g \end{bmatrix} \\ h{:}\ i \end{bmatrix} \\ q{:}\ r \end{bmatrix}$$

the path $p : c : d$ leads to the value $e$.

In mathematics, a PARTIAL FUNCTION is a function that yields a value for some arguments but not for others. We can view a path as a partial function which, given a feature structure, may or may not return a value. For example, in the structure above, $p : c : d$ has the value $e$, and $q$ has the value $r$, but $p : z : y$ has no value.

This suggests a different way of writing unification-based grammar rules. Instead of using variables in feature structures, we can specify that the values of certain paths have to be equal. I call this "equational style." For example, instead of

$$S \quad \rightarrow \quad \overset{NP}{\begin{bmatrix} pers{:}\ P \\ num{:}\ X \\ case{:}\ nom \end{bmatrix}} \quad \overset{VP}{\begin{bmatrix} pers{:}\ P \\ num{:}\ X \end{bmatrix}}$$

we can write

$$S \ \rightarrow \ NP\ VP$$
$$\langle NP\ pers \rangle = \langle VP\ pers \rangle$$
$$\langle NP\ num \rangle = \langle VP\ num \rangle$$
$$\langle NP\ case \rangle = nom$$

That is, the NP's *pers* equals the VP's *pers,* and the NP's *num* equals the VP's *num,* and the NP's *case* equals *nom.* This is the notation used by the computer program PATR-II (Shieber 1985).

We are about to develop an extension of Prolog called GULP in which both conventional and equational styles can be used. Here are two ways of writing the above rule in GULP:

```
s --> np(pers:P..num:X..case:nom), vp(pers:P..num:X).

s --> np(NPfeatures), vp(VPfeatures),
        { NPfeatures = pers:P,   VPfeatures = pers:P,
          NPfeatures = num:X,    VPfeatures = num:X,
          NPfeatures = case:nom }.
```

In both versions, np and vp each have a single Prolog term as an argument. In the first version, each of these arguments is a feature structure. In the second, the arguments are variables (NPfeatures and VPfeatures) which must then be unified with several feature structures; for example, NPfeatures is unified, in succession, with [*pers: P*], [*num: X*], and [*case: nom*]. This won't work in ordinary Prolog, of course, but GULP translates notations such as case:nom into structures that unify in the desired way.

Crucially, both GULP and PATR-II allow you to use paths. For example, in PATR-II, you could describe

$$NP$$
$$\left[\ agr:\ \left[\ case:\ nom\ \right]\ \right]$$

by saying ⟨*NP agr case*⟩ = *nom.* In GULP, you could say that NP has the feature agr:case:nom.

**Exercise 5.3.3.1**

Identify all the paths in

$$\left[\begin{array}{l} p: \left[\begin{array}{l} a:\ b \\ c: \left[\begin{array}{l} d:\ e \\ f:\ g \end{array}\right] \\ h:\ i \end{array}\right] \\ q:\ r \end{array}\right]$$

and give their values.

**Exercise 5.3.3.2**

Express

$$S\quad\rightarrow\quad \overset{NP}{\left[\ agr:\ \boxed{1}\left[\ case:\ nom\ \right]\ \right]}\quad \overset{VP}{\left[\ agr:\ \boxed{1}\ \right]}$$

in PATR-II equational style. (Hint: You will need to mention the path *NP agr case* in one of the equations.)

## 5.4 AN EXTENSION OF PROLOG FOR UBG

### 5.4.1 A Better Syntax for Features

So far we have implemented features in Prolog as arguments to nodes in DCGs. This works well as long as there are only a few features. Clearly, however, a wide-coverage parser for a human language will have many features, perhaps dozens of them. Most rules mention only a few features, but argument positions have to be provided for every feature so that terms will unify properly. It is easy to end up with grammar rules such as

```
s(_,_,_,_,Tns,_,_,s(Tree1,Tree2),_,_,_) -->
                np(_,_,_,_,_,N,Pers,Tree1,_,_,_),
                vp(_,_,_,_,Tns,N,Pers,Tree2,_,_,_).
```

which are hard both to read and to type correctly.

To make features less cumbersome we need to do three things:

- Collect all the features into feature structures. Then each node will have only one argument, a feature structure.

- Develop a convenient notation for writing feature structures in Prolog.

- Somehow get feature structures to unify properly.

The notation for feature structures is not too hard. All that is necessary is to define the infix operators ':' and '..' and write

$$
\begin{bmatrix}
\textit{case: nom} \\
\textit{person: P} \\
\textit{sem:} \begin{bmatrix} \textit{pred: bark} \\ \textit{arg1: fido} \end{bmatrix}
\end{bmatrix}
$$

as `case:nom..person:P..sem:(pred:bark..arg1:fido)`. That is, ':' joins a feature to a value, and '..' joins one feature-value pair to the next.[2] The value of a feature can be any Prolog term, or another feature structure. This is known as GULP notation because it was first used in a program known as *Graph Unification Logic Programming* (Covington 1989). Fig. 5.2 shows further examples of GULP notation.

The next question is how to get feature structures to unify. There are two possibilities:

- We could write our own unifier that will handle feature structures written in GULP notation; or

---

[2]By using colons, we make the Prolog module system unavailable, but this is only a minor limitation; a different character could easily be used. Some Prologs may require you to use something other than the colon. In Arity Prolog 4, a blank is required before each left parenthesis within a feature structure.

$$\begin{bmatrix} num:\ sg \end{bmatrix} \quad = \quad \texttt{num:sg}$$

$$\begin{bmatrix} num:\ sg \\ subcat:\ 2 \\ tense:\ present \end{bmatrix} \quad = \quad \texttt{num:sg..subcat:2..tense:present}$$

$$\begin{bmatrix} a:\ p \\ b:\ q \\ c:\ \begin{bmatrix} d:\ p \\ e:\ f \end{bmatrix} \end{bmatrix} \quad = \quad \texttt{a:p..b:q..c:(d:p..e:f)}$$

$$\begin{bmatrix} p:\ \begin{bmatrix} a:\ b \\ c:\ \begin{bmatrix} d:\ e \\ f:\ g \end{bmatrix} \\ h:\ i \end{bmatrix} \\ q:\ r \end{bmatrix} \quad = \quad \texttt{p:(a:b..c:(d:e..f:g)..h:i)..q:r}$$

**Figure 5.2**   Examples of GULP notation.

- We could write a translator that will convert GULP feature structures into something that the ordinary Prolog unifier handles in the desired way.

Johnson and Klein (1986) and others have taken the first approach; here we take the second.

All we really have to do is map names of features onto positions in a list. For example, if *case, person,* and *number* are the only features in our grammar, we can represent each feature structure as a list

```
[C,P,N]
```

where C stands for the case, P stands for the person, and N stands for the number. Then in order to unify

$$\begin{bmatrix} case:\ nom \\ person:\ 3 \end{bmatrix} \quad \text{and} \quad \begin{bmatrix} case:\ nom \\ number:\ sg \end{bmatrix}$$

we simply unify `[nom,3,_]` with `[nom,_,sg]` and everything comes out right.

So far, so good. Our translator will read a Prolog program, scan it for GULP feature structures, and convert them all into lists with each value in the right position. To keep these lists from being mistaken for ordinary lists in the translated program, we will mark them with the functor `g_/1`; the resulting structure will be called a `g_`-list. For example:

```
case:C..person:P..number:N    translates to    g_([C,P,N])
```

Every list will be long enough to accommodate all the features in the grammar; this means that in most lists, many positions are never instantiated. For example:

> `case:C..number:N`   translates to   `g_([C,_,N]).`

This assumes that *case, person,* and *number* are the only features in the grammar. If any other features were ever used, there would have to be positions for them in every list.

Crucially, the order of the feature-value pairs does not matter; `case:C..number:N` translates to exactly the same thing as `number:N..case:C`.

### Exercise 5.4.1.1

Write each of the following feature structures in GULP notation.

1. $\begin{bmatrix} num:\ sg \\ case:\ acc \end{bmatrix}$

2. $\begin{bmatrix} case:\ nom \\ person:\ 3 \\ num:\ pl \end{bmatrix}$

3. $\begin{bmatrix} case:\ C \\ person:\ P \\ num:\ sg \end{bmatrix}$

4. $\begin{bmatrix} a:\ b \\ c: \begin{bmatrix} d:\ e \\ f:\ g \\ h: \begin{bmatrix} i:\ j \\ k:\ l \end{bmatrix} \end{bmatrix} \end{bmatrix}$

5. $\begin{bmatrix} semantics: \begin{bmatrix} pred:\ chases \\ tense:\ present \end{bmatrix} \\ syntax: \begin{bmatrix} person:\ 3 \\ num:\ sg \end{bmatrix} \end{bmatrix}$

### Exercise 5.4.1.2

Lists are not necessarily the best internal representations for feature structures; they are just the simplest to build. Suggest some alternative data structures that could be used instead, and indicate how they would work.

## 5.4.2 Translating a Single Feature Structure

What we want to build is a translator program, called Mini-GULP, which will accept Prolog programs (including DCGs) that use GULP notation, and will translate the feature structures from GULP notation into g_-lists while leaving the rest of the program unaltered.

The translator program will begin with the op declarations

```
:- op(600,xfy,':').
:- op(601,xfy,'..').
```

so that as soon as it is loaded, all subsequent Prolog code, including input accepted through `read/1`, can use GULP notation.

At the beginning of the program to be translated, we will ask the user to supply a set of *schemas* that map features onto positions in a list. Some examples:

```
g_schema(case:X,    [X,_,_]).
g_schema(person:X,  [_,X,_]).
g_schema(number:X,  [_,_,X]).
```

Creation of schemas could easily be automated, and in the full GULP system, it is. Here, however, we're trying to keep things simple.

Each schema then provides the translation of one feature-value pair, except that 'g_/1' is left out. For example:

```
?- g_schema(number:plural,What).
What = [_,_,plural]
```

To translate a series of feature-value pairs, such as

```
case:nom..person:3..number:plural
```

all we need to do is translate the individual feature-value pairs, then unify the translations with each other, and add 'g_/1' at the beginning. That is, we need to obtain the translations

```
[nom,_,_]
[_,3,_]
[_,_,plural]
```

and unify them, thereby obtaining `[nom,3,plural]`, and then add 'g_' giving `g_([nom,3,plural])`. So far, then, the translator needs two clauses:

```
% g_translate(+FeatureStructure,-g_(List)) (FIRST VERSION)
%   Translates FeatureStructure to internal representation g_(List).

% Case 1: A single feature-value pair
%
g_translate(F:V,g_(List)) :-
    g_schema(F:V,List).
```

```
% Case 2: A series of feature-value pairs
%
g_translate(First..Rest,g_(List)) :-
   g_translate(First,g_(List)),
   g_translate(Rest,g_(List)).
```

This produces the translations that we want, such as:

```
?- g_translate(case:nom..number:plural,What).
What = g_([nom,_,plural])
```

The alert reader will have noticed that all functors that have special meaning for Mini-GULP begin with 'g_' to avoid conflict with anything in the user's program.

### Exercise 5.4.2.1

Suppose a Prolog neophyte says, "I don't understand how g_translate adds 'g_' to the translation. There isn't a step in it to do that." How would you respond?

### Exercise 5.4.2.2

Get g_translate working. (Remember that the op declarations go in the translator program.) Then supply schemas for a grammar containing the features *case, number, person, sem, pred,* and *arg1* and give the translations produced by g_translate for:

```
case:nom
case:acc..person:2
person:2..case:acc
number:singular..sem:(pred:chases..arg1:fido)..person:3
```

What is unsatisfactory about the last of these?

### Exercise 5.4.2.3

Modify g_translate so that if the input contains a feature for which there is no schema, an error message will be produced. (This modification is *very* helpful in doing the subsequent exercises, and in working with Mini-GULP generally. Everyone misspells a feature or leaves out a schema sooner or later.)

## 5.4.3 Translating Terms of All Types

So far, our translator has two serious limitations:

- It won't translate general Prolog terms, only feature structures.
- It won't accept a feature structure within a feature structure.

For Mini-GULP to be useful, both of these problems have to be corrected. Let's tackle the first one first.

The user's program is nothing more than a series of terms, most of which have the principal functor ':-' or '-->'. What we want to do is search through each term, translating all the feature structures wherever they occur, but otherwise leaving things unchanged. From this perspective, we need to look for *four* kinds of terms, not just two:

- Feature-value pairs. We already know how to handle these, except that we need to *translate* the value, rather than just inserting it into the list unchanged. That will take care of feature structures within feature structures.

- Sequences of feature-value pairs joined by '. .'. Just translate all the feature-value pairs and merge the results, as we're already doing.

- Structures. Break the structure up into functor and arguments, recursively translate all the arguments, then reassemble the result.

- Variables and atomic terms. Leave these unchanged. Actually, we check for these *first,* because a variable would match anything, and also because these involve the least work.

Note that this is fully recursive. A feature structure can occur inside any other kind of term, and any other kind of term can occur within a feature structure. Here are the clauses to implement it:

```
% g_translate(+FeatureStructure,-g_(List)) (SECOND VERSION)
%   Translates FeatureStructure to internal representation g_(List).

% Case 1: A variable or atomic term
%
g_translate(X,X) :-
   (var(X) ; atomic(X)), !.

% Case 2: A single feature-value pair
%
g_translate(F:V,g_(List)) :-
   !,
   g_translate(V,TranslatedV),
   g_schema(F:TranslatedV,List).

% Case 3: A series of feature-value pairs
%
g_translate(First..Rest,g_(List)) :-
   !,
   g_translate(First,g_(List)),
   g_translate(Rest,g_(List)).

% Case 4: A structure
%
g_translate(Structure,Result) :-
```

```
Structure =.. [Functor|Args],
!,
g_translate_aux(Args,NewArgs),   % translate all args
Result =.. [Functor|NewArgs].
```

Here `g_translate_aux/2` translates, in succession, all the elements in a list, like this:

```
g_translate_aux([T|Terms],[NewT|NewTerms]) :-
   g_translate(T,NewT),
   g_translate_aux(Terms,NewTerms).

g_translate_aux([],[]).
```

### Exercise 5.4.3.1

Why doesn't `g_translate` need another clause to deal with lists?

### Exercise 5.4.3.2

Get `g_translate` working and use it to translate the same feature structures as in Exercise 5.4.2.2.

## 5.4.4 Translating While Consulting

We want the translator to accept programs like that shown in Fig. 5.3. We will write a procedure called `g_consult` to load such programs into memory, translating GULP notation into g_-lists as it does so. The `g_consult` procedure will read terms from a file one by one and process them, thus:

- If the term is `end_of_file`, stop. (Recall that this is what `read` returns when it hits end of file.)
- If the term is a `g_schema`, assert it into memory.
- If the term is a grammar rule (with principal functor '`-->`'), translate it, then pass it through the DCG rule translator and assert the result into memory.
- If the term is anything else, translate it and then assert it.

The top level of this processing is easy:

```
% g_consult(+File)
%  Reads clauses from File, translating as appropriate.

g_consult(File) :-
   see(File),
   repeat,
     read(Term),
     g_consult_aux(Term),    % handle it appropriately
```

```
% DCG parser for the grammar in Section 5.2.
% To be processed by Mini-GULP.
% Demonstrates number agreement, case assignment,
% and verb subcategorization.

g_schema(case:X,   [X,_,_]).
g_schema(num:X,    [_,X,_]).
g_schema(subcat:X,[_,_,X]).

pronoun(case:nom..num:sg) --> [he].
pronoun(case:acc..num:sg) --> [him].
pronoun(num:sg)           --> [it].
pronoun(case:nom..num:pl) --> [they].
pronoun(case:acc..num:pl) --> [them].

n(num:sg)   -->  [dog]; [cat].
n(num:pl)   -->  [dogs];[cats].

d(_)        -->  [the].
d(num:sg)   -->  [a].
d(num:pl)   -->  [two].

v(num:sg..subcat:1) --> [barks].
v(num:pl..subcat:1) --> [bark].
v(num:sg..subcat:2) --> [scares].
v(num:pl..subcat:2) --> [scare].

np(num:N) --> d(num:N), n(num:N).
np(num:N..case:C) --> pronoun(num:N..case:C).

vp(num:N) --> v(subcat:1..num:N).
vp(num:N) --> v(subcat:2..num:N), np(case:acc).

s --> np(case:nom..num:N), vp(num:N).
```

**Figure 5.3**  Example of a program to be input to Mini-GULP.

```
   Term == end_of_file,
   !,
   seen.

g_consult(_) :-      % if something went wrong in previous clause
   seen,
   write('g_consult failed.'),
   nl.
```

All the decision-making is relegated to `g_consult_aux`, which looks like this:[3]

```
g_consult_aux(end_of_file) :- !.

g_consult_aux(g_schema(X,Y)) :-
    !,
    assertz(g_schema(X,Y)).

g_consult_aux((X-->Y)) :-
    !,
    g_translate((X-->Y),Rule),
    expand_term(Rule,NewRule),    % DCG translator
    assertz(NewRule).

g_consult_aux(Term) :-
    g_translate(Term,TranslatedTerm),
    assertz(TranslatedTerm).
```

Now Mini-GULP is ready for use. The normal way to use it is as follows:

1. Get into Prolog.
2. Type '?- consult(*filename*).' to load Mini-GULP into memory. This executes the op declarations so that GULP syntax becomes legal.
3. Type '?- g_consult(*filename*).' to translate and load your program.
4. Type whatever queries your program expects. For example, '?- s([two,cats,bark],[]).' would be appropriate for the program in Figure 5.3.

**Exercise 5.4.4.1**

What happens if you g_consult the same file twice in succession?

**Exercise 5.4.4.2**

Get g_consult working and use it to translate and run the program in Figure 5.3. (Your translator program should now contain the op declarations, followed by g_translate, g_consult, and g_consult_aux.)

**Exercise 5.4.4.3**

Why is the second clause of g_consult necessary?

### 5.4.5 Output of Feature Structures

There's still one thing missing: a neat way to output feature structures. This is important because many of our parsers will report their results by building a feature structure.

---

[3]In ALS Prolog, expand_term/2 is called `builtins:dcg_expand/2`, and you have to `consult(dcgs)` to make it available.

Sticking with the program in Figure 5.3, let's take a simple example. If you want to find out the features of [$_{NP}$ *him* ], you can type

```
?- np(Features,[him],[]).
```

but you'll merely get

```
Features = g_([acc,sg])
```

which doesn't give the names of the features. In a large grammar with dozens of features, output in this format would be almost useless.

One way to get the computer to report names with the features is to use g_schema like this:

```
?- np(g_(Features),[him],[]), g_schema(FV,Features).
FV = case:acc  ;
FV = num:sg ;
no
```

Notice that 'g_' has been added in the first argument of np, so that Features is now just a list. Now we get the names and values of all the features, one at a time, as alternative solutions to the g_schema subgoal.

That's still rather clumsy, but we can do better. The built-in predicate setof will gather all these alternative solutions into a list, like this:

```
?- np(g_(Features),[him],[]), setof(FV,g_schema(FV,Features),L).
L = [case:acc,num:sg]
```

That's *almost* what we need. The problem is that, in most feature structures in most real grammars, most of the features are uninstantiated, so in a larger grammar you'd get something like

```
[person:_001,case:acc,gender:_002,tense:_003,num:pl,sem:_004]
```

which is hardly ideal.

Let's develop a predicate g_write/1 that outputs feature structures in readable form. Basically, here's what g_write will do:

- Output a g_-list by converting it into a series of feature-value pairs (using g_write recursively to write the values, and skipping the ones whose values are uninstantiated).
- Output anything else by calling write/1.

The alert reader will notice that this is only partly recursive: g_write can handle feature structures inside feature structures, and other terms inside feature structures, but not feature structures inside other kinds of terms. For most purposes, this is enough, and it greatly simplifies the program. Here, then, is `g_write`:

```
%  g_write(+g_(List))
%  Produces legible output of a feature structure in internal form.
%  Assumes all necessary schemas are present.
%  Imperfect; limitations are noted in text.

g_write(g_(Features)) :-
   !,
   write('('),
   setof(FV,g_schema(FV,Features),FVList),
   g_write_aux(FVList),
   write(')').

g_write(X) :-
   write(X).

g_write_aux([]) :-
   !.

g_write_aux([_:V|Rest]) :-
   var(V),
   !,
   g_write_aux(Rest).

g_write_aux([F:V|Rest]) :-
   !,
   write(F),
   write(':'),
   g_write(V),
   write('..'),
   g_write_aux(Rest).

g_write_aux(X) :-
   write(X).
```

This is good enough to output most feature structures, but (apart from not being completely recursive) it has a couple of flaws: it writes an extra '. .' after the last feature-value pair, and it fails to correctly write a variable or an empty list (and thus is not a perfect substitute for `write`). But at least we can now do things like this:

```
?- np(Features,[she],[]), g_write(Features).
(person:3..number:singular..)
```

and thus we will be able to look at the feature structures produced by more complex grammars.

**Exercise 5.4.5.1**

Get `g_write` working. A good way to test it is to write a program that consists of a set of schemas such as:

```
g_schema(person:X,[X,_,_]).
g_schema(number:X,[_,X,_]).
g_schema(sem:X,   [_,_,X]).
```

followed by some clauses such as:

```
test1 :- g_write(person:1).
test2 :- g_write(person:3..number:plural).
test3 :- g_write(sem:(person:3)..number:singular).
```

Then load the program through `g_consult` in order to turn all the feature structures into `g_`-lists, and see if `g_write` translates them back correctly when `test1`, `test2`, etc., are executed.

**Exercise 5.4.5.2**

Modify `g_write` so that '?- `g_write([])`.' will output '`[]`' and '?- `g_write(X)`.' will output a representation of an uninstantiated variable (something like `_001`, or whatever your Prolog normally produces).

**Exercise 5.4.5.3**

Modify `g_write` so that there will not be an extra '`..`' after the last feature-value pair. Note that the last feature-value pair to be printed is not necessarily the last one in the `g_`-list, because features with uninstantiated values are skipped.

## 5.5 UBG IN THEORY AND PRACTICE

### 5.5.1 A More Complex Grammar

It's time to look at, and implement, a more elaborate unification-based grammar. Here is a grammar based on the four PS rules:

$$
\begin{array}{rcl}
NP & \rightarrow & \textit{Fido, Felix, he, him, they, them} \\
V & \rightarrow & \textit{chase, chases, sleep, sleeps} \\
VP & \rightarrow & \textit{V (NP)} \\
S & \rightarrow & \textit{NP VP}
\end{array}
$$

To these we will add features to handle the following things:

- Case assignment (*he chases me,* not *\*him chases I*);
- Subject-verb agreement (*Fido sleeps,* not *\*Fido sleep*);

- Verb subcategorization (*Fido chases Felix*, not *\*Fido sleeps Felix*);
- Semantics (we will build a primitive semantic representation of the sentence—too primitive for practical use, but adequate to illustrate some techniques).

All together, the features that we use will be *agr, sem, num, case, pred, arg1, arg2,* and *subcat*. So the parser has to start with a set of schemas:

```
g_schema(agr:X,    [X,_,_,_,_,_,_,_]).
g_schema(sem:X,    [_,X,_,_,_,_,_,_]).
g_schema(num:X,    [_,_,X,_,_,_,_,_]).
g_schema(case:X,   [_,_,_,X,_,_,_,_]).
g_schema(pred:X,   [_,_,_,_,X,_,_,_]).
g_schema(arg1:X,   [_,_,_,_,_,X,_,_]).
g_schema(arg2:X,   [_,_,_,_,_,_,X,_]).
g_schema(subcat:X,[_,_,_,_,_,_,_,X]).
```

Now for the grammar itself. Let's look first at the lexical entries for the NPs. These endow each NP with a semantic representation of sorts, plus a group of *agr* features (number, and case if case is marked).

$$\begin{matrix} & NP & & \\ \begin{bmatrix} agr: \begin{bmatrix} num:\ sg \end{bmatrix} \\ sem:\ fido \end{bmatrix} & \rightarrow & Fido \end{matrix}$$

$$\begin{matrix} & NP & & \\ \begin{bmatrix} agr: \begin{bmatrix} num:\ sg \end{bmatrix} \\ sem:\ felix \end{bmatrix} & \rightarrow & Felix \end{matrix}$$

$$\begin{matrix} & NP & & \\ \begin{bmatrix} agr: \begin{bmatrix} num:\ sg \\ case:\ nom \end{bmatrix} \\ sem:\ he \end{bmatrix} & \rightarrow & he \end{matrix}$$

$$\begin{matrix} & NP & & \\ \begin{bmatrix} agr: \begin{bmatrix} num:\ sg \\ case:\ acc \end{bmatrix} \\ sem:\ him \end{bmatrix} & \rightarrow & him \end{matrix}$$

$$\begin{matrix} & NP & & \\ \begin{bmatrix} agr: \begin{bmatrix} num:\ pl \\ case:\ nom \end{bmatrix} \\ sem:\ they \end{bmatrix} & \rightarrow & they \end{matrix}$$

$$\begin{matrix} & NP & & \\ \begin{bmatrix} agr: \begin{bmatrix} num:\ pl \\ case:\ acc \end{bmatrix} \\ sem:\ them \end{bmatrix} & \rightarrow & them \end{matrix}$$

They go into DCG with GULP straightforwardly:

```
np(agr:(num:sg)..sem:fido)          --> [fido].
np(agr:(num:sg)..sem:felix)         --> [felix].
np(agr:(num:sg..case:nom)..sem:he)  --> [he].
np(agr:(num:sg..case:acc)..sem:him) --> [him].
np(agr:(num:pl..case:nom)..sem:they) --> [they].
np(agr:(num:pl..case:acc)..sem:them) --> [them].
```

As before, we have two subcategories of verbs:

$$
\begin{bmatrix} V \\ subcat:\ 1 \\ agr:\ [\ num:\ sg\ ] \\ sem:\ sleeps \end{bmatrix} \rightarrow \quad sleeps
$$

$$
\begin{bmatrix} V \\ subcat:\ 1 \\ agr:\ [\ num:\ pl\ ] \\ sem:\ sleep \end{bmatrix} \rightarrow \quad sleep
$$

$$
\begin{bmatrix} V \\ subcat:\ 2 \\ agr:\ [\ num:\ sg\ ] \\ sem:\ chases \end{bmatrix} \rightarrow \quad chases
$$

$$
\begin{bmatrix} V \\ subcat:\ 2 \\ agr:\ [\ num:\ pl\ ] \\ sem:\ chase \end{bmatrix} \rightarrow \quad chase
$$

These, too, go into GULP straightforwardly:

```
v(subcat:1..agr:(num:sg)..sem:sleeps)  --> [sleeps].
v(subcat:1..agr:(num:pl)..sem:sleep)   --> [sleep].
v(subcat:2..agr:(num:sg)..sem:chases)  --> [chases].
v(subcat:2..agr:(num:pl)..sem:chase)   --> [chase].
```

Notice that our approach to semantics here is extremely naive—we're just writing each word itself in place of its semantic representation. This is enough to show that we can get the symbols to come out in the right places; we'll explore semantics in depth in Chapters 7 and 8.

The VP rules must enforce subcategorization and, if there is an object, assign accusative case to it. Here's what they look like, in UBG and in GULP:

$$
\begin{array}{ccc}
VP & & V \\
\left[\begin{array}{l} agr:\ X \\ sem:\ \left[\ pred:\ P\ \right] \end{array}\right] & \rightarrow & \left[\begin{array}{l} subcat:\ 1 \\ agr:\ X \\ sem:\ P \end{array}\right]
\end{array}
$$

$$
\begin{array}{cccc}
VP & & V & NP \\
\left[\begin{array}{ll} agr:\ X \\ sem: & \left[\begin{array}{l} pred:\ P \\ arg2:\ A2 \end{array}\right] \end{array}\right] & \rightarrow & \left[\begin{array}{l} subcat:\ 2 \\ agr:\ X \\ sem:\ P \end{array}\right] & \left[\begin{array}{ll} agr: & \left[\ case:\ acc\ \right] \\ sem:\ A2 \end{array}\right]
\end{array}
$$

```
vp(agr:X..sem:(pred:P)) -->
   v(subcat:1..agr:X..sem:P).

vp(agr:X..sem:(pred:P..arg2:A2)) -->
   v(subcat:2..agr:X..sem:P),
   np(agr:(case:acc)..sem:A2).
```

Notice what these rules do. Besides enforcing subcategorization, percolating *agr,* and assigning case to the direct object, they also build a semantic representation. The semantics of the verb (*P*) and of the noun (*A2*) get combined into a structure representing the semantics of the VP, such as

$$
\left[\begin{array}{l} pred:\ chases \\ arg2:\ fido \end{array}\right]
$$

if the VP is *chases Fido.* As you might guess, the S rule is going to add an *arg1,* so that *Felix chases Fido* will come out as:

$$
\left[\begin{array}{l} pred:\ chase \\ arg1:\ felix \\ arg2:\ fido \end{array}\right]
$$

The S rule itself takes the form

$$
\begin{array}{cccc}
S & & NP & VP \\
\left[\ sem:\ \boxed{1}\left[\ arg1:\ A1\ \right]\ \right] & \rightarrow & \left[\begin{array}{ll} agr:\ \boxed{2}\left[\ case:\ nom\ \right] \\ sem:\ A1 \end{array}\right] & \left[\begin{array}{l} agr:\ \boxed{2} \\ sem:\ \boxed{1} \end{array}\right]
\end{array}
$$

Here the S has a single feature, *sem,* which is the same as the *sem* feature of the VP except that it also has to unify with *arg1: A1* (which is how the semantics of the subject gets into it). NP and VP share all their *agr* features and are required to contain *case: nom.* To express this rule in GULP, we have to use equational style:

```
s(Sfeatures) --> np(NPfeatures), vp(VPfeatures),
   { Sfeatures   = sem:(arg1:A1), NPfeatures = sem:A1,
     Sfeatures   = sem:S,         VPfeatures = sem:S,
     NPfeatures = agr:X,          VPfeatures = agr:X,
     NPfeatures = agr:case:nom                        }.
```

It's also possible to use a style that is only partly equational, like this:

```
s(sem:S) --> np(agr:X..sem:A1), vp(agr:X..sem:S),
  { S = arg1:A1,
    X = case:nom }.
```

Here the second line means, "In addition to the value that S already has, S must be unified with `arg1:A1`," and likewise for X and `case:nom`.

Notice that, since the *sem* of the S and of the VP are unified with each other, *arg1* gets added to the *sem* of the VP as well as of the S. This is harmless and, in fact, correctly reflects the fact that the meaning of the verb is incomplete until the meaning of the subject is added.

To parse a sentence, issue a query such as:[4]

```
?- s(Features,[felix,chases,fido],[]), g_write(Features).
(sem:(arg1:felix..arg2:fido..pred:chases))
```

All you're doing here is invoking a DCG parser in the usual way and telling it to parse `[fido,chases,felix]` and end up with `[]`. The argument of s is `Features`, a GULP feature structure which is then printed out by `g_write`. In this grammar, the features of S contain a primitive semantic representation of the sentence.

You can equally well parse any other constituent, for example a VP, like this:

```
?- vp(Features,[chases,fido],[]), g_write(Features).
(agr:(num:sg)..sem:(arg2:fido..pred:chases))
```

This highlights an important fact:

> *Unification-based grammar is not sentence based.*

In UBG, the sentence is just one of many constituents that can be described and parsed. This contrasts sharply with transformational grammar, in which many transformations apply only to the whole S, and the grammar does not correctly generate NPs, VPs, etc., unless they are embedded in their proper places in sentences.

**Exercise 5.5.1.1**

Draw trees (with features) for the following sentences generated by this grammar:

**1.** *Fido chases him.*

---

[4]The output as shown here assumes that the behavior of **g_write** has been cleaned up as suggested in the exercises. Otherwise there will be a redundant '..' at the end.

**2.** *They sleep.*

**3.** *He chases Fido.*

In doing this by hand, it is probably best to work bottom-up. First write down the words and apply the lexical entries. Then group the words into phrases, performing appropriate unifications as you go.

### Exercise 5.5.1.2

Get this grammar working, as a DCG parser, on your computer. Parse the three sentences from the previous exercise, and give the features of the S.

### Exercise 5.5.1.3

Modify this grammar so that every node has another feature, *tree,* whose value is a representation of the parse tree below it. This will work very much like the tree-building parser in Chapter 3. Parse the same three sentences again and show the value of *tree* for S.

### Exercise 5.5.1.4

Construct and implement a UBG to parse sentences such as

*Who did Max say ␣ thought Fido barked?*

(as in Section 3.4.5), constructing a representation of the tree in which *who* is associated with (or moved into) the position of the missing NP.

## 5.5.2 Context-Free Backbones and Subcategorization Lists

So far, every UBG that we've worked with has had a CONTEXT-FREE BACKBONE—that is, if you strip away all the features, you get context-free PS rules.

Notice that the node labels themselves can be treated as features. Instead of

$$NP$$
$$\begin{bmatrix} case:\ nom \\ num:\ pl \end{bmatrix}$$

we can write

$$\begin{bmatrix} cat:\ np \\ case:\ nom \\ num:\ pl \end{bmatrix}$$

So far so good; the grammar still has a context-free backbone *if* every node in every rule has a *cat* feature whose value contains no variables. (Normally the value of *cat* is an atomic symbol such as *np,* but Jackendoff (1977) and Gazdar et al. (1985) explore what can be accomplished by using feature structures there.)

If we let *cat* be a variable, we pass into interesting territory. For one thing, we can handle verb subcategorization by giving each verb a feature which is a *list* of complement categories. Consider the rules:

$$\begin{bmatrix} cat\text{:} \ vp \\ subcat\text{:} \ Y \end{bmatrix} \ \rightarrow \ \begin{bmatrix} cat\text{:} \ vp \\ subcat\text{:} \ [X \mid Y] \end{bmatrix} \ \begin{bmatrix} cat\text{:} \ X \end{bmatrix}$$

$$\begin{bmatrix} cat\text{:} \ s \end{bmatrix} \ \rightarrow \ \begin{bmatrix} cat\text{:} \ np \end{bmatrix} \ \begin{bmatrix} cat\text{:} \ vp \\ subcat\text{:} \ [] \end{bmatrix}$$

The first rule is effectively *VP → VP X*, where *X* comes from the *subcat* list of the VP. It applies recursively, picking off values of *X* one by one until there are none left. Then the second rule, *S → NP VP*, is allowed to apply.

With these rules we use lexical entries such as the following:

$$\begin{bmatrix} cat\text{:} \ vp \\ subcat\text{:} \ [] \end{bmatrix} \ \rightarrow \ \text{bark(s)} \qquad\qquad (\textit{bark} \text{ takes no complement})$$

$$\begin{bmatrix} cat\text{:} \ vp \\ subcat\text{:} \ [np] \end{bmatrix} \ \rightarrow \ \text{chase(s)} \qquad\qquad (\textit{chase} \text{ takes one NP})$$

$$\begin{bmatrix} cat\text{:} \ vp \\ subcat\text{:} \ [np,np] \end{bmatrix} \ \rightarrow \ \text{give(s)} \qquad\qquad (\textit{give} \text{ takes two NPs})$$

$$\begin{bmatrix} cat\text{:} \ vp \\ subcat\text{:} \ [np,s] \end{bmatrix} \ \rightarrow \ \text{tell(s)} \qquad\qquad (\textit{tell} \text{ takes an NP and an S})$$

The resulting structures are as shown in Fig. 5.4.

This analysis follows a proposal by Shieber (1985:27–32) except that we use Prolog notation for lists, and the subject of the verb is not listed among its complements. Note that a verb here is a VP, not a V. Note also that the elements of a subcategorization list could be feature structures.

Unfortunately we can't implement this with a top-down DCG parser. The obvious way to approach it is to give all nodes the same label (let's use z) and encode the real node labels in the *cat* feature, rendering the first rule thus:

```
z(cat:vp..subcat:Y) --> z(cat:vp..subcat:[X|Y]), z(cat:X).
```

The problem is that, parsing top-down, this rule creates an endless loop. In order to parse z(cat:vp..subcat:[X|Y]), with X and Y uninstantiated, this rule simply calls itself. We will return to this point in the next chapter.

Are subcategorization lists a good idea? That depends. To use subcategorization lists is to claim (with Gross 1979) that verbs do not necessarily fall into classes and thus that the complements of each verb must be listed in its lexical entry. Many generative

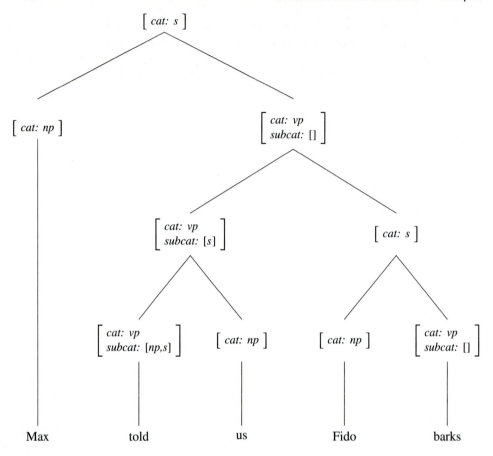

**Figure 5.4**  Tree showing how subcategorization lists work.

linguists, however, believe (with Gazdar et al. 1985) that verbs fall into a finite, though possibly large, set of classes, and thus that subcategorization with numbers (as pointers to classes) is more appropriate.

**Exercise 5.5.2.1**

Using the rules developed in this section, draw trees for the sentences:

1. Fido chases Felix.
2. Felix gives Fido a hard time.

Assume any other PS rules that are necessary.

### 5.5.3 Negative and Disjunctive Features

The alert reader will notice that we have been ignoring the *person* feature of the English verb. There's a good reason. Every regular present tense verb has two forms: with *-s* in the third person singular, and without *-s* elsewhere. Thus we get:

|              | Singular          |        | Plural   |        |
|--------------|-------------------|--------|----------|--------|
| 1st person   | *(I)*             | *bark* | *(we)*   | *bark* |
| 2nd person   | *(you)*           | *bark* | *(you)*  | *bark* |
| 3rd person   | *(he, she, it)*   | *barks*| *(they)* | *bark* |

In UBG as formulated so far, the best we can do is list the form with *-s* once, and the form without *-s* three times:

$$\left[\left[ agr: \begin{array}{c} V \\ \left[ \begin{array}{l} person:\ 3 \\ num:\ sg \end{array} \right] \end{array} \right]\right] \quad \rightarrow \quad barks$$

$$\left[\left[ agr:\ \left[\ person:\ 2\ \right]\ \right]\right]^{V} \quad \rightarrow \quad bark$$

$$\left[\left[ agr:\ \left[\ person:\ 1\ \right]\ \right]\right]^{V} \quad \rightarrow \quad bark$$

$$\left[\left[ agr:\ \left[\ num:\ pl\ \right]\ \right]\right]^{V} \quad \rightarrow \quad bark$$

It would be more convenient if we could collapse the last three of these into one rule like this:

$$\left[\left[ agr:\ \mathbf{not} \begin{array}{c} V \\ \left[ \begin{array}{l} person:3 \\ num:sg \end{array} \right] \end{array} \right]\right] \quad \rightarrow \quad bark$$

Here **not** means "This feature must ultimately have a value that will not unify with the value shown here." This is called a NEGATIVE feature.

Or consider the forms of the German word for "the" (*der, die, das,* etc.). A striking pattern emerges: the form is *die* whenever:

- the case is nominative or accusative (not genitive or dative), *and*
- the gender is feminine *or* the number is plural (or both).

We could sum this up as:

$$
\begin{array}{c}
D \\
\left[
\begin{array}{l}
\textit{case: nom } \textbf{or } \textit{acc} \\
\textit{agr:} \quad \left[ \textit{ num: pl } \right] \textbf{ or } \left[ \textit{ gen: fem } \right]
\end{array}
\right] \quad \rightarrow \quad \textit{die}
\end{array}
$$

Here we've moved *case* outside the *agr* group, and **or** means "the actual value must unify with one of these values, or the other, or both." Features joined with **or** are called DISJUNCTIVE features.

Obviously the Prolog unifier will not handle negative or disjunctive features. Johnson (1991) discusses them lucidly and offers an analysis based on classical logic, leading to a unifier based on a theorem-proving algorithm.

**Exercise 5.5.3.1**

Using negative and/or disjunctive features, write concise lexical entries for the English copula:

|              | Singular        |     | Plural  |     |
|--------------|----------------:|-----|---------|-----|
| 1st person   | *(I)*           | *am*  | *(we)*    | *are* |
| 2nd person   | *(you)*         | *are* | *(you)*   | *are* |
| 3rd person   | *(he, she, it)* | *is*  | *(they)*  | *are* |

**Exercise 5.5.3.2**

If negative and disjunctive features were implemented, what should be the result of unifying each of the following pairs of feature structures? Explain your answers and relate them to what you know about logic.

**1.** $\left[ \textit{ person: } \textbf{not } \textit{3} \right]$     and     $\left[ \textit{ person: 2 } \right]$

**2.** $\left[ \textit{ person: 1 } \textbf{or } \textit{2} \right]$     and     $\left[ \textit{ person: 2 } \right]$

**3.** $\left[ \textit{ a: b } \textbf{or } \textit{c} \right]$     and     $\left[ \textit{ a: c } \textbf{or } \textit{d} \right]$

**4.** $\left[ \textit{ a: b } \textbf{or } \textit{c} \right]$     and     $\left[ \textit{ a: } \textbf{not } \textit{b} \right]$

**Exercise 5.5.3.3   (project)**

Implement a unifier for negative and/or disjunctive feature structures. (See Johnson (1991) for guidance.)

# CHAPTER 6

# Parsing Algorithms

## 6.1 COMPARING PARSING ALGORITHMS

So far, all our parsers have relied on Prolog's built-in DCG translator as discussed in Chapter 3. In this chapter we will implement a number of parsing algorithms for ourselves. Parts of this chapter are heavily indebted to Pereira and Shieber (1987), who describe several algorithms in more detail.

We will take advantage of the fact that, in Prolog, backtracking is automatic. This makes Prolog ideal for implementing parsers and seeing clearly how they work. Most parsers need to backtrack, but most programming languages make backtracking rather hard to implement. This means that, in ordinary programming languages, the core of any parser is likely to be hidden under a large, cumbersome backtracking mechanism.

All our parsers will use the grammar shown in Figure 6.1, except for certain rules that particular parsing algorithms can't handle.

## 6.2 TOP-DOWN PARSING

Let's start with top-down recursive-descent parsing. This is the same algorithm used by the DCG system, but we will implement it differently. The DCG system is a COMPILER for

$S \rightarrow NP\ VP$

$NP \rightarrow D\ N$
$NP \rightarrow NP\ Conj\ NP$     (not for top-down parsers)

$VP \rightarrow V\ NP\ (PP)$

$PP \rightarrow P\ NP$

$D \rightarrow \emptyset$     (not for bottom-up parsers)
$D \rightarrow$ *the, all, every*

$P \rightarrow$ *near*

$Conj \rightarrow$ *and*

$N \rightarrow$ *dog, dogs, cat, cats, elephant, elephants*

$V \rightarrow$ *chase, chases, see, sees, amuse, amuses*

**Figure 6.1**    A sample grammar for experimenting with parsers.

grammar rules—it translates them directly into executable Prolog clauses. For example,

$$s \rightarrow np,\ vp.$$

goes into memory as something like this:

$$s(L1,L) :\!-\ np(L1,L2),\ vp(L2,L).$$

What we're going to build is an INTERPRETER for grammar rules. Instead of executing the rules directly, it will store them as facts in a knowledge base and look them up as needed. Execution will be a little slower, but the parser will be much easier to modify. We'll represent PS rules as

```
rule(s,[np,vp]).
rule(np,[d,n]).
rule(d,[]).
```

and the like. Lexical entries will look like this:

```
word(d,the).
word(n,dog).       word(n,dogs).
word(n,cat).       word(n,cats).
word(v,chase).     word(v,chases).
```

This format works conveniently with a variety of parsing algorithms; we'll be able to transfer the set of rules with little or no change from one parser to another.

Now recall how top-down parsing works. To parse *The dog barked,* the parser, in effect, says to itself:

— I'm looking for an S.
— To get an S, I need an NP and a VP.
— To get an NP, I need a D and an N.
— To get a D, I can use *the* ... Got it.
— To get an N, I can use *dog* ... Got it.
— That completes the NP.
— To get a VP, I need a V.
— To get a V, I can use *barked* ... Got it.
— That completes the VP.
— That completes the S.

To get a feel for what's going on, try drawing the tree as you work through these steps. Figure 6.2 shows the order in which a top-down parser discovers the various parts of the tree.

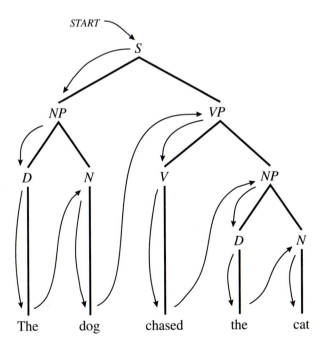

**Figure 6.2**  Top-down parsing. The parser discovers the nodes of the tree in the order shown by the arrows.

Like the DCG system, our parser will work through the input string, accepting words one by one.  Let C represent the kind of constituent the parser is looking for at any particular moment (an S, NP, V, or whatever). Then the algorithm to parse a constituent of type C is:

- If C is an individual word, look it up in the lexical rules and accept it from the input string.
- Otherwise, look in the PS rules to expand C into a list of constituents, and parse those constituents one by one.

Or, putting it into Prolog:

```
% parse(?C,?S1,?S)
%   Parse a constituent of category C
%   starting with input string S1 and
%   ending up with input string S.

parse(C,[Word|S],S) :-
   word(C,Word).

parse(C,S1,S) :-
   rule(C,Cs),
   parse_list(Cs,S1,S).
```

Here `parse_list` is just like `parse` except that it takes a list of constituents and parses all of them:

```
parse_list([C|Cs],S1,S) :-
   parse(C,S1,S2),
   parse_list(Cs,S2,S).

parse_list([],S,S).
```

That's the whole parser. The query to parse a sentence looks like this:

```
?- parse(s,[the,dog,barked],[]).
```

Notice that backtracking, where needed, occurs automatically.

**Exercise 6.2.0.1**

Get this parser working and equip it with all the grammar rules in Figure 6.1 except for *NP → NP Conj NP*. Use it to parse sentences such as *All dogs amuse the elephant.*

**Exercise 6.2.0.2**

In this parser, why is *D → ∅* encoded as a PS-rule rather than as a lexical entry?

**Exercise 6.2.0.3**

By adding arguments to nodes (as in Chapter 3, section 3.4), make the parser enforce subject-verb number agreement and build a representation of the parse tree. (Hint: This is easy; only the rules need to be modified.)

**Exercise 6.2.0.4**

*(Not for courses that skipped Chapter 5.)* Combine Mini-GULP with this parser. Account for number agreement of subject and verb, and of determiner and noun, using GULP feature structures.

**Exercise 6.2.0.5**

Modify the parser so that it always builds a representation of the parse tree, even with the rules in their original form (without arguments). (Hint: Add extra arguments to `parse` and `parse_list`.)

## 6.3 BOTTOM-UP PARSING

### 6.3.1 The Shift-Reduce Algorithm

A familiar limitation of top-down parsers is that they loop on LEFT-RECURSIVE rules of the form $A \rightarrow A\ B$ ("to parse an A, parse an A and then ..."). Yet, as we saw in Chapter 4, such rules occur in natural language; one example is *NP → NP Conj NP*, where *Conj* is a conjunction such as *and* or *or*.

One way to handle left-recursive rules is to parse BOTTOM-UP. A bottom-up parser accepts words and tries to combine them into constituents, like this:

— Accept a word ... it's *the*.
— *The* is a D.
— Accept another word ... it's *dog*.
— *Dog* is an N.
— D and N together make an NP.
— Accept another word ... it's *barked*.
— *Barked* is a V.
— V by itself makes a VP.
— NP and VP make an S.

Again, try drawing a tree while working through these steps. (During most of the process it will of course be a set of partial trees not yet linked together.) You'll find that you encounter the various parts of the tree in the order shown by the arrows in Figure 6.3.

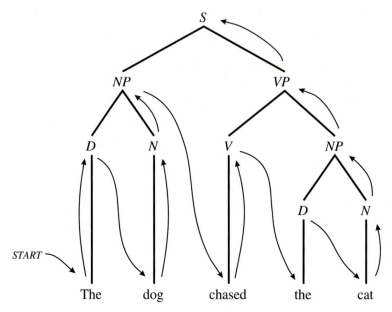

**Figure 6.3**  Bottom–up parsing. The parser discovers the nodes of the tree in the order shown by the arrows.

Because its actions are triggered only by words actually found, this parser does not loop on left-recursive rules. But it has a different limitation: it cannot handle rules like

$$D \rightarrow \emptyset$$

because it has no way of responding to a null (empty, missing) constituent. It can only respond to what's actually there.

The bottom-up algorithm that I've just sketched is often called SHIFT-REDUCE parsing. It consists of two basic operations: to SHIFT words onto a stack, and to REDUCE (simplify) the contents of the stack. Here's an example:

| Step | Action | Stack | Input string |
|---|---|---|---|
| | (Start) | | *the dog barked* |
| 1 | Shift | *the* | *dog barked* |
| 2 | Reduce | D | *dog barked* |
| 3 | Shift | D *dog* | *barked* |
| 4 | Reduce | D N | *barked* |
| 5 | Reduce | NP | *barked* |
| 6 | Shift | NP *barked* | |
| 7 | Reduce | NP V | |
| 8 | Reduce | NP VP | |
| 9 | Reduce | S | |

So the shift-reduce algorithm is as follows:

**1.** Shift a word onto the stack.
**2.** Reduce the stack repeatedly using lexical entries and PS rules, until no further reductions are possible.
**3.** If there are more words in the input string, go to Step 1. Otherwise stop.

A noteworthy feature of shift-reduce parsing is that it has no expectations. That is, you can give it an input string and say, "What kind of constituent is this?" and get an answer. You do not have to say "Parse this as an S" or "Parse this as an NP."

**Exercise 6.3.1.1**

By hand, using the grammar in Figure 6.1, do shift-reduce parsing on the following input strings:

**1.** *the dogs amuse the elephants*
**2.** *see the cat near the dog*
**3.** *the dogs and the cats*
**4.** *the dogs the dogs the dogs*

What happens in the last of these?

## 6.3.2 Shift-reduce in Prolog

Efficient shift-reduce parsing in Prolog requires a couple of subtle techniques. The first of these is to build the stack backward. That is, shift words from the beginning of the input string to the *beginning* of the stack, so that they end up in reverse order, thus:

```
Start:      []                [the,dog,barked]
Shift:      [the]             [dog,barked]
Reduce:     [d]               [dog,barked]
Shift:      [dog,d]           [barked]
Reduce:     [n,d]             [barked]
Reduce:     [np]              [barked]
Shift:      [barked,np]       []
Reduce:     [v,np]            []
Reduce:     [vp,np]           []
Reduce:     [s]               []
```

This is efficient because all the action is at the beginning of each list; there is no need to work all the way along a list to get to the end.

The second subtlety is that the "reduce" step goes a lot faster if the rules, too, are stored backward. For example,

$$NP \rightarrow D\ N$$

goes into Prolog as

```
brule([n,d|X],[np|X]).
```

Here `brule` stands for "backward rule." The first argument, `[n,d|X]`, directly matches the stack to which this rule applies, and `[np|X]` is what the stack becomes after reduction. With the rule written this way, unification does all the work.

So the "reduce" step in the parser is very simple: if there is an applicable rule, use it, and then try to reduce again; otherwise leave the stack unchanged. The rest of the parser is even simpler; the whole thing is shown in Figure 6.4.

**Exercise 6.3.2.1**

Using the parser in Figure 6.4, what is the effect of each of the following queries? Consider all possible solutions.

```
?- parse([the,dog,chases,the,cat],[s]).
?- parse([the,dog,chases,the,cat],[What]).
?- parse([the,dog,chases,the,cat],What).
```

**Exercise 6.3.2.2**

Why isn't there a cut in the first clause of `reduce`?

**Exercise 6.3.2.3**

Extend the parser in Figure 6.4 to contain all the grammar rules in Figure 6.1 except for $D \to \emptyset$. Then use it to parse the input strings from Exercise 6.3.1.1.

**Exercise 6.3.2.4**

Add features to the shift-reduce parser to enforce subject-verb number agreement and build a representation of the parse tree. As before, only the rules need to be modified.

**Exercise 6.3.2.5**

*(Not for courses that skipped Chapter 5.)* Combine Mini-GULP with this parser. Account for number agreement of subject and verb, and of determiner and noun, using GULP feature structures.

**Exercise 6.3.2.6**

What, exactly, does a shift-reduce parser do if it tries to use a rule like $D \to \emptyset$?

## 6.4 LEFT-CORNER PARSING

### 6.4.1 The Key Idea

Left-corner parsers are often described as bottom-up, but left-corner parsing is actually a combination of bottom-up and top-down strategies. This technique was popularized

```
% Bottom-up shift-reduce parser

% parse(+S,?Result)
%   parses input string S, where Result
%   is list of categories to which it reduces.

parse(S,Result) :-
  shift_reduce(S,[],Result).

% shift_reduce(+S,+Stack,?Result)
%   parses input string S, where Stack is
%   list of categories parsed so far.

shift_reduce(S,Stack,Result) :-
  shift(Stack,S,NewStack,S1),       % fails if S = []
  reduce(NewStack,ReducedStack),
  shift_reduce(S1,ReducedStack,Result).

shift_reduce([],Result,Result).

% shift(+Stack,+S,-NewStack,-NewS)
%   shifts first element from S onto Stack.

shift(X,[H|Y],[H|X],Y).

% reduce(+Stack,-ReducedStack)
%   repeatedly reduces beginning of Stack
%   to form fewer, larger constituents.

reduce(Stack,ReducedStack) :-
  brule(Stack,Stack2),
  reduce(Stack2,ReducedStack).

reduce(Stack,Stack).

% Phrase structure rules

brule([vp,np|X],[s|X]).
brule([n,d|X],[np|X]).
brule([np,v|X],[vp|X]).

brule([Word|X],[Cat|X]) :- word(Cat,Word).

% Lexicon

word(d,the).

word(n,dog).        word(n,dogs).
word(n,elephant).   word(n,elephants).

word(v,chase).      word(v,chases).
word(v,see).        word(v,sees).
% etc.
```

**Figure 6.4**  Shift-reduce parser.

by Rosenkrantz and Lewis (1970) and Aho and Ullman (1972:310–314), all of whom attribute it to Irons (1961).

The key idea is to accept a word, figure out what kind of constituent it marks the beginning of, and then parse the rest of that constituent top-down. The tree is thus discovered starting at the lower left corner, as shown in Figure 6.5.

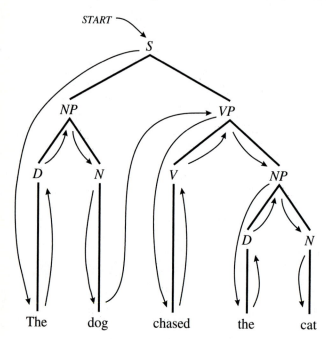

**Figure 6.5**  Left-corner parsing. Note that some nodes are visited twice, once working top-down and once working bottom-up.

Like a top-down parser, a left-corner parser is always expecting a particular constituent and therefore knows that only a few of the grammar rules are relevant. This can give it an efficiency advantage over straight bottom-up parsing.

But like a bottom-up parser, the left-corner parser can handle rules like $A \rightarrow A\ B$ without looping, because it starts each constituent by accepting a word from the input string.

### 6.4.2 The Algorithm

The algorithm consists of two parts: accepting and identifying a word, and then completing the constituent.

**To parse a constituent of type C:**

1. **Accept** a word from the input string and determine its category. Call its category W.

2. **Complete** C. If W = C, you're done. Otherwise,

- Look at the rules and find a constituent whose expansion begins with W. Call that constituent P (for "phrase"). For example, if W is Determiner, use the rule $NP \rightarrow D\ N$ and let P be Noun Phrase.
- Recursively left-corner-parse all the remaining elements of the expansion of P. (This is the top-down part of the strategy.)
- Last, put P in place of W, and go back to the beginning of step 2 (i.e., start over trying to complete C).

All of this is easier to describe in Prolog than in English. Rules will be represented as they were with our top-down parser:

```
rule(s,[np,vp]).
rule(np,[d,n]).   % etc.

word(n,dog).  word(n,dogs).
word(n,cat).  word(n,cats).  % etc.
```

and so on. To tackle any constituent, the parser first accepts a word, then completes the constituent, thus:

```
% parse(+C,+S1,-S)
%  Parse a constituent of category C
%  starting with input string S1 and
%  ending up with input string S.

parse(C,[Word|S2],S) :-
  word(W,Word),
  complete(W,C,S2,S).
```

Again, we have `parse_list`, which parses a list of constituents:

```
parse_list([C|Cs],S1,S) :-
   parse(C,S1,S2),
   parse_list(Cs,S2,S).

parse_list([],S,S).
```

The only nontrivial procedure is `complete`, defined as follows:

```
% complete(+W,+C,+S1,-S)
%  Verifies that W can be the first subconstituent
%  of C, then left-corner-parses the rest of C.

complete(C,C,S,S).   % if C=W, do nothing.

complete(W,C,S1,S) :-
```

```
rule(P,[W|Rest]),
parse_list(Rest,S1,S2),
complete(P,C,S2,S).
```

**Exercise 6.4.2.1**

Get this parser working with all the grammar rules from Figure 6.1 except $D \rightarrow \emptyset$.

**Exercise 6.4.2.2**

Add arguments to the nodes in the rules so that this parser will build a representation of the tree and enforce subject-verb number agreement. (Easy—just copy the modified rules from Exercise 6.2.0.3.)

**Exercise 6.4.2.3**

Modify this parser so that it builds a representation of the tree by itself, without requiring any arguments in the rules.

**Exercise 6.4.2.4**

*(Not for courses that skipped Chapter 5.)* Combine Mini-GULP with this parser. Account for number agreement of subject and verb, and of determiner and noun, using GULP feature structures. (Easy—copy the rules from Exercise 6.2.0.4.)

**Exercise 6.4.2.5**

Modify `complete` so that it can handle null constituents in the portion of the tree that it encounters top-down. Then modify the grammar so that the only rule expanding NP is $NP \rightarrow D\ N\ PP$ where $PP \rightarrow \emptyset$. In your modified parser, `rule(pp,[])` should allow the parser to skip the PP without trying to parse it.

**Exercise 6.4.2.6**

What does the left-corner parser do when asked to "generate a sentence" by a query such as the following?

```
?- parse(s,What,[]).
```

Recall that this query does indeed generate a sentence with the original top-down parser.

## 6.4.3 Links

As described so far, the left-corner parser is only partly able to handle rules that introduce null constituents, such as $D \rightarrow \emptyset$.

If the null constituent is encountered while parsing top-down, there is no problem. The left-corner parser works just like a top-down parser. This is the situation with rules of the form

$$
\begin{array}{ccc}
A & \rightarrow & B\ C \\
C & \rightarrow & \emptyset
\end{array}
$$

because the C gets parsed top-down. All that is necessary is to tell `parse/3` that if it's looking for a C, it can simply skip ahead without parsing anything. This could be accomplished by encoding the rules as

```
rule(a,[b,c]).
rule(c,[]).
```

and adding the following clause to `parse`:

```
parse(C,S2,S) :-
  rule(W,[]),
  complete(W,C,S2,S).
```

That is: "If W is a category that can be a null constituent, then it is permissible to 'complete' a W at any time by doing nothing."

Unfortunately, this is not what we need for English. Our best-established null constituent is the null determiner, which occurs at the *beginning* of a noun phrase and will therefore be parsed bottom-up. That is, the rules are

$$S \quad \rightarrow \quad NP\ VP$$
$$NP \quad \rightarrow \quad D\ N$$
$$D \quad \rightarrow \quad \emptyset$$

and these tell the parser to accept the null determiner as the very first step of parsing an S or NP.

With rules like these, the parser loops. The problem arises whenever it tries a parse that does not succeed. Suppose the parser is looking for a VP but the VP isn't there. This means the parser can't accept the first word of the VP, which could only be a verb. Instead, it "accepts" a null determiner and hypothesizes the structure:

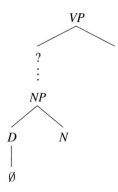

Next it tries to complete the NP by parsing the N top-down. But suppose the N isn't there either. The parse ought to have failed by now, but in fact the parser has an alternative:

it can "accept" another null determiner and try to complete another phantom NP. And of course this will again fail the same way, and the same action will occur over and over.

The problem is that, like a bottom-up parser, the left-corner parser is allowed to "accept" null constituents anywhere it wants to. The solution is to constrain the parser by adding a table of LINKS. Besides solving the null-constituent problem, the links make the parser more efficient.

The table of links specifies what kinds of constituents can appear at the beginning of what. For example, from the rules

$$
\begin{array}{rcl}
S & \rightarrow & NP\ VP \\
NP & \rightarrow & D\ N \\
VP & \rightarrow & V\ NP
\end{array}
$$

we can infer the links:

```
link(np,s).
link(d,np).
link(d,s).
link(v,vp).
link(X,X).
```

The last of these says that any constituent can begin with itself; it applies when, for example, the parser is looking for an N and is also about to accept an N.

We modify `parse/3` so that there has to be a link between the constituent it is looking for and the word it is trying to accept, thus:

```
parse(C,[Word|S2],S) :-
   word(W,Word),
   link(W,C),
   complete(W,C,S2,S).

parse(C,S2,S) :-
   rule(W,[]),    % for null constituents
   link(W,C),
   complete(W,C,S2,S).
```

This solves the problem because now the parser can only accept a null determiner if it's already looking for an S or an NP. It can't "accept" null determiners willy-nilly in arbitrary locations.

A left-corner parser can still loop on a set of rules of the form

$$
\begin{array}{rcl}
A & \rightarrow & B\ A \\
B & \rightarrow & \emptyset
\end{array}
$$

but in this case the looping is really the fault of the rules, not of the parser. These rules really do specify an infinite number of different parses for each string: an A can consist of a null B followed by another A, or of two null Bs followed by another A, or of three null Bs followed by another A, ad infinitum. So infinite backtracking is really the correct thing to do with a grammar of this form. When the grammar specifies an infinite number of parses, one can hardly fault the parser for trying to find them all.

**Exercise 6.4.3.1**

Add $D \rightarrow \emptyset$ to your left-corner parser and observe what happens. Try to parse both grammatical and ungrammatical sentences.

**Exercise 6.4.3.2**

Construct a table of links for the entire grammar in Figure 6.1. Add the table of links to your parser and demonstrate that the entire grammar can now be parsed.

**Exercise 6.4.3.3**

Define a predicate `generate_links/0` that looks at the rules in a grammar, generates the links automatically, and asserts them into memory.

**Exercise 6.4.3.4**

Even in grammars without null constituents, links can make the parser more efficient. Give an example of how this is so.

### 6.4.4 BUP

Perhaps the best-known implementation of left–corner parsing in Prolog is BUP, developed by Matsumoto, Tanaka, Hirakawa, Miyoshi, and Yasukawa (1983).

In BUP, each PS rule goes into Prolog as a clause whose head is not the mother node, but rather the leftmost daughter. Thus

$$NP \rightarrow D N PP$$

becomes

```
d(C,S1,S) :- parse(n,S1,S2), parse(pp,S2,S3), np(C,S3,S).
```

That is: "If you've just completed a D, then parse an N and PP. Then call the procedure for dealing with a completed NP." Here C is the higher constituent that the parser is trying to complete, and S1, S2, S3, and S are the input string at various stages.

In addition to a clause for each of the PS rules, BUP needs a "terminating clause" for every kind of constituent, for example:

```
np(np,S,S).
n(n,S,S).
d(d,S,S).
vp(vp,S,S).
v(v,S,S).
s(s,S,S).
```

Each of these means something like, "If you've just accepted an NP and an NP is what you were looking for, you're done."

BUP gets its efficiency from the fact that the hard part of the search—i.e., figuring out what to do with a newly completed leftmost daughter—is handled by Prolog's fastest search mechanism, namely the mechanism for finding a clause given the predicate.

Figure 6.6 shows a complete, working BUP parser, without links. Note that, as required by most Prologs, all the clauses with a particular predicate are grouped together. Matsumoto and colleagues use the names `goal` and `dict` for the predicates that we have called, respectively, `parse` and `word`. Their full BUP implementation includes

```
% BUP left-corner parser, without links, without chart

% parse(+C,+S1,-S)
%   Parse a constituent of category C starting with input
%   string S1 and ending up with input string S.

parse(C,S1,S) :-
  word(W,S1,S2),
  P =.. [W,C,S2,S],
  call(P).


% PS rules and terminating clauses

np(C,S1,S) :- parse(vp,S1,S2), s(C,S2,S).      % S --> NP VP
np(np,X,X).

d(C,S1,S)  :- parse(n,S1,S2), np(C,S2,S).      % NP --> D N
d(d,X,X).

v(C,S1,S)  :- parse(np,S1,S2), vp(C,S2,S).     % VP --> V NP
v(v,X,X).

s(s,X,X).
vp(vp,X,X).
pp(pp,X,X).
n(n,X,X).

% Lexicon

word(d,[the|X],X).
word(n,[dog|X],X).
word(n,[cat|X],X).
word(v,[chases|X],X).    % etc.
```

**Figure 6.6**   A working BUP parser.

links and a chart (see next section). For subsequent developments, see also Okunishi et al. (1988).

**Exercise 6.4.4.1**

Add rules to the parser in Figure 6.6 to cover the complete grammar from Figure 6.1, except for $D \rightarrow \emptyset$. Demonstrate that the parser works.

**Exercise 6.4.4.2**

In your parser from the previous exercise, add arguments to nodes to enforce subject-verb number agreement and build a representation of the tree during parsing.

**Exercise 6.4.4.3**

Add links to BUP by putting calls to `link/2` in each phrase structure rule as well as in the clause for `goal` itself.

**Exercise 6.4.4.4   (small project)**

The slow part of BUP is now the execution of '`=..`' and `call/1` in `parse`. Eliminate them. This requires major rearranging because now W (in `parse`) cannot be the predicate of the procedure that gets called; instead it must be an argument. Use first-argument indexing to good advantage. Compare the speed of the old and new parsers.

**Exercise 6.4.4.5   (project)**

Write a program that accepts a set of PS rules, in whatever notation you find most convenient, and generates a BUP parser for them.

## 6.5 CHART PARSING

### 6.5.1 The Key Idea

Consider the rule

$$VP \rightarrow V\ NP\ (PP)$$

This goes into DCG as two rules:

```
vp --> v, np.
vp --> v, np, pp.
```

Now consider the query:

```
?- vp([chased,the,cat,into,the,garden],[]).
```

The parser tries the first rule, works through the structure

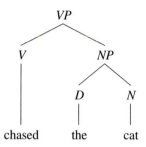

and then realizes it hasn't used up all the words. So it backs up, forgets all the work it has just done, chooses the second VP rule, and *parses the same structure again.* Then it goes ahead and parses the PP, giving:

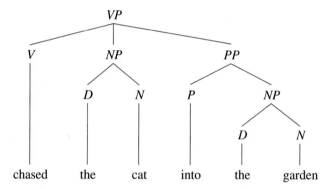

Crucially, the parser had to parse the same V and NP twice. And that could have been a lot of work—recall how complicated an NP can be.

A CHART PARSER or TABULAR PARSER is a parser that remembers substructures that it has parsed, so that if it has to backtrack, it can avoid repeating its work. For example, the first time through, a chart parser would make a record that *the cat* is an NP. The second time through, when looking for an NP at the beginning of *the cat into the garden,* it would look at its records (the CHART) before using the NP rule. On finding [NP *the cat* ] in the chart it would not have to work through the process of parsing the NP.

### 6.5.2 A First Implementation

To save each constituent, the parser must record:

- what kind of constituent it is;
- where it begins; and
- where it ends.

One way to represent this information is to store, in the knowledge base, clauses such as:

```
chart(np,[the,cat,into,the,garden],[into,the,garden]).
```

This means: "If you remove an NP from the beginning of *the cat into the garden* you're left with *into the garden*." That is, *the cat* is a noun phrase.

The two lists represent positions in the input string. This is not the most concise or efficient way to represent positions, but it is the most readable to human eyes, and we will stick with it through most of this chapter.

Now let's modify our original top-down parser (Section 6.2) to use a chart. To do this, we modify `parse/3` so that it looks like this:

```
parse(C,[Word|S],S) :-
    word(C,Word).

parse(C,S1,S) :-
    chart(C,S1,S).

parse(C,S1,S) :-
    rule(C,Cs),
    parse_list(Cs,S1,S),
    asserta(chart(C,S1,S)).
```

The first clause deals with individual words, as in the original top-down parser. It's faster to look up single words in the lexicon than to try to get them into the chart.

The second clause says, "If what you're looking for is already in the chart, don't parse it." The third clause, using `rule`, is like the original except that it asserts a fact into the chart at the end.

Also, we need a way to discard the chart before starting a new sentence:

```
clear_chart :- abolish(chart/3).
```

Otherwise the chart would become cluttered with obsolete information. So now the usual query to parse a sentence looks like this:

```
?- clear_chart,
    parse(s,[the,dog,chased,the,cat,near,the,elephant],[]).
```

Finally, there is a minor technical problem to be dealt with. Normally, a chart parser will look at the chart before any clauses of `chart` have been asserted. In some Prologs, this causes an error message, which can be prevented by including, at the beginning of the program, a line such as

```
:- unknown(_,fail).        % in Quintus Prolog

'?ERROR'(2,_) :- fail.     % in LPA (Quintus DOS) Prolog
```

to tell the Prolog system that queries to nonexistent predicates should simply fail, rather than raising error conditions. It is not sufficient to declare `chart` as `dynamic`, because when `clear_chart` abolishes `chart`, it will abolish the dynamic declaration too.

**Exercise 6.5.2.1**

> Get the chart parser working and use it to parse *The dog chases the cat near the elephant.* What information is in the chart at the end of the parse?

**Exercise 6.5.2.2**

> Modify your chart parser to display a message whenever the first clause of *chart* succeeds. This will let you know when the chart is actually saving the parser some work. Parse *The dog chases the cat near the elephant* again. What output do you get?

**Exercise 6.5.2.3   (small project)**

> Chart parsers need not be top-down. Implement a bottom-up (shift-reduce) chart parser.

## 6.5.3 Representing Positions Numerically

We noted that storing whole lists in the chart, as in

```
chart(np,[the,cat,into,the,garden],[into,the,garden]).
```

is inefficient. The lists represent positions in the input string; they can be replaced by word counts (0 for the beginning of the string, 1 for the position after the first word, and so on), so that chart entries look like this:

```
chart(np,0,2).
```

That is: "The NP begins when 0 words have been accepted, and ends when 2 words have been accepted." Numbers are more efficient than lists because they are smaller, can be compared more quickly, and can be distinguished by first-argument indexing.

If we do this, we can get rid of the input "string" altogether, and replace it by a set of facts about what words are in what positions. For example:

```
c(the,0,1).
c(dog,1,2).
c(sees,2,3).
c(the,3,4).
c(cat,4,5).
c(near,5,6).
c(the,6,7).
c(elephant,7,8).
```

It's quicker to look these up than to repeatedly pick a list apart.

All this requires almost no change to the parser. The only difference is that `parse/3` uses a slightly different method to accept a word:

```
parse(C,S1,S) :-
   chart(C,S1,S).

parse(C,S1,S) :-
   c(Word,S1,S),    % this is the only change
   word(C,Word).

parse(C,S1,S) :-
   rule(C,Cs),
   parse_list(Cs,S1,S),
   asserta(chart(C,S1,S)).
```

In one brief test, making this change sped up the parser about 30% with a simple grammar. If the grammar is more complex, the speed-up could be greater. On the other hand, it takes time to convert each sentence into a set of `c/3` clauses.

Having introduced this technique, we will now put it aside, because in the rest of this chapter, it is much more important for the examples to be readable than for them to run fast. Converting the various chart parsers to use numeric positions is left as an exercise for the implementor.

**Exercise 6.5.3.1**

Get this parser working and measure the speed-up on your computer. To do this, you will probably have to parse the same sentence hundreds or thousands of times; be sure to clear the chart in between.

### 6.5.4 Completeness

As implemented so far, the chart parser can remember what it found, but it can't remember what it failed to find. For example, it can remember that *the cat* is an NP, but it can't remember that *the cat* is not a PP. This means that with a complex grammar, the parser can waste more time than it saves.

To parse any constituent, the parser first looks at the chart. If the chart doesn't contain the constituent that it's looking for, then the parser proceeds to do all the work that it would have done if there had been no chart in the first place. In such a case the chart doesn't save it any work.

This situation arises mainly with fairly large grammars. Here is a simple example. Consider the phrase-structure rules

$$
\begin{aligned}
VP &\rightarrow V\ NP\ (PP)\ (Adv) \\
NP &\rightarrow D\ N\ (PP) \\
PP &\rightarrow P\ NP
\end{aligned}
$$

This is really four VP rules—with and without PP and with and without Adv—as well as two NP rules, with and without PP.

Suppose the parser is parsing [<sub>VP</sub> *saw the boy yesterday* ]. Two different rules allow a PP to come after *boy*. Accordingly, the parser will make two attempts to find a PP at that position, and both attempts will fail. Each attempt will consist of a fair bit of work (invoking $PP \rightarrow P\ NP$, then looking at lexical entries for P, and failing to find *yesterday* among them). If, the first time through, the chart could record that a PP is definitely *not* present at that position, the second attempt to find one would be unnecessary.

There is also another reason why the chart needs to store negative information: unwanted alternatives. Every parse that can be found in the chart can also be found without using the chart. This means that, upon backtracking, the parser can often get the same constituent more than one way, and the number of alternatives to try grows exponentially.

A much better approach is to use the chart only if it is *complete* for a particular constituent type in a particular position. That is, if you're looking for an NP at the beginning of *the cat near the elephant,* use the chart only if it is known to contain all possible NPs in that position. Otherwise, ignore the chart and parse conventionally. And if, when parsing conventionally, you fail to find what you're looking for, then assert that the chart is complete for that constituent in that position, because there are no more alternatives to be found.

We can record completeness by asserting facts such as

```
complete(np,[the,cat,into,the,garden]).
```

Modified to work this way, `parse` looks like this:

```
parse(C,[Word|S],S) :-
   word(C,Word).

parse(C,S1,S) :-
   complete(C,S1),
   !,
   chart(C,S1,S).

parse(C,S1,S) :-
   rule(C,Cs),
   parse_list(Cs,S1,S2),
   asserta(chart(C,S1,S2)),
   S2 = S.

parse(C,S1,_) :-
   asserta(complete(C,S1)),
   fail.
```

The first clause is as before. The second clause is as before except that it requires the chart to be complete, and if the chart is complete, it performs a cut so that the subsequent clauses won't be used. The third clause is as before except that it passes S2 to `parse_list` uninstantiated, in an attempt to get as many alternatives into the chart as possible, and then checks afterward whether S2=S. The last clause asserts that the chart is complete if all the other clauses have failed.

It is also necessary to modify `clear_chart` to erase `complete` as well as `chart`, thus:

```
clear_chart :- abolish(chart/3), abolish(complete/2).
```

**Exercise 6.5.4.1**

Demonstrate the problem of unwanted alternatives. Using the parser from Section 6.5.2 (without completeness checking), execute the query:

```
?- parse(s,[the,dog,chases,the,cat,near,the,elephant],[]),
   write(y),
   fail.
```

How many y's do you get? Why?

**Exercise 6.5.4.2**

Modify the parser to include the completeness check and try the same query.

**Exercise 6.5.4.3**

Why can't there be a cut in the second clause of `parse` if the parser does not check for completeness? That is, in the parser in Section 6.5.2, why couldn't that clause have been as follows?

```
parse(C,S1,S) :- chart(C,S1,S), !.
```

(Hint: Parse *the dog chases the cat near the elephant.*)

**Exercise 6.5.4.4**

As implemented, the chart parser tries to parse single-word categories (N, V, etc.) with `chart` and `rule` as well as with `word`. We can make `parse` faster by changing its first clause to:

```
parse(C,[Word|S],S) :-
   word(C,_),
   !,
   word(C,Word).
```

What does this do to the search process? How does it affect the way we have rendered $D \rightarrow \emptyset$?

### 6.5.5 Subsumption

If nodes have arguments, chart parsing runs into another problem. Suppose the parser is looking for np(X) and the chart contains np(singular) at the right position. Should the parser use this chart entry? Definitely not. Doing so would instantiate X to the value singular, which might be wrong.

To illustrate this problem is not particularly easy; there are no simple examples in English. It's the kind of thing that crops up suddenly in the middle of a large project after dozens of other rules have worked correctly.

For the determined reader, however, here is a somewhat contrived example. Recall that one way to handle verb subcategorization is to assign the verbs to numbered classes. Consider, then, the following PS rules. For legibility, they are written in DCG format, although in our actual parser they would be clauses of rule/2.

```
vp --> verbal(0).
vp --> verbal(X), rest_of_vp(X).

rest_of_vp(1) --> np.
rest_of_vp(2) --> np, np.    % etc.

verbal(X) --> v(X).

v(0) --> [sleep].
v(1) --> [see].
v(2) --> [give].  % etc.
```

Assume the usual expansions of np. Now execute the query:

```
?- clear_chart, parse(vp,[see,the,dog],[]).
```

This parse should succeed, but it doesn't. The first VP rule looks for a verbal(0) and, of course, doesn't find it. So the chart is marked as complete for verbal(0) in that position:

```
complete(verbal(0),[see,the,dog]).
```

Now the second VP rule looks for verbal(X) in the same position, with X uninstantiated. And verbal(X) matches the stored verbal(0), so the parser thinks the chart is complete for verbal(X) as well.

The problem, of course, is that *unifying* verbal(X) with the stored verbal(0) is the wrong thing to do. The parser should instead check whether the stored category SUBSUMES the one it is looking for. We say that term A subsumes term B if and only if:

- A can be unified with B;
- When this is done, B is no more instantiated than it was before.

For example, f(X,b) subsumes f(a,b), but f(a,b) does not subsume f(X,b) because performing the unification would instantiate X.

The Quintus Prolog built-in predicate `subsumes_chk/2` succeeds if its first argument subsumes its second argument. With subsumption checking added, the second clause of `parse` becomes:

```
parse(C,S1,S) :-
   complete(C0,S1),
   subsumes_chk(C0,C), !,
   C0 = C,
   chart(C,S1,S).
```

Figure 6.7 gives an implementation of `subsumes_chk` for other Prologs.

```
% Subsumption checker.
% Based on code by R. A. O'Keefe
% in shared Edinburgh (later Quintus) library.

% subsumes_chk(?T1,?T2)
%   Succeeds if term T1 subsumes T2, i.e.,
%   T1 and T2 can be unified without further
%   instantiating T2.

subsumes_chk(T1,T2) :-
   \+ ( numvars(T2), \+ (T1 = T2) ).

% numvars(+Term)
%   Instantiates each variable in Term to a unique
%   term in the series vvv(0), vvv(1), vvv(2)...

numvars(Term) :- numvars_aux(Term,0,_).

numvars_aux(Term,N,N) :- atomic(Term), !.

numvars_aux(Term,N,NewN) :-
   var(Term), !,
   Term = vvv(N),
   NewN is N+1.

numvars_aux(Term,N,NewN) :-
   Term =.. List,
   numvars_list(List,N,NewN).

numvars_list([],N,N).

numvars_list([Term|Terms],N,NewN) :-
   numvars_aux(Term,N,NextN),
   numvars_list(Terms,NextN,NewN).
```

**Figure 6.7**   Implementation of `subsumes_chk` for Prologs in which it is not built in.

**Exercise 6.5.5.1**

Demonstrate the problem. Use the parser from the previous section with the grammar in this section, and show what goes wrong upon trying to parse *see the dog*.

**Exercise 6.5.5.2**

Solve the problem by adding subsumption checking, and demonstrate that your modified parser works correctly.

**Exercise 6.5.5.3**

Why does `parse` use the subsumption checker when calling `complete` but not when calling `chart`?

**Exercise 6.5.5.4**

With the grammar in this section, the modification suggested in Exercise 6.5.4.4 no longer works correctly. Explain why, and make the necessary changes.

**Exercise 6.5.5.5**

Modify the grammar by adding arguments to nodes to account for subject-verb number agreement and to build a representation of the tree. (This is simple; just copy the modified grammar from Exercise 6.2.0.3.)

**Exercise 6.5.5.6**

*(Not for courses that skipped Chapter 5.)* Combine Mini-GULP with this parser. Account for number agreement of subject and verb, and of determiner and noun, using GULP feature structures. (Easy—copy the rules from Exercise 6.2.0.4.)

## 6.6 EARLEY'S ALGORITHM

### 6.6.1 The Key Idea

Earley (1970) introduced a chart parsing algorithm with the following characteristics:

- It parses $n$-word sentences in, at most, time proportional to $n^3$, which is near the best possible performance.
- It handles null constituents correctly.
- It does not loop on left-recursive rules ($A \rightarrow A\ B$).
- It uses a combination of top-down parsing ("prediction") and bottom-up parsing ("completion").
- It is an ACTIVE CHART PARSER, i.e., the chart stores work in progress as well as completed work.
- The parser does not backtrack; instead, it pursues all alternatives concurrently, and at the end, all alternative parses are in the chart.

The key idea of Earley's algorithm is that the chart can store unfinished constituents as well as constituents that have been completely parsed. To understand how this is possible, recall that in DCG, the rule $S \rightarrow NP\ VP$ goes into Prolog as:

```
s(S1,S) :- np(S1,S2), vp(S2,S).
```

Now consider the query

```
?- s([the,dog,barked],[]).
```

Imagine combining the query with the rule, like this:

```
s([the,dog,barked],[]) :- np([the,dog,barked],S1), vp(S1,[]).
```

This could be an Earley chart entry. Now imagine that the parser has processed the NP *the dog*. Then this same rule can be simplified to:

```
s([the,dog,barked],[]) :- vp([barked],[]).
```

That is: If *barked* is a VP, then *the dog barked* is an S. And after the VP is parsed, the rule simplifies further to:

```
s([the,dog,barked],[]).
```

which indicates that the entire sentence has been parsed.

## 6.6.2 An Implementation

In Earley's original notation, these three chart entries just mentioned would have the form:

$$S \rightarrow \bullet\ NP\ VP \quad 0 \quad 0$$
$$S \rightarrow NP \bullet VP \quad 0 \quad 2$$
$$S \rightarrow NP\ VP \bullet \quad 0 \quad 3$$

The dot in the PS rule indicates which subconstituent is to be parsed next. The two numbers are word counts; they indicate, respectively, the position of the beginning of the S, and the position of the dot, relative to the input string.

To implement Earley's algorithm in Prolog, we will store chart entries in yet a different form, like this:

```
chart(s,[the,dog,barked],[np,vp],[the,dog,barked]).
chart(s,[the,dog,barked],[vp],[barked]).
chart(s,[the,dog,barked],[],[]).
```

These save space by leaving out the predictable part of the Prolog clauses that we used initially. The four arguments are:

- The constituent originally being sought;
- The position at which that constituent was supposed to begin;
- The subconstituents (GOALS) currently being sought (we'll call the first goal in each list the CURRENT GOAL); and
- The CURRENT POSITION in the input string, where the current goal should begin.

Obviously, an Earley parser has many current goals, one corresponding to each chart entry at the current position. (The inefficient representation of positions is deliberate; see section 6.5.3.)

Earley's algorithm parses entirely by manipulating the chart. This means that the `parse` procedure is very simple—put the input string and initial goal into the chart, let the parser do its thing, and then see whether it has produced a successful parse:

```
parse(C,S1,S) :-
  clear_chart,
  store(chart(start,S1,[C],S1)),
  process(S1),
  chart(C,S1,[],S).
```

Here `process` steps through the input string, calling the three parts of the parser at each position:

```
process([]) :- !.

process(Position) :-
  predictor(Position),
  scanner(Position,NewPosition),
  completer(NewPosition),
  process(NewPosition).
```

The three parts of the parser itself are:

- The PREDICTOR, which looks for rules that expand current goals, and uses them to create new goals;
- The SCANNER, which accepts a word from the input string and uses it to satisfy current goals; and
- The COMPLETER, which looks at the output of the scanner and determines which, if any, larger constituents have been completed.

All three of these produce chart entries. For example, given

```
chart(s,[the,dog,barked],[np,vp],[the,dog,barked]).
```

the predictor will use *NP → D N* to produce

```
chart(np,[the,dog,barked],[d,n],[the,dog,barked]).
```

Then the scanner will accept *the*, giving:

```
chart(np,[the,dog,barked],[n],[dog,barked]).
```

Now the completer executes, but can't do anything because nothing has been completed; then the predictor executes, but can't do anything because there are no rules expanding n. So the scanner gets to execute again; it accepts *dog*, giving:

```
chart(np,[the,dog,barked],[],[barked]).
```

Now the NP is complete and the completer takes note of this fact, modifying the chart entry for S appropriately:

```
chart(s,[the,dog,barked],[vp],[barked]).
```

In a similar way the predictor, scanner, and completer process the VP. Then the S is complete and the last thing put into the chart is:

```
chart(s,[the,dog,barked],[],[]).
```

Since S was the original goal and the input string is empty, the parse is complete.

The predictor, scanner, and completer communicate mainly through the chart, except that each of them has to know the current position in the input string (and the scanner changes it). Here is a more precise description of what they do:

**Predictor**

For each current goal at the current position,

look up all the rules expanding it

and use them to make more chart entries.

(This creates additional current goals at the current position;

do the same thing to all of them.)

**Scanner**

Accept a word from the input string and determine its category.

Look for all chart entries for the current position

whose active goal is that category.

Make, from each of them, a new chart entry,

removing the first goal and the first word of the input string.

**Completer**

Look for constituents that have just been completed,

and use them to complete higher-level constituents.

(Upon completing a constituent this way,

do the same thing with the result.)

Figure 6.8 shows, in detail, the process of parsing *The dog chases the cat.* For simplicity, lots of irrelevant syntax rules are ignored in the example. With a larger grammar, there would be somewhat more entries in the chart and more work at each stage.

**Exercise 6.6.2.1**

By hand, work through the process of parsing *The dogs chase the cat near the elephant* using Earley's algorithm and the grammar in Figure 6.1. Include all chart entries, including those from rules that do not contribute to a successful parse. Show your results in the format of Figure 6.8.

### 6.6.3 Predictor

The predictor looks at all the chart entries that apply to the current position in the input string, and constructs, from each of them, new chart entries expanding their current goals. This work is done by two predicates, `predictor` and `predict`, both of which use `fail` to make execution backtrack through all possibilities:

```
predictor(Position) :-
   chart(_,_,[Goal|_],Position),     % For every chart entry of this
   predict(Goal,Position),           % kind do all possible
   fail.                             % predictions

predictor(_).                        % then succeed with no further
                                     % action.


predict(Goal,Position) :-
   rule(Goal,[H|T]),                 % For every rule expanding Goal
   store(chart(Goal,Position,
               [H|T],Position)),     % make a new chart entry and
   predict(H,Position),              % make predictions from it too
   fail.

predict(_,_).                        % then succeed with no further
                                     % action.
```

There are two predicates here because `predict` has to call itself in order to make further predictions from the chart entries it creates.

The alert reader will notice that `predictor` looks for chart entries at `Position`, and `predict`, which it calls, is constantly adding chart entries at the same `Position`.

**Start with:**    chart(start,[the,dog,chases,the,cat],[s],[the,dog,chases,the,cat] ).

**Predict:**    Use *S → NP VP* and *NP → D N.*
chart(s,[the,dog,chases,the,cat],[ np,vp],[the,dog,chases,the,cat]).
chart(np,[the,dog,chases,the,cat],[d,n],[the,dog,chases,the,cat]).

**Scan:**    Accept *the.*
chart(np,[the,dog,chases,the,cat],[n],[dog,chases,the,cat]).

**Complete:**    Nothing to do; no phrase has been completed.

**Predict:**    Nothing to do; there are no rules expanding N.

**Scan:**    Accept *dog.*
chart(np,[the,dog,chases,the,cat],[],[chases,the,cat]).

**Complete:**    An NP has now been parsed.
chart(s,[the,dog,chases,the,cat],[vp],[chases,the,cat]).

**Predict:**    Use *VP → V* and *VP → V NP.*
chart(vp,[chases,the,cat],[v],[chases,the,cat]).
chart(vp,[chases,the,cat],[v,np],[chases,the,cat]).

**Scan:**    Accept *chases.*
chart(vp,[chases,the,cat],[],[the,cat]).
chart(vp,[chases,the,cat],[np],[the,cat]).

**Complete:**    According to *VP → V,* a VP and hence the S have now been parsed.
chart(s,[the,dog,chases,the,cat],[],[the,cat]).
chart(start,[the,dog,chases,the,cat],[],[the,cat]).

**Predict:**    The other VP rule is still looking for an NP. Expand it...
chart(np,[the,cat],[d,n],[the,cat]).

**Scan:**    Accept *the.*
chart(np,[the,cat],[n],[cat]).

**Complete:**    Nothing to do—no phrase has been completed.

**Predict:**    Nothing to do—there are no rules expanding N.

**Scan:**    Accept *cat.*
chart(np,[the,cat],[],[]).

**Complete:**    Now the NP, and hence the VP and S, have been parsed.
chart(vp,[chases,the,cat],[],[]).
chart(s,[the,dog,chases,the,cat],[],[]).
chart(start,[the,dog,chases,the,cat],[],[]).
All done.

**Figure 6.8**   Earley's algorithm in action.

Why doesn't it get into a loop trying to process its own output? Or at least, why call `predict` recursively to process the new entries, if they would have been found by backtracking anyway?

For two reasons. First, `store` (which we haven't defined yet) uses `asserta`, not `assertz`, and thus the new entries are added before the one presently being looked at. Second, even if `store` didn't do this, most Prologs would never see the new entries, because in most Prologs, newly added clauses cannot become alternatives for a query that is already in progress. Upon starting any query, Prolog determines which facts and rules can satisfy it, and any further rules that get asserted during the processing of the query will be ignored.

**Exercise 6.6.3.1**

Get the predictor working and show that it can execute the first part of the parse in Figure 6.8, up to the point where the scanner is needed. Temporarily use `asserta` in place of `store`.

### 6.6.4 Scanner

The scanner is very simple:

```
scanner([W|Words],Words)  :-
   chart(C,PC,[G|Goals],[W|Words]),   % for each current goal at
                                      % current position
   word(G,W),                         % if category of W matches it
   store(chart(C,PC,Goals,Words)),    % make a new chart entry
   fail.

scanner([_|Words],Words).             % then succeed with no further
                                      % action.
```

Traditionally, the predictor predicts individual words. We do not do this here, because it would add a vast number of unnecessary predictions to the chart. Instead, the scanner determines the category of each word at the time the word is accepted.

**Exercise 6.6.4.1**

Add the scanner to the predictor that you have already gotten working. Show that your scanner and predictor can execute the first two steps of the parse in Figure 6.8, up to the point where the completer is needed.

**Exercise 6.6.4.2**

Why doesn't second clause of `scanner` have anonymous variables in place of `Words`?

### 6.6.5 Completer

The completer looks at all chart entries at the current position that have no goals—i.e., all completed constituents—and tries to use them to complete larger constituents. Normally the scanner produces one completed constituent (a single word, such as [$_N$ *dog* ]), and the completer tries to use this to complete something larger, such as an NP.

Again, there are two predicates, because the completer has to call itself on its own output:

```
completer(Position) :-
    chart(C,PC,[],Position),     % For every chart entry with no
    complete(C,PC,Position),     % goals, complete all possible
    fail.                        % higher constituents,

completer(_).                    % then succeed with no further
                                 % action.

complete(C,PC,Position) :-
    chart(C0,PC0,[C|Goals],PC),  % For every constituent that can be
    store(chart(C0,PC0,          % completed make a new chart entry,
            Goals,Position)),
    Goals == [],                 % then fail here if Goals not empty,
    complete(C0,PC0,Position),   % or process new entry the same way
    fail.

complete(_,_,_).                 % then succeed with no further
                                 % action.
```

The difference is that, unlike `predict`, `complete` does not *always* call itself on its own output—it does so only if its output is itself a chart entry with no goals, and hence a completed constituent. Recall that the completer is responsible for creating

```
chart(s,[the,dog,chases,the,cat],[vp],[chases,the,cat]).
```

when the NP is finished and then

```
chart(s,[the,dog,chases,the,cat],[],[]).
```

when the VP is finished. Only the second of these completes a constituent and thereby justifies a recursive call to the completer.

**Exercise 6.6.5.1**

Get the completer working and add it to the predictor and scanner that you have already implemented. Test it. Use a grammar that does not include any left-recursive rules.

### 6.6.6 How Earley's Algorithm Avoids Loops

We haven't defined `store` yet. Its definition is the key to the way Earley's algorithm keeps from looping on left-recursive rules. Specifically, `store` fails upon attempting to put something in the chart that is already there:

```
store(chart(A,B,C,D)) :-
  \+ chart(A,B,C,D),
  asserta(chart(A,B,C,D)).
```

Consider how the predictor handles the rules

$$NP \quad \rightarrow \quad D\,N$$
$$NP \quad \rightarrow \quad NP\;Conj\;NP$$

when parsing *the dog and the cat.* At the start, there is no way to tell which rule applies, so the predictor makes two chart entries:

```
chart(np,[the,dog,and,the,cat],[d,n],[the,dog,and,the,cat]).
chart(np,[the,dog,and,the,cat],[np,conj,np],[the,dog,and,the,cat]).
```

Recall that the predictor is supposed to apply to its own output, i.e., the chart entries that it generates. The first of these chart entries has d as its current goal; d is not a phrase; so no further predictions are made from it. The second chart entry has current goal np, which can be expanded by either of two rules, giving two more chart entries:

```
chart(np,[the,dog,and,the,cat],[d,n],[the,dog,and,the,cat]).
chart(np,[the,dog,and,the,cat],[np,conj,np],[the,dog,and,the,cat]).
```

But these entries are *already* in the chart. This means that store fails, and the predictor doesn't get to call itself recursively on them. Thus the rule is blocked.

To put it more succinctly: *Earley's algorithm will never predict a constituent at a position, if it has already predicted the same constituent at the same position.*

But the completer is welcome to use the same chart entry more than once when completing a recursively embedded phrase. Thus long phrases such as *the dog and the cat and the elephant* are parsed with no problem.

**Exercise 6.6.6.1**

Determine (by hand or using the computer) the chart entries for parsing *the dog and the cat and the elephant.* Show them in the order in which they are added to the chart.

## 6.6.7 Handling Null Constituents

As shown, our parser still has trouble with the rule $D \rightarrow \emptyset$, which we represent as

```
rule(d,[]).
```

because the predictor insists that the second argument of rule be a nonempty list.

We have two choices. We can recast $D \rightarrow \emptyset$ as word(d,[]) and modify the scanner to handle it; or we can leave it as it is and modify the predictor.

We choose the first of these, and add a clause for `predict`:

```
predict(Goal,Position) :-
  rule(Goal,[]),
  store(chart(Goal,Position,[],Position)),
  complete(Goal,Position,Position),
  fail.
```

This comes between the two clauses already defined. This clause generates a new chart entry in the same way as the first clause, but then it calls the completer—necessary because a constituent has been completed, of course, and the completer now needs to work on it at *this* position in the input string. Normally the completer would not get to work until after the scanner had advanced the current position to the next word.

**Exercise 6.6.7.1**

Get an Earley parser working which includes the whole grammar in Figure 6.1.

**Exercise 6.6.7.2**

Add features to the nodes in the grammar to enforce subject-verb number agreement and build a representation of the tree structure (as in Exercise 6.2.0.3).

## 6.6.8 Subsumption Revisited

Like all chart parsers, Earley's algorithm needs a subsumption check. This turns out to be just a simple modification to `store`: instead of checking for pre-existing chart entries that *match* the new one, check for entries that *subsume* it.

```
store(chart(A,B,C,D)) :-
  \+ (chart(A1,B,C1,D), subsumes_chk(A1,A), subsumes_chk(C1,C)),
  asserta(chart(A,B,C,D)).
```

Here we save some time by looking only at A and C, which are the only parts of the chart entry in which uninstantiated arguments can appear.

Recall that `subsumes_chk` is not built in. If you need to define `subsumes_chk` for yourself but forget to do so, the parser will still work but the chart will contain superfluous entries, because all the calls to `subsumes_chk` will fail.

**Exercise 6.6.8.1**

Demonstrate the need for a subsumption check in your Earley parser, using the same grammar as in Exercise 6.5.5.1. Then modify your parser to correct it.

**Exercise 6.6.8.2**

As you have done with all the other parsers, add arguments to the nodes to account for subject-verb number agreement and to build a representation of the tree. (See Exercise 6.2.0.3.)

**Exercise 6.6.8.3**

*(Not for courses that skipped Chapter 5.)* Combine Mini-GULP with the Earley parser. Account for number agreement of subject and verb, and of determiner and noun, using GULP feature structures. (Easy—copy the rules from Exercise 6.2.0.4.)

## 6.6.9 Restriction

Earley's algorithm can still loop on grammar rules where a daughter node has an argument that contains an argument of the mother node, like this:

```
a(X) --> a(f(X)).
```

Suppose $X = b$. Then the predictor will first predict `a(b)`, then `a(f(b))`, then `a(f(f(b)))`, then `a(f(f(f(b))))`, ad infinitum.

Here's a real-life example. Several grammatical theories equip each verb with an argument which is a list of constituents that should come after it:

```
v([])        --> [sleep]; [bark].
v([np])      --> [see]; [chase].
v([np,np]) --> [give].
v([np,pp]) --> [put].
```

Then a phrase-structure rule of the form

```
v(Y) --> v([X|Y]), X.            % (not a legal DCG rule)
```

picks apart these lists and generates the right things in the right places (Figure 6.9). (This is essentially the same as the example of subcategorization lists at the end of Chapter 5.)

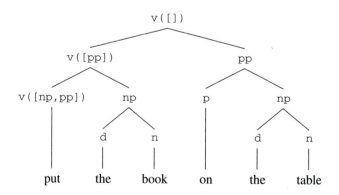

**Figure 6.9**  Parse tree with subcategorization lists.

Here we're using DCG notation for clarity, but this last rule is, of course, not legal in DCG, because one of the constituents (X) is a variable. Nevertheless, Earley's algorithm should be able to handle it, because as soon as the scanner accepts the verb, the value of X will be known.

Earley's algorithm loops for a different reason—the occurrence of the argument Y within the argument `[X|Y]`. Starting with

```
chart(v([]),[sees,the,dog],[v([X]),X],[sees,the,dog]).
```

the predictor will generate, in succession,

```
chart(v([X]),[sees,the,dog],[v([X1,X]),X1],[sees,the,dog]).
chart(v([X1,X]),[sees,the,dog],[v([X2,X1,X]),X2],[sees,the,dog]).
chart(v([X2,X1,X]),[sees,the,dog],[v([X3,X2,X1,X]),X3],[sees,the,dog]).
chart(v([X3,X2,X1,X]),[sees,the,dog],[v([X4,X3,X2,X1,X]),X4],[sees,the,dog]).
```

ad infinitum, where X, X1, X2... represent the variables that correspond to X on successive invocations of the v(Y) rule.

Shieber (1986) proposes a solution that he calls RESTRICTION: make the predictor ignore arguments whose values are not fully instantiated. By "ignore" we mean, in the context of our parser, that anonymous variables will be substituted for these arguments. (This makes the predictor overpredict, but no harm results because the spurious predictions are not used further.) With restriction, *sees the dog* is parsed as follows:

```
Predict:    chart(v([]),[sees,the,dog],v(_),[sees,the,dog]).
Scan:       chart(v([np]),[sees,the,dog],[],[the,dog]).
Complete:   chart(v([np,np]),[sees,the,dog],[np],[the,dog]).
```

and so on. Restriction applies only to the predictor; the scanner and completer look back at the rules and fill in the missing arguments. Gerdemann (1989, 1991) explores other uses of restriction.

In this context it is helpful to think of parsing with arguments as a twofold process—accepting the input string and building the arguments of the nodes. These processes go on concurrently, working, as it were, at right angles to one another. Earley's algorithm does a good job of loop-proofing the process of accepting the input string, but loops with argument-building are still possible. An important research topic at the moment is the discovery of linguistically motivated constraints on arguments.

### Exercise 6.6.9.1

Demonstrate that Earley's algorithm loops on the grammar shown.

### Exercise 6.6.9.2   (small project)

Implement restriction and use it to make Earley's algorithm handle this grammar successfully.

## 6.6.10 Improving Earley's Algorithm

The implementation of Earley's algorithm that we have developed is far from optimal. There are numerous ways to improve it from the standpoint of Prolog coding:[1]

- Represent positions in the sentence as numbers (word counts) rather than lists (as in Section 6.5.3).
- Use first-argument indexing. The parser spends much of its time searching through the chart or through the rules. Organize these so that they have distinctive first arguments that will speed the retrieval of the desired information.
- Reduce the use of `assert`; see what happens if (part of) the chart is kept in a list rather than stored in the knowledge base. This may be beneficial during some kinds of processing but not others.

Another tack is to improve the predictor. Except for the loop-check, the usual Earley predictor works just like a recursive-descent top-down parser. Like all top-down parsers, it makes plenty more predictions than are really necessary. Earley (1970) suggested letting the predictor look ahead to the next entry in the input string, and thereby narrow down the range of choices. Kilbury (1984) replaced the top-down predictor with one that works like a left-corner parser; Leiss (1990) discusses Kilbury's proposal and then presents his own, which works like a left-corner parser with links, thereby avoiding many spurious predictions.

**Exercise 6.6.10.1　(project)**

Implement a *good* Earley parser in Prolog, making as many improvements as possible.

## 6.6.11 Earley's Algorithm as an Inference Engine

Recall that when we introduced Earley's algorithm, we presented chart entries as stored Prolog rules and facts. This leads us to suspect that Earley's algorithm could serve as a general way to execute Prolog, instead of the normal search-and-backtracking process. And this suspicion is right. Pereira and Warren (1983) and Pereira and Shieber (1987:199–210) discuss "Earley deduction," which they attribute to an unpublished 1975 note by David H. D. Warren.

The basic idea is that any inference engine can store LEMMAS, or previously proved results, in order to keep itself from repeating work upon backtracking. This is the equivalent of chart parsing pure and simple. An Earley inference engine is loop-proof because it never stores a lemma, nor tries to derive further lemmas from it, if the same lemma, or one that subsumes it, is already in the knowledge base. Thus, with Earley deduction,

```
ancestor(X,Z) :- ancestor(X,Y), ancestor(Y,Z).
```

does not cause the infamous loop.

---

[1] In this section I am indebted to Joseph Knapka, who experimented with a number of these proposed improvements.

There are differences between parsing and deduction, of course. In Earley deduction, there is no input string and hence no scanner. Instead, both the completer and the predictor need to look at every clause that is added to the chart.

The predictor looks at each rule newly added to the chart, and expands that rule's first subgoal using every possible rule in the knowledge base, then does the same thing, if possible, to the results. Thus from

```
f(a)  :- g(a). (newly added)
g(X)  :- h(X), j(X). (in the knowledge base)
```

the predictor produces `g(a)  :- h(a), j(a).` and adds it to the chart.

The completer deletes subgoals by resolving them with facts. When a fact is added to the chart, the completer will resolve it against the first subgoal of every possible rule already in the chart, so that for example

```
h(a). (newly added)
k(X)  :- h(X), m(X). (already in the chart)
```

yields the new chart entry `k(a)  :- m(a).`

The completer also works on newly added rules, resolving them against facts in the chart or in the knowledge base. If for example

```
k(X)  :- h(X), m(X).
```

has just been added and

```
h(a).
```

is already in the chart or the knowledge base, the completer will produce `k(a)  :- m(a).` just as in the previous example.

Figure 6.10 shows this process in action. Clauses are arranged in sets. First the predictor works on a set, producing the next set of new clauses; then the completer works on all the clauses in that set, producing the next set; then the predictor operates again; and so on.

Earley deduction is slower and requires more memory than ordinary Prolog deduction. Even with simple computations, the chart can become quite large, and the process of searching it, quite time-consuming. Further, even Earley deduction can loop on rules of the form

```
f(X)  :- f(a(X)).
```

because neither X nor `f(X)` subsumes the other, leading to the same problem as with grammars in the previous section.

All this reminds us of the fact that Prolog was never meant to be a perfect inference engine in the first place; instead, it was a deliberate compromise between logical purity

| Knowledge base: | 1. | `a(a,b).` | |
| | 2. | `a(b,c).` | |
| | 3. | `a(X,Z) :- a(X,Y), a(Y,Z).` | |

| Query: | 4. | `start :- a(a,c).` | |

| Predictor: | 5. | `a(a,c) :- a(a,Y0), a(Y0,c).` | from 4 and 3 |
| | 6. | `a(a,Y0) :- a(a,Y1), a(Y1,Y0).` | from 5 and 3 |

(Loop checker intervenes here,
to prevent deriving a redundant clause
from 6 and 3.)

| Completer: | 7. | `a(a,c) :- a(b,c).` | from 5 and 1 |
| | 8. | `a(a,c).` | from 7 and 2 |
| | 9. | `start.` | from 8 and 4 |

(This is a solution to the original query;
computation could stop here, or continue
in order to look for other solutions.)

| Predictor: | 10. | `a(b,c) :- a(b,Y2), a(Y2,c).` | from 7 and 3 |
| | 11. | `a(b,Y2) :- a(b,Y3), a(Y3,Y2).` | from 10 and 3 |

(Loop checker intervenes here,
to prevent deriving a redundant clause
from 11 and 3.)

| Completer: | 12. | `a(b,c) :- a(c,c).` | from 10 and 2 |
| | 13. | `a(b,Y2) :- a(c,Y2).` | from 11 and 3 |

| Predictor: | 14. | `a(c,c) :- a(c,Y4), a(Y4,c).` | from 12 and 3 |
| | 15. | `a(c,Y2) :- a(c,Y5), a(Y5,Y2).` | from 13 and 3 |

(Loop checker intervenes.)

| Completer: | | No further action |

(nothing matches `a(c,Y4)` or `a(c,Y5)`).

| Predictor: | | No further action (no new clauses). |

**Figure 6.10**   Earley deduction in action. This computation would loop in ordinary Prolog.

and speed. By not storing lemmas or checking for loops, Prolog runs faster and in less memory than more sophisticated inference engines.

### Exercise 6.6.11.1    (project)

Implement Earley deduction as an inference engine for Prolog clauses that do not contain cuts. Evaluate the performance of your implementation.

## 6.7 WHICH PARSING ALGORITHM IS REALLY BEST?

### 6.7.1 Disappointing News about Performance

Table 6.1 presents a piece of sad news. It shows the times taken by the parsers in this chapter to parse, 100 times, the 24 sentences generated by the grammar

$$
\begin{array}{rcl}
S & \to & NP\ VP \\
NP & \to & D\ N \\
VP & \to & V\ NP \\
PP & \to & P\ NP \\
D & \to & \text{the} \\
P & \to & \text{near} \\
N & \to & \text{dog, cat} \\
V & \to & \text{chases, sees}
\end{array}
$$

which is a subset of the grammar in Figure 6.1.[2]

**TABLE 6.1**    COMPARISON OF SPEED OF VARIOUS PARSERS.

| | Time (in seconds) to parse 24 sentences 100 times* | |
|---|---|---|
| Parser | ALS Prolog 20-MHz 80386 | Quintus Prolog Sparcstation 1+ |
| DCG rules | 3.4 | 0.3 |
| Top-down interpreter | 6.0 | 1.2 |
| Bottom-up (shift-reduce) | 38.3 | 8.4 |
| Left-corner (no links) | 12.7 | 2.6 |
| Left-corner (with links) | 12.0 | 2.5 |
| BUP (no links, no chart) | 38.5 | 8.4 |
| Chart (no completeness check) | 47.2 | 20.5 |
| Chart (with completeness check) | 59.3 | 27.3 |
| Chart (with subsumption check) | 71.3 | 32.2 |
| Earley (no subsumption check) | 320.3 | 144.5 |
| Earley (with subsumption check) | 989.8 | 172.0 |

*CAUTION: These data were obtained with a very small grammar. See text before drawing any conclusions!

The sad news is that as the algorithms get "better" the parsing gets slower and slower. Top-down parsing is very fast; left-corner parsing is second best; but shift-reduce parsing and all the chart parsers are regrettably slow, to the point that Earley's algorithm with subsumption is intolerable.

---

[2]The procedure was to parse the set of 24 sentences once (to allocate memory), start timing, parse the same set 100 more times, and stop timing. The test routine performed a cut after parsing each sentence.

What's going on here? Several things:

- LACK OF OPTIMIZATION. Recall that the parsers in this chapter were not designed for speed. Only DCG and BUP compile the grammar rules into executable Prolog clauses; the others store the rules as Prolog facts and manipulate them at run time. Further, no attempt has been made to fully exploit first-argument indexing or to use the most efficient data structures.

- SMALL GRAMMARS. These tests were run with a very small grammar. That's one reason chart parsing comes out so badly. In the test sentences, there is little ambiguity and hence little benefit from using the chart. But the cost of constructing the chart is large, especially when it is built using `assert`. Pereira and Shieber (1987:196–210), Ross (1989:217–246), and Simpkins and Hancox (1990) present chart parsers in which the chart is passed along in arguments of procedures. In any case, the chart would be much more helpful with a larger grammar.

   But Shann (1991) reports that even with large grammars, Earley's algorithm remains quite slow; left-corner parsing and Tomita's bottom-up algorithm run much faster.

- SUBSUMPTION. A third factor is that subsumption checking is rather costly, for two reasons. First, the subsumption checker itself is inefficient (except in Quintus, where it is built in). Second, the subsumption check limits the use of first-argument indexing. Instead of looking directly at the chart for an entry that matches the current goal, the subsumption-checking parser must instead retrieve all the chart entries for the current position, one by one, and run them through the subsumption checker. This means that indexing can't prevent some unnecessary entries from being retrieved.

The lesson to be learned is that parsing isn't easy. Both backtracking, and charts that reduce backtracking, are costly. But there is another way to approach this problem. Any nondeterministic parser can be improved by adding an ORACLE or TABLE that keeps it from trying grammar rules that won't succeed. This is particularly the case with the shift-reduce parser, which otherwise spends too much time searching through all the rules. A parser with an oracle goes through a series of numbered states. In each state, the oracle looks ahead at the next word in the input string and tells the parser what grammar rule to use and what state to go into next. If this process were deterministic, it would be like the LR(1) parse tables commonly used by programming-language compilers (Aho and Ullman 1972:368–399), but as Nilsson (1986) points out, the language need not be deterministically parsable; Prolog can still backtrack if it needs to.

   Not only does an oracle reduce backtracking, it also enables a shift-reduce parser to handle null constituents ($D \rightarrow \emptyset$) without looping, because the parser can only "accept" a null constituent in places where the table allows one. For a clear exposition of shift-reduce parsing with an oracle, see Pereira (1985).

   In any case, the data in Table 6.1 should serve as a warning. Not every "efficient" parser is actually fast; testing is always appropriate.

**Exercise 6.7.1.1**

What is the difference between table-driven (oracle-driven) parsing and tabular parsing?

**Exercise 6.7.1.2    (project)**

Take one of the parsing algorithms presented in this chapter and make it work as efficiently as possible with a reasonably large grammar. Support your claims with actual tests.

**Exercise 6.7.1.3    (project)**

Test some published parsers written in Prolog for which efficiency is claimed, and see if they are as fast as DCG with a moderately large grammar.

## 6.7.2 Complexity of Parsing

Earley's algorithm made history because it proved that phrase-structure parsing could be done in POLYNOMIAL TIME, i.e., in time proportional to $n^k$, where $n$ is the length of the input string and $k$ is some constant. Further, Earley proved that $k \leq 3$.

This is important because recursive-descent and shift-reduce parsers take, in the worst case, EXPONENTIAL TIME, i.e., time proportional to $k^n$ (which, for large $n$, is much greater than $n^3$).

Recursive-descent and shift-reduce parsers take exponential time because they try out each possible parse tree separately. With some grammars, every string of $n$ words can have $k^n$ different parse trees, of which only the last one can be used in further parsing. Earley's algorithm gets around this limitation by trying all the parse trees concurrently, so that many of its actions apply to more than one parse tree.

Generally, polynomial-time algorithms reflect principled solutions to a problem, while exponential-time algorithms reflect brute-force combinatorial search. Thus, Earley's algorithm shows that parsing can be done in a principled way, not just by trying all possible combinations one after another.

These famous results are less important than they appear, for several reasons. First, natural-language parsers never face large values of $n$. Even exponential-time parsers can be quick when $n$ is small, and in real life, sentences of more than 30 words are uncommon. When long sentences do occur, they can usually be broken up into shorter sentences that are joined by words like *and,* and parsable separately.

Second, the $n^3$ and $k^n$ results apply only to the WORST CASE, i.e., the situation in which the parser "guesses wrong" as much as possible and uses the right rule only after trying all the wrong ones. It is common for a $k^n$-time parser to take much less than $k^n$ time on any particular parse, because it is almost certain to guess right some of the time and thereby avoid unnecessary work.

Third, and most importantly, the $n^3$ result holds only for grammars in which nodes do not have arguments. Barton, Berwick, and Ristad (1987) proved that parsing, in the general case, is NP-COMPLETE—that is, belongs to a class of problems that are believed to take exponential time—if grammars are allowed to have agreement features (i.e., arguments on nodes, such as `singular` and `plural`, together with agreement rules), and if words can be ambiguous (like *deer,* which is ambiguously singular or plural). And natural-language grammars do need these capabilities.

On consideration, this is not unreasonable. There *are* sentences which even human beings cannot parse. Consider Barton, Berwick, and Ristad's example:

BUFFALO BUFFALO BUFFALO BUFFALO BUFFALO

Give up? The structure is exactly like *Boston cattle bewilder Boston cattle.* Now that I've told you this, you probably have no trouble parsing it. And this is a hallmark of NP-complete problems: even though a solution cannot be *found* efficiently, nevertheless if you find a solution somehow, it can be *verified* quickly. What buffaloes us here is, of course, the multiple ambiguity of each of the words.

Progress in developing more efficient parsers, then, apparently depends on two things: the careful study of complexity in typical or average cases (not in the theoretical worst case, which is admittedly intractable), and the discovery of as-yet-unexploited constraints on natural-language grammars.

**Exercise 6.7.2.1**

Show that, with the grammar

$$
\begin{aligned}
NP &\rightarrow D\ N_{sg}\ (and\ NP) \\
NP &\rightarrow D\ N_{pl}\ (and\ NP) \\
D &\rightarrow the \\
N_{sg} &\rightarrow sheep,\ deer,\ quail\ (etc.) \\
N_{pl} &\rightarrow sheep,\ deer,\ quail\ (etc.)
\end{aligned}
$$

every NP containing $n$ ambiguous nouns (such as *the deer and the quail and the sheep*) has $2^n$ different parse trees. (Hint: What happens to the number of parse trees every time an ambiguous noun is added to the phrase?)

**Exercise 6.7.2.2**

Suppose that one parser takes $1.5^n$ seconds to parse an $n$-word sentence, while another parser takes $2.5 \times n^3$ seconds. For what values of $n$ is the exponential-time parser faster? (Compute some actual numbers and make a table.)

**Exercise 6.7.2.3**

(For students who know calculus.) Show that, for any constant $k > 1$ and for sufficiently large $n$, $k^n > n^k$. (Find the value at which $k^n = n^k$ and then compare the rates at which $k^n$ and $n^k$ grow as $n$ increases.)

**Exercise 6.7.2.4**

Examine some English sentences in an actual text (perhaps this book). How long is the longest sentence that does not break up into conjoined shorter sentences? What can you observe about the statistical distribution of sentence length?

**Exercise 6.7.2.5**

Consider the sentences:

> *There are pigs in the pen.*
> *There is ink in the pen.*

Clearly, *pen* needs two lexical entries, one with each of two meanings. What could be done to guide the parser to the right lexical entry in each case, so that it doesn't have to try both of them? (Hint: Consider what it is like when you, as a human being, hear and understand one of these sentences.)

### 6.7.3 Further Reading

Parsing is a big field, and this chapter has sampled only a small part of it. A vast number of different parsing techniques have been developed, some for natural language, some for programming languages, and some for both. Some good general surveys of natural-language parsing are Winograd (1983), Kay (1980), King (1983), Dowty, Karttunen, and Zwicky (1985), and Tomita (1991). On parsing in Prolog, see, besides the references given throughout this chapter, Dahl and Saint-Dizier (1985, 1988), Abramson and Dahl (1989), and Gal, Lapalme, Saint-Dizier, and Somers (1991).

In this chapter we have looked at parsers designed to handle arbitrary sets of PS rules. But human languages have a structure all their own. PS rules in human languages are constrained in ways that are not yet well understood, and human languages involve many phenomena that PS rules by themselves can't handle. Marcus (1978, 1980) inaugurates an important line of research on parsers designed specifically for human languages. Marcus' parser has no backtracking and limited lookahead; it gives special treatment to NP nodes; and its performance on structurally ambiguous sentences is surprisingly humanlike (see also Kac 1982). More recent "principle-based parsers" deduce the rules of grammar (PS rules, case assignment, etc.) from more abstract principles (Berwick, Abney, and Tenny 1991). Tomita (1986), with more modest goals, presents a bottom-up chart parser optimized to deal with the fact that natural-language utterances are short (usually under 30 words) but have a lot of structural ambiguity.

In many languages, word order is partly or completely variable. For example, the Russian translation of *the dog sees the cat* is *sobaka vidit koshku* with the three words in any order depending on the desired emphasis. PS rules do not work well for such languages, and a variety of other approaches have been taken; see Abramson and Dahl (1989:150–153), Covington (1990), and Kashket (1991).

# CHAPTER 7

# Semantics, Logic, and Model Theory

## 7.1 THE PROBLEM OF SEMANTICS

Semantics is the level at which language makes contact with the real world. This means that semantics is at once the most important part of natural language processing, and the most difficult. Many problems in computational semantics have, as yet, no widely accepted solutions. In principle, an entirely adequate theory of semantics would require a complete theory of human thought.

The goals of this chapter are more modest. In it, we will focus on how to translate English into Prolog or something close to it, mainly in order to answer database queries. Even though Prolog is not powerful enough to represent human knowledge as a whole, it is adequate and convenient for the kinds of information commonly stored in computers. Practically all computer databases map onto Prolog in a simple way.

The techniques used here are somewhat *ad hoc*, but there is a strong emphasis on the underlying logical theory. The model-theoretic semantics is largely based on the Discourse Representation Theory of Kamp (1981; for a readable exposition see Spencer-Smith 1987, and for an implementation, Covington, Nute, Goodman, and Schmitz 1988).

## 7.2 FROM ENGLISH TO LOGICAL FORMULAS

### 7.2.1 Logic and Model Theory

To describe the meanings of natural-language utterances, we need a precise way to describe the information that they contain. We can get this from logic and set theory; it's called MODEL-THEORETIC SEMANTICS. It relies on MODELS, which are precisely defined knowledge bases.

Consider a simple formula such as *chases*(*fido*, *felix*) ('Fido chases Felix'). This formula is part of a logical language. A MODEL for the language consists of a DOMAIN **D**, which is the set of individual people and things that can be talked about, plus an INTERPRETATION FUNCTION **I** which maps everything in the language onto something in the domain. Specifically:

- **I** maps logical constants (proper names) onto individual members of **D**. For instance, **I**(*fido*) is Fido.
- **I** maps predicates onto sets of tuples of elements of **D**. For example, **I**(*green*) picks out the 1-tuples consisting of elements of **D** that are green. **I**(*chases*) picks out all the pairs $\langle x, y \rangle$ of elements of **D** such that $x$ chases $y$. Similarly, **I** would map a three-place predicate onto a set of ordered triples, and so on.

Now we can define, in a precise way, what it means for a formula to be true:

- A formula of the form *predicate*($arg_1$, $arg_2$, ...) is true if and only if $\langle \mathbf{I}(arg_1), \mathbf{I}(arg_2), ... \rangle \in \mathbf{I}(predicate)$.
  For example, *chases*(*fido*, *felix*) is true when $\langle \mathbf{I}(fido), \mathbf{I}(felix) \rangle \in \mathbf{I}(chases)$.
- A formula that contains quantifiers or connectives such as $\neg, \wedge, \vee, \forall, \exists$ is true if it meets the conditions given by the definitions of the connectives and quantifiers (Table 7.1).

**TABLE 7.1**   LOGIC SYMBOLS.

| Symbol | Read as | Example | Meaning |
|--------|---------|---------|---------|
| $\neg$ | not | $\neg P$ | $P$ is not true |
| $\wedge$ | and | $P \wedge Q$ | $P$ is true and $Q$ is true |
| $\vee$ | or | $P \vee Q$ | $P$ is true or $Q$ is true, or both |
| $\rightarrow$ | implies | $P \rightarrow Q$ | if $P$ is true then so is $Q$ (either $P$ is false or $Q$ is true, or both) |
| $\forall$ | for all | $(\forall x)P$ | $P$ is true for all values of $x$ |
| $\exists$ | for some | $(\exists x)P$ | $P$ is true for at least one value of $x$ |
| $\lambda$ | lambda | $(\lambda x)p$ | the formula is incomplete and has no truth value until a value is supplied for $x$ |

For example, the definition of $\wedge$ says that $P \wedge Q$ is true if and only if $P$ and $Q$ are both true. The definition of $\forall$ says that $(\forall x)P$ is true if and only if $P$ is true for all possible values of $x$ (i.e., true no matter which element of $\mathbf{D}$ we assign to $x$)

Compared to other ways of evaluating logical formulas, model theory has two important advantages. First, it assigns meanings to all parts of every formula, rather than just assigning truth values to complete sentences. Second, model theory works with knowledge bases (models) without making any claims about the real world as a whole. This is important because it corresponds closely to computer manipulation of a database.

**Exercise 7.2.1.1**

Given the model

$$\mathbf{D} = \{\text{Fido, Felix, Max}\}$$
$$\mathbf{I}(\textit{fido}) = \text{Fido}$$
$$\mathbf{I}(\textit{felix}) = \text{Felix}$$
$$\mathbf{I}(\textit{max}) = \text{Max}$$
$$\mathbf{I}(\textit{animal}) = \{\langle\text{Fido}\rangle, \langle\text{Felix}\rangle\}$$
$$\mathbf{I}(\textit{chases}) = \{\langle\text{Fido, Felix}\rangle, \langle\text{Max, Fido}\rangle\}$$

determine whether each of the following formulas is true or false, and show how you obtained each result:

*(I/max) ∉ I(animal)*

$animal(max)$

$animal(fido)$

$animal(fido) \wedge chases(max, fido)$

$animal(max) \rightarrow animal(fido)$

$(\forall x)(animal(x) \rightarrow \neg chases(x, max))$

**Exercise 7.2.1.2**

Assume that it is true that Fido shows Felix to Max, and that *shows* is a three-place predicate. Supply $\mathbf{I}(\textit{shows})$.

## 7.2.2 Simple Words and Phrases

Table 7.2 shows logical formulas that represent a number of simple English words and phrases, along with a way of representing these formulas in Prolog. As in Chapters 2 and 3, we represent lambda as `^`, which is right-associative so that `Y^X^formula = Y^(X^formula)`.

The first thing to note is that names are logical constants ('Max' = *max*), but common nouns, like adjectives, are predicates ('dog' = $(\lambda x)dog(x)$). Being a dog, like being green, is a *property,* not a thing.

This has to do with the distinction between sense and reference. A name can refer to only one individual, so we translate it directly into a logical constant.[1] But a

---

[1]At least for the moment. Montague (1973) and others argue that even names should be treated as denoting sets of properties.

**TABLE 7.2**   REPRESENTATIONS OF SIMPLE WORDS AND PHRASES.

| Type of constituent | Logical representation | As written in Prolog |
|---|---|---|
| **Proper noun** | Logical constant | |
| *Max* | *max* | `max` |
| *Fido* | *fido* | `fido` |
| **Common noun** | 1-place predicate | |
| *dog* | $(\lambda x)dog(x)$ | `X^dog(X)` |
| *professor* | $(\lambda x)professor(x)$ | `X^professor(X)` |
| **Adjective** | 1-place predicate | |
| *green* | $(\lambda x)green(x)$ | `X^green(X)` |
| *big* | $(\lambda x)big(x)$ | `X^big(X)` |
| **Noun with adjectives** | 1-place predicates joined by 'and' | |
| *green dog* | $(\lambda x)(green(x) \wedge dog(x))$ | `X^(green(X),dog(X))` |
| **Verb phrase** | 1-place predicate | |
| *barked* | $(\lambda x)barked(x)$ | `X^barked(X)` |
| *chased Felix* | $(\lambda x)chased(x, felix)$ | `X^chased(X,felix)` |
| **Transitive verb** | 2-place predicate | |
| *chased* | $(\lambda y)(\lambda x)chased(x, y)$ | `Y^X^chased(X,Y)` |
| **Copular verb phrase** | 1-place predicate | |
| *is a dog* | $(\lambda x)dog(x)$ | `X^dog(X)` |
| *is green* | $(\lambda x)green(x)$ | `X^green(X)` |
| **Prepositional phrase** | 1-place predicate | |
| *with Max* | $(\lambda x)with(x, max)$ | `X^with(X,max)` |
| **Preposition** | 2-place predicate | |
| *with* | $(\lambda y)(\lambda x)with(x, y)$ | `Y^X^with(X,Y)` |

common noun such as 'dog' can refer to many different individuals, so its translation is the property that these individuals share. The referent of 'dog' in any particular utterance is the value of $x$ that makes $dog(x)$ true.

Second, note that different verbs require different numbers of arguments. The intransitive verb 'barked' translates to a one-place predicate $(\lambda x)barked(x)$. A transitive verb translates to a two-place predicate; a ditransitive verb such as *give* translates to a three-place predicate such as $(\lambda z)(\lambda y)(\lambda x)give(x, y, z)$.

These arguments are filled in, step by step, as you progress up from verb to VP and then S, thus:

| Verb | *chases* | $(\lambda y)(\lambda x)chases(x, y)$ |
| Verb phrase | *chases Felix* | $(\lambda x)chases(x, felix)$ |
| Sentence | *Fido chases Felix* | $chases(fido, felix)$ |

We saw this process in action in Chapter 3.

Some sentences correspond to formulas with logical connectives in them:

| *Fido does not chase Felix* | $\neg chases(fido, felix)$ |
| *Fido and Felix are animals* | $animal(fido) \wedge animal(felix)$ |

Note in Table 7.2 that the copula (*is*) is unusual among verbs because it has no semantic representation. To put this another way, *is X* means the same thing as *X*. The representation for 'is a dog' is the same as for 'dog.'

Last, note that Table 7.2 does not cover the whole of English. Neither does first-order predicate logic. Here are some examples where first-order logic is not sufficient to represent English:

- Predicate with a predicate as argument:

   *Max has an unusual property.*
   $(\exists p)(p(max) \wedge unusual(p))$

- Predicate with a whole proposition as an argument:

   *Fido believes Felix is human.*
   $believes(fido, human(felix))$

- Context in which reference is blocked:

   *John is looking for a unicorn.*
   (It's not clear how to represent "a unicorn" here. Any formula that contains $(\exists x)\ldots unicorn(x)$ is wrong because this unicorn need not exist.)

We will not try to deal with such cases here, but they are all-pervasive; you cannot analyze much natural-language text without running into them. Fortunately, if you confine yourself to texts whose information content can be represented in a computer database, first-order logic or something close to it is usually sufficient.

**Exercise 7.2.2.1**

Using Tables 7.1 and 7.2, represent each of the following sentences as a logical formula:

   *Max is angry.*
   *Fido chased Felix.*
   *Felix did not chase Fido.*
   *Either Felix is green, or Fido is blue, or both.*

*Fido is a dog and Felix is a cat.*

*If Max is angry then Fido is angry.*

*Fido is a green dog.*

*Fido is either a dog or a cat, but not both.*

### 7.2.3 Semantics of the N$^1$ Constituent

Now let's do something practical. Recall the syntax rules:

$$N^1 \quad \rightarrow \quad Adj\ N^1$$
$$N^1 \quad \rightarrow \quad N$$

The N$^1$ constituent is a common noun together with zero or more adjectives, but no determiner, such as *big green dog* or *fat professor.*

Let's implement the semantics of the N$^1$. Adjectives and common nouns alike translate to one-place predicates. What we want to do is combine all the predicates in the N$^1$, joining them with $\wedge$ ('and'). From

$$
\begin{aligned}
big &= (\lambda x)big(x) \\
green &= (\lambda x)green(x) \\
dog &= (\lambda x)dog(x)
\end{aligned}
$$

we want to get:

$$big\ green\ dog = (\lambda x)(big(x) \wedge green(x) \wedge dog(x)).$$

Switching to Prolog notation, we want to combine `X^big(X)`, `X^green(X)`, and `X^dog(X)` to get `X^(big(X),green(X),dog(X))`. Crucially, we have to ensure that the variables get unified with each other; it would be quite unsatisfactory if we got `(big(X),green(Y),dog(Z))`.

All this is easy to accomplish through arguments on DCG rules. First the lexical entries for particular words:

```
adj(X^big(X))     --> [big].
adj(X^brown(X))   --> [brown].
adj(X^little(X))  --> [little].
adj(X^green(X))   --> [green].

n(X^dog(X)) --> [dog].
n(X^cat(X)) --> [cat].
```

Now for the PS rules. The rule $N^1 \rightarrow N$ is easy to handle, since in this case the semantics of the whole N$^1$ is the same as that of the noun:

```
n1(Sem) --> n(Sem).
```

Finally, here is the rule that combines an adjective with an N$^1$:

```
n1(X^(P,Q)) --> adj(X^P), n1(X^Q).
```

Notice that this rule is recursive. After combining one adjective with an N$^1$, it can combine another adjective with the resulting N$^1$, and so on, as shown in Figure 7.1.

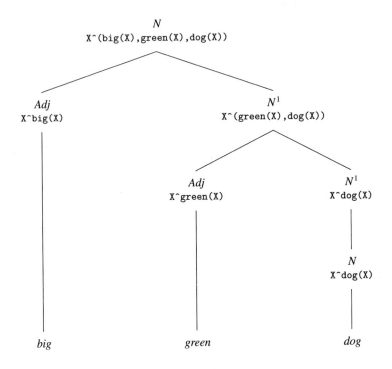

**Figure 7.1** Constructing the semantics of an N$^1$.

### Exercise 7.2.3.1

What would happen if, in place of

```
n1(X^(P,Q)) --> adj(X^P), n1(X^Q).
```

the last rule were written as follows?

```
n1((P,Q)) --> adj(P), n1(Q).
```

### Exercise 7.2.3.2

Using the rules just given, get a small parser working and show that it generates the correct semantics for the phrases *cat*, *big cat*, *big brown dog*, and *big green cat*.

**Exercise 7.2.3.3**

Extend this small parser so that:

- It handles NPs whose determiner is *a* or *an,* so that, for example, the semantics of *a big green dog* is the same as that of *big green dog.*
- It handles sentences of the form *Name is NP,* such as *Felix is a big brown cat,* and generates correct semantics, in this case
  ```
  (big(felix),brown(felix),cat(felix)).
  ```

## 7.3 QUANTIFIERS (DETERMINERS)

### 7.3.1 Quantifiers in Language, Logic, and Prolog

Determiners in natural language correspond to quantifiers in formal logic; we shall use the terms *quantifier* and *determiner* almost interchangeably.[2]  Table 7.3 shows some sentences that contain quantifiers and their semantic representations.

The alert reader will notice that the quantifier $\exists$ normally goes with the connective $\land$, and $\forall$ with $\rightarrow$. In our Prolog renditions of the logical formulas, the connectives are implicit. We write `all(X,Goal1,Goal2)` to mean that all values of X which satisfy Goal1 also satisfy Goal2. A predicate to test this, in database queries, can be defined as follows:

```
all(_,Goal1,Goal2) :-
  \+ (Goal1, \+ Goal2).
```

That's very simple: verify that there is no way to satisfy Goal1 that cannot be extended (by instantiating more variables) to satisfy Goal2. The argument X is not actually used; we include it only so that `all` will have the same argument structure as other quantifiers to be defined later on.

But wait a minute—what if there is no way to satisfy Goal1 at all? Then `all(X,Goal1,Goal2)` succeeds, and that's probably not what we want. In logic, $(\forall x)(p(x) \rightarrow q(x))$ is true in the situation where $p(x)$ is always false. But in natural language, we don't want to claim that *all unicorns are green* is true when there are no unicorns in the knowledge base. Accordingly, we should modify `all` to test that there is indeed at least one solution to Goal1, and then cut to prevent pointless backtracking:

```
% all(-X,+Goal1,+Goal2)
%   Succeeds if all values of X that satisfy Goal1
%   also satisfy Goal2.
```

---

[2]Some authors say that a quantifier consists of a determiner plus its restrictor; that is, a determiner by itself is not a complete quantifier, but only an ingredient for making one. On this view, for example, 'most dogs' is a quantifier but 'most' is not. See the next section.

```
all(_,Goal1,Goal2) :-
  \+ (Goal1, \+ Goal2),
  Goal1,
  !.
```

The definition of some is even simpler, because all we have to do is find *one* solution of Goal1 and Goal2. Again, we use a cut to prevent pointless backtracking:

```
% some(-X,+Goal1,+Goal2)
%  Succeeds if there is a value of X that
%  satisfies Goal1 and Goal2.

some(_,Goal1,Goal2) :-
  Goal1,
  Goal2,
  !.
```

**Exercise 7.3.1.1**

Referring to Table 7.3 as needed, express each of the following sentences as a logical formula, and as the Prolog representation of that formula.

> *All unicorns are animals.*
> *One or more unicorns are purple.*
> *A cat chased Fido.*
> *Every cat chased Fido.*
> *Every cat is an animal.*
> *Every cat chased a dog.*

**Exercise 7.3.1.2**

When all/3 succeeds, does it instantiate its first argument? If so, explain how.

**Exercise 7.3.1.3**

What is the purpose of the cut in some/3?

**Exercise 7.3.1.4**

Given the knowledge base

```
dog(fido).
cat(felix).
cat(leo).
animal(leo).
animal(felix).
animal(fido).
```

**TABLE 7.3**   QUANTIFIERS DETERMINE THE OVERALL SEMANTIC
STRUCTURE OF THE SENTENCE.

| Sentence | Representations |
|---|---|
| *Fido barked.* | *barked*(*fido*) |
| | barked(fido) |
| *A dog barked.* | $(\exists x)(dog(x) \wedge barked(x))$ |
| | some(X,dog(X),barked(X)) |
| *Every dog barked.* | $(\forall x)(dog(x) \rightarrow barked(x))$ |
| | all(X,dog(X),barked(X)) |
| *Fido chased a cat.* | $(\exists x)(cat(x) \wedge chased(fido, x))$ |
| | some(X,cat(X),chased(fido,X)) |
| *Fido chased every cat.* | $(\forall x)(cat(x) \rightarrow chased(fido, x))$ |
| | all(X,cat(X),chased(fido,X)) |
| *A dog chased a cat.* | $(\exists x)(dog(x) \wedge (\exists y)(cat(y) \wedge chased(x, y)))$ |
| | some(X,dog(X),some(Y,cat(Y),chased(X,Y))) |
| *A dog chased every cat.* | $(\exists x)(dog(x) \wedge (\forall y)(cat(y) \rightarrow chased(x, y)))$ |
| | some(X,dog(X),all(Y,cat(Y),chased(X,Y))) |
| *Every dog chased a cat.* | $(\forall x)(dog(x) \rightarrow (\exists y)(cat(y) \wedge chased(x, y)))$ |
| | all(X,dog(X),some(Y,cat(Y),chased(X,Y))) |
| *Every dog chased every cat.* | $(\forall x)(dog(x) \rightarrow (\forall y)(cat(y) \rightarrow chased(x, y)))$ |
| | all(X,dog(X),all(Y,cat(Y),chased(X,Y))) |

predict (without using the computer) the outcomes of the queries:

```
?- some(X,dog(X),animal(X)).
?- all(X,cat(X),animal(X)).
?- all(X,animal(X),cat(X)).
```

Then use the computer to confirm your results.

## 7.3.2 Restrictor and Scope

We noted already that $\exists$ is somehow associated with $\wedge$ and $\forall$ with $\rightarrow$. In fact, in Prolog, we left out the latter connective and treated each quantifier as a relationship between a quantified variable and two Prolog goals.

Let's pursue this idea further. Consider the formulas

$(\exists x)(cat(x) \wedge animal(x))$    'At least one cat is an animal.'
$(\forall x)(cat(x) \rightarrow animal(x))$    'Every cat is an animal.'

These can be written another way. Let $(\forall x : cat(x))$ mean 'For all $x$ such that $x$ is a cat.' Then, using this notation, we can write:

$$(\exists x : cat(x))animal(x) \quad \text{'At least one cat is an animal.'}$$
$$(\forall x : cat(x))animal(x) \quad \text{'Every cat is an animal.'}$$

Notice that the connectives $\wedge$ and $\rightarrow$ have disappeared.

In this new notation, $cat(x)$ is called the RESTRICTOR (or RANGE) of the quantifier $\exists x$ or $\forall x$; it restricts the set of values of $x$ that the quantifier can pick out. The rest of the formula, here $animal(x)$, is the SCOPE of the quantifier; it is the proposition that is supposed to be true for the appropriate values of $x$.

From this perspective we can look at each quantifier as a relation between quantified variable, scope, and restrictor:

- $(\exists x)$ means that *at least one* value of $x$ that makes the restrictor true will also make the scope true;
- $(\forall x)$ means that *every* value of $x$ that makes the restrictor true will also make the scope true.

More precisely, for any quantified variable $x$, the quantifier is a relation between the set of values of $x$ that satisfy the restrictor, and the set of values of $x$ that satisfy both the restrictor and the scope.

It's easy to invent other quantifiers, such as:

- (*two x*), meaning that exactly two of the values of $x$ that satisfy the restrictor also satisfy the scope;
- (*most x*), meaning that more than half of the values of $x$ that satisfy the restrictor also satisfy the scope;

or whatever you like. These are called GENERALIZED QUANTIFIERS and are essential for analyzing natural language.

We can represent generalized quantifiers in Prolog with three-place predicates such as `two(X,Goal1,Goal2)`, `most(X,Goal1,Goal2)`, and so forth. Now it is obvious why X has to be an argument (even though `some` and `all` didn't use it): quantifiers like `two` and `most` have to count the values of X that satisfy the goals, and they have to make sure they are indeed counting values of X rather than values of some other variable.

**Exercise 7.3.2.1**

Rewrite each of your formulas from Exercise 7.3.1.1 in restrictor-scope format (both in logical notation and in Prolog).

**Exercise 7.3.2.2**

Consider the knowledge base:

```
dog(fido).
cat(felix).
```

```
cat(leo).
chases(fido,felix).
chases(fido,leo).
```

How many solutions are there to the query '?- dog(X),cat(Y),chases(X,Y).'? How many dogs are cat-chasers? Why aren't these the same number, and what does this tell us about the right way to implement generalized quantifiers?

**Exercise 7.3.2.3**

Define the generalized quantifier two in Prolog using setof (see section 7.4.2.)

**Exercise 7.3.2.4**

In ordinary English, does *two* mean 'exactly 2' or does it mean '2 or more'? Discuss and cite evidence.

### 7.3.3 Structural Importance of Determiners

Determiners affect more of the *semantic* structure than the *syntactic* structure would suggest.

Consider for example *Fido chases every cat.* On the syntactic level, *every* modifies *cat.* You might therefore expect that on the semantic level, when *every* is converted into an all(...,...,...) structure, only *cat* will be inside it.

But such an expectation would be wrong. On the semantic level, *every* has scope over the entire sentence, even though syntactically it only modifies *cat.* Figure 7.2 shows part of the process by which the semantic structure is built up.

Or consider *Every dog chases a cat,* which we represent as:

```
all(X,dog(X),some(Y,cat(Y),chases(X,Y)))
```

Here the constituent *every dog* gives rise to an all structure that contains not only the representation of the NP (where *every* occurs), but also the representation of the VP.

Does this mean that our enterprise of building semantic structures constituent-by-constituent is doomed? No; it means only that some careful use of lambda expressions is required.

**Exercise 7.3.3.1**

Draw diagrams like Figure 7.2 for the sentences:

> *Every cat chased Fido.*
> *Some dog chased every cat.*

### 7.3.4 Building Quantified Structures

Now for the implementation. Despite their complexity, the semantic structures that we need can still be built through unification of arguments in DCG rules.

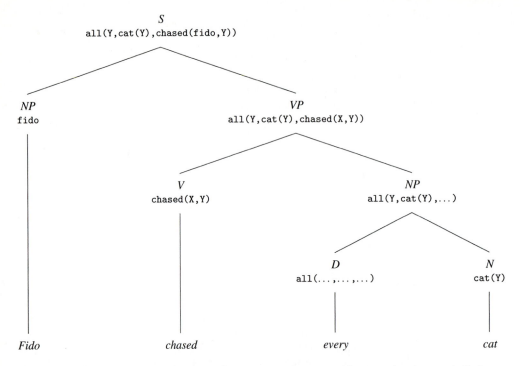

**Figure 7.2** The quantifier *all* dominates the semantic representation, even though syntactically it belongs only to the last NP. (This structure is incomplete; all lambdas are left out.)

Our representation of verbs and common nouns will be the same as before. For brevity we will omit the N¹ node. This gives us some lexical entries:

```
n(X^dog(X)) --> [dog].
n(X^cat(X)) --> [cat].

v(X^meowed(X))        --> [meowed].
v(Y^X^chased(X,Y)) --> [chased].
v(Y^X^saw(X,Y))      --> [saw].
```

The key question at this point is how to represent determiners. For our purposes, a determiner is something that takes a scope and a restrictor, and puts them together. So the semantic representation of every determiner will have the form (X^Res)^(X^Sco) ^Formula—that is, "Give me a restrictor and a scope and I'll make a formula out of them." The variable X is explicit here so that the corresponding variables in different terms will be unified. Thus we get the lexical entries:

```
d((X^Res)^(X^Sco)^all(X,Res,Sco))  --> [every].
d((X^Res)^(X^Sco)^some(X,Res,Sco)) --> [a];[some].
```

Now that we know what a determiner is, what's an NP? The same thing as a determiner, except that the restrictor has been supplied, as in the structure:

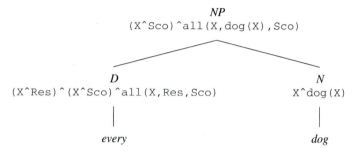

The D and NP are alike except that the NP is only awaiting the scope, not the restrictor. The grammar rule for NP is

```
np((X^Sco)^Pred) --> d((X^Res)^(X^Sco)^Pred), n(X^Res).
```

or, more concisely,

```
np(Sem) --> d((X^Res)^Sem), n(X^Res).
```

There are two VP rules. If the verb has no object, then the semantics of the VP is the same as that of the V:

```
vp(Sem) --> v(Sem).
```

That gives us [VP *meowed*] = X^meowed(X) and the like.

But if there is an object NP within the VP, the verb becomes the scope of that NP, thus:

```
vp(X^Pred) --> v(Y^X^Sco), np((Y^Sco)^Pred).
```

This accounts for structures such as:

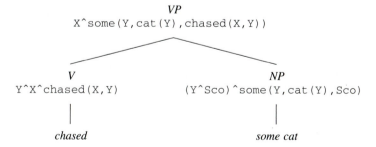

Finally, the S rule takes the NP (which is waiting for a scope) and the VP (which is waiting for an argument), and puts them together:

```
s(Sem) --> np((X^Sco)^Sem), vp(X^Sco).
```

This accounts for structures like this:

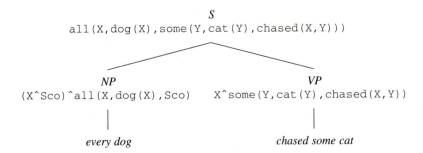

Notice how things have changed: in Chapters 3 and 5 we treated the subject as an argument of the VP, and now we're doing it the other way around, so that determiners (and NPs containing them) will always have control of the overall semantic structure.

That's enough to handle many common sentence structures. Figure 7.3 shows, in detail, how the structure of *Every dog chased some cat* is built up.

One last problem remains. We can no longer represent proper names as constants; instead, they have to be structures that accept a VP as scope. Instead of

```
np(fido) --> [fido].
```

we have to write

```
np((fido^Sco)^Sco) --> [fido].
```

Here `(fido^Sco)^Sco` is an expression that receives `X^Sco` from the verb phrase, instantiates the lambda variable to `fido`, and returns `Sco` with no other changes.

### Exercise 7.3.4.1

Get a parser working that uses the grammar rules introduced in this section, plus other rules as necessary, in order to generate correct semantic representations for the sentences:

*Fido barked.*

*A dog barked.*

*Every dog barked.*

*Fido chased Felix.*

*A dog chased Felix.*

*Felix chased a cat.*

*Every dog chased Felix.*

*Felix chased every cat.*

*A dog chased every cat.*

*Every dog chased a cat.*

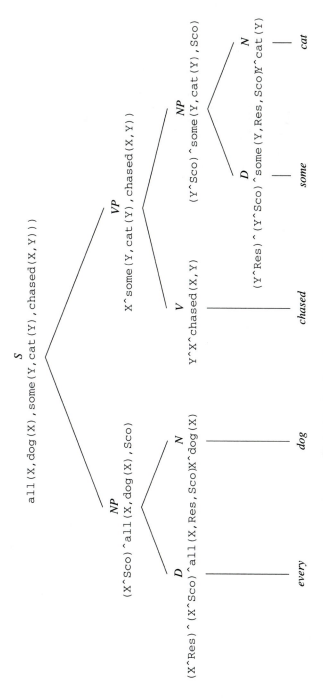

**Figure 7.3** Building semantic structure, in detail.

### 7.3.5 Scope Ambiguities

The alert reader will have noticed that *A dog chased every cat* is ambiguous. Here are its two readings:

*A dog chased every cat* =

   (1)  `some(X,dog(X),all(Y,cat(Y),chased(X,Y)))`
       'There is a dog that chased all cats'

   (2)  `all(Y,cat(Y),some(X,dog(X),chased(X,Y)))`
       'Each cat was chased by some dog (not necessarily the same dog)'

The first of these is what our rules so far generate. The second can be derived from the first by a transformation known as QUANTIFIER RAISING:

```
some(X,dog(X),all(Y,cat(Y),chased(X,Y)))
⇓
all(Y,cat(Y),some(X,dog(X),chased(X,Y)))
```

or, more generally:

```
Q1(V1,R1,Q2(V2,R2,S2))                    (QUANTIFIER RAISING FROM SCOPE)
⇓
Q2(V2,R2,Q1(V1,R1,S2))
```

where `Q1` and `Q2` stand for the quantifiers[3] and `R2` does not contain any variable other than `V2`.

    It's also possible to raise a quantifier from the restrictor, like this:

*Someone who sees every dog laughs.* =

   (1)  `some(X,all(Y,dog(Y),sees(X,Y)),laughs(X))`
       'There is someone who sees all the dogs and laughs'

   (2)  `all(Y,dog(Y),some(X,sees(X,Y),laughs(X)))`
       'For each dog, there is someone who sees it and laughs'

This time the general schema is:

```
Q1(V1,Q2(V2,R2,S2),S1)                    (QUANTIFIER RAISING FROM RESTRICTOR)
⇓
Q2(V2,R2,Q1(V1,R1,S1))
```

---

[3]Of course real Prolog does not allow a variable in this position.

Actually these two schemas are instances of a more general pattern. In fact almost *any* quantifier anywhere within the scope or restrictor—no matter how deep down—can be raised to have scope over the entire sentence. Here's how to do it:

- Pick the quantified structure to be raised; call it $Q(V,R,S)$.
- Replace $Q(V,R,S)$ with $S$. Call the resulting formula $F$.
- The result of raising is then $Q(V,R,F)$.

That describes how to raise *one* quantifier from anywhere in the sentence. In real life, more than one quantifier can be moved, because quantifier raising is recursive. There is considerable debate as to how far the recursion should be allowed to go.

In principle, a sentence with $n$ quantifiers could have $n!$ ($n$-factorial) readings. To see that this is so, consider that you can choose any of the $n$ quantifiers to be raised to the topmost position. Having done this, you can then raise any of the $n-1$ quantifiers not yet raised; then any of the $n-2$ remaining, and so on, yielding $n \times (n-1) \times (n-2) \times \cdots$ alternatives.

In practice, we don't get this many, for several reasons. Some readings are blocked because they leave variables unbound (that is, they put variables outside the scope or restrictor of the quantifiers that bind them). Other readings are logically equivalent (for example, raising one `all` past another `all` has no effect on the truth conditions of the sentence). Still others are blocked by structural principles. For example, Hobbs and Shieber (1987) point out that in English, it is not permissible to take a quantifier from outside an NP and put it between two quantifiers that originated in that NP.

Further, there are differences in the ease with which various quantifiers can be raised. Specifically, *each* almost always raises; *some, all,* and *every* can raise but need not do so; *any* tends not to raise; and numerals generally do not raise.

The *especially* alert reader will now notice that quantifier raising is what we've been doing all along. The whole point of Figures 7.2 and 7.3 was that quantifiers get raised out of individual NPs so that they have scope over the complete sentence. So it makes sense to build an initial semantic representation with the quantifiers still *in* the NPs, and then require that they be raised far enough to give well-formed logical formulas, with further raising then being optional.

That is in fact now the standard approach to quantifier scoping (Cooper 1983, Hornstein 1984, Chierchia and McConnell-Ginet 1990 chapter 3). Hobbs and Shieber (1987) give an algorithm that raises quantifiers from NP positions, generating all and only the scopings that are structurally possible in English.

**Exercise 7.3.5.1**

Give formulas for the two readings of *Every man loves a woman.*

**Exercise 7.3.5.2**

Explain why quantifier raising has no effect on the truth conditions of *Every dog chased every cat.*

**Exercise 7.3.5.3**

Express the sentence

> *Everyone who hates a dog loves two cats.*

as a formula. Derive two more formulas from it (by raising from the scope and from the restrictor respectively) and explain the meaning of the sentence that corresponds to each of your three formulas.

**Exercise 7.3.5.4**

Implement quantifier raising from scope and from restrictor. That is, implement a predicate `raise_quantifier/2` which, when given a formula, will perform raising from the scope or from the restrictor, whichever is possible, and will also have a solution in which no raising is performed. For example:

```
?- raise_quantifier(some(X,dog(X),all(Y,cat(Y),chased(X,Y))),What).
What = all(Y,cat(Y),some(X,dog(X),chased(X,Y))) ;
What = some(X,dog(X),all(Y,cat(Y),chased(X,Y)),What).
```

When given the formula from the previous exercise, `raise_quantifier` should get all three readings. You need not check whether variables are left unbound (in these examples they won't be).

**Exercise 7.3.5.5**

Define a predicate `interpret/2` that parses a sentence using your parser, then optionally applies quantifier raising, so that if you give it `[every,dog,chased,a,cat]` you get two alternative formulas.

## 7.4 QUESTION ANSWERING

### 7.4.1 Simple Yes/No Questions

We have now implemented enough semantics to be able to answer, from a knowledge base, plain-English questions such as:

> *Did Fido chase Felix?*
> *Did every cat meow?*
> *Did every dog chase a cat?*

All we need to do is change the grammar rules so that questions can be parsed. To do this, we replace the S rule

```
s(Sem) --> np((X^Sco)^Sem), vp(X^Sco).
```

with one appropriate for questions,

```
s(Sem) --> [did], np((X^Sco)^Sem), vp(X^Sco).
```

and we add the "plain" forms of the verbs (without final *-ed*), thus:

```
v(X^meowed(X))      --> [meowed];[meow].
v(Y^X^chased(X,Y)) --> [chased];[chase].
v(Y^X^saw(X,Y))     --> [saw];[see].
```

Now *Did every dog chase a cat?* translates directly into the query

```
?- all(X,dog(X),some(Y,cat(Y),chased(X,Y))).
```

which can be answered from a suitable knowledge base.

**Exercise 7.4.1.1**

Using the grammar rules presented so far, the definitions of some and all, and the knowledge base

```
cat(felix).    cat(leo).
dog(fido).     dog(bucephalus).
saw(felix,fido).
saw(leo,felix).
chased(fido,felix).
chased(bucephalus,leo).
```

write a Prolog program that will accept and answer the questions

> *Did Leo see Felix?*
> *Did every cat see a dog?*
> *Did a cat see a dog?*
> *Did every dog chase a cat?*

and others of similar form. You need not handle scope ambiguities.

## 7.4.2 Getting a List of Solutions

To go further and answer questions that contain *which* or *how many,* we will need a way to get a list of solutions to a Prolog query. Two approaches are possible.

The built-in predicate setof/3 returns a list of all solutions to a query. More precisely,

```
?- setof(X,Goal,L).
```

will instantiate L to a list of all the values of X that occur in solutions to Goal. The list is sorted in alphabetical order and duplicates are removed. For example:

```
dog(fido).
dog(bucephalus).

?- setof(X,dog(X),L).
L = [bucephalus,fido]
```

That's *almost* what we need. The problem is that if Goal contains a variable other than X, setof will return only the solutions in which that variable has one particular value. On backtracking, setof will then let that variable have another value, and so on. With the knowledge base

```
f(a,c).
f(b,c).
f(c,d).
f(d,d).
```

we get:

```
?- setof(X,f(X,Y),L).
Y = c    L = [a,b] ;
Y = d    L = [c,d] ;
```

What we want is to get all the values of X into a single list. Otherwise, there are some queries we can't answer, such as how many dogs chase any cat (not necessarily the same cat).

Fortunately setof provides a way to work around this.[4] If we write

```
?- setof(X,Term^Goal,L).        % here ^ does not denote lambda
```

then setof works as before, except that all the variables in Term are allowed to take on all possible values, like this:

```
?- setof(X,Y^f(X,Y),L).
L = [a,b,c,d]
```

(assuming the same knowledge base as before).

What we want, of course, is this kind of treatment for all the variables in Goal, so we simply write Goal^Goal. We'll encapsulate this trick by defining the predicate solutions/3:

---

[4]At least in ALS, Arity, and Quintus (UNIX) Prolog, and in the draft ISO standard; not in LPA Prolog 3.10 (Quintus Prolog for MS-DOS).

```
% solutions(-X,+Goal,-List)
%   Returns, in List, all the values of X that satisfy Goal.
%   Free variables in Goal are allowed to take all possible values.
%   List contains no duplicates.

solutions(X,Goal,List) :-
    setof(X,Goal^Goal,List).  % here ^ does not denote lambda
```

A few Prologs either do not have `setof`, or do not accept the `Goal^Goal` trick. These Prologs have, instead, a built-in predicate `findall/3` that works like `setof`, but allows the free variables to take on all values, thus:

```
?- findall(X,f(X,Y),L).
L = [a,b,c,d]
```

The trouble with `findall` is that it doesn't remove duplicates. If we're counting the cat-chasing dogs, we don't want to count Fido twice merely because he chases two cats. So we'll need to define `solutions` as:

```
solutions(X,Goal,List) :-
    findall(X,Goal,L),
    remove_duplicates(L,List).
```

You will have to define `remove_duplicates` also.

**Exercise 7.4.2.1**

> Get `solutions/3` working on your computer. Using a small knowledge base, verify that it works correctly.

**Exercise 7.4.2.2**

> Using `solutions/3`, define the following generalized quantifiers:
>
> - `two(X,Res,Sco)`, true if there are exactly two values of X that satisfy `Res` and also satisfy `Sco`;
> - `three(X,Res,Sco)` and `four(X,Res,Sco)`, analogous to `two`;
> - `most(X,Res,Sco)`, true if more than half of the values of X that satisfy `Res` also satisfy `Sco`.
>
> Be sure you compare the number of values that satisfy `Res` to the number of values that satisfy *both* `Res` and `Sco` (not just `Sco` by itself). If there are three dogs and two green objects (not dogs) in the knowledge base, you would not want to conclude that two dogs are green.

### 7.4.3  *Who/What/Which* **Questions**

Now we can tackle questions that contain the "WH-words" *who, what, which,* and *how many.* Syntactically, *who* and *what* are pronouns; roughly they mean 'which person' and 'which thing'. *Which* and *how many* are determiners and are the words we will focus on here.

We can handle *which* and *how many* like quantifiers, except that when they occur in a query, the Prolog system will display the values on the screen rather than just testing the truth of a statement:

```
which(X,Res,Sco) :-
    solutions(X,(Res,Sco),L),
    write(L),
    nl.

how_many(X,Res,Sco) :-
    solutions(X,(Res,Sco),L),
    length(L,N),
    write(N),
    nl.
```

The main syntactic peculiarity of WH-words is that they always occur at the beginning of the sentence. Of course, sometimes they would have been there anyway; structures like

> *Which cat saw a dog?*
>
> *How many cats saw a dog?*

are no problem. In other cases, however, the WH-word moves to sentence-initial position and takes the rest of its NP with it. Instead of

> *Fido chased which cat?*

we normally get

> *Which cat did Fido chase ⊔?*

where, as in Chapter 3, ⊔ denotes a missing NP. The moved NP can be associated with its original position using the same techniques as in Chapter 3.

WH-words are also subject to scope ambiguities. In English, *Which dogs chased a cat?* can mean either 'Which dogs chased one particular cat?' or 'Which dogs chased any cat (we don't care which one)?' These require the same techniques, and present the same puzzles, as the ambiguities of *all* and *some* already noted.

**Exercise 7.4.3.1**

Extend your parser from Exercise 7.4.1.1 to answer queries such as:

> *Which cat saw Fido?*
>
> *How many dogs chased some cat?*
>
> *Fido chased how many cats?*

You need not deal with scope ambiguities, nor with plurals whose determiner is anything other than *which* or *how many*.

**Exercise 7.4.3.2   (small project)**

Extend your parser so that it also handles WH-movement and will answer queries such as:

*How many cats did Fido chase?*
*Which cats did every dog see?*

Again, you need not handle scope ambiguities, nor plurals with determiners other than *which* or *how many.*

## 7.5 FROM FORMULA TO KNOWLEDGE BASE

### 7.5.1 Discourse Referents

When we move from question answering to actually building a knowledge base from English input, a problem immediately arises. Consider how to render the sentence

*Max owns a dog.*

into Prolog. A first guess would be to use the two facts:

```
dog(X).          % wrong!
owns(max,X).
```

That's not right; in Prolog, these facts say 'Anything is a dog' and 'Max owns any-thing.' They would succeed with queries as bizarre as '?- dog(qwertyuiop).' and '?- owns(max,new_york).'

Since the dog doesn't have a name, we have to give it one. That is, we have to recognize the dog as a DISCOURSE REFERENT (a thing that can now be talked about)[5] and give it a unique name (a DISCOURSE MARKER), such as x123 or x(123). Then what we want to say is:

```
dog(x(123)).
owns(max,x(123)).
```

We will also need some kind of TABLE OF IDENTITY so that if we ever find out this dog's name, or find out that it is identical to some other dog with a different discourse marker, we can keep track of it properly.

An even bigger problem arises with statements like *Every farmer owns a dog.* What we want is something like this,

```
dog(Y)     :- farmer(X).    % wrong!
owns(X,Y) :- farmer(X).
```

---

[5] See Karttunen (1969), an account still well worth reading. In this section I follow Covington, Nute, Goodman, and Schmitz (1988) and the sources cited there.

but here the variables are obviously doing the wrong things. What we need is to generate a different discourse referent for each farmer's dog. We can do this by letting the dog's name be a structure that has the farmer's name in it, like this:

```
dog(x(124,X))      :- farmer(X).
owns(X,x(124,X)) :- farmer(X).
```

Then if Max is a farmer, his dog is temporarily known as `x(124,max)`; Bill's dog is `x(124,bill)`; and so on. Each dog has a unique name. This is a form of SKOLEMIZA-TION (Skolem 1920), the replacement of ∃-quantified variables with terms whose values depend on the values of all the other variables. In effect, we are changing

$$(\forall x)(farmer(x) \rightarrow (\exists y)(dog(y) \land owns(x, y)))$$

into

$$(\forall x)(farmer(x) \rightarrow (dog(f(x)) \land owns(x, f(x))))$$

where $f$ is a function that maps each farmer onto (a name for) the appropriate dog.

**Exercise 7.5.1.1**

Define a procedure `generate_marker/1` which will create new discourse markers by instantiating its argument to a different discourse marker every time it is called, thus:

```
?- generate_marker(What).
What = x(1)
?- generate_marker(What).
What = x(2)
?- generate_marker(What).
What = x(3)
```

and so on. (Hint: Use `assert` and `retract`.)

**Exercise 7.5.1.2**

Translate into Prolog facts and rules, by hand, using discourse markers where necessary:

> *A dog barked.*
> *Felix chased a dog.*
> *Felix chased every dog.*
> *A dog chased a cat.*

**Exercise 7.5.1.3   (small project)**

Write a program that will take the formulas

```
some(X,dog(X),barked(X))
some(X,dog(X),chased(felix,X))
all(X,dog(X),chased(felix,X))
some(X,dog(X),some(Y,cat(Y),chased(X,Y)))
```

(which are, of course, representations of the sentences in the previous exercise) and translate each of them into one or more Prolog clauses using discourse markers wherever appropriate.

## 7.5.2 Anaphora

ANAPHORA is the use of pronouns (ANAPHORS) to refer to people, places, or things previously mentioned. For example:

> *Max$_i$ photographed himself$_i$.*
> *Then he$_i$ photographed Sharon$_j$*
> *and she$_j$ photographed him$_i$.*

The subscripts $i, j, \ldots$ identify words that are COREFERENTIAL (refer to the same person).

In order for an anaphor to be understood, it must be matched up with the appropriate pre-existing discourse referent. This is called RESOLVING the anaphoric reference[6] and is often done by looking for the ANTECEDENT of the anaphor, i.e., the previous mention of the thing that the anaphor refers to. Anaphora resolution is still an area of ongoing research, but several important principles have emerged.

First, *anaphors stand for discourse referents, not for words or phrases.* Consider the example:

> *Max found a trail and followed it.*

Clearly this means that Max found a trail and then followed the same trail. But if *it* were merely a substitute for the words *a trail,* then

> *Max found a trail and followed a trail.*

would mean the same thing, which it doesn't (in the latter sentence the two trails need not be the same). Evidently, then, an anaphor stands for the same referent, not merely the same words, as its antecedent.

Occasionally the antecedent of the anaphor is something that has not been mentioned, but has been brought to the hearer's attention some other way. This is called PRAGMATIC ANAPHORA. For an example, imagine hearing a loud noise and asking someone, *What was it?* The antecedent of *it* is the noise, which has not been mentioned.

Second, *the antecedent almost always precedes the anaphor.* This is simple but important. The obvious way to search for the antecedent of an anaphor is to start with the most recently introduced discourse referent, and search backward until a suitable antecedent is found.

Occasionally the anaphor and antecedent are in reverse order; that is, the anaphor comes first. This is called BACKWARDS ANAPHORA or CATAPHORA and the classic example is:

> *Near him$_i$, John$_i$ saw a snake.*

---

[6]Not to be confused with "resolution" in theorem proving.

Cataphora apparently requires the pronoun and antecedent to be in the same sentence, with the pronoun more deeply embedded (farther from the S node at the top), as noted by Ross (1967) and many others since (see Carden 1986).

Third, *the gender and number of the anaphor restrict the set of possible antecedents.* In English, we use *he/him* to refer to singular males, *she/her* for singular females, *it* for singular inanimate objects, and *they/them* for plurals.[7]

This suggests a general algorithm for finding antecedents:

- Keep a list (or a series of Prolog facts) listing all the discourse referents, newest first, and tagging each of them as masculine, feminine, or inanimate, and as singular or plural.

- Upon finding an anaphor, search through the discourse referents to find the most recent antecedent with appropriate gender and number.

And in fact this strategy works well; Allen (1987:339–354) explores it at some length. Hobbs (1978) found that it is not usually necessary to search back very far, because 98% of all antecedents are within the current or the previous sentence.

There's more. *The form of the anaphor indicates whether the antecedent is in the same sentence.* In English, intrasentential anaphors (REFLEXIVES) end in *-self*. For example:

> $John_i$ saw $himself_i$.
> $John_i$ saw $him_j$.      $(j \neq i)$

Here we know that *him* in the second sentence cannot be coreferential with *John* because it does not end in *-self*.

Actually, "in the same sentence" is not quite the right criterion; the exact syntactic criteria are more complicated, and are not fully understood. Note the contrast between:

> $John_i$ baked a cake for $himself_i$.   (not $him_i$)
> $John_i$ saw a snake near $him_i/himself_i$.

The problem of formulating the exact conditions for the use of reflexives has been an important stimulus for research in generative grammar (Chomsky 1982:218 ff., 288 ff.).

Finally, *semantics and real-world knowledge can help choose between possible antecedents,* as in Jespersen's macabre example:[8]

> If the $baby_i$ does not thrive on raw $milk_j$, boil $it_j$.

Here you have to know that milk can be boiled and babies can't.

---

[7] We will get to plural discourse referents in the next section.

[8] Jespersen (1954:143), cited by Hobbs (1978).

Computational linguists who are daunted by the challenges of anaphora can take solace in the fact that native speakers have problems too, especially when expressing themselves in writing. Unclear or misleading antecedents are a common problem in poorly written English.

### Exercise 7.5.2.1

Consider the following short text:

> *Without considering whether he would offend vegetable growers, the president said he hated broccoli and didn't have to eat it if he didn't want to. And sure enough, they were offended. As a protest, they sent him a huge amount of it.*

(a) Use subscripts to indicate the coreferential nouns and pronouns.

(b) Point out an instance of cataphora.

(c) What kinds of information do you rely on when identifying the antecedent of each anaphor? What kinds of indicators mentioned in the text are not necessary here?

### Exercise 7.5.2.2

Consider now the much simpler text:

> *Cathy photographed Fred.*
> *Then she photographed herself.*
> *Finally Fred looked at Sharon and she photographed him.*

which goes into formulas as:

```
photographed(cathy,fred).
photographed(she,herself).
looked_at(fred,sharon).
photographed(she,him).
```

Define a procedure `resolve_anaphors/2` that will accept this series of formulas (in a Prolog list) and will replace all the anaphors with the names of their most likely referents, thus:

```
?- resolve_anaphors([photographed(cathy,fred),
                     photographed(she,herself)],What).
```

```
What = [photographed(cathy,fred),photographed(cathy,cathy)]
```

(and likewise for the complete list, and for other similar lists).

As real-world knowledge, your procedure can assume that Cathy and Sharon are female and Fred is male. You can further assume that each formula corresponds to a single sentence, and that all anaphors refer to individuals that have been named (so that there is no need for discourse markers).

### 7.5.3 Definite Reference (*the*)

Although we've analyzed lots of determiners, we still haven't said anything about *the*. What does an NP like *the cat* really mean?

The classic analysis, due to Bertrand Russell (1905), is that *the* is a quantifier (written $\exists!$ or $\iota$) which means 'there is exactly one.' On this analysis, *The king is bald* corresponds to the formula

$$(\exists!x : king(x))bald(x)$$

and means 'There is exactly one value of $x$ which satisfies $king(x)$ and also satisfies $bald(x)$.'

But Russell's analysis captures only part of the picture. Quite often, definite NPs (NPs with *the*) refer to discourse referents already mentioned, thus:

> *A dog$_i$ barked and a cat$_j$ howled.*
>
> *Then the dog$_i$ chased the cat$_j$ away.*

If the second sentence had said *A dog chased a cat away* it would have suggested that the second dog and cat are not the same as the first ones. Using *the* makes it clear that the dog and the cat are the ones already mentioned. It is as if *the dog* were an anaphor that can only refer to dogs.

It turns out that treating definite NPs as anaphors is a good idea, with the proviso that pragmatic anaphora is common, and that the antecedent is often in the hearer's background knowledge (or assumed background knowledge) rather than in his or her immediate awareness. I can say *the king of Lesotho* without previously having mentioned him; you will react to this by assuming (if you did not know already) that Lesotho does indeed have a king. That is, you will ACCOMMODATE to my pragmatic anaphora by introducing a discourse referent with appropriate properties. Russell's analysis of *the* does a good job of characterizing the effect of *the* in just this special case where no antecedent is available.

**Exercise 7.5.3.1**

Modify `resolve_anaphors` from the previous exercise so that it will also resolve the referents of NPs bound by *the*, treating them as anaphors whose referents must satisfy a particular predicate. This time, use the text:

> *Henry III knighted Robin Hood.*
>
> *Then Friar Tuck petitioned the king*
>
> *and the king knighted the friar too.*

The formulas that correspond to the sentences are

```
knighted(henry_iii,robin_hood).
the(X,king(X),petitioned(tuck,X)).
the(X,king(X),the(Y,friar(Y),knighted(X,Y))).
```

and the relevant background knowledge is that Henry III is a king, Tuck is a friar, and Robin Hood is neither one.

The output from `resolve_anaphors` should contain the following formulas (in a list, of course):

```
knighted(henry_iii,robin_hood).
petitioned(tuck,henry_iii).
knighted(henry_iii,tuck).
```

### 7.5.4  Plurals

The correct semantics for natural-language plurals is still a matter of debate. Webber (1983) points out that in *Three boys bought five roses,* each plural NP has three readings:

- DISTRIBUTIVE (there were 3 boys and each bought 5 roses);
- COLLECTIVE (the 3 boys, as a group, bought a group of 5 roses);
- CONJUNCTIVE (a total of 3 boys bought roses, and a total of 5 roses were bought).

The distributive reading is what our quantifier rules already give us, and the conjunctive reading could be derived from it by a transformation not unlike quantifier raising.

The collective reading is the interesting one because it introduces a new concept: SETS or COLLECTIVES. The key idea is that at least on the collective reading of

*Three men sang.*

and possibly on all three readings, the set of three men is itself a discourse referent, with several attributes:

- ELEMENTS (although in this sentence they are not identified);
- CARDINALITY (the number of elements, in this case 3); and
- DISTRIBUTED PROPERTIES, i.e., properties that all the elements share (in this case $(\lambda x)man(x)$).

Figure 7.4 shows a strategy for representing collectives in a knowledge base. Note that collectives can be denoted by conjoined singulars (such as *Curly, Larry, and Moe*) as well as by plurals.

**Exercise 7.5.4.1**

Give formulas for the distributive and conjunctive readings of *Three boys bought five roses.*

**Exercise 7.5.4.2**

Consider the knowledge base:

```
collective(x(4)).
element(x(4),curly).
element(x(4),larry).
distprop(x(4),X^man(X)).
```

*Curly, Larry, and Moe sang (together).*

```
collective(x(1)).
element(x(1),curly).
element(x(1),larry).
element(x(1),moe).
cardinality(x(1),3).
sang(x(1)).
```

---

*Three men sang (together).*

```
collective(x(2)).
distprop(x(2),X^man(X)).
cardinality(x(2),3).
sang(x(2)).
```

---

*Some cats howled (together).*

```
collective(x(3)).
distprop(x(3),X^cat(X)).
howled(x(3)).
```

**Figure 7.4**   Representation of collectives in a knowledge base.

This implies that Curly is a man, but the query '?- man(curly).' does not succeed from it.

Define a predicate prove/1 that attempts to satisfy any query, not only by executing it in Prolog in the usual way, but also by making inferences from distprop and element. Your code should have the form

```
prove(Goal) :- call(Goal).
prove(Goal) :- ...something else...
```

and the query '?- prove(man(curly)).' should succeed using the knowledge base above.

**Exercise 7.5.4.3**

The middle knowledge base in Figure 7.4 asserts that the *group* of three men sang. What would it mean if instead of `sang(x(2))` it said `distprop(x(2),X^sang(X))`? Using this as a hint, how could you represent the distributive reading of *Three million men sang* without using three million discourse markers?

## 7.5.5 Mass Nouns

If plurals are a puzzle, mass nouns such as *water* or *gold* are an even bigger puzzle. In sentences like

*Gold is an element.*

*This ring is made of gold.*

it makes sense to treat *gold* like a proper name: there is only one substance called *gold* in the entire universe, and these sentences make assertions about it (cf. Chierchia 1982). So they can be rendered in a knowledge base as something like this:

```
element(gold).
made_of(x(5),gold).    % x(5) is discourse marker for the ring
```

But in other instances a mass noun denotes a PORTION of a substance (Parsons 1970). A portion is somewhat like a collective except that it has no elements and no cardinality. Instead it has a QUANTITY, which maps onto real numbers using standard units. Such an interpretation is necessary in order to represent sentences such as:

*There is an ounce of water in the glass.*

```
portion(x(1)).
distprop(x(1),X^water(X)).     % x(1) is a portion of water ...
quantity(x(1),29.6,mL).        % comprising 29.6 milliliters ...
in(x(1),x(2)).                 % and is in x(2), the glass.
```

Often, only relations between quantities are known, not actual values:

*There is more water in the glass than in the cup.*

Finally, note that mass nouns can often be CONVERTED (changed without alteration of form) into count nouns denoting kinds of the original substance: *the wines of California, the heavy metals.*

The semantics of mass nouns is an area of ongoing research. Ojeda (1991) and the papers in Pelletier (1979) describe a number of current approaches.

**Exercise 7.5.5.1**

Identify the underlined noun in each of the following examples as either a count noun, a mass noun denoting a substance, or a mass noun denoting a portion of a substance. (Hint: Count nouns distinguish singular from plural; mass nouns do not. Further, it makes sense to ask "how much?" when the mass noun denotes a portion but not when it denotes a substance.)

> *Every cat eats meat.*
> *We got some cat food at the store.*
> *The cat food was mainly made of tuna.*

**Exercise 7.5.5.2**

> How might you express *John has more money than Jack does* in Prolog, sticking as close as possible to the formalism used in this section?

## 7.6 NEGATION

### 7.6.1 Negative Knowledge

So far we have said nothing about how to represent negative statements such as

> *Fido does not bark.*

We're handicapped by the fact that Prolog itself has no way to encode negative knowledge. Extensions of Prolog that do so have been developed but are beyond the scope of this book.[9] One approach is to proceed as follows:

- Store negative facts in the knowledge base explicitly: `neg(barks(fido))`.
- Define a procedure that creates the COMPLEMENT of each query by adding `neg` if `neg` is absent, or removing it if it is present.
- Answer each query by trying to prove both the query itself, and its complement. This gives any of four results: *yes, no, don't know* (neither the query nor its complement succeeds), or *contradiction* (both the query and its complement succeed).

In a database-querying situation we can get by with something much simpler: NEGATION AS FAILURE, the approach used by Prolog itself. We can assume that a query is false if it cannot be proved true. This is sufficient to answer queries such as:

> *Is there a dog that does not bark?*

```
?- dog(X), \+ barks(X).
```

and is the approach that will be used here.

**Exercise 7.6.1.1**

> Assume that you are using an extension of Prolog with explicit negation as described above.
>     (a) What is the complement of `barks(fido)`? Of `neg(barks(fido))`?
>     (b) Given the knowledge base

---

[9]See Nute (1988); Covington, Nute, and Vellino (1988, ch. 11); Naish (1986); Pearce and Wagner (1991).

```
barks(fido).
howls(felix).
neg(howls(leo)).
neg(howls(felix)).
```

what answer ('yes,' 'no,', 'contradiction,' or 'don't know') should you get to each of the following queries?

```
?- barks(fido).
?- howls(fido).
?- howls(leo).
?- howls(felix).
```

### Exercise 7.6.1.2   (project)

Implement an extension of Prolog with explicit negation.

### Exercise 7.6.1.3

Why is contradiction impossible in ordinary Prolog?

## 7.6.2 Negation as a Quantifier

Consider now the sentence:

*No dog barks.*

Here *no* is a quantifier, and we can render this sentence into logic as:

```
no(X,dog(X),barks(X))
```

('there is no X which is a dog and barks').

More formally, `no(Var,Scope,Res)` is true if and only if there is no value of `Var` that satisfies `Scope` and `Res`. In Prolog:

```
no(_,Scope,Res) :- \+ (Scope,Res).
```

To get the truth value we do not need to identify `Var`, nor to distinguish scope from restrictor. We do these things only so that, during the structure-building process, *no* can be handled like the other quantifiers.

Negation of the main verb (with *not* or *does not*) works like *no* except that it has the whole sentence within its scope, thus:

*Max does not bark.*

```
no(_,true,barks(max))
```

Here `true` is the Prolog built-in predicate that always succeeds; we use it to express an "empty" restrictor with no content.

As expected, *no* participates in scope ambiguities. An example:

*All dogs do not bark.*

(1)   `all(X,dog(X),no(_,true,barks(X)))`
      All dogs are non-barkers.

(2)   `no(_,true,all(X,dog(X),barks(X)))`
      Not all dogs bark.

Ambiguities like these sometimes confuse native speakers, and some people are uneasy with any quantifier raising that involves negation.

**Exercise 7.6.2.1**

What does *All that glitters is not gold* normally mean? Could it be interpreted as meaning something else? Explain why it is ambiguous.

**Exercise 7.6.2.2**

Extend your parser from Exercises 7.4.1.1, 7.4.3.1, and 7.4.3.2 so that it can answer questions of the form:

> *Is it true that no dog barks?*
> *Is it true that every cat chased no dog?*
> *Is it true that no dog chased every cat?*

Here you can treat *is it true that* as a prefix that turns any statement into a question.

**Exercise 7.6.2.3**

Does *Doesn't Fido bark?* mean the same thing as *Is it true that Fido does not bark?* If not, what does it mean, and what is the function of the negative marker (*n't*)?

## 7.6.3 Some Logical Equivalences

Negation gives us many ways to create formulas that are logically equivalent to each other. The most obvious is DOUBLE NEGATION:

`no(_,true,no(_,true,S))` $\equiv$ S

where S is any formula. There are also interactions of negation with quantifiers:

`some(V,R,no(_,true,S))`   $\equiv$   `no(_,true,all(V,R,S))`
*Some dogs do not bark*                *Not all dogs bark*

```
all(V,R,no(_,true,S))  ≡  no(_,true,some(V,R,S))
```
*All dogs do not bark*                  *It is not true that some dogs bark*
*(All dogs are non-barkers)*            *(No dogs bark)*

and perhaps most importantly of all,

```
no(_,true,some(V,R,S)) ≡ no(V,R,S)
```

Notice that this is not quantifier raising; no ambiguities or changes of meaning are involved. The formulas that we are interconverting have exactly the same truth conditions.

As long as negation occurs only in database queries, these alternative forms are not a practical problem; the inference engine will get the right answers with any of them. But if we want to store negative information in the knowledge base, it is important to convert each formula into a standard form so that the same information will always be expressed the same way.

What to use for a standard form is up to the implementor. One could choose to move all negatives to the outermost, or perhaps the innermost, possible position. Another possibility is to eliminate a quantifier: any system that has `no` and `all` can do without `some`, or if it has `no` and `some` it can do without `all`.

### Exercise 7.6.3.1

Simplify the formula

```
no(_,true,some(X,dog(X),no(_,true,bark(X))))
```

to the simplest logically equivalent form. (To avoid bumping into a discrepancy between our definition of `all` and the standard one, assume that there is at least one dog in the knowledge base.)

### Exercise 7.6.3.2

Define a predicate `simplify/2` that will do the previous exercise for you. That is, define a predicate that will "simplify" a formula containing negation, as follows:

- Transform double negation, `no(_,true,no(_,true,S))`, into S.
- If `no` occurs in the scope of another quantifier, move it out and change the quantifier, so that:
  `some(V,R,no(_,true,S))` becomes `no(_,true,all(V,R,S))` and
  `all(V,R,no(_,true,S))` becomes `no(_,true,some(V,R,S))`;
- Do both of these things recursively; that is, before simplifying any formula, attempt to simplify its scope.

### Exercise 7.6.3.3

Explain why a system that has `no` and `all` does not need `some`.

## 7.7 FURTHER READING

Of the many available introductions to first-order logic, that of Barwise and Etchemendy (1991) meshes especially well with the material covered in this chapter. It covers topics such as Skolemization that are left out of more traditional texts. McCawley (1981) is also useful because of its length (Its explanations are fuller than usual) and because of its emphasis on natural language semantics.

Aside from logic texts, books on semantics are of two kinds: some cover mainly word meanings (Palmer 1981) while others treat syntactic and logical issues. A good introduction of the latter type is Chierchia and McConnell-Ginet (1990).

A good example of semantic analysis in action is Horn (1989), a comprehensive but readable study of negation that treats many other phenomena along the way. Dowty (1979) gives insightful analyses of a wide range of phenomena, many of which can easily be adapted into frameworks other than Dowty's.

For an introduction to model theory, see Bach (1989). The classic paper on generalized quantifiers is Barwise and Cooper (1981), but Peres' account (1991) is shorter and more accessible to the beginner.

# CHAPTER 8

# Further Topics in Semantics

## 8.1 BEYOND MODEL THEORY

There is much more to natural-language understanding than just translating English into logical formulas. Unfortunately, the area beyond simple model theory is a realm of fundamental mysteries and unsolved problems. Here computational linguistics becomes inseparably bound up with knowledge representation and the general question of how people think.

This chapter will briefly sketch three major topics that lie in this realm: language translation, word-sense disambiguation, and understanding of events. Coverage will be far from complete; parts of this chapter will have the atmosphere of a whirlwind tour. I shall refrain from going deeply into knowledge representation, since doing so would require another book at least as long as the present one.

## 8.2 LANGUAGE TRANSLATION

### 8.2.1 Background

Attempts at computer translation of human languages are as old as computers themselves (Buchmann 1987). Practical techniques were foreseen by Trojanskij in 1933, and a word-by-word French-to-Spanish translation program was implemented by Booth and Ritchens in 1948. By 1955 "machine translation" (MT) was an up-and-coming technology heavily supported by the U.S. Government. In 1966, however, a National Academy of Sciences committee declared MT to be impractical and most support for research was withdrawn.

The committee's mistake was to expect instant results. In the 1950s and 1960s, many mathematical and clerical activities—banking, engineering calculations, and the like—had been computerized almost overnight. The committee failed to realize that MT was not simply a matter of applying computers to a mechanical procedure already well understood. Nobody really knows how human translators do their work; they certainly don't just look up words in a dictionary and write down the equivalents in another language, which is what some of the earliest MT programs tried to do.

There has been a resurgence in MT since 1980, spurred by cheap computer power and advances in computational linguistics. One of the most successful projects is TAUM-METEO, which translates Canadian weather reports from English into French (Thouin 1982).

### 8.2.2 A Simple Technique

The essential steps in language translation are ANALYSIS of the input, TRANSFER (restructuring), and GENERATION of the output. Since the earliest days of MT, there have been two rival approaches: to map one language onto another directly, or to translate the input into an INTERLINGUA (intermediate language) which can then be translated into the output language.

In what follows we will develop a translator that uses logical formulas as an interlingua. We will take advantage of the fact that semantic analyzers written in Prolog can be made REVERSIBLE, i.e., the same program can not only translate English into formulas, but also translate formulas back into English (or whatever language the parser handles). Then, to translate a sentence, one simply analyzes it in one language and re-generates it in the other.

For example, the semantic analyzer from Section 7.3.4, reproduced in Figure 8.1, is reversible:

```
?- s(What,[every,dog,barked],[]).
What = all(X,dog(X),barked(X))

?- s(all(X,dog(X),barked(X)),What,[]).
What = [every,dog,barked]
```

So in order to translate languages, all we have to do is build the semantic structure using a grammar for one language, and then turn the semantics back into a sentence using a grammar for the other language. What could be simpler?

**Exercise 8.2.2.1**

Get the program in Figure 8.1 working (again) and verify that it is reversible. Use it to translate

```
all(X,dog(X),all(Y,cat(Y),saw(X,Y)))
```

into an English sentence.

```
% Semantics of sentences with quantifiers on NPs.

s(Sem) --> np((X^Sco)^Sem), vp(X^Sco).

np(Sem) --> d((X^Res)^Sem), n(X^Res).

vp(Sem) --> v(Sem).
vp(X^Pred) --> v(Y^X^Sco), np((Y^Sco)^Pred).

d((X^Res)^(X^Sco)^all(X,Res,Sco))  --> [every].
d((X^Res)^(X^Sco)^some(X,Res,Sco)) --> [a];[some].

n(X^dog(X)) --> [dog].
n(X^cat(X)) --> [cat].

v(X^meowed(X))      --> [meowed].
v(Y^X^chased(X,Y)) --> [chased].
v(Y^X^saw(X,Y))     --> [saw].
```

**Figure 8.1**   Reversible semantic analyzer.

**Exercise 8.2.2.2   (for discussion)**

Under what conditions does a Prolog program fail to be reversible? That is, how can you recognize a non-reversible program? Discuss.

### 8.2.3 Some Latin Grammar

In what follows we will turn the semantic analyzer into an English-to-Latin translation program.[1] (We choose Latin rather than French, Spanish, or German because Latin grammar is quite a bit different from English, so that translating word by word is impossible.) To begin with, we need a DCG parser for Latin, shown in Figure 8.2. So that this can be merged with an English parser without conflict, all the node labels have been prefixed with x, so that instead of s, np, vp, we call the Latin nodes xs, xnp, xvp, and so on.

Table 8.1 shows some English sentences with their Latin equivalents. Looking both at the grammar and at the table, note that:

- Latin word order is different from English: the verb comes at the end of the sentence, and one kind of determiner (here called xd2) follows rather than precedes its noun.
- Case is marked on all nouns; 'cat' is *felis* in subject position but *felem* in object position (and likewise 'dog' is *canis* or *canem* respectively).
- Determiners agree with nouns in case (*omnis felis* versus *omnem felem*).

---

[1] I am indebted to R. A. O'Keefe for suggesting an exercise of this type; he is absolved of all responsibility for what is actually presented here.

```
xs --> xnp(_,nom), xvp.

xvp --> xv.
xvp --> xnp(_,acc), xv.

xnp(Gender,Case) --> xd(Gender,Case), xn(Gender,Case).
xnp(Gender,Case) --> xn(Gender,Case), xd2(Gender,Case).

xd(_,_)   --> [].
xd(_,nom) --> [omnis].
xd(_,acc) --> [omnem].

xd2(masc,nom) --> [quidam].
xd2(masc,acc) --> [quendam].
xd2(fem,nom)  --> [quaedam].
xd2(fem,acc)  --> [quandam].

xn(masc,nom)  --> [canis].
xn(masc,acc)  --> [canem].
xn(fem,nom)   --> [felis].
xn(fem,acc)   --> [felem].

xv --> [ululavit];[vidit];[agitavit].
```

**Figure 8.2**   A parser for a few Latin sentences.

**TABLE 8.1**   SOME LATIN SENTENCES AND THEIR ENGLISH EQUIVALENTS.

| | |
|---|---|
| *Felis ululavit.* | A cat meowed. (= Some cat meowed.) |
| *Felis quaedam ululavit.* | A cat meowed. (= Some cat meowed.) |
| *Omnis felis ululavit.* | Every cat meowed. |
| | |
| *Canis felem agitavit.* | A dog chased a cat. |
| *Canis quidam felem agitavit.* | A dog chased a cat. |
| *Canis quidam felem quandam agitavit.* | A dog chased a cat. |
| | |
| *Felis canem vidit.* | A cat saw a dog. |
| *Felis quaedam canem vidit.* | A cat saw a dog. |
| *Felis quaedam canem quendam vidit.* | A cat saw a dog. |
| | |
| *Omnis felis canem quendam agitavit.* | Every cat chased some dog. |
| *Omnis canis omnem felem agitavit.* | Every dog chased every cat. |

- Latin has arbitrary gender: *felis* 'cat' is normally feminine (unless you're specifically talking about a male cat) and *canis* 'dog' is normally masculine.
- Some determiners are marked for gender as well as case: we get *felis quaedam* (feminine) but *canis quidam* (masculine).
- There is a null determiner, and it means 'some'.

Purists will note that many details of Latin grammar are being glossed over; the word order is actually variable, the null determiner can also mean 'the', and there are several more ways of saying 'some'. But we have enough Latin grammar here to make a start.

**Exercise 8.2.3.1**

Get this parser working and verify that it parses all the Latin sentences in Table 8.1.

**Exercise 8.2.3.2**

By hand, translate into English:

> *Felis canem agitavit.*
> *Felis omnem canem vidit.*
> *Canis quidam ululavit.*

## 8.2.4  A Working Translator

Figure 8.3 shows the Latin parser with arguments added to make it build semantic representations just like those used by the English parser. This parser is reversible, like the English one:

```
?- xs(Sem,[felis,ululavit],[]).
Sem = some(X,cat(X),meowed(X))

?- xs(some(X,cat(X),meowed(X),What,[]).
What = [felis,ululavit]
```

There is some nondeterminism, because the Latin parser has two ways to say 'some' (the appropriate form of *quidam* or the null determiner); similarly, there is nondeterminism on the English side because *some* and *a* are treated as equivalent.

To translate a sentence, all we need to do is run it through one parser forward and then the other parser backward:

```
english_latin(E,L) :- s(Sem,E,[]), xs(Sem,L,[]).
```

For example:

```
?- english_latin([a,cat,meowed],What).
What = [felis,ululavit]
```

**Exercise 8.2.4.1**

Get the translation program working and use it to translate the sentences in Table 8.1.

**Exercise 8.2.4.2**

Will `english_latin/2` also translate Latin into English? If so, is it more efficient in one direction than in the other? Explain.

```
xs(Sem) --> xnp(_,nom,(X^Sco)^Sem), xvp(X^Sco).

xvp(Sem) --> xv(Sem).
xvp(X^Pred) --> xnp(_,acc,(Y^Sco)^Pred), xv(Y^X^Sco).

xnp(Gender,Case,Sem) -->
xd(Gender,Case,(X^Res)^Sem), xn(Gender,Case,X^Res).
xnp(Gender,Case,Sem) -->
xn(Gender,Case,X^Res),xd2(Gender,Case,(X^Res)^Sem).

xd(_,_,(X^Res)^(X^Sco)^some(X,Res,Sco))  --> [].
xd(_,nom,(X^Res)^(X^Sco)^all(X,Res,Sco)) --> [omnis].
xd(_,acc,(X^Res)^(X^Sco)^all(X,Res,Sco)) --> [omnem].

xd2(masc,nom,(X^Res)^(X^Sco)^some(X,Res,Sco)) --> [quidam].
xd2(masc,acc,(X^Res)^(X^Sco)^some(X,Res,Sco)) --> [quendam].
xd2(fem,nom,(X^Res)^(X^Sco)^some(X,Res,Sco))  --> [quaedam].
xd2(fem,acc,(X^Res)^(X^Sco)^some(X,Res,Sco))  --> [quandam].

xn(masc,nom,X^dog(X))  --> [canis].
xn(masc,acc,X^dog(X))  --> [canem].
xn(fem,nom,X^cat(X))   --> [felis].
xn(fem,acc,X^cat(X))   --> [felem].

xv(X^meowed(X))      --> [ululavit].
xv(Y^X^chased(X,Y))  --> [agitavit].
xv(Y^X^saw(X,Y))     --> [vidit].
```

**Figure 8.3**   Reversible semantic analyzer for Latin.

**Exercise 8.2.4.3   (small project)**

Implement your own translation program that will translate a comparable set of sentences from English into some other language.

## 8.2.5 Why Translation Is Hard

Translation by reversible unification-based grammar is an up-and-coming technology. The general idea is to analyze a sentence into a feature structure (which can be more than just a semantic representation), manipulate the feature structure as appropriate to suit the target language, and then use it to generate a sentence. Estival (1990a,b) reports some research in this area. Of course many older techniques are also still being pursued.

But there is much more to translation that just the mapping of one grammar onto another. There are several main challenges:

- *Words do not have exact equivalents in different languages.* The common Spanish word *simpático* 'friendly, easy to get along with' has no exact English translation;

it takes a while even to explain the concept in English. Many English words such as *picturesque* lack equivalents in other languages.

- *Even in a single language, the same word means different things in different contexts.* This is the problem of WORD SENSE DISAMBIGUATION; more about it in the next section.

- *Different languages require different amounts of information to be expressed.* In Spanish, *llegó* means either 'he arrived' or 'she arrived', but in order to translate it into English, you have to choose *he* or *she* on the basis of context and background knowledge. Again, French, Spanish, and German distinguish 'familiar' and 'polite' forms of the word *you*; English has only one form. Japanese has 'polite' markers for nouns as well (which bad translations sometimes render as 'honorable'). A translator translating from English into one of these languages must guess where the 'polite' forms should go, based on background knowledge and knowledge of the culture.

This seems to paint a very gloomy picture of the prospects of MT. But in fact there are situations in which MT works well. For example, MT is quite practical if the languages are closely related (such as Norwegian and Swedish), so that substantial differences of culture or world-view are rare. MT also works well if the subject matter is restricted (e.g., Canadian weather reports, or certain kinds of business documents).

Finally, MT works well if imperfect translations are tolerable. Computers don't produce *good* translations, but they can grind out *rough* translations cheaply and quickly. These can be polished by a human translator, or used in their rough form by someone who needs only the gist of the text, not all the details.

**Exercise 8.2.5.1**

Using a foreign language familiar to you, give an example of:

- a word that has no exact equivalent in English;
- a simple instance in which the foreign language and English convey different amounts of information while saying essentially the same thing (like Spanish *llegó* versus English *he arrived*).

## 8.3  WORD-SENSE DISAMBIGUATION

### 8.3.1  The Problem

So far we have blithely assumed that each word has exactly one meaning. This assumption holds only in the simplest database-querying applications. In the English vocabulary as a whole, ambiguity runs rampant. The *Concise Oxford Dictionary* lists 54 senses of *run*, 38 senses of *go*, and even three senses of the seemingly unambiguous word *bachelor*. Ambiguities are of three main types:

- HOMONYMY, in which two senses have no relationship that an ordinary speaker can recognize, so that they are in effect two words that sound alike.
  Example: the *bark* of a tree versus the *bark* of a dog.

- POLYSEMY, in which the senses of a word are distinct but connected in the speaker's mind, often by metaphor. There is great variation as to what relationships a particular speaker will recognize.
  Example: the *kernel* of a nut versus the *kernel* of an operating system.

- ARGUMENT AMBIGUITY or THETA-ROLE AMBIGUITY, in which two senses denote essentially the same thing, but with a different mapping from syntax to semantic arguments.
  Example: *Mary is cooking* (subject = agent) versus *The potatoes are cooking* (subject = theme).

The amazing thing about ambiguity is that people hardly notice it. Research suggests that the human mind resolves ambiguities by working on at least three levels:

- CONTEXTS or SPECIALIZED VOCABULARIES. Many word senses belong to specific domains of discourse. For example, *bark* means one thing when you're talking about dogs and another when you're talking about trees.

- SELECTIONAL RESTRICTIONS, i.e., restrictions on the semantic arguments of a word. For example, *arrest* has different meanings depending on whether its object is a person or a physical change (*arrest the burglar* vs. *arrest the decay*). Selectional restrictions are particularly helpful with argument ambiguities, where context is little help.

- INFERENCE FROM REAL-WORLD KNOWLEDGE. For example, Hirst (1987:80) points out that in order to disambiguate *head* in the sentence

  *Nadia swung the hammer at the nail and the head flew off*

  we have to think about how hammers work, because not only does the hammer have a head, but so do the nail and Nadia.

The problem, of course, is that it's hard to draw a line between selectional restrictions and real-world knowledge; further, there's no limit to the amount of real-world knowledge or inference that may be required. Imagine, for instance, a detective novel that begins with the words *The house blew it,* found on a piece of paper at the scene of the crime, and in which the whole story is devoted to figuring out what those words mean (Weizenbaum 1976:187).

### 8.3.2 Disambiguation by Activating Contexts

In this section we can do no more than sketch one approach to disambiguation—an approach that is admittedly inadequate, but suffices to give you a taste of the problem. Consider the sentences:

*There are pigs in the pen.*    (*pen* = enclosure*)*

*There is ink in the pen.*    (*pen* = writing instrument*)*

The two senses of *pen* are distinguished by the prior context: *pigs,* which calls up the context of farming, or *ink,* which calls up the context of writing. That is, *pigs* and *ink* serve as CUES for the appropriate contexts. From the sentences

*The pen is full of pigs.*

*The pen is full of ink.*

we see that the cues need not precede the ambiguous words. These facts suggest a disambiguation algorithm:

- Keep a list of CONTEXTS (specialized vocabularies) that are in use.
- Scan the sentence for words that serve as cues, and activate the appropriate context for each.
- Then scan the sentence again, replacing each ambiguous word by a representation of its meaning in the currently active context(s).

For simplicity, we'll completely ignore parsing and semantic analysis; we'll view the sentence as a simple string of words. Naturally, a more satisfactory disambiguator would take morphology, syntax, and semantics into account.

First we need a table of cues, and also a table of ambiguous words indicating what they mean in each context:

```
% cue(?Word,?Context)
%   Word is a cue for Context

cue(farmer,     farm).
cue(pigs,       farm).
cue(ink,        writing).
cue(airport,    aircraft).
cue(carpenter,  woodworking).


% mic(?Word,?Meaning,?Context)
%   Word has specified Meaning in Context

mic(pen,       pen_for_animals,   farm).
mic(pen,       writing_pen,       writing).
mic(plane,     plane_tool,        woodworking).
mic(plane,     airplane,          aircraft).
mic(terminal,  airport_terminal,  aircraft).
mic(terminal,  computer_terminal, computer).
```

Here `mic` stands for *meaning in context*. The "meanings" such as `pen_for_animals` are merely symbols that stand for the various senses of a word.

Next we need a procedure to go through the sentence and activate all the contexts for which there are cues:

```
% collect_cues(+Words,+Contexts,-NewContexts)
%   scans Words looking for cues, and adding appropriate
%   contexts to Contexts giving NewContexts.

collect_cues([],Contexts,Contexts).

collect_cues([W|Words],Contexts,NewContexts) :-
  cue(W,C),
  \+ member(C,Contexts),
  !,
  collect_cues(Words,[C|Contexts],NewContexts).

collect_cues([_|Words],Contexts,NewContexts) :-
  collect_cues(Words,Contexts,NewContexts).
```

The first clause is for the end of the list; the second is for activating a new context; and the third clause deals with words that are not cues, and cues for contexts already active. Here's an example of what it does:

```
?- collect_cues([the,carpenter,put,the,pigs,in,the,pen],[],What).
What = [woodworking,farm]
```

Here the initial argument `[]` is a list of contexts *already* active, if any; it allows contexts to be carried along from sentence to sentence.

Once `collect_cues` has done its work, the next step is to go through the sentence again, disambiguating each ambiguous word by looking up its meaning in the active context or contexts:[2]

```
% disambiguate_words(+Words,-DWords,+Contexts)
%   goes through Words using Contexts to disambiguate them.

disambiguate_words([],[],_).

disambiguate_words([W|Words],[D|DWords],Contexts) :-
  mic(W,D,C),      % W is ambiguous and means D in context C
  member(C,Contexts),
  disambiguate_words(Words,DWords,Contexts).

disambiguate_words([W|Words],[W|DWords],Contexts) :-
```

---

[2]Recall that **member** is not built in, but is defined in Appendix A.

```
\+ mic(W,_,_),  % W is not listed as ambiguous
disambiguate_words(Words,DWords,Contexts).
```

Here again we have three clauses: one for the end of the list, one for an ambiguous word that can be disambiguated in an active context, and one for words that are not ambiguous. The main procedure, then, looks like this,

```
disambiguate(Words,DWords,Contexts) :-
  collect_cues(Words,[],Contexts),
  disambiguate_words(Words,DWords,Contexts).
```

and an example of a query is:

```
?- disambiguate([there,are,pigs,in,the,pen],DWords,Contexts).
DWords = [there,are,pigs,in,the,pen_for_animals]
Contexts = [farm]
```

**Exercise 8.3.2.1**

Get the disambiguation program working and use it to disambiguate the following sentences:

> *There are pigs in the pen.*
> *There is ink in the pen.*
> *The pen is full of pigs.*
> *The pen is full of ink.*
> *The carpenter built a pen for the pigs.*
> *The carpenter used a plane.*
> *The plane is at the airport.*
> *The carpenter found a pig at the airport.*

In which sentences does more than one context get activated?

**Exercise 8.3.2.2**

What does the program in this section do with each of the following sentences? Why?

> *The carpenter found a plane at the airport.*
> *The plane is at the terminal.*

**Exercise 8.3.2.3**

Extend the disambiguation program to disambiguate *star* in the following sentences:

> *The astronomer photographed the star.*
> *The film publicist photographed the star.*
> *The star of the show was a previously unheard-of actress.*

*What does this program do with* The astronomer married the star *and with* The astronomer made a film about the star*? Are these sentences unambiguous to human listeners?*

### 8.3.3 Finding the Best Compromise

The algorithm developed so far assumes that cues are sharply distinct from the words that need to be disambiguated. But this distinction does not hold up, because ambiguous words can serve as cues for each other. Consider the sentence:

*The plane is at the terminal.*

Without further context, most people interpret this as 'The airplane is at the airport terminal' even though *plane* and *terminal* are both ambiguous.

The reason that particular interpretation is preferred is that it activates only one specialized context, not two. Consider the possibilities:

| Interpretation | Context list |
|---|---|
| 'The aircraft is at the airport terminal' | `[aircraft]` |
| 'The aircraft is at the computer terminal' | `[aircraft,computers]` |
| 'The woodworking tool is at the airport terminal' | `[woodworking,aircraft]` |
| 'The woodworking tool is at the computer terminal' | `[woodworking,computers]` |

Generally, the reading with the fewest active contexts is preferred.

Looking at disambiguation this way, a cue is a word that activates one context; an ambiguous word is a word that activates any of several contexts depending on which sense is chosen. This suggests a different disambiguation algorithm:

- Find all possible ways of disambiguating the sentence, activating the appropriate contexts with each one.
- Choose the reading that has the fewest contexts active.

Finding *one* way of disambiguating the sentence is easy. First we list all the cues and ambiguous words in a single "meaning-in-context" (`mic`) table:

```
%    WORD       MEANING          CONTEXT
mic(farmer,    farmer,          farm).
mic(pigs,      pigs,            farm).
mic(ink,       ink,             writing).
mic(airport,   airport,         aircraft).
mic(carpenter, carpenter,       woodworking).
mic(pen,       pen_for_animals, farm).
mic(pen,       writing_pen,     writing).
mic(plane,     plane_tool,      woodworking).
```

```
mic(plane,     airplane,            aircraft).
mic(terminal,  airport_terminal,    aircraft).
mic(terminal,  computer_terminal,   computer).
```

The ambiguous words have multiple entries here; the cues have only one entry each.

Then we work through the sentence, and upon encountering a word that is in the `mic` table, choose a sense for it and add the appropriate context to the context list if it is not already there. Here's the procedure that does all this:

```
% dis1(Words,DWords,Contexts,NewContexts)
%  Find 1 disambiguated reading of Words, placing it in DWords,
%  adding newly activated contexts to Contexts giving NewContexts.

dis1([],[],Contexts,Contexts).   % end of list

dis1([W|Words],[D|DWords],Contexts,NewContexts) :-
  mic(W,D,C),
  member(C,Contexts),    % W means D in a context already active
  dis1(Words,DWords,Contexts,NewContexts).

dis1([W|Words],[D|DWords],Contexts,NewContexts) :-
  mic(W,D,C),
  \+ member(C,Contexts),  % W means D by activating a new context
  dis1(Words,DWords,[C|Contexts],NewContexts).

dis1([W|Words],[W|DWords],Contexts,NewContexts) :-
  \+ mic(W,_,_),          % W is not ambiguous
  dis1(Words,DWords,Contexts,NewContexts).
```

Now the challenge is to compare *all* the potential disambiguations and select the one with the fewest contexts active. Here we take advantage of a very high-level feature of Prolog, the built-in predicate `setof`.

Recall that `setof` finds all the solutions to a query and places them in a list in alphabetical order. Thus if Kermit and Gonzo are animals, `setof` works like this:

```
?- setof(X,animal(X),L).
L = [gonzo,kermit]
```

To be precise, `?- setof(X,Goal,List)` makes a sorted list of instantiations of `X` corresponding to solutions to `Goal`. Here `X` need not be a variable; it can be a structure that has one or more variables in common with `Goal`. For example:

```
?- setof(f(X),animal(X),L).
L = [f(gonzo),f(kermit)]
```

Further, the "alphabetical" order of the solutions is more than just alphabetical; it includes the ability to compare numbers and other types of terms. When structures have the same functor, they are "alphabetized" by arguments, first argument first, so that for example `f(9,z)` comes out before `f(10,a)`.[3]

To get `setof` to put the disambiguations with the fewest contexts at the beginning of the list, we will represent each disambiguation as a structure of the form

```
reading(1,[there,are,pigs,in,the,pen_for_animals],[farm])
```

where the first argument is the number of contexts. The whole main procedure of the program, then, is:

```
disambiguate(Words,Readings) :-
    setof(reading(N,Contexts,DWords),
          (dis1(Words,DWords,[],Contexts),length(Contexts,N)),
          Readings).
```

Note that the middle argument of `setof` is a compound goal. The output of `disambiguate/2` looks like this:

```
?- disambiguate([the,plane,is,at,the,terminal],What).
What =
[reading(1,[aircraft],[the,airplane,is,at,the,airport_terminal]),
 reading(2,[aircraft,woodworking],[the,plane_tool,is,at,the,airport_terminal])
 reading(2,[computer,aircraft],[the,airplane,is,at,the,computer_terminal]),
 reading(2,[computer,woodworking],[the,plane_tool,is,at,the,computer_terminal]
```

### Exercise 8.3.3.1

Get this disambiguation program working and use it to disambiguate all the sentences in Exercise 8.3.2.1, as well as *The plane is at the terminal.*

### Exercise 8.3.3.2

What does this program do with *The carpenter found a plane at the airport?*

### Exercise 8.3.3.3

Extend this disambiguation program to handle *star* in:

> *The astronomer photographed the star.*
> *The film publicist photographed the star.*

What does the program do with *The astronomer made a film about the star?* Is this a reasonable thing to do? Explain.

---

[3]The way in which `setof` compares terms is not standardized, and some Prologs may behave differently than described here.

### 8.3.4 Spreading Activation

Our programs so far make an unjustified assumption about contexts. They assume that the vocabulary is divided up into a set of discrete sub-vocabularies which we have labeled `farm`, `aircraft` and the like. This assumption does not stand up under examination. Why is `farm` a context while `pig` is not? Why does *pig* activate the context `farm` and not `animal`? It turns out that there is no good reason to divide words up into the particular contexts that we did, except that it happened to work well with our example sentences.

Instead, we need to look at relationships between the concepts that words stand for. Figure 8.4 shows a number of concepts arranged in a SEMANTIC NET. The net shows several relationships, of which 'is a' is the most important: a farmer *is a* person, a pig *is a* domesticated animal, and so on. Other important relations are *contains* and *uses*.

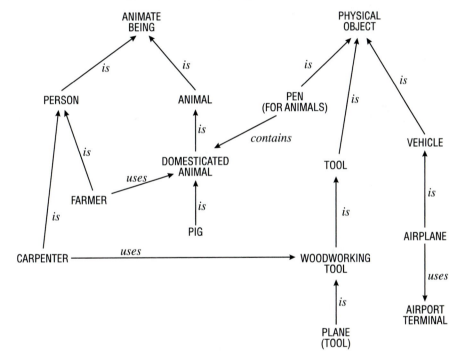

**Figure 8.4**    A semantic network.

Every meaning of every word is a node in the net. The "context" for a meaning consists of the other nodes that are near it. The reason *pig* and *farmer* seem to belong to the same context is that they are connected by a short path through the net. Neither of them is connected very closely to *airplane,* which is why *airplane* does not seem to belong to the same context.

Semantic networks were introduced by Quillian (1967) for the purpose of disambiguating words. The key idea is that to activate a context, one activates not only the particular word sense involved, but also the other senses that are close to it in the network. That is, activation SPREADS from one node to another. The most likely reading of an ambiguous sentence is the one that activates the smallest portion of the network (thereby sticking to a relatively well-defined context).

To keep from activating the entire network at once, there have to be limits on how activation spreads: typically it can only spread along the arrows (so that *pig* activates *animal* but not vice versa) and/or can only spread a limited number of steps.

Semantic nets with spreading activation are not a complete solution to the disambiguation problem, but they are a good start. Selectional restrictions and real-world knowledge also have to be taken into account. Still, there is good evidence that semantic nets model a portion of what the brain actually does when processing language, and semantic nets are an ongoing research topic in psycholinguistics as well as computational linguistics.

**Exercise 8.3.4.1**

Express Figure 8.4 as a set of Prolog clauses such as:

```
is(carpenter,person).
uses(carpenter,woodworking_tool).
...
```

**Exercise 8.3.4.2**

Using the results of the previous exercise, define a predicate `related/2` which will tell you whether it is possible to get from one sense to another by following the arrows in the network. For example, '`?- related(pig,animal).`' should succeed but '`?- related(plane,carpenter).`' should fail.

**Exercise 8.3.4.3**

Using the results of the previous two exercises, define `near/2` which is like `related/2` except that the two senses have to be no more than two nodes apart (that is, have no more than one other node between them). For example, '`?- near(carpenter,physical_object).`' should fail.

**Exercise 8.3.4.4  (small project)**

Implement a disambiguation program comparable to the one in the previous section, but using spreading activation through a semantic net.

## 8.4 UNDERSTANDING EVENTS

### 8.4.1 Event Semantics

Consider the two sentences:

> *Mary believes Brutus stabbed Caesar.*
> *Mary saw Brutus stab Caesar.*

The first of these goes into logic straightforwardly as:

```
believes(mary,stabbed(brutus,caesar))
```

That is, Mary believes the PROPOSITION that Brutus stabbed Caesar. So far, so good.

Now try the second sentence. It's tempting to translate it as

```
saw(mary,stabbed(brutus,caesar))
```

but, as Terence Parsons has pointed out, problems immediately arise.[4]  Consider the context:

> *Mary saw Brutus stab Caesar,*
>> *but she didn't know that the first man was Brutus,*
>> *nor that the second man was Caesar,*
>> *nor that he was stabbing him.*

Clearly, Mary did not see the *proposition* or *fact* that Brutus stabbed Caesar. She saw an *event,* and we know (though she didn't) that the event was a stabbing and the protagonists were Brutus and Caesar.

Events are a lot like discourse referents; we can represent them with EVENT MARKERS analogous to discourse markers. Then *Brutus stabbed Caesar* goes into Prolog as a set of facts rather than a single fact:

```
stab(e(34)).                    % Event e(34) is a stabbing
agent(e(34),brutus).            % Brutus did it
theme(e(34),caesar).            % Caesar was the victim
```

If we get more information, we can represent it as additional facts:

```
place(e(34),forum).
instrument(e(34),knife).
```

And if Mary saw the event, we can record that fact too:

```
see(e(35)).                     % Event e(35) is an act of seeing
experiencer(e(35),mary).        % Mary experienced it
theme(e(35),e(34)).             % What she saw was event e(34)
```

and so on. This is essentially the theory of Parsons (1990) implemented in Prolog.

The relations *agent, theme,* etc. are called THEMATIC RELATIONS or THETA ROLES and go back originally to the work of Gruber (1965), Fillmore (1968), and Jackendoff (1972). Many linguists use thematic relations in a haphazard way; Table 8.2 shows the system I prefer, which is approximately that of Parsons. See also Dowty (1989).

---

[4]This exact argument is taken from a talk given by Parsons in Tübingen in 1987. See Parsons (1990).

**TABLE 8.2**     THEMATIC RELATIONS.

| | |
|---|---|
| AGENT | Person or thing that causes or actively permits an event<br>*Max kicked Bill.*<br>*General Motors raised prices.* |
| THEME | Person or thing affected or described<br>Present in (almost?) every sentence<br>*Max kicked Bill.*<br>*Felix is a cat.*<br>*Clouds formed on the horizon.* |
| GOAL | Result, intended result, or destination<br>*I went to New York.*<br>*We painted the house red.*<br>*Max turned into a unicorn.* |
| SOURCE | Point of origin; opposite of goal.<br>*I came from New Haven.*<br>*It changed from red to green.* |
| BENEFACTIVE | Person for whose benefit something is done<br>*We gave an award to the leader.*<br>*They threw him a party.* |
| EXPERIENCER | Person who experiences or perceives something<br>*We slept.*<br>*The noise surprised us.*<br>*We heard it several times.* |
| INSTRUMENT | Means with which something is accomplished<br>*I opened it with a crowbar.*<br>*The wrench got it open.*<br>*It was only soluble by induction.* |

Crucially, each verb can have at most one argument in each theta role. No verb ever has two different agents or themes at once. Other pieces of information such as place, time, and manner *can* be doubled up, and Parsons calls them MODIFIERS. An example of a sentence with two time modifiers is *Call me* [ *on Tuesday* ]$_{time}$ [ *at noon* ]$_{time}$.

**Exercise 8.4.1.1**

Consider the following sentences:

> *Fido chased Felix from Atlanta to Boston.*
> *Felix hated Boston.*
> *He went back to Atlanta on a train.*

(a) Identify all the thematic relations in each sentence.

(b) Encode the three sentences in Prolog in the manner described in this section, assigning an event marker to each event. (Some fine details, such as the difference between *went* and *went back,* will end up being ignored.)

### 8.4.2 Time and Tense

Every event occurs at a particular time which may or may not be known. The internal representation of a text should include the same information about time as the text itself. For example:

> *Fido barked at midnight. Then Felix howled.*

```
bark(e(1)).              % first event
agent(e(1),fido).
time(e(1),midnight).     % ... occurred at midnight

howl(e(2)).              % second event
agent(e(2),felix).
precedes(e(1),e(2)).     % ... e(1) preceded e(2)
```

*At midnight* tells us when Fido barked (assuming for the moment that *midnight* picks out a time unambiguously; recall that there are 365 midnights every year). *Then* tells us that Felix's howl came after Fido's bark, and that no significant event intervened.

That's not all. The verbs are in the past tense, which tells us that both `e(1)` and `e(2)` precede the speech act that describes them:

```
precedes(e(1),speech_act).
precedes(e(2),speech_act).
```

What we have, in general, is a PARTIAL ORDERING of events—we know the relative order of some of them but not necessarily all of them.

Different kinds of events relate to time in different ways. We have already implicitly distinguished events that occur at specific times from STATES, such as 'Gold is an element,' which we have viewed as timeless. Besides this, some events take (or seem to take) only a moment, while others occupy specific periods of time.

Table 8.3 shows a classification of verbs proposed by Vendler (1957) and subsequently refined by many other semanticists.[5] It is important to note that most events can be conceived of more than one way, and, in context, verbs are easily converted from one class to another.

Fleck (1988) argues convincingly that time as viewed by human beings is not normally a continuum. Humans prefer to divide a continuous stretch of time into a series of discrete states divided by events. Words like *then* and *next* tell us that there

---

[5]See especially Dowty (1979, ch. 2) and Fleck (1988, ch. 7). The felicitous substitution of the term STATE CHANGE for ACHIEVEMENT is due to Fleck.

**TABLE 8.3**   VENDLER'S FOUR CLASSES OF ENGLISH VERBS.

| | |
|---|---|
| STATE | *John knows Latin.* |
| | *Gold is an element.* |

True timelessly or for a specified period.
Not used in present participle (*\*John is knowing Latin*).

| | |
|---|---|
| ACHIEVEMENT | *John found a penny.* |
| (STATE CHANGE) | *Fido barked (once).* |

Instantaneous; has no duration; cannot be prolonged or interrupted.

| | |
|---|---|
| ACTIVITY | *John sang songs.* |
| | *Fido barked (continually).* |

Can continue any length of time with no definite endpoint.
Present tense usually expressed with *–ing* (*John is singing songs*).
"When did it start?" and "When did it stop?" are appropriate questions.

| | |
|---|---|
| ACCOMPLISHMENT | *John composed a symphony.* |
| | *Fido hunted down a rabbit.* |

Like an activity ending with a state change.
Finishing is not the same thing as stopping.
"How long did it take?" is an appropriate question.

is no other event between the two events being referred to; rather than being timeless, states persist until an event changes them.

**Exercise 8.4.2.1**

*Reasoning with a partial ordering:* Define `before/2` such that `before(e(1),e(2))` succeeds if `e(1)` is before `e(2)` in the partial ordering defined by `precedes`. Also define `after`. Can you define `simultaneous` in terms of `precedes`? Explain why or why not.

**Exercise 8.4.2.2**

Classify each of the following underlined verbs as denoting a state, an activity, a state change, or an accomplishment:

> *Fido chased Felix from Atlanta to Boston.*
> *They got there at sundown.*
> *Fido likes Boston.*
> *He met a famous person there.*

**Exercise 8.4.2.3**

Cite evidence that *find* normally denotes a state change in English. Then give an example in which *find* is used to denote an activity or an accomplishment.

## 8.4.3 Scripts

A SCRIPT is a representation of how an event is composed of sub-events. Given an incomplete description of a birthday party, a shopping trip, or an election, for instance, you can immediately infer many sub-events that may not have been mentioned. If I tell you I got a scarf at Macy's, you presume that I went there and paid for it.

Research on scripts was pioneered by Roger Schank and his students at Yale University in the 1970s and early 1980s (Charniak 1973; Schank 1975; Schank and Abelson 1977; Schank and Riesbeck 1981; for overview see especially Lehnert 1988). At that time, theoretical linguistics had little to say about semantics. Accordingly, Schank's group had to invent their own semantic formalism, which they called CONCEPTUAL DE-PENDENCY (CD).

An important goal of CD is to always represent the same event the same way even though different words can be used to describe it. Accordingly, CD translates all verbs into a small set of PRIMITIVE ACTIONS, of which the ones that concern us here are PTRANS (transfer a physical object) and ATRANS (transfer ownership, possession, or some other abstract relationship).[6] Often, a single verb denotes a whole set of primitive actions connected in particular ways; commonly, one event is the CAUSE or INSTRUMENT of another.

Each PTRANS or ATRANS has four arguments: Actor, Object, Destination-From, and Destination-To (or, in modern terms, Agent, Theme, Source, and Goal). For brevity, we will express these as arguments of a Prolog functor, and we will ignore the distinction between names and common nouns. Here, then, are some CD encodings of simple sentences, with uninstantiated variables standing for unknowns:

| | |
|---|---|
| *John removed the book from the shelf.* | `ptrans(john,book,shelf,_).` |
| *John went to New York.* | `ptrans(john,john,_,new_york).` |
| *John came from the library.* | `ptrans(john,john,library,_).` |
| *John became the owner of a house.* | `atrans(_,house,_,john).` |

Given this kind of representation, applying a script is a simple matter: match up the events in the script with the events obtained from natural-language input, and let the script fill in any that are missing. Script application is especially easy in Prolog because pattern matching, variable instantiation, and backtracking are built in. Figure 8.5 shows a much-shortened Prolog translation of a Lisp program given by Cullingford (1981), and Figure 8.6 shows the results of using it.

Crucially, this is a "miniature" script applier, designed only to illustrate the idea; a real script applier would be much more powerful, and would be able to choose among appropriate scripts, verify that the chosen script is indeed suitable (e.g., by verifying that Macy's is a store), provide alternative paths through a complex script, and construct more than just a list of events as output.

This in turn is only a preliminary to the *real* challenge, which is to derive scripts from knowledge of a more general kind. Relatively few real-world event sequences actually fit scripts that could be known in advance in enough detail to be useful. Accordingly,

---

[6]The others are MTRANS (transfer information), PROPEL, EXPEL, INGEST, SPEAK, GRASP, MOVE, ATTEND (pay attention to something), and MBUILD (build a mental representation). In addition to actions, there are a variety of STATES in various versions of CD.

```
% Miniature script-applier based on McSAM (Cullingford 1981)

% apply_script(+Events,-Result)
%  takes a list of events and applies a script to them,
%  giving a more detailed list of events.

apply_script(Events,Result) :-
   script(Script),
   apply_aux(Script,Events,Result).

apply_aux([E|Script],[E|Events],[E|Result]) :-
   apply_aux(Script,Events,Result).
   % Event in script matches actual event, so use it

apply_aux([S|Script],[E|Events],[S|Result]) :-
   \+ (E = S),
   apply_aux(Script,[E|Events],Result).
   % Event in script matches no actual event,
   % so add it to the list.

apply_aux(Script,[],Script).
   % If events are used up, fill in the rest of the
   % script (which may be empty) and stop.


% Script for buying something at a store

script([[ptrans(Actor,Actor,_,Store),       % go to store,
         ptrans(Actor,Item,_,Actor),        % get an item,
         atrans(Actor,Money,Actor,Store),   % pay for it,
         atrans(Store,Item,Store,Actor),    % obtain ownership,
         ptrans(Actor,Actor,Store,_)]]).    % go away.
```

**Figure 8.5**   Simple script-applying program.

Schank and his group have worked extensively on modeling goal-directed behavior, human responses to novel situations, and narrative themes (see Dyer 1983, who reviews earlier work).

Computer programs that use Schank's techniques can be viewed as expert systems for understanding particular kinds of events. They are often strikingly successful within their limited domains. For example, the program CYRUS (Kolodner 1984) could read incoming news stories from a wire service and use them to maintain its own database about the activities of then-Secretary of State Cyrus Vance. It could even refine its scripts by exploiting patterns found in the data.

Obviously, scripts and script generation are important; but just as obviously, they are not confined to the understanding of *language,* because the same mechanisms would be needed to understand events through, for instance, visual perception. Here, then, we

```
% "John went to Macy's, got a scarf, and went home."

?- apply_script([ptrans(john,john,_,macys),
                 ptrans(john,scarf,_,john),
                 ptrans(john,john,_,home)],What).

What = [ptrans(john,john,_401,macys),
        ptrans(john,scarf,_423,john),
        atrans(john,_481,john,macys),
        atrans(macys,scarf,macys,john),
        ptrans(john,john,macys,home)]


% "John went to Macy's and spent $5 there."

?- apply_script([ptrans(john,john,_,macys),
                 atrans(john,'$5',john,macys)],What).

What = [ptrans(john,john,_401,macys),
        ptrans(john,_339,_341,john),
        atrans(john,'$5',john,macys),
        atrans(macys,_339,macys,john),
        ptrans(john,john,macys,_385)]
% "John went from his home to Macy's."

?- apply_script([ptrans(john,john,home,macys)],What).

What = [ptrans(john,john,home,macys),
        ptrans(john,_135,_137,john),
        atrans(john,_149,john,macys),
        atrans(macys,_135,macys,john),
        ptrans(john,john,macys,_181)]


% "John got a scarf from Macy's."

?- apply_script([ptrans(john,scarf,macys,john)],What).

What = [ptrans(john,john,_211,_213),
        ptrans(john,scarf,macys,john),
        atrans(john,_237,john,_213),
        atrans(_213,scarf,_213,john),
        ptrans(john,john,_213,_269)]
```

**Figure 8.6** Examples of using the script applier to convert partial narratives into complete ones.

have definitely crossed the border into knowledge representation and cognitive modeling; and since this is a natural language processing textbook, here we must stop.

### Exercise 8.4.3.1

For each of the examples in Figure 8.6, express both the input and output of `apply_script` in English.

### Exercise 8.4.3.2

Get `apply_script` working and show that it can process the incomplete narratives in Figure 8.6, as well as other similar ones.

### Exercise 8.4.3.3   (open-ended project)

Starting with the "miniature" Lisp programs in Schank and Riesbeck (1981), implement further Schankian techniques in Prolog. Build a working natural language understander for a limited domain.

### Exercise 8.4.3.4

One of Schank's criticisms of early natural language processing was that computational linguists wanted to do all the syntactic parsing of a sentence first, and only then begin to build a semantic representation. Schank pointed out that human beings have immediate access to the meaning of each part of a sentence as soon as they hear it; they don't wait until the sentence is complete before interpreting it, and in fact if they did, some ambiguities would be excessively hard to resolve.

To what extent does this criticism apply to the newer parsing techniques presented in this and the previous chapter?


## 8.5 FURTHER READING

Numerous references have already been given in the text. In addition, Allen (1984) and many of the papers in Grosz et al. (1986) address semantic topics at length. Palmer (1990) presents a fine example of semantics implemented in Prolog for a specific domain (physics word problems).

The literature of machine translation is large and varied; at one time several entire journals were devoted to it. Hutchins (1986) reviews the long history of the field, and Nirenburg (1987) presents examples of current work.

On word-sense disambiguation and semantic nets, see Hirst (1987), several of the articles in Brachman and Levesque (1985), and all the articles in Evens (1988). Because of its data-driven nature and the acceptability of approximate results, word-sense disambiguation lends itself to neural network implementation, on which see Cottrell (1989). Wilks (1975) and Slator and Wilks (1991) explore disambiguation via selectional restrictions. Bartsch (1987) makes a pioneering effort to integrate word sense disambiguation with model-theoretic semantics.

The literature on events, scripts, and plans was extensively surveyed in the text. Two sources of additional information are Allen (1983), on temporal reasoning, and Herzog and Rollinger (1991), on current techniques.

# CHAPTER 9

# Morphology and the Lexicon

## 9.1 HOW MORPHOLOGY WORKS

### 9.1.1 The Nature of Morphology

We noted in Chapter 1 that morphology consists of two kinds of processes:

- INFLECTION, which creates the various forms of each word (singular and plural, present and past tense, or whatever); and
- DERIVATION, which creates new words from pre-existing words, often of different syntactic categories.

Perhaps the biggest difference between morphology and syntax is that, in most languages at least, morphology is finite. You can make a list of all the forms of every word in the language. In some languages this would be grossly wasteful—every Finnish verb, for example, has perhaps 12,000 inflected forms, all predictable by rule—but the point is that it's possible.[1]

---

[1] A few languages do have recursive word-formation processes, but even then the recursion is highly restricted (Anderson 1988b:149). Anyhow, we can force morphology to be finite by handling the recursive processes in the syntax.

What this means is that you don't have to implement morphology on the computer at all. You can, if you wish, list all the forms of every word in the lexicon. This has often been done for English.

What's more, morphology is riddled with IRREGULARITY. There are plenty of inflected or derived forms that *have* to be listed in the lexicon because they are not predictable by rules. No rule will tell you that the plural of English *child* is *children,* or that the plural of *corpus* is *corpora.*

This means that in dealing with morphology on the computer, you have to face a practical question: how much of it should you handle by means of rules, and how much should you simply list in the lexicon?

It's a matter of trade-offs. Listing every form of every word is obviously inefficient; morphological rules can certainly save space. But an overly elaborate rule system can be inefficient in the opposite way; it can be faster to work with an incomplete set of rules, looking up some forms in the lexicon, than to work with a more complex set of rules that captures everything. Unlike the theoretical linguist, the computer implementor is not required to track down every regular pattern and reduce it to a rule.

In languages like English, it is much more important to implement inflection than to implement derivation. The reason is that English inflection is very regular, but most cases of derivation are irregular, at least on the semantic level, and therefore have to be listed in the lexicon anyhow. If you take an English verb that ends in *ate* and change the ending to *ation,* you get a noun, but only the lexicon can tell you whether the noun denotes an activity (*rotate : rotation*), the result of an act (*create : creation*), or an abstract property (*locate : location*). The only reason to implement the *ate → ation* rule would be the ability to recognize newly coined words.

But some derivational processes are highly regular. Take almost any English adjective and add *ness*; you get an abstract noun that denotes the same property as the original adjective. Implementing this morphological rule could eliminate the need for a lot of lexical entries. Some languages have numerous derivational processes that are as regular as this, and it would make no sense not to implement them as rules.

There is as yet no standard approach to computational morphology. In this chapter we will develop a somewhat *ad hoc* practical implementation of English inflection, adaptable to many but not all other languages. Then we'll look briefly at more abstract models of morphology and at Koskenniemi's two-level morphological parsing algorithm.

**Exercise 9.1.1.1**

English has a suffix *er* which, when attached to a verb, produces a noun denoting a person or thing that does whatever the verb describes (*teach : teacher, learn : learner,* etc.).

Should a parser for English implement a rule that adds *er* to verbs, or should it simply list all the *er* words in the lexicon? Make a recommendation and give reasons for it.

## 9.1.2 Morphemes and Allomorphs

Any morphologically complex word can be broken up into several meaningful units called MORPHS. For example:

$$dogs \qquad = \quad dog + s$$
$$dishes \qquad = \quad dish + es$$
$$undoing \qquad = \quad un + do + ing$$
$$unrealities \quad = \quad un + real + ity + s$$

If two morphs are equivalent, we say they are ALLOMORPHS of the same MORPHEME. For example, the *s* in *dogs* and the *es* in *dishes* are equivalent to each other; they have exactly the same syntactic and semantic effect. We therefore classify them as allomorphs of the English plural morpheme.

To put this another way: MORPHS are the smallest meaningful segments into which a word is divided; MORPHEMES are morphs that have been identified (treating equivalent morphs alike); and ALLOMORPHS are the various forms of any morpheme.

An English word consists of zero or more PREFIXES, followed by the ROOT and then zero or more SUFFIXES:

|  | | Prefix | | Root | | Suffix | | Suffix |
|---|---|---|---|---|---|---|---|---|
| *untouchables* | = | *un* | + | *touch* | + | *able* | + | *s* |

Some languages also have INFIXES, which are inserted into the root (as in Tagalog *s+um+ulat,* a form of the verb *sulat* 'write'). Prefixes, suffixes, and infixes together are called AFFIXES.

Some languages also use VOWEL CHANGE as a morphological process. English does this in words such as *begin : began : begun, mouse : mice,* and *foot : feet.* The Semitic languages (Hebrew, Arabic, and their kin) use vowel change as the basis of their whole morphological system; here are some Hebrew examples:

| | | | |
|---|---|---|---|
| *katav* | 'wrote' | *kotev* | 'writing' |
| *ahav* | 'loved' | *ohev* | 'loving' |
| *bakhar* | 'chose' | *bokher* | 'choosing' |
| *amar* | 'said' | *omer* | 'saying' |

Here each verb form obviously consists of two parts, but the parts cannot be segmented into morphs in the usual way. One part of each verb form is the root, consisting of two or three consonants ($k-t-v$, $-h-v$, $b-kh-r$, or $-m-r$); the other part is the set of vowels, $-a-a-$ for past tense or $-o-e-$ for present participle.

Some words in some languages never appear without inflectional affixes. Consider Latin *casa* 'house':

| | |
|---|---|
| Nominative | *cas-a* |
| Accusative | *cas-am* |
| Genitive | *cas-ae*   (etc.) |

But *cas−* by itself is not a word; there is no way to say 'house' without marking it as nominative, accusative, genitive, or some other case. Instead, we say that *cas−* is the STEM of all the forms of the word for 'house'.

Finally, some inflections and derivations are expressed by nothing at all; when this happens, we call them ZERO MORPHS. For example, in English the plural of *sheep* is *sheep*. On one analysis, the plural should be viewed as *sheep*+∅ where ∅ is the invisible plural morph that appears in place of the usual *s*.

Like the phoneme, the morpheme is a descriptive concept from early twentieth-century descriptive linguistics (Bloomfield 1933). A list of morphemes and allomorphs is not nowadays considered to be an adequate analysis of the morphology of a language; the real question is *why* the allomorphs are what they are. But segmentation into morphs, and classification of morphs into morphemes, is always a good first step in analyzing an unfamiliar language.

**Exercise 9.1.2.1**

Break each of the following English words into morphs: *childish, indescribable, repeating, blessedness.* Give the meaning and/or grammatical function of each morpheme.

**Exercise 9.1.2.2**

Identify the morphological process involved in each of the following examples:

1. English *black* : *blackness*
2. Greek *philō* 'I love' : *philoumen* 'we love'
3. Greek *philoumen* 'we love' : *ephiloumen* 'we loved'
4. Navaho *dibááh* : *dišbááh* (two forms of the verb 'start off for war')
5. English *begin* : *began*
6. English *run* (present tense) : *run* (past participle)

## 9.2 ENGLISH INFLECTION

### 9.2.1 The System

Later in this chapter we will implement a morphological parser for English inflection. First, let's review how English inflection works.

**Verbs.**    Each English verb has only a few forms. Four of them are unproblematic:

- The PLAIN FORM, with no ending, as in *Fido will bark*;
- The S FORM, used in the third person singular, as in *Fido barks*;
- The ING FORM, used both as an adjective (*a barking dog*) and as a noun (*his loud barking*); and
- The ED FORM, used in the past tense (*Fido barked*).

But English also has plenty of IRREGULAR VERBS ("strong verbs") with two peculiarities:

- The past tense does not end in *ed*; instead it is formed by vowel change (*sing : sang, eat : ate*).
- There is usually a fifth verb form, which we will call the the EN FORM, used after *has* and other auxiliary verbs:

    *Fido has <u>eaten</u>.*   (not <u>*ate*</u>)

Regular verbs don't have a special form for this situation; they use the *ed* form (*Fido has barked*).

Immediately we find ourselves in an analytical dilemma. Should we say that regular verbs have no *en* form, or should we say that their *en* form is the same as their *ed* form?

The question is basically whether to complicate the syntax or the morphology. If we say that regular verbs have no *en* form, then the syntactic component is going to have to know whether each verb is regular, so that it can specify an *en* form in *Fido has eaten* but an *ed* form in *Fido has barked*. If we say that regular verbs *do* have *en* forms which are identical in form with their *ed* forms, the syntax becomes simpler but the morphology has to deal with the fact that every verb that ends in *ed* is ambiguous: *barked* = both *bark+ed* and *bark+en*.

We will take the second option, but with no great confidence that it is the best analysis of modern English. Table 9.1 shows the forms of a number of regular and irregular verbs, classified the way our morphological parser will analyze them.

**TABLE 9.1**    FORMS OF ENGLISH VERBS.

| Form | Examples | | | Example of use |
|---|---|---|---|---|
| plain | *bark* | *eat* | *run* | Fido wants to *bark / eat / run*. |
| *s* form | *barks* | *eats* | *runs* | Fido *barks / eats / runs*. |
| *ing* form | *barking* | *eating* | *running* | Fido is *barking / eating / running*. |
| *ed* form | *barked* | *ate* | *ran* | Fido *barked / ate / ran*. |
| *en* form | *barked* | *eaten* | *run* | Fido has *barked / eaten / run*. |

**Adjectives and adverbs.**    English adjectives, and some kinds of adverbs, take the inflectional suffixes *er* and *est* to form, respectively, the comparative and the superlative. These are used only on one- or occasionally two-syllable words (*bigger, happier,* but not *\*beautifuler*).

Just to keep down the total number of rules, we will not implement inflection of adjectives or adverbs. Rules to handle it are easy to add.

**Nouns.**    Most English nouns form the plural from the singular by adding *s* or *es*. Some nouns are irregular (*child : children, ox : oxen*) and some (denoting edible animals) have the plural the same as the singular (*deer, sheep*). Nouns borrowed from other languages sometimes use the plural morphology of the original language (*bacterium : bacteria, seraph : seraphim, chateau : chateaux*).

For our purposes it will be sufficient to treat everything except the *s/es* suffix as irregular, listing all irregular plurals in the lexicon. A more ambitious morphological parser might recognize some of the foreign patterns, such as *um : a*.

**Possessive *'s* as clitic, not suffix.**     There is abundant evidence that the possessive ending *'s* is not an inflectional suffix for nouns, but rather a CLITIC, i.e., a syntactically separate word that is always pronounced as part of the previous word.

If *'s* were a noun inflection, it would never appear on anything other than a noun. But in English it is at least marginally possible to say

> *the boy who came early's lunch*

and *early* is definitely not a noun (it is an adverb). This example may not be fully grammatical, but the point is that if *'s* were a noun inflection, attaching *'s* to an adverb would be flatly impossible, not just slightly deviant.

Further, if *'s* were a noun inflection denoting possessive case, it would always attach to the noun that denotes the possessor. But in the phrase

> [$_{NP}$ *the dictator of Ruritania* ] *'s crimes*

the crimes are definitely those of the dictator, not of the country. Thus it is evident that what we have is not a "possessive case" of *Ruritania,* but rather a separate word, spelled *'s,* which comes at the end of a complete noun phrase, and makes the whole noun phrase possessive.

The tokenizers in Appendix B already split off *'s* and treat it as a separate word. We will ignore it in the morphological analysis to be done in this chapter.

**Exercise 9.2.1.1**

Identify all the inflectional (but not derivational) morphology in the following sentences. Distinguish *ed* forms from *en* forms of verbs even when they look alike.

> *Two elephants, surrounded by deer, marched into the garden.*
> *Having bellowed loudly, the larger one knelt and its rider dismounted.*
> *Then the tallest of the deer ran toward the chateaux.*

## 9.2.2 Morphographemics (Spelling Rules)

English has a number of rules that change the spellings of various morphemes depending on the context. These are called MORPHOGRAPHEMIC RULES. The main ones that we have to deal with are as follows:

1. FINAL E DELETION: Silent final *e* disappears before any suffix that begins with a vowel, as in *rake+ing = raking, rake+ed = raked.* (We will assume that any final *e* that is preceded by a consonant is silent. Exceptions are rare enough to be listed individually in the lexicon.)

2. Y-TO-I RULE: Final *y* changes to *i* before any suffix that does not begin with *i*: *carry+ed = carried,* but *carry+ing = carrying.* This occurs only when the final *y* is not preceded by a vowel (*delay+ed = delayed,* not *\*delaied*).

3. **S-TO-ES RULE:** The suffix *s,* on both nouns and verbs, appears as *es* after *s, z, x, sh, ch,* and after *y* which has changed to *i.* Thus *grass+s = grasses, dish+s = dishes, carry+s = carries.*

4. **FINAL CONSONANT DOUBLING:** Generally, a single final consonant doubles before any suffix that begins with a vowel; thus *grab+ed = grabbed, grab+ing = grabbing, big+er = bigger.* There are exceptions (*offering, chamfering*) but they are infrequent enough to list in the lexicon.

Notice that these rules do not all operate in the same direction. Specifically,

- Rules 1, 2, and 4 operate RIGHT-TO-LEFT: the form of the second morph (the suffix) influences the form of the first morph.
- Rule 3 operates LEFT-TO-RIGHT: the form of the first morph influences the second.

All of these rules could be refined somewhat, but this is enough to get us started. English is unusual in having this much right-to-left influence; some languages, such as Latin, are easily analyzed without postulating any right-to-left morphographemic rules at all.

Of course the most unusual thing about English here is that the spelling follows different rules than the pronunciation. In most languages we would have few or no MORPHOGRAPHEMIC (spelling) rules; instead we would have MORPHOPHONEMIC (pronunciation) rules which are reflected directly in the spelling.

**Exercise 9.2.2.1**

Indicate which morphographemic rules, if any, are involved in forming each of the following words:

> *amazing*
>
> *matching*
>
> *portrayed*
>
> *whizzing*
>
> *churches*
>
> *merrier*
>
> *bacteria*

Which words involve more than one rule?

## 9.3 IMPLEMENTING ENGLISH INFLECTION

### 9.3.1 Lexical Lookup

For morphological analysis, we want to look at the individual characters of each word. This means that we will represent words, not as atoms, but as CHARLISTS (lists of one-character atoms, `[[l,i,k,e],[t,h,i,s]]`). We could have used strings (lists of

ASCII codes), but then our code would be hard to read. (Quick, does [_,115] match
"es"?)[2] A tokenizer that produces charlists is given in Appendix B. ISO Standard
Prolog will encourage the use of charlists.

The next question is how to store the lexicon. Recall that Prolog has a very efficient
indexing (hashing) scheme for finding the first argument of any predicate. Accordingly,
we *could* convert every word to an atom when we want to look it up, and store the
lexicon like this:

```
lex(dog, ...information about 'dog'... ).
lex(cat, ...information about 'cat'... ).
```
$\vdots$

The indexing scheme would find dog, cat, etc., very quickly.

But there's a good reason not to do this. Imagine what happens when we find
the word *babies.* First we have to look up babies in the lexicon to see if it's an
irregular form. Then we have to try various morphological rules; maybe it's the plural
of *babie*...no, there's no such word...not the plural of *babi* either... so finally we look
for *baby* and find it.

Now recall how the Prolog symbol table works. Whenever an atom is created, it's
stored in the symbol table. But most Prologs do not GARBAGE-COLLECT the symbol table;
that is, they don't remove atoms that no longer exist in the program. In the process of
looking up *babies* in the manner just described, the program would use not one, but four
atoms (*babies, babie, babi,* and *baby*). If you do a lot of morphological analysis this
way in a highly inflected language, you'll eventually fill up the symbol table with useless
material.

Fortunately, there's an alternative: a structure called a LETTER TREE, CHARACTER
TREE, or *trie* [short for *retrieval;* see de la Briandais (1959), Fredkin (1960), Knuth
(1973:481-505)]. Figure 9.1 shows how it works. The idea is to look at each word letter
by letter, and choose the appropriate branch of the tree each time. Eventually, if the
word is in the tree, you get to the place where its lexical entry is stored.

**Exercise 9.3.1.1**

Draw, in the style of Figure 9.1, a letter tree for the words:

*aardvark   abacus   baker   bark   bee   beef   book*

### 9.3.2 Letter Trees in Prolog

Figure 9.2 shows the same letter tree represented in Prolog. We store the tree as the
argument of a Prolog fact so that we can retrieve it easily.

The exact form of the tree bears explaining. Crucially, to progress from one letter
to the next, we move *into* the list (i.e., into lists within lists). To search among alternative

---

[2]Some Prologs let you write the ~a, ~b, etc., or 0'a, 0'b, etc., for the numeric ASCII codes of a,
b, etc. This solves the readability problem but isn't portable.

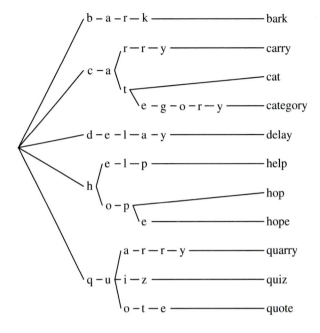

**Figure 9.1**  Letter tree for the words *bark, carry, cat, category, delay, help, hop, hope, quarry, quiz,* and *quote.*

```
ltree([ [b, [a, [r, [k, bark]]]],
        [c, [a, [r, [r, [y, carry]]],
                [t, cat,
                    [e, [g, [o, [r, [y, category]]]]]]]]],
        [d, [e, [l, [a, [y, delay]]]]],
        [h, [e, [l, [p, help]]],
            [o, [p, hop,
                    [e, hope]]]],
        [q, [u, [a, [r, [r, [y, quarry]]]],
                [i, [z, quiz]],
                [o, [t, [e, quote]]]]]
      ]).
```

**Figure 9.2**  Letter tree from Figure 9.1, in Prolog.

letters we move *along* the list (from one element to another). If *cat* were the only word in the tree, it would be represented as `[[c,[a,[t,cat]]]]` so that each letter could be reached by moving deeper into each succeeding element. Here the atom `cat` is the lexical entry; in real life this could be a much larger data structure containing many kinds of information about the word.

All this needs to be defined more formally. We'll define a TREE to be a list of BRANCHES. Each branch is the portion of the tree that is relevant if a particular letter has been found in a particular position:

- A branch is a list.
- The first element of the list is a letter.
- Each succeeding element is either another branch, or the lexical entry for a word.
- The elements are in a specific order: the lexical entry (if any) comes first, and branches are in alphabetical order by their first letters.

So a branch representing *cat, category,* and *cook* would look like this:

```
[c,[a,[t,cat,
        [e,[g,[o,[r,[y,category]]]]]]]],
    [o,[o,[k,cook]]]]
```

All this is probably easier to see than to describe. Note in particular that if you take the first element off a branch, you get a tree. That is, trees contain branches which contain trees which contain branches, and so on recursively.

The procedure to find a word in a tree is simple. In principle, all we need is:[3]

```
% find_word(+Word,+Tree,-LexEntry) -- First version
%   Finds Word in Tree retrieving LexEntry.

find_word([H|T],Tree,LexEntry) :-
    member([H|Branches],Tree),
    find_word(T,Branches,LexEntry).

find_word([],Tree,LexEntry) :-
    member(LexEntry,Tree),
    \+ (LexEntry = [_|_]).
```

That is: To find a word, find (in the current tree) the branch whose first element matches the word's first letter. Then continue the search using the tail of that branch instead of the original tree, and looking at the next letter of the word. When you run out of letters, look for a non-list (i.e., a lexical entry) in whatever tree you've gotten to.

In fact, however, member/2 fails to exploit the fact that the branches are in alphabetical order. If the program finds a branch whose first letter is alphabetically *after* the letter it's looking for, it should give up—that word definitely isn't there, or the program would have found it already.

The built-in predicate @< will compare two atoms for alphabetical order. Accordingly, here's a more efficient version of find_word, replacing member with find_branch:

```
% find_word(+Word,+Tree,-LexEntry)
%   Finds Word in Tree retrieving LexEntry.
```

---

[3] Here member/2 is as defined in Appendix A.

```
find_word([H|T],Tree,LexEntry) :-
   find_branch(H,Tree,SubTree),
   find_word(T,SubTree,LexEntry).

find_word([],[LexEntry|_],LexEntry) :-
   \+ (LexEntry = [_|_]).

% find_branch(+Letter,+Tree,-LexEntry)
%  Given a letter and a tree, returns the
%  appropriate (unique) subtree.  Deterministic.

find_branch(Letter,[[Letter|LexEntry]|_],LexEntry) :- !.
  % Found it; there is only one.

find_branch(Letter,[[L|_]|_],_) :- Letter @< L, !, fail.
  % Went past where it should be; don't search any further.

find_branch(Letter,[_|Rest],LexEntry) :-
  find_branch(Letter,Rest,LexEntry).
  % Haven't found it yet, so advance to next branch.
```

Notice that this version of find_word also exploits the fact that the lexical entry, if any, comes right at the beginning of the subtree.

**Exercise 9.3.2.1**

Get find_word working. Then take your letter tree from the previous exercise, express it in Prolog, and show that find_word searches it correctly.

**Exercise 9.3.2.2**

Implement a predicate mparse/2 that takes a word (expressed as a charlist) and gives its morphological analysis. Start as follows:

```
mparse(Word,Result) :-
  ltree(Tree),
  find_word(...)...
```

You will use mparse extensively in what follows.

**Exercise 9.3.2.3**

Modify find_word so that a word can have more than one lexical entry, like this:

```
[r,[a,[k,[e,noun(rake),verb(rake)]]]]
```

Assume that all the lexical entries are at the beginning of the list, immediately after the last letter of the word, before any other branches.

### 9.3.3  How to Remove a Suffix

By adding one more clause to `find_word` we can start parsing suffixes. Recall that `find_word` works through each word one letter at a time. When trying to parse `[d,e,l,a,y,e,d]`, for example, it will eventually be looking at `[e,d]`. At this point it should recognize the suffix *ed*, then try to parse `[]` (i.e., find a word that ends at the point in the letter tree that it's presently looking at) in order to find the root. Here's the clause that does this:

```
% Additional rule for suffix

find_word(Ending,Tree,Result+Suffix) :-
   suffix(Ending,Suffix),
   find_word([],Tree,Result).
```

Of course now we need a table of suffixes, like this:

```
% suffix(?Chars,?Morpheme)
%  Chars is a suffix, Morpheme is the representation
%  of it (identifying the morpheme).

suffix([s],s).
suffix([e,d],ed).
suffix([e,d],en).     % Ambiguous verb suffix
suffix([i,n,g],ing).
```

Recall that *ed* marks both the *ed* form and the *en* form of regular verbs; that's why it's in the table twice. If the suffixes were more numerous, it would pay to put them in a letter tree too.

**Exercise 9.3.3.1**

Get this extension to `find_word` working. Show that your program will successfully analyze *barks, barked, hops, carrying, delayed,* and *cats.*

**Exercise 9.3.3.2**

Add the adjective suffixes *er* and *est* to `suffix/2` and add the roots *odd* and *sweet* to the letter tree. Show that your program will correctly analyze *sweeter, sweetest, odder,* and *oddest.*

### 9.3.4  Morphographemic Templates and Rules

Now for morphographemics. The morphographemic rules that we formulated in Section 9.2.2 work *forward;* that is, they start with the root and the suffix, and derive the actual correctly spelled form. What we want to do now is work *backward,* taking the observed form and picking it apart into root and suffix.

This isn't especially easy, for several reasons. For one, English morphographemics has a lot of right-to-left influence; the root itself changes form depending on what suffix follows it. Second, there are plenty of words in which more than one rule applies; *quizzes,* for example, undergoes both consonant doubling and the *s-to-es* change.

Fortunately, in English the total number of inflectional suffixes and the total number of morphographemic rules is small. We can make a chart (Table 9.2) showing the effects of all the rules with each suffix on roots of various forms.

**TABLE 9.2**   SOME ENGLISH
INFLECTIONAL ENDINGS,
SHOWING THE EFFECT OF ALL
MORPHOGRAPHEMIC RULES.

| Ending | | Analysis | Example |
|--------|---|----------|---------|
| *s*      | = | *s*      | *barks*    |
| *ses*    | = | *s+s*    | *glasses*  |
| *zes*    | = | *z+s*    | *klutzes*  |
| *xes*    | = | *x+s*    | *foxes*    |
| *shes*   | = | *sh+s*   | *dishes*   |
| *ches*   | = | *ch+s*   | *churches* |
| *Cies*   | = | *Cy+s*   | *hobbies*  |
| *ed*     | = | *ed*     | *barked*   |
| *ed*     | = | *e+ed*   | *raked*    |
| *Cied*   | = | *Cy+ed*  | *worried*  |
| *ing*    | = | *ing*    | *barking*  |
| *ing*    | = | *e+ing*  | *raking*   |
| *VCCed*  | = | *VC+ed*  | *grabbed*  |
| *VCCing* | = | *VC+ing* | *grabbing* |
| *Vzzes*  | = | *Vz+s*   | *quizzes*  |

**Note:**  Throughout, *V* denotes any vowel,
and *C* denotes any consonant.

This suggests a shortcut: simply use the endings in Table 9.2 as templates, match them to a word, and thereby extract the root and suffix. Fortunately, we don't need quite as many templates as are shown in the table, because many suffixes act alike. Doubling occurs before any suffix that begins with a vowel, and *y* changes to *i* before any suffix that doesn't begin with *i*.

What we need is a predicate called `split_suffix` that extracts a suffix from the ending of a word, or fails if there is no suffix. Figure 9.3 shows its clauses.

To distinguish consonants from vowels, `split_suffix` relies on this predicate:

```
% vowel(?Char)
%   Char is a vowel.

vowel(a).  vowel(e).  vowel(i).  vowel(o).  vowel(u).  vowel(y).
```

The code for `suffix/1` remains as before, but we need to get rid of the clause of `find_word` that recognizes a suffix directly, and replace it with a clause that calls

```
split_suffix:

find_word(Chars,Tree,Root+Suffix) :-
   split_suffix(Chars,Stem,Suffix),
   find_word(Stem,Tree,Root).
```

**Exercise 9.3.4.1**

> Get all this new code working and show that it correctly parses *carries, carried, carrying, categories, hopping, hoping, quizzes,* and *quoting* as well as all of the words correctly parsed by the previous version.

**Exercise 9.3.4.2**

> Using the code in this section, how many analyses of *hoping* do you get? Why?

**Exercise 9.3.4.3**

> Add the adjectives *big* and *large* to the letter tree, and add the adjective suffixes *er* and *est* to `suffix/2` if you have not already done so. Then show that your program correctly parses *big, bigger, biggest, large, larger,* and *largest.*

### 9.3.5 Controlling Overgeneration

So far our implementation still overgenerates—that is, it parses plenty of forms that don't really exist. (The term "overgenerate" is used both for generators and for recognizers.) Specifically:

- It lets you put any suffix on any word. In correct English, nouns don't take *ing* or *ed*, and irregular forms such as *went* don't take any suffixes at all.
- It doesn't recognize that certain morphographemic changes are obligatory. This leads to misinterpretations. For example, our implementation doesn't know that *hoping* is not a form of *hop* (that is, it doesn't know that the doubling in *hopping* is obligatory).

We can fix the first problem by enriching the lexical entry of each word, so that each lexical entry looks like this:

```
word(Morpheme,Category,Infl)
```

Here `Morpheme` identifies the word; `Category` is `noun` or `verb` (etc.); and `Infl` is 1 if the word takes inflectional endings and 0 if it does not. This enables us to check that *ed* and *ing* appear only on verbs, not on nouns. It also lets us ensure that irregular forms such as *went* don't take any affixes at all. Figure 9.4 shows the letter tree with lexical entries in this form and with a few irregular forms added.

We also need to modify the last clause of `split_suffix`—the one that adds a suffix with no morphographemic changes—so that it won't apply if doubling should have

```
% split_suffix(+Characters,-Root,-Suffix)
%   Splits a word into root and suffix.
%   Fails if there is no suffix.

% Suffixes with doubled consonants in root
split_suffix([V,z,z,e,s],[V,z],s).    % "quizzes", "whizzes"
split_suffix([V,s,s,e,s],[V,s],s).    % "gasses" (verb)
split_suffix([V,C,C,V2|Rest],[V,C],Suffix) :-
    vowel(V), \+ vowel(C), vowel(V2), suffix([V2|Rest],Suffix).

% y changing to i and -s changing to -es simultaneously
split_suffix([C,i,e,s],[C,y],s) :- \+ vowel(C).

% y changes to i after consonant, before suffix beg. w vowel
split_suffix([C,i,X|Rest],[C,y],Suffix) :-
    \+ vowel(C), \+ (X = i), suffix([V|Rest],Suffix).

% -es = -s after s (etc.)
split_suffix([s,h,e,s],[s,h],s).
split_suffix([c,h,e,s],[c,h],s).
split_suffix([s,e,s],[s],s).
split_suffix([z,e,s],[z],s).
split_suffix([x,e,s],[x],s).

% Final e drops out before a suffix beg. with a vowel
split_suffix([C,V|Rest],[C,e],Suffix) :-
    \+ vowel(C), vowel(V), suffix([V|Rest],Suffix).

% Ending of word exactly matches suffix.
split_suffix(Ending,[],Suffix) :- suffix(Ending,Suffix).
```

**Figure 9.3**  Implementation of templates to recognize suffixes and undo morphographemics.

applied. (Actually, it shouldn't apply if *any* other rule should have applied, but filtering
out just the cases where doubling should apply is sufficient for our present purposes.)

Figure 9.5 shows `split_suffix`, `suffix`, and `find_word` in final form. (The
predicates `find_branch` and `vowel` are not shown because they haven't changed.)
Notice that we allow the suffix *s* to attach to any syntactic category. Strictly speaking,
that's not correct, since it attaches only to nouns and verbs. But if we were to list it
twice—as a suffix for nouns, and as a suffix for verbs—a lot of needless backtracking
would take place. As it is, the slight remaining overgeneration is not troublesome.

### Exercise 9.3.5.1

Get these predicates working and show that they still parse all the words that were correctly
parsed by previous versions; also show that they no longer accept *hoped* as a form of *hop,*
or *quizes* as a form of *quiz.*

```
ltree([ [b, [a, [r, [k, word(bark,verb,1)]]]],
        [c, [a, [r, [r, [y, word(carry,verb,1)]]]],
            [t, word(cat,noun,1),
                [e, [g, [o, [r, [y, word(category,noun,1)]]]]]]]]]]],
        [d, [e, [l, [a, [y, word(delay,verb,1)]]]]]],
        [g, [o, word(go,verb,0),
                [n, [e, word(go+en,verb,0)]]]]],
        [h, [e, [l, [p, word(help,verb,1)]]]],
            [o, [p, word(hop,verb,1),
                    [e, word(hope,verb,1)]]]]],
        [q, [u, [a, [r, [r, [y, word(quarry,verb,1)]]]]],
            [i, [z, word(quiz,verb,1)]],
            [o, [t, [e, word(quote,verb,1)]]]]]]],
        [w, [e, [n, [t, word(go+ed,verb,0)]]]]]
    ]).
```

**Figure 9.4**   Revised letter tree with more information in the lexical entries.

**Exercise 9.3.5.2**

Modify `split_suffix` further so that *carryed* and *hopeing* will not be accepted.

## 9.4 ABSTRACT MORPHOLOGY

### 9.4.1 Underlying Forms

The frustrating thing about our morphological parser so far is that we weren't able to implement the morphographemic rules directly; instead we had to figure out their effects, define templates, and combine some of the templates into rules of a new kind. In so doing, we find that the program no longer expresses how the rules really work.

Traditionally, morphophonemics (or morphographemics, in the written language) is the relationship between UNDERLYING and SURFACE forms. Underlying forms are listed in the lexicon; surface forms are what actually occur. The morphophonemic rules map one onto the other. An example:

Underlying form    *quiz+s*
                       $\Downarrow$        $s \rightarrow es$ after $z$
              *quiz+es*
                       $\Downarrow$        $z$ doubles before suffix beginning with vowel
Surface form       *quizzes*

This analysis has three levels; besides the underlying and surface forms, there's a level in between, needed because the doubling rule can't be triggered until the vowel *e* has been inserted.

```
% split_suffix(+Characters,-Root,-Suffix,-Category)
%  Splits a word into root and suffix.
%  Fails if there is no suffix.
%  Instantiates Category to the syntactic category
%  to which this suffix attaches.

% Suffixes with doubled consonants in root
split_suffix([V,z,z,e,s],[V,z],s,_).  % "quizzes", "whizzes"
split_suffix([V,s,s,e,s],[V,s],s,_).  % "gasses" (verb)
split_suffix([V,C,C,V2|Rest],[V,C],Suffix,Cat) :-
    vowel(V), \+ vowel(C), vowel(V2), suffix([V2|Rest],Suffix,Cat).

% y changing to i and -s changing to -es simultaneously
split_suffix([C,i,e,s],[C,y],s,_) :- \+ vowel(C).

% y changes to i after consonant, before suffix beg. w vowel
split_suffix([C,i,X|Rest],[C,y],Suffix,Cat) :-
    \+ vowel(C), \+ (X = i), suffix([V|Rest],Suffix,Cat).

% -es = -s after s (etc.)
split_suffix([s,h,e,s],[s,h],s,_).
split_suffix([c,h,e,s],[c,h],s,_).
split_suffix([s,e,s],[s],s,_).
split_suffix([z,e,s],[z],s,_).
split_suffix([x,e,s],[x],s,_).

% Final e drops out before a suffix beg. with a vowel
split_suffix([C,V|Rest],[C,e],Suffix,Cat) :-
    \+ vowel(C), vowel(V), suffix([V|Rest],Suffix,Cat).

% Ending of word exactly matches suffix.
% (Does not apply if Doubling was required to apply.
%  This eliminates spurious ambiguities such as hoped=hop+ed.)
split_suffix([A,B,C|Rest],[A,B],Suffix,Cat) :-
    suffix([C|Rest],Suffix,Cat),
    \+ (vowel(A), \+ vowel(B), vowel(C)).  % Doubling

% suffix(?Chars,?Morpheme,?Category)
%  If Chars is a suffix, Morpheme is the description of it,
%  and Category is the syntactic category it attaches to.

suffix([s],s,_).              % let it attach to any category
suffix([e,d],ed,verb).
suffix([e,d],en,verb).       % ambiguous suffix
suffix([i,n,g],ing,verb).
```

**Figure 9.5**  Morphological parsing predicates in final form (`find_branch` and `vowel` are unchanged). (Continues on page 274.)

```
%  find_word(+Word,+Tree,-LexEntry)
%   Finds Word in Tree retrieving LexEntry
%   where LexEntry = word(Form,Category,Inflectable).

find_word([],[LexEntry|_],LexEntry)  :-
   \+ (LexEntry = [_|_]).

find_word([H|T],Tree,LexEntry)  :-
   find_branch(H,Tree,SubTree),
   find_word(T,SubTree,LexEntry).

find_word(Chars,Tree,word(Form+Suffix,Cat,0))  :-
   % use split_suffix, but only with inflectable roots
   split_suffix(Chars,Stem,Suffix,Cat),
   find_word(Stem,Tree,word(Form,Cat,1)).
```

**Figure 9.5   cont.**

Multilevel morphophonemics goes back at least to Bloomfield (1939). Here's a Finnish example (from Anderson 1988a) that needs *four* levels:

| | | |
|---|---|---|
| Underlying form | *karakha+i+ta* | |
| | ⇓ | $a \rightarrow o$ before *i* |
| | *karakho+i+ta* | |
| | ⇓ | *t* disappears between vowels |
| | *karakho+i+a* | |
| | ⇓ | $i \rightarrow j$ between vowels |
| Surface form | *karakhoja* | |

Why so many levels? Because, to a considerable extent, morphophonemic rules reflect context-dependent sound changes that have actually occurred in the history of the language. At one time, *karakhoja* probably *was* pronounced as *karakhaita* or something close. Again, here's a simple example from Classical Greek:

| | | |
|---|---|---|
| Underlying form | *phile+ete* | |
| | ⇓ | $ee \rightarrow ei$ |
| Surface form | *phileite* | |

The rule that changes *ee* to *ei* is needed in Classical Greek to explain why a large number of suffixes have the forms that they do. But if we look at the Greek of Homer, a few hundred years earlier, we find that the word corresponding to classical *phileite* is actually written *phileete*. The change of *e+e* to *ei* was a historical event, not just an analytic abstraction. Not all morphophonemic rules reflect historic changes like this, but sound change is at least part of the reason why morphophonemic rules exist.

**Exercise 9.4.1.1**

> Show, step by step, how morphographemic rules generate the English words *hopping, hoping, quizzing,* and *carried* from their underlying forms.

**Exercise 9.4.1.2**

> Hebrew has a rule that *nt* is always realized on the surface as *tt*. Accordingly, give both the underlying and the surface forms for the missing verb in this table:

|          |            |   |            |            |
|----------|------------|---|------------|------------|
| *shamar* | 'he kept'  | : | *shamarti* | 'I kept'   |
| *pa'al*  | 'he did'   | : | *pa'alti*  | 'I did'    |
| *nathan* | 'he gave'  | : | __?__      | 'I gave'   |

## 9.4.2 Morphology as Parsing

It would seem that the obvious way to do morphological parsing is to run all these rules backward, level by level. That, however, is difficult because so many of the rules introduce ambiguity by deleting letters or making different forms look alike. Consider the English rule that drops final *e*. It's easy to work forward using this rule and convert *rake+ing* to *raking*. But when it's working backward, how can the parser recognize the final *e*'s that aren't there?

Without guidance about where a silent final *e* can occur—guidance that cannot come from within the *e*-deleting rule itself—the parser can waste a lot of time hypothesizing deleted *e*'s where none are called for.

The same goes for deleted *t*'s in Finnish, or *ei* reflecting underlying *ee* in Greek, and so on. Generally, the underlying form contains more information than the surface form, and the parser cannot reconstruct the missing information out of thin air.

Crucially, morphological analysis is quite different from syntactic parsing. The syntactic parser's job is mainly to group and classify the elements of its input. The morphological analyzer, on the other hand, often has to deal with elements that aren't there, or appear in quite different forms than are listed in the lexicon.

**Exercise 9.4.2.1**

> Of the four English morphographemic rules that we've been studying, which ones introduce ambiguity (i.e., create a surface form that could have had more than one different underlying form)? Give examples.

**Exercise 9.4.2.2   (Small project)**

> Write a Prolog predicate `apply_morphographemics/2` that will apply the morphographemic rules, working forward, given a charlist that represents the underlying form. For example:
>
> ```
> ?- apply_morphographemics([c,a,r,r,y,+,e,d],What).
> What = [c,a,r,r,i,e,d]
> ```
>
> Assume that + will mark all morpheme boundaries in the input string.

### 9.4.3 Two-Level Morphology

What we need is a morphological analyzer that is guided by the lexicon—one that determines as early as possible what word it's looking at, and chooses morphological rules taking this knowledge into account. For example, we don't want it to hypothesize a deleted final *e* unless the input so far is consistent with a real word that actually has one.

What we face, in fact, is a problem of string comparison. We want to step through the surface form, letter by letter, and simultaneously step through the underlying form, making sure that the two forms correspond in the way that the rules require, like this:

```
u n + r a k e + e d
| | | | | | | | | |     (every correspondence sanctioned by rules)
u n 0 r a k 0 0 e d
```

Here 0 denotes a null (absent) character in the surface form, and + marks morpheme boundaries. We'll have to restrict the rules so that only these two levels (underlying and surface) are needed, and not any intervening ones.

The underlying forms are stored in a letter tree, and the system will have to backtrack whenever the wrong underlying form has been chosen. This is unavoidable. Until it reads the final *l*, the system has no way to know that *spiel* is not a form of *spy*. But choice of lexical item and choice of prefix or suffix will be the *only* sources of backtracking; the system will never waste time hypothesizing morphological changes that are not actually appropriate in the (apparent) context.

This is the essence of the TWO-LEVEL MORPHOLOGY developed by Koskenniemi (1983) and implemented by Karttunen (1983) in the computer program KIMMO.[4] Koskenniemi's original insights were that:

- No more than two levels are needed, because successive rules that require intermediate levels can be combined;

- Most rules are independent of each other and can operate in parallel, simultaneously;

- Each rule can be implemented efficiently as a DETERMINISTIC FINITE-STATE TRANSDUCER (to be explained shortly).

The results have been fruitful: KIMMO and its derivatives have been used to implement successful morphological parsers for English (Karttunen and Wittenburg 1983, Pulman et al. 1988, Ritchie et al. 1992), Japanese (Alam 1983), French (Lun 1983), Finnish (the language on which Koskenniemi originally worked), German (Trost 1991), and other languages. That's a wide variety.

**Exercise 9.4.3.1**

How many levels are used in our original system (`split_suffix` and its kin)? Is it a one-level system, a two-level system, or what? Explain why.

---

[4] An IBM PC implementation of KIMMO was released in 1990 by the Summer Institute of Linguistics, 7500 West Camp Wisdom Road, Dallas, Texas 75236.

### 9.4.4 Rules and Transducers

Here is our final-*e*-deletion rule expressed in KIMMO's framework:

e:0  ⟺  C:C _ +:0 V:V        where C is any consonant and V is any vowel.

Here the notation 'x:y' means 'underlying x corresponding to surface y.' So the rule as a whole says: e:0 (that is, underlying *e* corresponding to surface null) occurs if and only if preceded by C:C (that is, a consonant) and followed by +:0 (morpheme boundary corresponding to surface null) and then V:V (a vowel).

Figure 9.6 shows this same rule expressed as a DETERMINISTIC FINITE-STATE TRANS-DUCER, i.e., a state-transition network that steps through the two strings, accepting or rejecting them, and never backtracks. The transducer can be described by either a diagram or a table, and both are shown.[5]

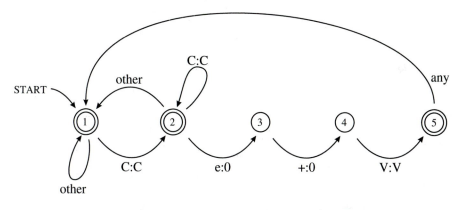

| State | C:C | V:V | e:0 | +:0 | other | Can stop? |
|-------|-----|-----|-----|-----|-------|-----------|
| 1     | 2   |     |     |     | 1     | yes       |
| 2     | 2   |     | 3   |     | 1     | yes       |
| 3     |     |     |     | 4   |       | no        |
| 4     |     | 5   |     |     |       | no        |
| 5     |     |     |     |     | 1     | yes       |

**Figure 9.6**  Finite-state transducer for final *e* deletion, shown as a diagram and as a table.

This transducer has five states. It starts in state 1 and must finish in state 1, 2, or 5, denoted by double circles. The states are linked by ARCS, and the transducer goes from one state to another by accepting the pair of underlying and surface characters indicated

[5]On transition networks see also the end of Chapter 3.

on the arc. An arc labeled 'other' can only be taken if none of the other arcs leading out of the same node is applicable.

The idea is to run the transducer like a machine, feeding it letters (or rather underlying-surface letter pairs), and check that it ends up in state 1, 2, or 5 at the end of the word. If it finishes in some other state, or if it BLOCKS (gets into a state from which there is no arc corresponding to the next character), then the proposed underlying and surface strings can't go together; the parser must back up and try a different lexical item if one is available.

Suppose, for example, we feed it the strings:

```
r a k e + e d
| | | | | | |
r a k 0 0 e d
```

Here's what happens:

> —*Start in state 1.*
> —*Accept* r:r *(a consonant); go to state 2.*
> —*Accept* a:a *(which matches only the 'other' arc); go back to state 1.*
> —*Accept* k:k *(a consonant); go to state 2.*
> —*Accept* e:0 *and go to state 3.*
> —*Accept* +:0 *and go to state 4.*
> —*Accept* e:e *(a vowel) and go to state 5.*
> —*Accept* d:d *and go to state 1.*
> —*Encounter end of word. Stopping in state 1 is permissible, so the word is accepted.*

Notice that if the underlying or the surface form is unknown, either one can be obtained from the other by simply running the transducer. That is, the transducer serves both to parse and to generate forms.

In KIMMO, the transducers for all the rules run simultaneously, in parallel, and a pair of strings is accepted only if none of the transducers reject it. Further, KIMMO has an automatic compiler to translate rules into transducers.

**Exercise 9.4.4.1**

What does this transducer do when given each of the following inputs?

```
r a k e + e d
| | | | | | |
r a k e 0 e d

r a k e + i n g
| | | | | | | |
r a k 0 0 i n g
```

```
a b c d e f g
| | | | | | |
a b c d e f g
```

**Exercise 9.4.4.2**

> Our *y*-to-*i* rule says that underlying *y* must be realized as surface *i* when preceded by a consonant and followed by a morpheme boundary and then a vowel other than *i*.
>
> > (a) Express this rule in KIMMO's notation.
> > (b) Convert this rule into a finite-state transducer and draw a diagram of it.

## 9.4.5 Finite-State Transducers in Prolog

Space and time preclude giving a full implementation of two-level morphology here, but we can at least implement a bit of it. [For a full KIMMO system in Prolog see Boisen 1988].

Figure 9.7 shows our finite-state transducer (from Figure 9.6) implemented in Prolog. It's surprisingly simple, consisting mostly of a table of how to get from one state to another. Notice that when there are multiple clauses starting in the same state (corresponding to multiple arcs), each of them except the last contains a cut. This allows the last clause—the 'other' arc—to be taken only if none of the preceding ones match the input.

This transducer succeeds if given an acceptable pair of input strings, and fails if given an unacceptable pair, like this:

```
?- transduce(1,State,[r,a,k,e,+,e,d],[r,a,k,0,0,e,d]).
State=1
yes

?- transduce(1,State,[r,a,k,e,+,e,d],[r,a,k,e,0,e,d]).
no
```

What's more, in fine KIMMO tradition, it can find either one of the strings given the other one:

```
?- transduce(1,State,[r,a,k,e,+,e,d],What).
State=1
What=[r,a,k,0,0,e,d]

?- transduce(1,State,What,[r,a,k,0,0,e,d]).
State=1
What=[r,a,k,e,+,e,d]
```

Notice that deterministic finite-state transducers run fast and never backtrack.

**Exercise 9.4.5.1**

> Get the transducer working as shown, modify it to output information about each state transition that it performs, and use it to check your work from the first exercise of the previous section.

```
% state(+Old,-New,?Undl,?Surf)
%   Allows moving from state Old to state New
%   by accepting Undl and Surf characters.

state(1,2,C,C) :- \+ vowel(C), !.
state(1,1,X,X).
state(2,3,e,0) :- !.
state(2,2,C,C) :- \+ vowel(C), !.
state(2,1,X,X).
state(3,4,+,0).
state(4,5,V,V) :- vowel(V).
state(5,1,X,X).

% final_state(?N)
%   N is a state in which the transducer can stop.

final_state(1).
final_state(2).
final_state(5).

% vowel(V)
%   V is a vowel.

vowel(a).  vowel(e).  vowel(i).  vowel(o).  vowel(u).  vowel(y).

% transduce(Start,Finish,UndlString,SurfString)

transduce(Start,Finish,[U|UndlString],[S|SurfString]) :-
  state(Start,Next,U,S),
  transduce(Next,Finish,UndlString,SurfString).

transduce(Start,Start,[],[]) :-
  final_state(Start).
```

**Figure 9.7**   Finite-state transducer from Figure 9.6, in Prolog.

### Exercise 9.4.5.2

Add a clause to `transduce` that allows it to "accept" a null without actually accepting any characters. This will allow us to write [r,a,k,e,d] instead of [r,a,k,0,0,e,d] (very important for practical parsing). Verify that this works and use it to find the underlying string corresponding to *raked*. How many alternative answers do you get? Is this correct behavior? Explain why or why not.

### Exercise 9.4.5.3

In a previous exercise you expressed the *y*-to-*i* rule as a finite-state transducer. Now implement it in a program similar to that in Figure 9.7, and show that it correctly parses *carrying*.

**Exercise 9.4.5.4    (small project)**

> Now that you have two transducers, make them apply in parallel to the same input. That is, as you step through the strings, feed each pair of characters to both transducers. Verify that the resulting program accepts *raked* and *carried* and rejects *rakeed* and *carryed*.

**Exercise 9.4.5.5    (project)**

> Implement all four English morphographemic rules as transducers; also implement true lexical search (that is, instead of being given an underlying form as input, the program should search the character tree or the set of suffixes as appropriate). The result should be a very satisfactory parser for English inflection.

## 9.4.6 Critique of Two-Level Morphology

All in all, KIMMO looks very promising. How satisfied should we be with it?

The big question is whether two levels are really enough. Of course it's *possible* to make do with two levels—or even with no levels at all, by listing everything in the lexicon. But are two levels enough to capture the way a morphological system really works?

Perhaps so. Some analyses don't really need as many levels as they seem to. Recall that our three-level analysis *quiz+s* → *quiz+es* → *quizzes* was motivated by the fact that doubling can't be triggered until the vowel is put in. We were assuming that each rule could only look at the level immediately above it. By letting every rule look at *both* the underlying and surface forms, KIMMO avoids this problem; the doubling can be triggered by the following vowel that is, in some sense, "already there" in the surface though not the underlying form.

On the other hand, there are undeniably a lot of clear, insightful analyses that can only be stated by using more than two levels. Anderson (1988a) points out that KIMMO's Finnish lexicon does in fact treat some forms as irregular that could have been predicted by multilevel rules. So it would be premature to conclude that two levels are entirely adequate for describing the structure of a morphological system.

Another strike against KIMMO is that finite-state transducers are not the guarantee of simplicity that they seem to be. Barton, Berwick, and Ristad (1987) have proved that KIMMO's formalism is powerful enough to encode NP-complete problems, i.e., problems that require gigantic amounts of computer time. This is not a fatal objection, because no cases of apparent NP-completeness have shown up in real morphological systems. Apparently, and not surprisingly, human language is constrained in ways that KIMMO does not yet recognize.

Still less serious are the objections that KIMMO does not yet have some needed mechanisms. So far KIMMO has no good way to deal with discontinuous morphemes (such as Hebrew vowel patterns), nor with syntactic conditioning of morphophonemics [as when the French suffix *e* causes consonant doubling on adjectives but not on verbs, (Ritchie et al. 1992:185)]. Nor can it refer to phonological features (such as the feature [+labial] that distinguishes *p, b,* and *m* from all the other consonants); instead it has to use explicit lists or sets of phonemes (or letters). If KIMMO's basic approach proves adequate, additional mechanisms to do these jobs can easily be added.

## 9.5 FURTHER READING

Sproat (1992) is a fine introduction to morphology in general and computational morphology in particular. To get more acquainted with morphological phenomena, read the opening chapters of Spencer (1991), or the whole of Matthews (1991), and/or the appropriate parts of a descriptive linguistics text (even Bloomfield 1933); then, to learn about computer implementations, proceed to Wallace (1988) (available from UCLA), and Ritchie, Black, Russell, and Pulman (1992).

Morphology is an oddly placed branch of linguistics. In traditional generative grammar, morphology is not a separate level; morphophonemics is subsumed into phonology. The classic work in this genre is Chomsky and Halle (1968), which is now widely considered to be too abstract, and certainly does not lend itself to computer implementation. For reviews of present-day phonological and morphological theory, and references to further reading, see the articles in Newmeyer (1988, vol. 1) as well as the later chapters of Spencer (1991).

# Review of Prolog

## A.1  BEYOND INTRODUCTORY PROLOG

This appendix is not intended to teach you Prolog, but rather to review the language and present some topics that are often skipped in introductory courses. Some knowledge of Prolog is presumed from the beginning.

The emphasis will be on the data-structuring features of Prolog. I won't say much about how these features are used in natural language processing (that's what the rest of the book is for). In fact I will use plenty of examples that do not, by themselves, do anything useful at all. This is intentional. To understand what Prolog actually makes the computer do, it helps to look at the features of the language outside their usual context.

An important concern here will be to show that Prolog is simpler than you probably thought. Many details which you probably learned separately will turn out to be instances of just a few systematic principles.

## A.2  BASIC DATA TYPES

### A.2.1  Terms

Prolog is a language for data as much as for procedures. Every data item that can exist in Prolog has a written representation. In this respect Prolog is like Lisp and unlike languages such as Pascal, in which some data types, such as arrays, have no written representations (though their elements do).

Prolog data items are called TERMS. The syntax of terms in Prolog is modeled on the syntax of expressions in C. Terms are of three kinds: *variables, atomic terms* (NUMBERS and ATOMS), and compound terms (STRUCTURES).

Notice a difference between Prolog and Lisp terminology. In Lisp, the word *atom* refers both to symbols such as ABC and to numbers such as 45. In Prolog, *atom* normally means 'symbol.' Numbers are atomic terms, but they are not atoms.

Atoms normally begin with a lowercase letter and contain letters, digits, and/or the character '_'. Examples are x, xAB_cDE, and a1anda2.

Any series of characters enclosed in single quotes is an atom. Thus:

```
'this is a long atom with spaces and @#$!#$ in it'
```

A zero-length atom is written ' '.

Single quotes occurring within single quotes are written double. In some implementations, backslashes within single quotes are also written double; consult your manual.

An atom consisting entirely of special characters from the set

```
+ - * / \ ^ < = > ~ : . ? @ # $ &
```

does not need quotes. Thus :-, -->, and \+ are (or can be) atoms. (See your manual to confirm that your Prolog uses exactly this set of characters.)

**Exercise A.2.1.1**

Which of the following are Prolog atoms (symbols)?

| abc123 | list_all | list-all | 'ab cd' | "ab cd" | ?- |
| -----> | --def--> | 23 | '23' | '2+2' | (2+2) |

**Exercise A.2.1.2**

Which of the items in the previous exercise are atomic terms?

**Exercise A.2.1.3**

Why are there quotes in write('One') but not in write(one)?

**Exercise A.2.1.4**

Are abc and 'abc' the same atom? Use the computer to make sure of your answer, and state how you did so.

## A.2.2 Internal Representation of Atoms

Atoms are not character strings; they are locations in a symbol table. That is, the computer stores only one copy of each atom, no matter how many times it occurs in the program. All occurrences of the atom in the program are then replaced by pointers to its location in the symbol table.

This means that, during program execution, the comparison

```
abracadabraabracazam = abracadabraabrashazam
```

takes no more time than

```
a = b
```

because in each case, the pointers get compared rather than the strings of characters. The real comparison—that is, the determination whether the strings were identical—was done once and for all when the atoms were first placed in the symbol table.

Placing atoms in the symbol table is known as INTERNING or TOKENIZING the atoms. At every moment the symbol table contains all the atoms that exist—whether they are part of the program itself, or data being processed by the program, or anything else.

**Exercise A.2.2.1**

Which of the following built-in Prolog predicates can cause new atoms to be added to the symbol table? Explain why.

```
read/1     write/1     consult/1     reconsult/1     name/2     assert/1
```

### A.2.3 Compound Terms (Structures)

A STRUCTURE consists of a *functor* with one or more ARGUMENTS, such as `f(a,b,c)`. The arguments can be terms of any type, including other structures. The functor is an atom with a specific number of argument positions; `f` with one argument and `f` with two arguments are not the same functor.

In Prolog, a functor is merely a data-structuring device; it does not refer to a procedure that is to be applied to the arguments. It is just a kind of label. A structure such as `f(g(h,i),j(k,l))` represents a treelike data object that could be diagrammed as:

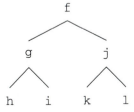

The ARITY of a functor is the number of arguments it takes. To refer to a functor, instead of saying "f, with 3 arguments" or "f, with arity 3" you can say `f/3`.

When a structure contains other structures, such as `f(a,b(c,d),e)`, the outermost functor (`f/3`, in this case) is called the PRINCIPAL FUNCTOR of the structure.

**Exercise A.2.3.1**

Draw tree diagrams of the following structures:

```
pred(a1,a2,a3,a4)      g(x(y,z,w),q(p,r(e(f))))      2+3*4
```

(Hint: Recall that + and * are functors that are written between their arguments.)

**Exercise A.2.3.2**

Suppose you are creating a Prolog knowledge base about a family tree. Would it make sense to use both `parent/2` and `parent/1` in the same program? What would each of them mean?

## A.2.4 Internal Representation of Structures

In the computer, a structure is a linked tree made of pointers to its substructures and to entries in the symbol table. For example, the structure `f(a(b,c),a,d)` is represented as:

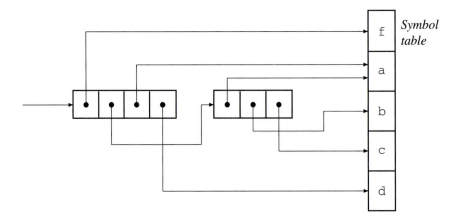

That is, each structure is represented by a CELL containing pointers to the functor and the arguments. The functor is always represented by an atom, i.e., an entry in the symbol table; the arguments can be terms of any type. The cell also contains other information not shown in the diagram, such as the arity of the functor. [If you are not familiar with this type of diagram, consult a data structures textbook. See also Covington, Nute, and Vellino (1988, ch. 7), and O'Keefe (1990, ch. 3).]

**Exercise A.2.4.1**

Draw both a tree diagram, and a cell-and-pointer diagram like the diagram above, for each of the following terms:

```
f(a,b)+g(c,d)      f(f(f(f(f(f(g)))))))      2+3*4
```

Note that to represent a number, Prolog does not use a pointer; instead it stores the number itself in the cell. Note also that, unlike the symbol table, the tree diagram of `f(f(a))` contains `f` in two different places.

**Exercise A.2.4.2**

Which structure takes more memory, `f(a,b,c,d,e)` or `f(abcde,abcde,abcde)`? Explain how you can answer this question without knowing the amount of memory needed for a character, a pointer, or a cell on any particular computer.

## A.2.5 Lists

A very useful kind of structure takes the form

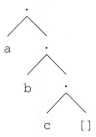

This structure consists of a, b, and c strung together; it is called a LIST. Here `[]` (pronounced "nil") is a special atom that denotes the end of the list. By itself, `[]` denotes an EMPTY LIST (a list with no elements).

Notice that the first argument of each dot functor (.) is an element, and the second argument is another list. That is: *every list consists of an element plus another list or* `[]`. If the whole thing does not end in `[]` it is called an IMPROPER LIST (like a dotted pair in Lisp).

There is a shorthand notation for lists, illustrated on the right below:

```
.(a,[])                =    [a]
.(a,.(b,.(c,[])))      =    [a,b,c]
.(a,b)                 =    [a|b]         % an improper list
.(a,.(b,.(c,d)))       =    [a,b,c|d]     % another improper list
```

Every nonempty list has the dot (.) as its principal functor.

The big advantage of lists over multiargument structures is that you can process a list without knowing how many elements it has. Any nonempty list will unify with `.(X,Y)` (more commonly written `[X|Y]`), regardless of the number of elements.

**Exercise A.2.5.1**

What is the most concise way of writing `[x,y|[]]`?

**Exercise A.2.5.2**

Write `.(.(a,.(b,[])),.(c,[]))` in ordinary list notation (with square brackets and commas) and draw a tree diagram of it.

### A.2.6 Internal Representation of Lists

Assuming the dot functor works as just described, the internal representation of the list
[a,b,c] should be:

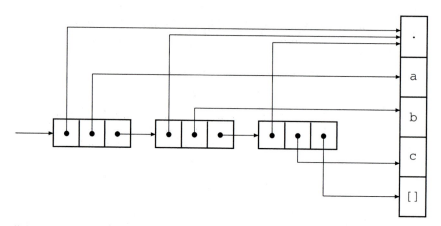

But lists are very common in Prolog, and all those pointers to the dot functor waste
space. Accordingly, almost all Prologs use a more compact representation of lists in
which [a,b,c] would be represented instead as

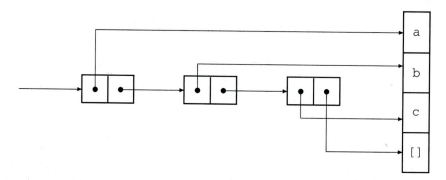

which is like the internal representation used in Lisp. That is, the dot functor is, internally,
no functor at all.

Regardless of which representation your Prolog uses, lists will behave *as if* they
were held together by the dot functor in the originally described way. But the compact representation saves memory. In particular, it makes [a,b,c] take up less
space than a listlike structure held together by some functor other than the dot, such
as f(a,f(b,f(c,[]))).

### Exercise A.2.6.1

Assuming that each pointer occupies 4 bytes, how much space is saved by representing
[a,b,c,d,e,f,g,h,i,j] the compact way instead of the original way?

## A.2.7 Strings

A string such as `"abc"` is simply another way of writing a list of the ASCII codes of the characters, in this case `[97,98,99]`. Do not be deceived; a string *is* a list of numbers, not characters. Like a list, a string can have zero length (written `""`).

The built-in predicate `name/2` interconverts atoms and strings. Some examples:

```
?- name(abc,What).
What = [97,98,99]        % that is, "abc"

?- name(What,"abc").
What = abc
```

This gives you a way to retrieve the character representation of an atom, or to construct a new atom out of characters strung together. (In C-Prolog, Quintus Prolog, and Arity Prolog, a string that validly represents a number, such as `"-234.5"`, will be converted into a Prolog number, not an atom. In ALS Prolog, ESL Prolog-2, and LPA Prolog, `name/2` always converts strings into atoms, not numbers.)

**Exercise A.2.7.1**

What is displayed by the Prolog query '`?- write("abc").`'? Why?

**Exercise A.2.7.2**

In what situation does `name/2` produce a zero-length atom?

**Exercise A.2.7.3**

Show how to use `name/2` to convert `"abracadabra"` into an atom.

**Exercise A.2.7.4**

Show how to use `name/2` to find out the ASCII code of the letter q.

## A.2.8 Charlists

The draft ISO standard (Scowen 1992) does not contain strings. Instead, programmers are encouraged to use lists of one-character atoms, `[l,i,k,e,' ',t,h,i,s]`, which I call *charlists*. The obvious advantages of charlists is that they are always output in readable form, and they do not rely on ASCII numeric codes.

The proposed standard calls for a built-in predicate `atom_chars/2` that interconverts atoms and charlists:

```
?- atom_chars(abc,What).
What = [a,b,c]

?- atom_chars(What,[a,b,c]).
What = abc
```

Quintus Prolog presently has a built-in predicate called `atom_chars`, but it doesn't do what the standard calls for; instead, it interconverts atoms and strings.

**Exercise A.2.8.1**

Define a recursive procedure `string_chars/2` that will interconvert strings and charlists. (Its first argument should be a string, and its second argument, a charlist; either argument can be uninstantiated.) (Hint: only two clauses are needed.)

**Exercise A.2.8.2**

Using `string_chars/2`, implement `atom_chars/2`. Don't worry about correct handling of numbers (e.g., `"23"`).

## A.3 SYNTACTIC ISSUES

### A.3.1 Operators

Some functors such as + can be written between their arguments, in which case no parentheses are needed. Thus `2+3` is equivalent to `+(2,3)`. Such functors are called INFIX OPERATORS.

In Prolog, opera*tors* need not stand for opera*tions*. Thus `2+3` does not mean 'add 2 and 3'—it's just a data structure with functor + and arguments 2 and 3. The built-in predicate `is`, and some others, can be used to evaluate the structure `2+3`, giving the number 5. Apart from this, `2+3` has nothing to do with 5. Here Prolog differs from most other programming languages, which evaluate '2+3' as '5' immediately wherever it occurs.

There are also PREFIX operators, which come before their arguments, and POSTFIX operators, which come after their arguments. An infix operator has two arguments; a prefix or postfix operator has only one.

The built-in predicate `display/1` displays any structure in ordinary (non-infix) notation, treating any operators within it as if they were ordinary functors.

**Exercise A.3.1.1**

What is displayed by the query '?- `display(2+[a,b])`.'? Try it on the computer and explain your results.

**Exercise A.3.1.2**

Consult the manual for the Prolog system that you are using, and give examples of predefined prefix and postfix operators (if any).

### A.3.2 The Deceptive Hyphen

Unlike the underscore mark, the hyphen ('-') cannot occur in an atom or variable name. If you try to put it there, you will get a structure in which the hyphen is an infix operator. That is, `abc-def` is not an atom; it's the structure `-(abc,def)`.

Because structures can occur in most of the places where atoms can occur, the compiler will not notice that you have made a mistake, but you will eventually get unexpected results.

**Exercise A.3.2.1**

Draw a tree diagram of `this-functor(a,b)`.

**Exercise A.3.2.2**

Consider the following knowledge base, in which the programmer has put hyphens in functors even though Prolog does not permit them there.

```
in-usa(X)  :- in-texas(X).              % Caution: risky syntax!
in-usa(X)  :- in-georgia(X).
in-texas(amarillo).
in-georgia(macon).
```

In spite of the syntax error, the knowledge base answers queries correctly. Why?

## A.3.3 The Dual Role of Parentheses

Parentheses serve two purposes in Prolog: to enclose the arguments of a functor, and to show how a term is to be divided up. The parentheses in `a+(b+c)` show that `b+c` is a term. Otherwise it wouldn't be; the first `+` would join `a` to `b` and the second `+` would join `a+b` to `c`.[1]

You are free to write parentheses around any term at any time. For example, `(((a)))` is the same term as `a`. The extra parentheses in

```
?- display( (b,c) ).
```

show that 'b,c' is to be treated as a single term even though it contains a comma. Otherwise `display` would be taken as having two arguments.

**Exercise A.3.3.1**

Demonstrate, using the computer, that `(((a)))` is equivalent to `a`.

## A.3.4 The Triple Role of Commas

This, of course, begs the question of what that comma is doing if it isn't separating arguments. The comma is, in fact, a right-associative infix operator. The term `(a,b,c,d,e,f)` is really `a,(b,(c,(d,(e,f))))` (analogous to `a+(b+(c+(d+(e+f))))`, but with commas instead of pluses). The Prolog rule

```
a :- b, c, d.
```

---

[1]In early versions of Arity Prolog, `a+(b+c)` has to be written as `a+ (b+c)`, because if any functor is written immediately before '(', Arity Prolog assumes that it is a functor of the ordinary kind (not an operator) with its arguments following in parentheses. This problem has been corrected in version 5.0.

is really

```
a :- (b, c, d).
```

or rather:

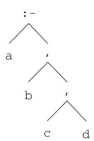

Knowing this structure is crucial if you want to write a Prolog program that processes other Prolog programs.

The comma has yet a third role in lists. In `[a,b,c]` the comma is neither an argument separator nor an infix operator; it is a list-element separator. Whenever a Prolog compiler encounters a comma, it has to figure out which of these three roles the comma is playing.

Some nonstandard versions of Prolog use the comma only as the argument separator; they use `&` as the infix operator, and something else as the list element separator.

**Exercise A.3.4.1**

Does `a :- b, c, d` unify with `X :- Y`?

**Exercise A.3.4.2**

Give an example of a Prolog term in which there are all three kinds of commas.

**Exercise A.3.4.3**

If a comma is in a position where it can be either an argument separator or an infix operator, which does your computer take it to be? How do you know?

## A.3.5 Op Declarations

You can define operators for yourself by specifying the functor you wish to make into an operator, its associativity, and its precedence.

For example, `a+b+c+d` is interpreted as `((a+b)+c)+d`, so `+` is said to be LEFT-ASSOCIATIVE. And `a+b*c` is interpreted as `a+(b*c)`, so `+` is said to have higher PRECEDENCE than `*` (the operator with higher precedence has larger parts of the term as arguments).

To make `&` into a right-associative infix operator with precedence 500, execute the query:

```
:- op(500,xfy,'&').
```

Here ':-' is what you write at the beginning of a query that is to be *executed*—not stored in the knowledge base—as the program is read in. See your Prolog manual for further details.

Note that by itself this op declaration does not give any meaning to '&'; it merely allows it to be written between its arguments.

### Exercise A.3.5.1

Which has higher precedence, - or / ?

### Exercise A.3.5.2

Which has higher precedence, :- or the comma?

### Exercise A.3.5.3

We said earlier that (a,b,c) = (a,(b,c)). Is the comma left-associative or right-associative?

## A.4 VARIABLES AND UNIFICATION

### A.4.1 Variables

Prolog variable names begin with upper-case letters or '_'. Examples are X, Y, WhatEver, _123.

Like-named variables occurring in the same term are considered to be the same variable. (Recall that a rule or a fact is one term.) Apart from this, variable names have no significance. In fact, in memory, variables have no names, only locations. This explains why, if you ask Prolog to output a term containing variables, the variables will have arbitrary names such as _0123.

The anonymous variable, written '_', is considered unique wherever it occurs; successive anonymous variables are not the same variable even if they occur in the same term.

### Exercise A.4.1.1

Of the three terms f(X,Y,Y), f(_3,_q,_q), and f(X,Y,_), which two are equivalent?

### A.4.2 Unification

Two terms can be UNIFIED (matched) if they are alike or can be made alike by INSTANTIATING (giving values to) variables. (Here instantiation includes the ability to make one variable the same as another.) For example:

f(X,Y) *unifies with* f(a,b) *instantiating* X=a, Y=b.

f(X,Y) *unifies with* f(Z,Z) *by making* X, Y, *and* Z *become the same variable.*

f(X,X) *does not unify with* f(a,b) *because* X *cannot have two different values at the same time in the same term.*

Unification is order-independent; if you unify a set of terms, you get the same result regardless of the order in which the terms are encountered. Much of the power of Prolog, particularly for natural language processing, comes from the order-independence of unification.

**Exercise A.4.2.1**

> Unify the following pairs of terms, or show why the unification cannot be performed:

```
f(X,Y)       with  f(a,b)
f(X,Y)       with  g(X,Y)
f(a,b,c)     with  f(a,X)
f(a,b,c)     with  f('a',X)
f(a,b,c)     with  f('a  ',X)
f(a,b,c)     with  f((('a')),X)
[a,b,c,d]    with  [Q|_234]
[a,b,c,d]    with  [X,Y|Z]
[a,X,b,Y]    with  [Z,a,B,b]
[a,X,Y,Y]    with  [Z,a,b,c]
[a,b,c,d]    with  [X,Y,Z]
(2+3)+X      with  Q+R
(2+3)+X      with  2+(3+4)
```

## A.5  PROLOG SEMANTICS

### A.5.1  Structure of a Prolog Program

A Prolog program is a file containing clauses and/or queries in the appropriate format for the Prolog reader.

CLAUSES contain information to be stored in the knowledge base. Clauses are of two kinds. FACTS are atoms or structures whose principal functor is not ':–' or '?–':

```
green(kermit).
ready_to_go.
kermit likes piggy.      (assuming likes is an infix operator)
```

RULES consist of a term, then the symbol ':–', then one or more terms joined by commas:

```
green(X)  :- wet(X).
piggy likes X :- handsome(X), amphibian(X).
```

For some purposes the fact green(kermit) is equivalent to the rule green(kermit) :– true, where true is a built-in predicate that succeeds with no other action.

The HEAD of a rule is the term to the left of ':–'; the BODY is the term on the right (which can be a series of terms joined by commas). The body of a fact is true.

A PREDICATE is defined by a set of one or more clauses whose heads have the same principal functor. A predicate or one of its clauses is often referred to as a PROCEDURE. Unlike other languages, Prolog lets the same procedure have more than one definition; each clause is one of its definitions. Sometimes the clauses give ways of handling different arguments; sometimes they give alternative ways of handling the same argument.

A QUERY is a request for the computer to do something. When a query occurs in the program file, it is preceded by ':-' (with nothing else on the left) thus:

```
:- write('Program is loading...').
```

The Prolog system loads (CONSULTS) a file by reading clauses and queries from it one by one. The clauses get stored in memory; the queries get executed immediately, the moment they are encountered.

The draft ISO standard does not specify how to consult a file. Traditionally, Prolog has had three built-in predicates:

- consult (*filename*) reads the file into memory for the first time;
- reconsult (*filename*) reads the file again after it has been edited; it discards previously existing predicates from memory when it encounters new definitions of the same predicates;
- compile (*filename*), if available, is like reconsult except that the code is compiled rather than interpreted, and thus will run faster.

In most Prologs, if you consult the same file twice, you will end up with two copies of each clause in memory. This does not happen with reconsult, but in some older Prologs (such as Arity 4.0), reconsult requires all the clauses for each predicate to be contiguous, and if they aren't, it will discard all but the last contiguous group. In Quintus Prolog, consult and reconsult are exactly alike; neither of them will produce duplicates if done repeatedly, and neither of them requires clauses to be contiguous (but if style checking is turned on, you will get warnings about discontiguous predicates).

**Exercise A.5.1.1**

What is the head of each of the following clauses?

```
green(kermit).
green(X) :- wet(X).
kermit likes piggy.
```

**Exercise A.5.1.2**

Explain what happens when the following file is consulted. Assume that the knowledge base is initially empty.

```
:- write('Starting'), nl.
:- green(kermit), write('Succeeded the first time'), nl.
green(kermit).
:- green(kermit), write('Succeeded the second time'), nl.
```

## A.5.2 Execution

Here is how Prolog executes a query.

- If the query is a series of terms joined by commas, the individual terms are treated as queries (SUBGOALS) and executed one by one, in sequence. That is, to execute

```
?- green(X), write(X).
```

  the Prolog system executes `green(X)` and then `write(X)`. Notice that the whole query is itself a term, and hence the two X's here are the same variable.

- If the principal functor of the query is a built-in predicate, the system performs the appropriate system-defined action:

```
?- write(hello).
```

- Otherwise, the system finds the first clause whose head can unify with the query and performs the unification. If the clause is a fact, no other action is performed. If the clause is a rule, its right-hand side is treated as a new query. Thus the rule

```
a(X)  :- b(X), c(X).
```

  transforms the query

```
?- a(zzz).
```

  into the query

```
?- b(zzz), c(zzz).
```

A fact by itself can do useful work. The query '`?- green(X).`' can be answered by the fact `green(kermit)`, which instantiates X to `kermit`.

**Exercise A.5.2.1**

Show how the query '`?- amphibian(kermit).`' is transformed into other queries, and ultimately solved, in the following knowledge base:

```
amphibian(X)  :-
    'Latin name'(X,Genus,Species),
    class('Amphibia',Genus).

'Latin name'(kermit,'Rana',catesbiana).

class('Amphibia','Rana').
```

**Exercise A.5.2.2**

Do the same for the query '?- amphibian(Who).'

## A.5.3 Backtracking

If at any point there is no clause to match the current query, that query is said to FAIL. Execution then backs up to the nearest BACKTRACK POINT (untried alternative), undoing any unifications that took place subsequent to that point, and proceeds forward again along an alternative path.

Alternatives exist because more than one clause can match the same query. Whenever execution enters a clause and there is another clause (as yet untried) that would have matched the same query, the Prolog system records a backtrack point.

**Exercise A.5.3.1**

Given the knowledge base

```
a(X)  :- b(X).
a(X)  :- c(X).
b(Z)  :- d(Z).
b(Z)  :- e(Z).
c(Y)  :- h(Y).
e(f).
```

show exactly what goals are tried, in what order, to solve the query '?- a(f).' (You may find it convenient to draw a treelike diagram.) Which backtrack points are left untried?

## A.5.4 Negation as Failure

If the query '?- p.' succeeds then the query '?- \+ p.' fails, and vice versa. The symbol '\+' is pronounced 'not' and was written not in older Prologs.

A query that fails does not leave a variable instantiated. By definition, either \+ p(X) fails or p(X) fails. Therefore the query '?- \+ p(X).' leaves X uninstantiated.

A double \+ is a handy way of finding out whether a query would succeed, without instantiating the variables in it. Thus '?- \+ \+ p(X).' succeeds if and only if p(X) would succeed, but does not leave X instantiated.

To force a clause to fail, put '!, fail' at the end of it. This is rarely necessary. Usually, rather than write a clause that will fail in a particular situation, you simply refrain from writing a clause that will succeed in that situation.

**Exercise A.5.4.1**

Is the clause f(X) :- \+ \+ \+ g(X). of any practical use? Why or why not?

**Exercise A.5.4.2**

What do the following clauses do? Suggest a more obvious way of doing the same thing.

```
not_a_list([_|_]) :- !, fail.
not_a_list(_).
```

## A.5.5 Cuts

The CUT predicate, written '!', tells the Prolog system to forget about some of the backtrack points. Specifically, it discards all backtrack points that have been recorded since execution entered the current clause. This means that, after executing a cut,

- it is no longer possible to try other clauses as alternatives to the current clause;
- it is no longer possible to try alternative solutions to subgoals preceding the cut in the current clause.

This applies, of course, only to the goal that caused execution to enter the current clause in the first place; it does not permanently change the knowledge base.

An example will make this clearer. Consider the program:

```
/* Clause 1 */   a(X) :- b(X).
/* Clause 2 */   a(w).
/* Clause 3 */   b(X) :- c(X), !, d(X).
/* Clause 4 */   b(y).
/* Clause 5 */   b(w).
/* Clause 6 */   c(w).
/* Clause 7 */   d(z).
```

The query '?- b(y).' succeeds. It first matches clause 3, but c(y) fails and execution backs out of clause 3 before the cut is executed, and then tries clause 4, successfully.

The query '?- b(w).' fails. Execution enters clause 3, c(w) succeeds, the cut is executed, and then d(w) fails. But because of the cut, it is impossible to try any other clauses for c or b, so the fact b(w) is ignored.

The query '?- a(w).' however succeeds. Clause 1 invokes clause 3, which fails just as before. However, the cut in clause 3 does not impair backtracking out of clause 1, so execution backtracks from clause 1 to clause 2 and then succeeds.

**Exercise A.5.5.1**

Given the knowledge base

```
f(X) :- g(X), !, h(X).
f(X) :- j(X).
g(a).
j(a).
```

what is the result of executing the query '?- f(a).'?

**Exercise A.5.5.2**

Given the knowledge base:

```
x(X)  :- a(X), b(X), !.
x(X)  :- c(X).
a(aa).
b(aa).
c(cc).
```

what is the effect of each of the following queries?

```
?- x(aa).
?- x(cc).
?- x(What), write(What), nl, fail.
```

**Exercise A.5.5.3**

Consider the knowledge base:

```
a :- b, my_cut, c(1).
a :- d.
b.
c(0).
d.
my_cut :- !.
```

What happens when the user types the query '?- a.'? What if my_cut in the first line is changed to '!'?

## A.5.6 Disjunction

If two subgoals are joined by a semicolon ( ; ) rather than a comma, they are alternatives. The Prolog system executes the first subgoal and remembers the second subgoal as an untried alternative. Thus

```
p :- q ; r.
```

is equivalent to

```
p :- q.
p :- r.
```

In this book the semicolon is rarely used. It is usually preferable to use alternative clauses.

### A.5.7 Control Structures Not Used in This Book

Most Prologs (including the draft ISO standard, but not Arity) have an "if-then" structure of the form `(p -> q ; r)` (pronounced "if p then q else r"). To execute this structure, the computer first tries to execute p. If p succeeds, it then executes q; otherwise it executes r. In either case it does not leave a backtrack point.

The "if-then" is not used in this book. Instead of

```
f :- (p -> q ; r).
```

this book uses

```
f :- p, !, q.
f :- r.
```

Arity Prolog has limited-scope cuts called "snips," written `[! !]`. Once execution has progressed through the closing snip `!]`, it is no longer possible to backtrack to any alternatives within the snips. To implement essentially the same thing in other Prologs, we can define a metapredicate `once`:[2]

```
once(Goal) :- Goal, !.
```

Here `Goal` can be a compound goal (a set of goals joined by infix commas). So the equivalent of `[!, p, q, r, !]` is `once((p,q,r))`, but `once` can be used in practically any Prolog, not just Arity. In the draft ISO standard, `once` is a built-in predicate.

### A.5.8 Self-Modifying Programs

Prolog programs can modify themselves. The built-in predicate `asserta/1` inserts a clause *before* the preexisting clauses for its predicate (if any). For example,

```
?- asserta( (f(X) :- g(X)) ).
```

inserts the rule `f(X) :- g(X)` in front of the first preexisting clause for `f/1`. (Notice the extra parentheses that are necessary whenever the argument of `asserta` contains ':-'.) The predicate `assertz/1` does the same thing, except that it would put `f(X) :- g(X)` *after* the preexisting clauses for `f/1`.

The built-in predicate `retract/1` removes a clause from the knowledge base. Specifically, it removes the first clause that matches its argument, or fails if there is no such clause. For example,

```
?- retract(green(X)).
```

---

[2]Some older Prologs require `Goal` on the right-hand side to be written as `call(Goal)`.

removes the first clause that matches `green(X)`, simultaneously unifying X with whatever was in the argument position. Because of this unification, `retract` can be used
to retrieve information while deleting it from the knowledge base. Like `asserta`,
`assertz`, and all other Prolog functors, `retract` requires extra parentheses if its
argument contains ':-' or a comma.

To retract all the clauses of `f/2`, you can use with either

```
?- abolish(f/2).
```

(or in ALS Prolog, `abolish(f,2)`).

One extremely important point must not be forgotten:

> `asserta`, `assertz`, and `retract` are *not* a general-purpose way of stor-
> ing temporary data.

Their use is justified only in situations that reflect a genuine, permanent change to the
knowledge contained in the program. The normal way to hold information temporarily
(analogous to storing it in a Pascal or C variable) is to pass it along in the arguments of
procedures (see the section on repetitive algorithms below).

### Exercise A.5.8.1

What would be in the knowledge base after execution of the following four queries? Assume
that beforehand, there were no clauses for `green`.

```
?- assertz(green(kermit)).
?- asserta(green(eggs+ham)).
?- assertz(green(cheese)).
?- asserta(green(grass)).
```

### Exercise A.5.8.2

Which of the following queries will successfully retract the clause '`f(X)  :- g(X),
h(X).`'? Explain why.

```
?- retract(f(X)).
?- retract((f(W)  :- g(W), h(W))).
?- retract((f(WXYZ)  :- g(WXYZ), h(Q))).
?- retract(f(X)  :- Y).
?- retract((f(X)  :- Y)).
?- abolish(f/1).
?- abolish(f/3).
```

### A.5.9 Dynamic Declarations

In Quintus Prolog and in the draft ISO standard, if any of the clauses for a predicate are to be asserted or retracted, the program must contain a declaration such as

```
:- dynamic f/2.
```

(where `f/2` stands for predicate `f` taking 2 arguments) before the clauses for the predicate (if any). This tells the compiler not to compile the clauses into a form that cannot be recognized at run time. In fact Quintus does not compile them at all; it runs them interpretively.

The only exception is that if a predicate is created entirely by asserting, it is automatically dynamic and need not be declared.

Dynamic declarations are not required by `abolish`; you can abolish any predicate, even a compiled one.

## A.6 INPUT AND OUTPUT

The input-output system described here is the traditional one from Edinburgh (DEC-10) Prolog. Virtually all present-day Prolog implementations support it, but the draft ISO standard introduces a different input-output system only partly compatible with the original one. When in doubt, check your manual.

### A.6.1 The Prolog Reader

Built into Prolog is a procedure for reading terms from input devices (files, the keyboard, etc.) and converting them into their internal representations. This procedure is called the READER and you can access it through the built-in predicate `read/1`. The reader is also used by `consult` and `reconsult` and by the routine that accepts queries that you type on the keyboard.

`read/1` reads, from the standard input file, exactly one Prolog term followed by a period, then unifies its argument with this term. The term can be of any kind whatsoever.

The reason for ending with a period is that a term can occupy more than one line. After the period there must be a blank, or a comment, or the end of the line; thus the period in the middle of the term `3.2` does not denote end of term.

The character `%` (not in quotes) makes the reader ignore everything until the beginning of the next line. The sequence `/*` makes it skip everything until after the following `*/`. Thus both `%` and `/* */` provide ways to delimit COMMENTS. Comments are permitted not only in programs, but in everything that the reader reads. Generally, however, you cannot put a comment within another comment.

Extra blanks and comments are permitted anywhere, so long as they do not interrupt a number, atom, functor, or quoted string, nor come between a functor and the parenthesis that introduces its arguments. Thus `f(a)` can be written `f( a )` but not as `f (a)`.

The reader recognizes variables but does not preserve their names. It *does* notice when two like-named variables occur in the same term. Thus, if you type [X,X] you get a list with two instances of the same variable in it. Notice that a Prolog clause such as

```
f(X) :- g(X), h(X).
```

is all one term, which is why all the occurrences of X in it are treated as the same variable.

When the reader tries to read past the end of a file, it behaves as if it has read the atom end_of_file. This is of course also what it reads if it encounters the characters

```
end_of_file.
```

which you can insert in the middle of a file to make the reader stop reading there.

**Exercise A.6.1.1**

What does '?- read(yes).' do if the user types 'yes.'? What if the user types 'no.' or 'Yes.'?

**Exercise A.6.1.2**

In your Prolog, is a/*comment*/b treated like ab or like a  b? State how you tested this.

**Exercise A.6.1.3**

What is printed by the query '?- write(f(X,Y,X)).'? Why? What does the reader have to do with this?

**Exercise A.6.1.4**

In the Prolog clauses

```
f(X) :- h(X).
g(X) :- z(X).
```

which occurrences of X are the same variable? Explain why the reader is responsible for this.

## A.6.2 The Writer

Corresponding to the reader there is, of course, a WRITER whose job is to produce a written representation of any term. The writer is usually accessed through write/1. Note, however, a possible problem:

```
?- write('hello there').
hello there
```

In this case the term 'hello there' is written out as hello there, which is not a term. Thus, in this case, output written by write is not suitable to be read back in by read.

The built-in predicate `writeq` remedies this problem. Everything that it writes is in legal Prolog syntax:

```
?- writeq('hello there').
'hello there'

?- writeq(2+3-4).
2+3-4
```

But there is still a potential problem. Suppose you have defined `likes` to be an infix operator. Then you can do the following:

```
?- writeq(kermit likes piggy).
kermit likes piggy
```

The reader will accept `kermit likes piggy` *if* it knows that `likes` is an infix operator. A subsequent program, reading this term back in from a file, would encounter difficulties if it did not have the same infix operator defined.

A third built-in predicate, `display`, remedies this problem too: `display` writes terms so that they can be read back in without relying on any operator declarations at all. For example:

```
?- display(2+3-4).
'-'('+'(2,3),4)

?- display(kermit likes piggy).
likes(kermit,piggy)
```

Finally, remember that if you are writing out terms to a file so that the reader can subsequently read them, you must put a period after each term.

### A.6.3 Character Input-Output

The built-in predicate `put/1` outputs the character whose ASCII code is given as its argument. For example, '`?- put(65).`' outputs the letter A.

The built-in predicate `get0/1` accepts a character from the input stream and unifies its argument with the ASCII code of that character. For example, '`?- get0(X).`' reads one character and unifies its code with X, and '`?- get0(65).`' reads a character and succeeds if that character is 'A' or fails otherwise.

Another built-in predicate, `get/1`, works like `get0` except that it skips over any nonprinting characters (blanks, returns, line feeds, etc.) and reads the first nonblank character. These predicates will be covered more fully in Chapter 3.

#### Exercise A.6.3.1

Define a predicate called `copy3` that accepts three characters from the keyboard and writes their ASCII codes (as numbers) on the screen. Experiment with its behavior using both `get` and `get0`.

### A.6.4 File Input-Output

Prolog normally reads from the keyboard and writes to the screen. These are referred to as STANDARD INPUT and STANDARD OUTPUT, respectively. Standard input and output can be REDIRECTED to files or to anything else that the operating system can treat as a file (such as a printer).

To redirect standard input, use `see(filename)`; to redirect standard output, use `tell(filename)`, where `filename` is a Prolog atom giving the name of the file. To close the files and cancel the redirection, use `seen` and `told`, respectively.

Whenever input or output is redirected to a file, the file is opened for reading or writing as the case may be. This means that redirected input always starts at the beginning of the file, and redirected output always starts by creating the file (and destroying any like-named file that already exists). It is, however, possible to have many files open at once. Here is an example:

```
test :-
    see(file1),         % start at beginning of file1
    read(T1),           % read a term
    see(file2),         % start at beginning of file2
    read(T2),           % read a term
    see(file1),         % switch back to file1
    read(T3),           % read second term on file1
    write([T1,T2,T3]),  % write results on the screen
    seen.               % close all files
```

Use `see(user)` or `tell(user)` to redirect input or output to the keyboard or screen without closing files. Use `seeing(F)` or `telling(F)` to find out the name of the file that input or output is currently using. Thus, the following code writes a message on the screen, then switches subsequent output back to wherever it had been redirected:

```
    :
    :
telling(F),
tell(user),
write('This is a message'),
tell(F),
    :
    :
```

Redirection can be dangerous, because if the program crashes while input or output is redirected, you may be unable to see the error messages or type any further input to the Prolog system. Almost all Prologs provide a way to read and write files without redirecting standard input or output. Unfortunately, such methods are not standardized and therefore cannot be used in this book.

All the built-in input-output predicates are DETERMINISTIC; that is, they do not yield alternative solutions upon backtracking.

**Exercise A.6.4.1**

Under what conditions must a file name be given in quotes?

**Exercise A.6.4.2**

Write a short program that accepts three terms (each followed by a period) from the keyboard, writes them out to a file named ECHO.DAT, and then reads them back in and displays them on the screen.

**Exercise A.6.4.3**

What does '?- read(X), fail.' do?

## A.7 EXPRESSING REPETITIVE ALGORITHMS

### A.7.1 `repeat` loops

The built-in predicate `repeat` is considered to have an infinite number of different solutions, so that execution can backtrack to it and go forward again an infinite number of times:

```
?- repeat,
      write('I run forever...'),
   fail.
```

More commonly, of course, the repetition is stopped by executing a cut after some test is passed. Here is a predicate that copies terms from standard input to standard output, up to and including `end_of_file`:

```
copy_terms :-
   repeat,
      read(X),
      write(X), nl,
      X == end_of_file,    % the test
   !.
```

Without the cut, repetition would still stop when `X == end_of_file` succeeds (because Prolog only backtracks from failures, not successes), but a subsequent failure might cause repetition to resume, as in a query like '?- copy_terms, z.' if z fails.

`repeat` loops are not as useful as you might think, because there is no way to carry information along from one pass to the next. All variable instantiations are undone as you backtrack through them. Also, execution will backtrack from any query that fails—not just the one you think of as the test.

In fact, the main use of `repeat` loops is to sift through input. There is a good reason for this. Something external has to change, from one repetition to the next, in order to ensure that the looping will terminate. So a `repeat` loop that does not look at something external, such as a file, will rarely be useful.

**Exercise A.7.1.1**

The following predicate is supposed to copy characters from standard input to standard output until a blank is encountered. After copying the blank it should stop.

```
copy_until_blank :-                      % Contains error!
    repeat,
        get0(Char),
        put(Char),
    [Char] == " ".
```

What did the programmer do wrong? Show how to demonstrate that the program does not work entirely as desired.

**Exercise A.7.1.2**

Define a predicate `get_lower_case_letter/1` that is like `get` except that, instead of just skipping nonprinting characters, it skips everything that is not a lower-case letter.

For example, '`?- get_lower_case_letter(X)`' should find the first lower-case letter on the input stream and instantiate X to the ASCII code of that letter. Likewise, '`?- get_lower_case_letter(100)`' should read the first lower-case letter on the input stream and succeed if that letter was code 100 ('d') or fail otherwise.

## A.7.2 Recursion

To do something repeatedly and carry information along from one pass to the next, use RECURSION—that is, make a procedure call itself. This is just like induction in logic. (Formal logic does not allow you to just "repeat" a line in a proof; instead, you must define one thing in terms of another so that you get the repetition you need.) Here's how to print the integers from 1 to 100:

```
count_from(X)  :-
    X > 100.           % succeed with no further action

count_from(X)  :-
    X =< 100,          % print this number, compute next one
    write(X), nl,
    NewX is X+1,
    count_from(NewX).

?- count_from(1).
```

Here X is called a STATE VARIABLE because it passes along information about the state of the computation. (State variables are also called ACCUMULATORS because they accumulate information.) Note that there's no way to change the value of X once it's instantiated, so instead of X the recursive call has `NewX`.

Often, in addition to the arguments that pass information into and out of a procedure, you will need other arguments for state variables. In such a case it is convenient
to define a second predicate (traditionally named something-aux and called an AUX-
ILIARY PREDICATE). The first predicate has only the arguments that are meaningful to
the user, and it calls the aux predicate, which has the full set of arguments. For
example:

```
reverse(List1,List2) :- reverse_aux(List1,[],List2).

reverse_aux([H|T],Stack,Result) :-
    reverse_aux(T,[H|Stack],Result).

reverse_aux([],Result,Result).
```

This is a classic list-reversal algorithm.

**Exercise A.7.2.1**

In reverse_aux/3 above, how does Result come to be instantiated?

**Exercise A.7.2.2**

Define a predicate add_up(X,Y,Z) which unifies Z with the sum of the integers from X
to Y inclusive. Do this by actually adding the integers, not by using a formula.

## A.7.3 Traversing a List

Here's an example of how to work through a list ("CDR down it," in Lisp parlance).
The task, in this case, is to make a copy of the list in which every occurrence of a is
replaced with b. The program logic will be very similar no matter what you are looking
for in the list, and whether or not you are making an altered copy.

```
rewrite(a,b) :- !.     % a rewrites as b
rewrite(X,X).          % anything else rewrites as itself

rewrite_list([],[]).

rewrite_list([First|Rest],[NewFirst|NewRest]) :-
    rewrite(First,NewFirst),
    rewrite_list(Rest,NewRest).
```

An example of its use:

```
?- rewrite_list([a,b,r,a,c,a,d,a,b,r,a],What).
What = [b,b,r,b,c,b,d,b,b,r,b]
```

The logic here is: To do something to a whole list, do it to the first element, then do it
to the list of remaining elements.

**Exercise A.7.3.1**

Define a recursive predicate `maximum(List,N)` which unifies `N` with the largest integer contained in `List`. Assume that all the elements of `List` are integers.

**Exercise A.7.3.2**

Define a recursive predicate `depth(List,N)` which unifies `N` with the depth of a list, defined as follows:

- Any term that is not a list has depth 0.
- The depth of any list is 1 + the depth of its deepest element.

Thus the depth of `a` is 0; the depth of `[a,b]` is 1; the depth of `[a,[b,c]]` and of `[[a,b],c]` is 2; and so on.

## A.7.4 Traversing a Structure

Often, instead of just lists, you'll need to process arbitrary terms, examining and possibly changing everything that is inside them. For example, if you implement an extension to Prolog (as was done in Chapter 5), you'll want to read every term in a program, searching for your special symbols and converting them into something else, while leaving the rest alone.

Here's how to generalize `rewrite_list/2` so it works for any term:

```
% rewrite_term(+Term1,?Term2)
%   Copies Term1 changing every atom or functor 'a' to 'b'
%   (using rewrite/2 from previous section).

rewrite_term(X,X) :-
    var(X),            % don't alter uninstantiated variables
    !.

rewrite_term(X,Y) :-
    atomic(X),         % 'atomic' means atom or number
    !,
    rewrite(X,Y).

rewrite_term(X,Y) :-
    X =.. XList,               % convert structures to lists
    rewrite_aux(XList,YList),  % process them
    Y =.. YList.              % convert back to structures

rewrite_aux([],[]).

rewrite_aux([First|Rest],[NewFirst|NewRest]) :-
    rewrite_term(First,NewFirst),    % note recursion here
    rewrite_aux(Rest,NewRest).
```

This procedure uses '=..' (pronounced "univ," which was its name in Colmerauer's early Prolog) to convert structures into lists and back; for example, `f(a,b,c) =.. [f,a,b,c]`. Either of the arguments of `=..` can be instantiated, and the other one will be given the appropriate value.

Even lists can be converted this way. For example,

```
[a,b,c] =.. ['.',a,[b,c]]
```

because the principal functor of every list is the dot. Thus, lists are a special case of structures and do not require a clause of their own in `rewrite_term/2`.

Notice that `rewrite_aux` (used by `rewrite_term`) is like `rewrite_list`, which we defined earlier, except that it uses `rewrite_term` recursively on the first element of each list. This ensures that structures within structures are all processed.

### Exercise A.7.4.1

Define `depth(Structure,N)` such that N will be unified with the depth of `Structure`. This time depth is defined as follows:

- An atomic term has depth 0.
- The depth of a structure is 1 + the depth of its deepest argument.

For example, the depth of `f(a,b(c,d(e),f),g)` is 3.

### Exercise A.7.4.2

What is the depth of a ten-element list according to the definition just given?

## A.7.5 Arrays in Prolog

Prolog has no arrays. However, it has two reasonable substitutes. First, if an array is to be used as a lookup table, replace it with a set of facts. For example:

```
nthprime(1,2).
nthprime(2,3).
nthprime(3,5).
nthprime(4,7).
    ⋮
```

This is a table for looking up the *n*th prime number. You can build it by executing a program that finds primes and uses `assertz`.

Second, a multi-argument structure acts like an array of Prolog terms or variables. For example,

```
f(A,B,C,D,E,F,G,H,I,J,K,L,M,N,O,P,Q,R,S,T,U,V,W,X,Y)
```

is like a 25-element array of variables; you can pass it around and instantiate or test the variables one by one.

To get to the *n*th argument without unifying the whole structure with anything, use the built-in predicate `arg(N,Structure,Arg)`, which unifies `Arg` with the Nth argument of `Structure`. For example,

```
?- arg(15,f(a,b,c,d,e,f,g,h,i,j,k,l,m,n,o,p,q,r,s,t,u,v,w,x,y),W).
```

unifies `W` with `o`. This is *much* faster than putting the whole structure through the unification process.

**Exercise A.7.5.1**

In C, a two-dimensional array is simply a one-dimensional array of one-dimensional arrays. What does this suggest about how to represent a two-dimensional array in Prolog? Give an example of a $3 \times 3$ matrix implemented this way.

**Exercise A.7.5.2**

Prolog implementations put a limit on the number of arguments in a structure—typically 256. What is the limit in the Prolog that you use? How did you find out?

## A.8  EFFICIENCY ISSUES

### A.8.1  Tail Recursion

Recursion eats up memory because, whenever one procedure invokes another, a record has to be kept of where to come back to when the second procedure finishes.

There is an exception: suppose the first procedure calls the second as its *very last step,* with no further actions to be performed and no backtrack points to be remembered. Then execution can simply jump into the second procedure without setting up a way for control to return to the first one. (At the end, control will instead end up wherever it was to have gone at the end of the first procedure.)

Recursion that satisfies this condition is called TAIL RECURSION. An example:

```
f(X) :- X < 100.                        % Tail recursive example
f(X) :- X >= 100, Y is X-1, f(Y).
```

If the recursive call isn't last, the procedure isn't tail recursive:

```
g(X) :- X >= 100, Y is X-1, g(Y), z.    % Not tail recursive
```

Nor is it tail recursive if there's still an untried alternative at the time the recursive call takes place. This is the case if the clauses in the example are in the opposite order:

```
h(X) :- X >= 100, Y is X-1, h(Y).       % Not tail recursive
h(X) :- X < 100.
```

When the first rule calls itself, the second rule hasn't yet been tried, so a backtrack point has to be stored on the stack. As the first rule calls itself over and over, the stack can eventually fill up. Try a query like '?- h(10000).' to see what happens.

In almost all Prologs, a cut will make such a procedure tail recursive after all, by eliminating the untried alternative:[3]

```
j(X) :- X >= 100, !, Y is X-1, j(Y).    % Tail recursive
j(X) :- X < 100.                        % because of cut
```

Place the cut so that it will be executed as soon as it is certain that execution has entered the right clause.

**Exercise A.8.1.1**

Rearrange the clauses in the following predicate definition and add cuts so that the predicate is tail recursive and never leaves behind an unnecessary backtrack point.

```
% contains_list(+L)
%    succeeds if L is a list that contains another list

contains_list([[]|_]).
contains_list([_|X]) :- contains_list(X).
contains_list([[_|_]|_]).
```

## A.8.2 Indexing

Almost all Prologs[4] can eliminate unnecessary backtrack points by looking ahead to see which clauses the query can match. For example, given the knowledge base

```
f(a(X),Y) :- f(X,Y).
f(b(X),Y) :- g(X,Y).
```

and the query '?- f(a(something),something).' the Prolog system will look ahead and see that the second clause cannot possibly match this query, so when it enters the first clause, it will not leave behind a backtrack point. As a result, this predicate becomes tail recursive even though it does not appear to be.

This feature is called *indexing*. Obviously, the Prolog system cannot predict with complete certainty which clauses will succeed; all it can do is rule out some obvious mismatches in advance.

Indexing normally looks only at the principal functor of the first argument. Thus indexing will distinguish f(a(X),Y) from f(b(X),Y), but it will not distinguish

---

[3]Exceptions include Arity Prolog Interpreter 4.0 and ESL Public Domain Prolog-2 version 2.3.5. In these implementations, the cut keeps the backtrack point from being used, but doesn't prevent it from being stored on the stack.

[4]Not ESL Public Domain Prolog-2 2.3.5.

`f(Y,a(X))` from `f(Y,b(X))`. This means that in order to take advantage of indexing, you should design your predicates so that the first argument has a variety of principal functors and is usually instantiated when the predicate is called.

**Exercise A.8.2.1**

Is the predicate

```
print_list([H|T]) :- write(H), put(32), print_list(T).
print_list([]).
```

tail recursive in a system with indexing? Why or why not? (And what does `put(32)` accomplish?)

**Exercise A.8.2.2**

By changing only the order of arguments, make the predicate

```
p(Y,f(Z)) :- p(Y,Z).
p(Y,[Y]).
```

tail recursive, assuming first-argument indexing.

## A.8.3 Computing by Unification Alone

Sometimes unification, by itself, can do the computation you need. Here's a predicate that tests whether its argument is a three-element list, and succeeds if so:

```
has_three_elements([_,_,_]).
```

Note that there is no call to `length/2` or anything like that. Unification does all the work.

Likewise, here's a predicate that takes any list and creates another list just like it with the first two elements swapped:

```
swap_first_two([A,B|Rest],[B,A|Rest]).
```

For example, the query '`?- swap_first_two([x,y,z],What).`' will instantiate `What` to `[y,x,z]`.

**Exercise A.8.3.1**

Define a predicate which, using unification alone, will convert `2+3` to `2-3`, or `(3+4)+f(x)` to `(3+4)-f(x)`, or, generally, any structure with principal functor `+` to the corresponding structure with principal functor `-`.

### A.8.4 Avoidance of Consing

Programs run more efficiently if they can avoid creating new structures and lists (an activity known to Lisp programmers as "consing").

It is much faster to instantiate a previously uninstantiated part of a structure, than to make a new copy of the whole structure in order to add information.

For example, if you want to build the list `[a,b,c,d]`, it is much faster to start with `[a,b,c|X]` and instantiate `X` to `[d]`, rather than starting with `[a,b,c]` and appending `[d]` to it.

A list with an uninstantiated tail, such as `[a,b,c|X]`, is called an OPEN LIST. Often you'll want to keep, outside the list, a pointer to the uninstantiated tail, so that you can get to the tail without searching through all the elements. This is called a DIFFERENCE LIST; an example is `f([a,b,c|X],X)`. Here `f` has no particular meaning; you could use any functor. Many people use the infix operator '`-`' or '`/`'.

The traditional predicate `append/3` can be a time waster; whenever you find yourself using it, see if the same work can be done more quickly with open lists or difference lists.

Another time waster is `=..` ("univ"), which builds a list from a structure. If you only need to retrieve part of the structure, it is much quicker to use `arg(N,Structure, Arg)`.

**Exercise A.8.4.1**

Define a predicate `open_list_length(OpenList,N)` which will unify `N` with the length of `OpenList` and will not instantiate any part of `OpenList` that was previously uninstantiated. For example, the length of `[a,b,c|X]` should be 3.

**Exercise A.8.4.2**

Define a predicate which, when given two difference lists such as `[a|X]-X` or `[a,b,c, d|Y]-Y`, will append them. For example, starting with `[a,b,c|X]-X` and `[d,e,f|Y] -Y`, the predicate that you define should create `[a,b,c,d,e,f|Y]-Y`.

**Exercise A.8.4.3**

Rewrite the following predicate to make it run faster.

```
second_argument_is_zero(X) :- X =.. [_,_,0|_].
```

## A.9 SOME POINTS OF PROLOG STYLE

### A.9.1 Predicate Headers

Every nontrivial Prolog predicate in this book begins with a comment (called the HEADER) that describes what it does. For example:

```
% member(?X,?Y)
%   X is an element of list Y.
```

```
member(X,[X|_]).
member(X,[_|Y]) :- member(X,Y).
```

The header must say succinctly:

- what the predicate does;
- what each argument is for;
- what type of term each argument should be, if it matters (in this case, Y is a list but X could be anything).

Auxiliary predicates do not require headers. Recall that an auxiliary predicate exists only to complete a recursive loop that starts in the main predicate; in this book auxiliary predicates have names ending in _aux.

Notice that the names of the arguments are not the same in the header as in the various clauses. (Nor are they the same from clause to clause.) In the header, the arguments are given whatever names will best explain how they work. Here I used X and Y because more meaningful names did not seem appropriate; perhaps I should have used Element and List or E and L.

The question marks on ?X and ?Y mean "This argument may or may not be instantiated when this predicate is called." A plus sign, as in +X, denotes an argument that must be instantiated at time of call; a minus, as in -X, means that the argument is normally uninstantiated. Note that in most situations where you write -X you could actually write ?X, because if X *does* happen to be instantiated, nothing goes wrong; the query succeeds if X has the right value and fails otherwise. It is rare indeed for a Prolog predicate to *require* an argument to be uninstantiated.

**Exercise A.9.1.1**

Write headers, in this format, for the built-in predicates write, read, and name.

## A.9.2 Order of Arguments

When defining a predicate with multiple arguments, it is generally best to put the known (instantiated) arguments first and the arguments that return results last. Thus, if widget/2 computes Y from X, it should be defined as widget(+X,-Y), not widget(-Y,+X). In addition to helping the human user remember where things go, this helps take advantage of first argument indexing.

O'Keefe (1990:14-15) takes this idea further and puts arguments in the following order:

- First, the input (the arguments that are always known, if any);
- Second, any intermediate data that the predicate passes along from one recursive call to the next;
- Third, any "leftovers" or partly processed input;
- Last, the output (the result desired by the user).

Some predicates, of course, are REVERSIBLE (they can compute either argument from the other one); an example is name/2. In this case the order of arguments should be whatever seems most natural to the human user.

**Exercise A.9.2.1**

Define a predicate find_max_min/3 that finds the largest and smallest numbers in a list. Include a standard header and put the arguments in an order consistent with the above principles.

**Exercise A.9.2.2   (project)**

Implement, in any programming language, a "lint checker" for Prolog. A lint checker is a program that reads another program and identifies statements which, although they may be syntactically correct, usually indicate mistakes on the part of the programmer. Examples of "lint" in Prolog might include:

- Hyphen (minus sign) between atoms (the programmer may have thought names could include hyphens);
- Operator : – inside a comment (a clause may have been commented out accidentally);
- End-of-line occurring within a quoted atom or quoted string (the closing quote may have been left out);
- Clause that does not begin at the beginning of a line (the programmer may have put a period instead of a comma between subgoals in the previous clause);
- Variable used only once in a clause (either it's misspelled, or an anonymous variable should have been used);
- Functor or atom used only once in entire program (it's probably misspelled).

This is an open-ended project, and your lint checker is probably something you'll keep adding to.

# APPENDIX B

# String Input and Tokenization

## B.1 THE PROBLEM

Prolog does not provide the kind of input routine that a natural-language system needs. The Prolog reader expects all its input to be expressed in Prolog syntax, but the users of NLP systems do not necessarily know Prolog. A user should be able to type

```
How many employees do we have?
```

and have Prolog process it as the list of atoms

```
[how,many,employees,do,we,have,'?']
```

or something similar. This chapter will present two predicates that solve the problem:

- `read_atomics/1`, which converts a line of input into a list of atomic terms `[like,this]`, and
- `read_charlists/1`, which renders each word as a list of one-character atoms `[[l,i,k,e],[t,h,i,s]]` so that morphological analysis can be performed.

Both predicates convert all capital letters to lower case.

## B.2 BUILT-IN SOLUTIONS

A few Prologs already provide solutions to this problem. For example, LPA Prolog on the Macintosh has a built-in predicate that puts up a window, prompts the user to type a sentence, accepts the sentence, removes the window, and delivers the result to the Prolog program as a list of atomic terms.

The Quintus Prolog library predicate `read_in/1` converts sentences into lists of atomic terms. Unlike `read_atomics`, `read_in` can accept more than one sentence at a time; it doesn't stop until a sentence ends at the end of the line. For example:

```
?- read_in(X).
This is an example. Notice that
reading does not stop until the end
of a sentence occurs at the end
of a line.

X = [this,is,an,example,.,notice,that,reading,does,not,stop,
      until,the,end,of,a,sentence,occurs,at,the,end,of,a,line,'.']
```

To use `read_in` in your program, include the directive

```
:- ensure_loaded(library(read_in)).
```

at the beginning. Also look at `read_sent/1`, which is similar to `read_in` but more customizable.

## B.3 IMPLEMENTING A TOKENIZER

A routine that breaks a string into words or other meaningful units (TOKENS) is called a TOKENIZER. Fig. B.1 shows a tokenizing input routine that works well in most Prologs.[1] The tokenizer classifies characters into four types:

- END characters, which mark end of line;
- BLANK characters, which separate words;
- ALPHANUMERIC characters (letters and digits), which can be part of words; and
- SPECIAL characters (punctuation marks), which are treated as words by themselves.

The predicate `char_type/3` performs this classification and also translates capital letters to lower case. It does all its work by examining and manipulating ASCII codes; even the translation to lower case is simply a matter of adding 32 to the code.

The tokenizer itself is a kind of parser; it is deterministic (does not backtrack) and relies on one character of lookahead (because it must see the next character in or-

---

[1]But not Arity Prolog, in which get and get0 receive every keystroke the moment the user types it and do not allow backspacing for corrections. Tokenizers for Arity Prolog are provided on the program disk that goes with this book. They are based on the built-in predicates `read_line(FileHandle,T)`, which reads a line of input into an Arity compact string, and `list_text(S,T)`, which converts a compact string into a list of ASCII codes. The rest of the tokenizer then processes the list.

```
% read_atomics(-Atomics)
%  Reads a line of text, breaking it into a
%  list of atomic terms: [this,is,an,example].

read_atomics(Atomics) :-
    read_char(FirstC,FirstT),
    complete_line(FirstC,FirstT,Atomics).

% read_char(-Char,-Type)
%  Reads a character and runs it through char_type/1.

read_char(Char,Type) :-
    get0(C),
    char_type(C,Type,Char).

% complete_line(+FirstC,+FirstT,-Atomics)
%  Given FirstC (the first character) and FirstT (its type), reads
%  and tokenizes the rest of the line into atoms and numbers.

complete_line(_,end,[]) :- !.                   % stop at end

complete_line(_,blank,Atomics) :-               % skip blanks
    !,
    read_atomics(Atomics).

complete_line(FirstC,special,[A|Atomics]) :-    % special char
    !,
    name(A,[FirstC]),
    read_atomics(Atomics).

complete_line(FirstC,alpha,[A|Atomics]) :-      % begin word
    complete_word(FirstC,alpha,Word,NextC,NextT),
    name(A,Word),   % may not handle numbers correctly - see text
    complete_line(NextC,NextT,Atomics).

% complete_word(+FirstC,+FirstT,-List,-FollC,-FollT)
%  Given FirstC (the first character) and FirstT (its type),
%  reads the rest of a word, putting its characters into List.

complete_word(FirstC,alpha,[FirstC|List],FollC,FollT) :-
    !,
    read_char(NextC,NextT),
    complete_word(NextC,NextT,List,FollC,FollT).
```

**Figure B.1**   Tokenizing input routine for most Prologs. (Continues on page 320.)

```
complete_word(FirstC,FirstT,[],FirstC,FirstT).
   % where FirstT is not alpha

% char_type(+Code,?Type,-NewCode)
%  Given an ASCII code, classifies the character as
%  'end' (of line/file), 'blank', 'alpha'(numeric), or 'special',
%  and changes it to a potentially different character (NewCode).

char_type(10,end,10)  :- !.          % UNIX end of line mark
char_type(13,end,13)  :- !.          % DOS end of line mark
char_type(-1,end,-1)  :- !.          % get0 end of file code

char_type(Code,blank,32)  :-         % blanks, other ctrl codes
   Code =< 32,
   !.

char_type(Code,alpha,Code)  :-       % digits
   48 =< Code, Code =< 57,
   !.

char_type(Code,alpha,Code)  :-       % lower-case letters

   97 =< Code, Code =< 122,
   !.

char_type(Code,alpha,NewCode)  :-    % upper-case letters
   65 =< Code, Code =< 90,
   !,
   NewCode is Code + 32.             %  (translate to lower case)

char_type(Code,special,Code).        % all others
```

**Figure B.1   cont.**

der to decide whether the current character is the last one in the word). Accordingly, `read_atomics/1` reads the first character and passes it to `complete_line`. Then `complete_line` looks at the type of the current character and does one of four things: stops if it is an end character, skips it if it is a blank, calls `complete_word` if it is alphanumeric, or makes it into a word by itself if it is a special character.

## B.4 HANDLING NUMBERS CORRECTLY

We want `read_atomics` to recognize numbers as numbers; if the user types 253 we want to get the number 253, not the atom '253'. This is important, because sentences typed by the user can contain numeric data (*Whose income is over 25000?* and the like).

Whether numbers are recognized depends on the behavior of the built-in predicate
name/2. In Quintus, Arity, and LPA Prolog, the query

```
?- name(What,"253").
```

does indeed produce the number 253, and all is well.  But in ALS Prolog and Expert
Systems Limited Prolog-2, name(What,253) creates the atom '253'.  This is not
satisfactory.

The solution is to change the last clause of complete_line, so that instead of
calling name, it calls our own number-interpreting routine, name_num/2, defined in
Fig. B.2.

```
% name_num(-AtomOrNumber,+String)
%  Used in place of name/2 in last clause of complete_atomics
%  in versions of Prolog where name/2 does not recognize numbers.

name_num(Number,String) :-
  nonvar(String),
  string_number(String,Number),
  !.

name_num(Atom,String) :-
  name(Atom,String).

% string_number(+S,-N)
%  Converts string to corresponding number, e.g. "234" to 234.
%  Fails if S does not represent a nonnegative integer.

string_number(S,N) :-
   string_number_aux(S,0,N).

string_number_aux([D|Digits],Total,Result) :-
   digit_value(D,V),
   NewTotal is 10*Total + V,
   string_number_aux(Digits,NewTotal,Result).

string_number_aux([],Result,Result).

% digit_value(+Code,-Value)
%  Maps ASCII code for a digit ("0"..."9") onto value (0...9).

digit_value(Code,Value) :-
   48 =< Code, Code =< 57,
   Value is Code - 48.
```

**Figure B.2**   Substitute for name for Prologs in which name does not recognize numbers.

The algorithm in `name_num` is very simple: keep a running total (initially 0), accept digits one by one, and each time, multiply the running total by 10 and then add the value of the current digit. Thus:

| Digit | | | Total |
|---|---|---|---|
| (start) | | | 0 |
| 2 | $(0 \times 10) + 2$ | $=$ | 2 |
| 5 | $(2 \times 10) + 5$ | $=$ | 25 |
| 3 | $(25 \times 10) + 3$ | $=$ | 253 |

The first clause of `name_num` tries to convert every string to a number this way. If the conversion fails, control drops to the second clause, which calls `name` in the usual way. Thus `name_num` can handle both numbers and words.

Thus modified, the tokenizer still does not handle numbers that contain a decimal point. Making it do so would require two changes:

- Modifying `name_num` to accept the decimal point and properly interpret the digits after it;
- Modifying `complete_word` to keep the whole number together (right now it splits `"23.4"` into `[23,'.',4]`).

The second of these is the larger change, because it requires two characters of lookahead. Consider the string `"2. ␣"` (where ␣ denotes a blank). The tokenizer cannot decide whether 2 is the last character of a token until it has read not only the period, but also the blank following it. Accordingly, decimal numbers are not implemented here.

More sophisticated tokenizers first gather all the characters of a line into a list, and then use any appropriate parsing algorithm (such as DCGs) to parse the characters into words. This allows as much lookahead as necessary.

## B.5  CREATING CHARLISTS RATHER THAN ATOMS

For morphological analysis, we want words to appear as lists of characters `[[l,i,k,e], [t,h,i,s]]` rather than atoms. Fig. B.3 shows a tokenizer that packages them this way. It is similar to the original tokenizer but with minor changes throughout. No attempt is made to handle numbers.

## B.6  USING THIS CODE IN YOUR PROGRAM

The most foolproof way to incorporate any of these predicates into your program is to actually copy the predicate definitions into your file.

```
% read_charlists(-Charlists)
%  Reads a line of text, breaking it into a list of lists
%  of one-character atoms, [[l,i,k,e],[t,h,i,s]].
%  Makes no attempt to recognize numbers.

read_charlists(Charlists) :-
   read_char(FirstC,FirstT),
   complete_line(FirstC,FirstT,Charlists).

% read_char(-Char,-Type)
%  Reads a character and runs it through char_type/1.

read_char(Char,Type) :-
   get0(C),
   char_type(C,Type,Char).

% complete_line(+FirstC,+FirstT,-Charlists)
%  Given FirstC (the first character) and FirstT (its type),
%  reads and tokenizes the rest of the line into charlists.

complete_line(_,end,[]) :- !.                    % stop at end

complete_line(_,blank,Charlists) :-              % skip blanks
   !,
   read_charlists(Charlists).

complete_line(FirstC,special,[[A]|Rest]) :-      % special char
   !,
   name(A,[FirstC]),
   read_charlists(Rest).

complete_line(FirstC,alpha,[Word|Rest]) :-       % begin word
   complete_word(FirstC,alpha,Word,NextC,NextT),
   complete_line(NextC,NextT,Rest).

% complete_word(+FirstC,+FirstT,-List,-FollC,-FollT)
%  Given FirstC (the first character) and FirstT (its type),
%  reads the rest of a word, putting its characters into List
%  as one-character atoms.

complete_word(FirstC,alpha,[C|List],FollC,FollT) :-
   !,
   name(C,[FirstC]),
   read_char(NextC,NextT),
   complete_word(NextC,NextT,List,FollC,FollT).
```

**Figure B.3**   Tokenizer that produces charlists. (Continues on page 324.)

```
complete_word(FirstC,FirstT,[],FirstC,FirstT).
   % where FirstT is not alpha

% char_type(+Code,?Type,-NewCode)
%  Given an ASCII code, classifies the character as
%  'end' (of line/file), 'blank', 'alpha'(numeric), or 'special',
%  and changes it to a potentially different character (NewCode).

char_type(10,end,10)  :- !.          % UNIX end of line mark
char_type(13,end,13)  :- !.          % DOS end of line mark
char_type(-1,end,-1)  :- !.          % get0 end of file code

char_type(Code,blank,32)  :-         % blanks, other ctrl codes
   Code =< 32,
   !.

char_type(Code,alpha,Code)  :-       % digits
   48 =< Code, Code =< 57,
   !.

char_type(Code,alpha,Code)  :-       % lower-case letters
   97 =< Code, Code =< 122,
   !.

char_type(Code,alpha,NewCode)  :-    % upper-case letters
   65 =< Code, Code =< 90,
   !,
   NewCode is Code + 32.             %  (translate to lower case)

char_type(Code,special,Code).        % all others
```

**Figure B.3   cont.**

The second most foolproof way is to include, at the beginning of your program file, the goal

```
:- reconsult('filename').
```

This makes the Prolog system reconsult the specified file every time it consults or reconsults your program. This technique is generally reliable, but it takes time and can get into a loop if you inadvertently create two files that reconsult each other.

In Quintus Prolog and in the draft ISO standard, the directive

```
:- ensure_loaded('filename').
```

reconsults the specified file only if it has not already been reconsulted (thus saving time) and does not loop if two files ask for each other.

# Bibliography

ABRAMSON, H., AND DAHL, V. (1989) *Logic grammars.* New York: Springer.

AHO, A. V., AND ULLMAN, J. D. (1972) *The theory of parsing, translation, and compiling,* vol. 1, *Parsing.* Englewood Cliffs, New Jersey: Prentice-Hall.

AKMAJIAN, A.; DEMERS, R. A.; FARMER, A. K.; AND HARNISH, R. M. (1990) *Linguistics: an introduction to language and communication.* 3rd ed. Cambridge, Massachusetts: MIT Press.

ALAM, Y. S. (1983) A two-level morphological analysis of Japanese. *Texas Linguistic Forum* 22:229–252.

ALLEN, J. F. (1983) Maintaining knowledge about temporal intervals. *Communications of the ACM* 26:832–843. Reprinted in BRACHMAN AND LEVESQUE (1985) 509–521.

ALLEN, J. F. (1987) *Natural language understanding.* Menlo Park, California: Benjamin-Cummings.

ANDERSON, S. R. (1988a) Morphology as a parsing problem. In WALLACE (1988) 4–21. Also published in *Linguistics* 26:521–544.

ANDERSON, S. R. (1988b) Morphological theory. In NEWMEYER (1988, vol. 1) 146–191.

BACH, E. W. (1989) *Informal lectures on formal semantics.* Albany, New York: State University of New York Press.

BARTON, G. E. (1985) On the complexity of ID/LP parsing. *Computational Linguistics* 11:205–218.

BARTON, G. E.; BERWICK, R. C.; AND RISTAD, E. S. (1987) *Computational complexity and natural language.* Cambridge, Massachusetts: MIT Press.

BARTSCH, R. (1987) Context-dependent interpretation of lexical items. In GROENENDIJK, J.; DE JONGH, D.; AND STOKHOF, M., eds., *Foundations of Pragmatics and Lexical Semantics* (Groningen-Amsterdam Studies in Semantics, 7), 1–26. Dordrecht: Foris.

BARWISE, J., AND COOPER, R. (1981) Generalized quantifiers and natural language. *Linguistics and philosophy* 4:159–219. Reprinted in KULAS ET AL. (1988), 241–301.

BARWISE, J., AND ETCHEMENDY, J. (1991) *The language of first-order logic.* (CSLI Lecture Notes, 23.) 2nd ed. Stanford: Center for the Study of Language and Information.

BATES, M. (1978) The theory and practice of augmented transition network grammars. In BOLC (1978) 191–259.

BERWICK, R. C.; ABNEY, S. P.; AND TENNY, C., EDS. (1991) *Principle-based parsing: computation and psycholinguistics.* Dordrecht: Kluwer.

BLOOMFIELD, L. (1933) *Language.* New York: Holt, Rinehart, Winston. Reprinted 1984, Chicago: University of Chicago Press.

BLOOMFIELD, L. (1939) Menomini morphophonemics. *Travaux du cercle linguistique de Prague* 8:105–115. Reprinted in MAKKAI, V. B., ED., *Phonological theory,* 58–64. New York: Holt, Rinehart, Winston, 1972.

BLUM, B. I. (1966) Free-text inputs to utility routines. *Communications of the ACM* 9:525–526.

BOBROW, D. G. (1968) Natural language input for a computer problem-solving system. In MINSKY (1968) 135–215.

BOISEN, S. (1988) Pro-KIMMO: a Prolog implementation of two-level morphology. In WALLACE (1988) 31–53.

BOLC, L., ed. (1978) *Natural language communication with computers.* (Lecture Notes in Computer Science, 63.) Berlin: Springer.

BRACHMAN, R. J., AND LEVESQUE, H. J. (1985) *Readings in knowledge representation.* Los Altos, California: Kaufmann.

BRESNAN, J., ed. *The mental representation of grammatical relations.* Cambridge, Massachusetts: MIT Press.

BUCHMANN, B. (1987) Early history of machine translation. In KING (1987) 3–21.

CARDEN, G. (1986) Blocked forwards coreference, unblocked forwards anaphora: evidence for an abstract model of coreference. *CLS 22,* Part 1, 262–276. Chicago Linguistic Society.

CHARNIAK, E. (1973) Jack and Janet in search of a theory of knowledge. *Advance papers from the Third International Joint Conference on Artificial Intelligence [IJCAI],* 337–343. Los Altos, California: Kaufmann. Reprinted in GROSZ ET AL. (1986) 331–337.

CHIERCHIA, G. (1982) Bare plurals, mass nouns, and nominalization. *Proceedings, First West Coast Conference on Formal Linguistics (WCCFL I),* 243–255. Stanford University.

CHIERCHIA, G., AND MCCONNELL-GINET, S. (1990) *Meaning and grammar: an introduction to semantics.* Cambridge, Massachusetts: MIT Press.

CHOMSKY, N. (1957) *Syntactic structures.* The Hague: Mouton.

CHOMSKY, N. (1965) *Aspects of the theory of syntax.* Cambridge, Massachusetts: MIT Press.

CHOMSKY, N. (1982) *Lectures on government and binding.* Dordrecht: Foris.

CHOMSKY, N., AND HALLE, M. (1968) *The sound pattern of English.* New York: Harper and Row.

CHURCH, A. (1941) *The calculi of lambda-conversion.* Princeton: Princeton University Press.

COLMERAUER, A. (1978) Metamorphosis grammars. In BOLC (1978) 133-189.

COOK, V. J. *Chomsky's universal grammar: an introduction.* Oxford: Blackwell.

COOPER, R. (1983) *Quantification and syntactic theory.* Dordrecht: Reidel.

COTTRELL, G. W. (1989) *A connectionist approach to word sense disambiguation.* London: Pitman.

COVINGTON, M. (1984) *Syntactic theory in the High Middle Ages.* Cambridge, England: Cambridge University Press.

COVINGTON, M. (1989) *GULP 2.0: an extension of Prolog for unification-based grammar.* Research Report AI-1989-01, Artificial Intelligence Programs, The University of Georgia.

COVINGTON, M. (1990) Parsing discontinuous constituents in dependency grammar. *Computational Linguistics* 16:234–236.

COVINGTON, M; NUTE, D.; GOODMAN, D.; AND SCHMITZ, N. (1988) *From English to Prolog via discourse representation theory.* Research Report 01-0024, Artificial Intelligence Programs, The University of Georgia.

COVINGTON, M.; NUTE, D.; AND VELLINO, A. (1988) *Prolog programming in depth.* Glenview, Illinois: Scott, Foresman. (Second edition in preparation, to be published by Prentice-Hall.)

CRYSTAL, D. (1987) *The Cambridge encyclopedia of language.* Cambridge, England: Cambridge University Press.

CULLINGFORD, R. (1981) SAM and Micro-SAM. In SCHANK AND RIESBECK (1981) 75–135.

DAHL, V., AND SAINT-DIZIER, P., eds. (1985) *Natural-language understanding and logic programming.* Amsterdam: North-Holland.

DAHL, V., AND SAINT-DIZIER, P., eds. (1988) *Natural-language understanding and logic programming, II.* Amsterdam: North-Holland.

DATE, C. J. (1990) *An introduction to database systems,* vol. 1. 5th ed. Reading, Massachusetts: Addison-Wesley.

DE LA BRIANDAIS, R. (1959) File searching by using variable length keys. *Proceedings of the Western Joint Computer Conference* 15:295–298. New York: Institute of Radio Engineers.

DENES, P. B., AND PINSON, E. N. (1963) *The speech chain: the physics and biology of spoken language.* Bell Telephone Laboratories.

DOWTY, D. R. (1979) *Word meaning and Montague grammar.* Dordrecht: Reidel.

DOWTY, D. R. (1989) On the semantic content of the notion 'thematic role.' In CHIERCHIA, G.; PARTEE, B. H.; AND TURNER, R., eds., *Properties, types, and meaning,* vol. 2: *Semantic issues,* 69–130. Dordrecht: Kluwer.

DOWTY, D. R.; KARTTUNEN, L.; AND ZWICKY, A. M., eds. (1985) *Parsing natural language.* Cambridge, England: Cambridge University Press.

DYER, M. G. (1983) *In-depth understanding: a computer model of integrated processing for narrative comprehension.* Cambridge, Massachusetts: MIT Press.

EARLEY, J. (1970) An efficient context-free parsing algorithm. *Communications of the ACM* 13:94–102. Reprinted in GROSZ ET AL. (1986) 25–33.

EMONDS, J. E. (1976) *A transformational approach to English syntax.* New York: Academic Press.

ESTIVAL, D. (1990a) Generating French with a reversible unification grammar. *Proceedings of the 13th International Conference on Computational Linguistics (COLING 90),* 106–112.

ESTIVAL, D. (1990b) ELU: an environment for machine translation (project note). *Proceedings of the 13th International Conference on Computational Linguistics (COLING 90),* 385–387.

EVENS, M. W., ed. (1988) *Relational models of the lexicon: representing knowledge in semantic networks.* Cambridge, England: Cambridge University Press.

FILLMORE, C. (1968) The case for case. In BACH, E., AND HARMS, R. T., EDS., *Universals in linguistic theory,* 1–88. New York: Holt, Rinehart, and Winston.

FLECK, M. M. (1988) *Boundaries and topological algorithms.* Technical Report 1065, MIT Artificial Intelligence Laboratory.

FREDKIN, E. (1960) Trie memory. *Communications of the ACM* 3:490–499.

FROMKIN, V., AND RODMAN, R. (1988) *An introduction to language.* 4th ed. New York: Holt, Rinehart, and Winston.

GAL, A.; LAPALME, G.; SAINT-DIZIER, P.; AND SOMERS, H. (1991) *Prolog for natural language processing.* Chichester, England: Wiley.

GAZDAR, G.; FRANZ, A.; OSBORNE, K.; AND EVANS, R. *Natural language processing in the 1980s: a bibliography.* (CSLI Lecture Notes, 12.) Stanford: Center for the Study of Language and Information.

GAZDAR, G.; KLEIN, E.; PULLUM, G.; AND SAG, I. (1985) *Generalized phrase structure grammar.* Cambridge, Massachusetts: Harvard University Press.

GAZDAR, G., AND MELLISH, C. (1989) *Natural language processing in Prolog: an introduction to computational linguistics.* Wokingham: Addison-Wesley.

GERDEMANN, D. (1989) Restriction as a means of optimizing unification parsing. *Studies in the Linguistic Sciences* 19.1:81–92.

GERDEMANN, D. (1991) *Parsing and generation of unification grammars.* Cognitive science technical report CS-91-06, The Beckman Institute, Urbana, Illinois.

GRICE, H. P. (1975) Logic and conversation. COLE, P. AND J. MORGAN, EDS., *Syntax and semantics,* vol. 3, 41–58. New York: Academic Press.

GROSS, M. (1979) On the failure of generative grammar. *Language* 55:859–885.

GROSZ, B. J.; SPARCK JONES, K.; AND WEBBER, B. L. (1986) *Readings in natural language processing.* Los Altos, California: Kaufmann.

GRUBER, J. S. (1965) *Studies in lexical relations.* Thesis, Ph.D., Massachusetts Institute of Technology. Published as Part 1 of GRUBER (1976).

GRUBER, J. S. (1976) *Lexical structures in syntax and semantics.* Amsterdam: North-Holland.

HALLE, M. (1959) *The sound pattern of Russian.* The Hague: Mouton.

HERZOG, O., AND ROLLINGER, C. R., eds. (1991) *Text understanding in LILOG: integrating computational linguistics and artificial intelligence.* (Lecture Notes in Artificial Intelligence, 546.) Berlin: Springer.

HIRST, G. (1987) *Semantic interpretation and the resolution of ambiguity.* Cambridge: Cambridge University Press.

HOBBS, J. R. (1978) Resolving pronoun references. *Lingua* 44:311-388. Reprinted in GROSZ ET AL. (1986) 339–352.

HOBBS, J. R., AND SHIEBER, S. M. (1987) An algorithm for generating quantifier scopings. *Computational Linguistics* 13:47–63.

HORN, L. R. (1989) *A natural history of negation.* Chicago: University of Chicago Press.

HORNBY, A. S. (1989) *Oxford advanced learner's dictionary of current English.* 4th ed. Oxford University Press.

HORNSTEIN, H. (1984) *Logic as grammar: an approach to meaning in natural language.* Cambridge, Massachusetts: MIT Press.

HUDDLESTON, R. (1988) *English grammar: an outline.* Cambridge, England: Cambridge University Press.

HUDSON, R. A. (1988) Coordination and grammatical relations. *Journal of Linguistics* 24:303–342.

HUTCHINS, W. J. (1986) *Machine translation: past, present, future.* Chichester: Ellis Horwood.

IRONS, E. T. (1961) A syntax directed compiler for ALGOL 60. *Communications of the ACM* 4:51–55.

ISO. See: SCOWEN (1992).

JACKENDOFF, R. S. (1972) *Semantic interpretation in generative grammar.* Cambridge, Massachusetts: MIT Press.

JACKENDOFF, R. S. (1977) $\overline{X}$ *syntax: a study of phrase structure.* Cambridge, Massachusetts: MIT Press.

JESPERSEN, O. (1949) *A modern English grammar on historical principles,* part VII: *Syntax* (completed by NIELS HAISLUND). Copenhagen: Munksgaard.

JOHNSON, M. (1991) Features and formulae. *Computational Linguistics* 17:131–151.

JOHNSON, M., AND KLEIN, E. (1986) *Discourse, anaphora, and parsing.* Report No. CSLI-86-63. Center for the Study of Language and Information, Stanford University. Also in *Proceedings of the 11th International Conference on Computational Linguistics (COLING 86),* 669–675.

KAC, M. (1982) Review of Marcus (1980). *Language* 58:447–455.

KAMP, H. (1981) A theory of truth and semantic representation. In GROENENDIJK, J., ET AL. (eds.) *Formal methods in the study of language,* 277–322. University of Amsterdam. Reprinted in GROENENDIJK, J., ET AL. (eds.), *Truth, interpretation, and information* (Groningen-Amsterdam Studies in Semantics, 2), 1–40. Dordrecht: Foris.

KARTTUNEN, L. (1969) Discourse referents. Reprinted in McCAWLEY, J. D., ED., *Syntax and Semantics,* vol. 7: *Notes from the linguistic underground,* 363–385. New York: Academic Press.

KARTTUNEN, L. (1983) KIMMO: a general morphological processor. *Texas Linguistic Forum* 22:165–186.

KARTTUNEN, L., AND KAY, M. (1985) Parsing in a free word order language. In DOWTY ET AL. (1985) 279–306.

KARTTUNEN, L., AND WITTENBURG, K. (1983) A two-level morphological analysis of English. *Texas Linguistic Forum* 22:217–227.

KASHKET, M. (1991) Parsing Warlpiri, a free-word-order language. In BERWICK ET AL. (1991) 123–151.

KAY, M. (1980) *Algorithm schemata and data structures in syntactic processing.* Research report, Xerox Palo Alto Research Center. Reprinted in GROSZ ET AL. (1986) 35–70.

KAY, M. (1985) Parsing in functional unification grammar. In DOWTY ET AL. (1985) 251–278.

KHAN, R. (1983) A two-level morphological analysis of Rumanian. *Texas Linguistic Forum* 22:253–270.

KILBURY, J. (1984) *Earley-basierte Algorithmen für direktes Parsen mit ID/LP-Grammatiken.* KIT-Report 16, Institut für angewandte Informatik, Technische Universität Berlin.

KING, M., ed. (1983) *Parsing natural language.* London: Academic Press.

KING, M., ed. (1987) *Machine translation today: the state of the art.* Edinburgh: Edinburgh University Press.

KNUTH, D. E. (1973) *The art of computer programming,* vol. 3: *Sorting and searching.* Reading, Massachusetts: Addison-Wesley.

KOLODNER, J. L. (1984) *Retrieval and organizational strategies in conceptual memory: a computer model.* Hillsdale, New Jersey: Erlbaum.

KOSKENNIEMI, K. (1983) *Two-level morphology: a general computational model for word-form recognition and production.* Publication No. 11, Department of General Linguistics, University of Helsinki.

KULAS, J.; FETZER, J. H.; AND RANKIN, T. L., eds. (1988) *Philosophy, language, and artificial intelligence.* Dordrecht: Kluwer.

LANE, A. (1987) DOS in English. *Byte* 12.14 (December 1987) 261–264.

LEHNERT, W. G. (1988) Knowledge-based natural language understanding. In SHROBE, H. E., ED., *Exploring artificial intelligence: survey talks from the National Conferences on Artificial Intelligence,* 83–131. San Mateo, California: Kaufmann.

LEISS, H. (1990) On Kilbury's modification of Earley's algorithm. *ACM Transactions on Programming Languages and Systems* 12:610–640.

LEVINSON, S. C. (1983) *Pragmatics.* Cambridge, England: Cambridge University Press.

LUN, S. (1983) A two-level morphological analysis of French. *Texas Linguistic Forum* 22:271–278.

MARCUS, M. P. (1978) A computational account of some constraints on language. In WALTZ, D., ED., *Theoretical issues in natural language processing—2* (Urbana, Illinois: Association for Computational Linguistics), 236–246. Reprinted in GROSZ ET AL. (1986) 89–99.

MARCUS, M. P. (1980) *A theory of syntactic recognition for natural language.* Cambridge, Massachusetts: MIT Press.

MATSUMOTO, Y.; TANAKA, H.; HIRAKAWA, H.; MIYOSHI, H.; AND YASUKAWA, H. (1983) BUP: a bottom-up parser embedded in Prolog. *New Generation Computing* 1:145–158.

MATTHEWS, P. H. (1991) *Morphology.* 2nd edition. Cambridge, England: Cambridge University Press.

MATTHEWS, P. H. (1981) *Syntax.* Cambridge, England: Cambridge University Press.

MCCAWLEY, J. D. (1981) *Everything that linguists have always wanted to know about logic.* Chicago: University of Chicago Press.

MINSKY, M., ed. (1968) *Semantic information processing.* Cambridge, Massachusetts: MIT Press.

MONTAGUE, R. (1973) The proper treatment of quantification in ordinary English. In HINTIKKA, J., ET AL., eds., *Approaches to Natural Language,* 221–242, Dordrecht: Reidel. Reprinted in THOMASON, R. H., ED., *Formal philosophy: selected papers of Richard Montague,* 247–270, New Haven: Yale University Press, 1974. Also reprinted in KULAS ET AL. (1988), 141–162.

MOYNE, J. A. (1985) *Understanding language: man or machine.* New York: Plenum.

NAISH, L. (1986) *Negation and control in Prolog.* (Lecture Notes in Computer Science, 238.) Berlin: Springer.

NEWMEYER, F. J. (1983) *Grammatical theory: its limits and possibilities.* Chicago: University of Chicago Press.

NEWMEYER, F. J. (1986) *Linguistic theory in America.* 2nd edition. Orlando: Academic Press.

NEWMEYER, F. J., ed. (1988) *Linguistics: the Cambridge survey.* 4 vols. Cambridge, England: Cambridge University Press.

NILSSON, U. (1986) AID: an alternative implementation of DCGs. *New Generation Computing* 4:383–399.

NIRENBURG, S., ED. (1987) *Machine translation: theoretical and methodological issues.* Cambridge, England: Cambridge University Press.

NORVIG, P. (1991) *Paradigms of artificial intelligence programming: Case studies in Common Lisp.* San Mateo, California: Kaufmann.

NUTE, D. (1988) Defeasible reasoning: a philosophical analysis in Prolog. In FETZER, J. H., ed., *Aspects of artificial intelligence* 251–288. Dordrecht: Kluwer.

OBERMEIER, K. K. (1989) *Natural language processing technologies in artificial intelligence: the science and industry perspective.* Chichester: Ellis Horwood.

OJEDA, A. E. (1991) Definite descriptions and definite generics. *Linguistics and Philosophy* 14:367–397.

O'KEEFE, R. A. (1985) On the treatment of cuts in Prolog source-level tools. *Proceedings, 1985 Symposium on Logic Programming,* 68–72. IEEE Computer Society.

O'KEEFE, R. A. (1990) *The craft of Prolog.* Cambridge, Massachusetts: MIT Press.

OKUNISHI, T.; SUGIMURA, R.; AND MATSUMOTO, Y. (1988) Comparison of logic programming based natural language parsing systems. In DAHL, V., AND SAINT-DIZIER, P., eds., *Natural language understanding and logic programming, II,* 1–14. Amsterdam: Elsevier.

O'SHAUGHNESSY, D. (1987) *Speech communication: human and machine.* Reading, Massachusetts: Addison-Wesley.

PALMER, F. R. (1981) *Semantics.* 2nd edition. Cambridge, England: Cambridge University Press.

PALMER, M. S. (1990) *Semantic processing for finite domains.* Cambridge: Cambridge University Press.

PARSONS, T. (1970) An analysis of mass terms and amount terms. *Foundations of Language* 6:362–388. Reprinted in PELLETIER (1979:137–166).

PARSONS, T. (1990) *Events in the semantics of English.* Cambridge, Massachusetts: MIT Press.

PEARCE, D., AND WAGNER, G. Logic programming with strong negation. In SCHROEDER-HEISTER, P., ed., *Extensions of Logic Programming* (Lecture Notes in Artificial Intelligence, 475), 311–326. Berlin: Springer.

PELLETIER, F. J., ed. (1979) *Mass terms: some philosophical problems.* Dordrecht: Reidel.

PEREIRA, F. C. N. (1981) Extraposition grammars. *Computational Linguistics* 7:243–256.

PEREIRA, F. C. N. (1985) A new characterization of attachment preferences. In DOWTY ET AL. (1985:307–319).

PEREIRA, F. C. N., AND SHIEBER, S. M. (1987) *Prolog and natural-language analysis.* (CSLI Lecture Notes, 10.) Stanford: Center for the Study of Language and Information.

PEREIRA, F. C. N., AND WARREN, D. H. D. (1980) Definite clause grammars for language analysis—a survey of the formalism and a comparison with augmented transition networks. *Artificial Intelligence* 13:231–278. Reprinted in GROSZ ET AL. (1986) 101–138.

PEREIRA, F. C. N., AND WARREN, D. H. D. (1983) Parsing as deduction. *Proceedings, 21st Annual Meeting (ACL '83)*, 137–144. Association for Computational Linguistics.

PERES, J. (1991) Basic aspects of the theory of generalized quantifiers. In FILGUEIRAS, M.; DAMAS, L.; MOREIRA, N.; AND TOMÁS, A. P., eds., *Natural language processing* (Lecture Notes in Artificial Intelligence, 476), 141–157. Berlin: Springer.

PETZOLD, C. (1987) And here comes HAL. *PC Magazine* 6.4:109–122.

PULMAN, S. G.; RUSSELL, G. J.; RITCHIE, G. D.; AND BLACK, A. W. (1988) Computational morphology of English. *Linguistics* 26:545–560.

QUILLIAN, M. R. (1967) Word concepts: a theory and simulation of some basic semantic capabilities. *Behavioral Science* 12:410–430. Reprinted in BRACHMAN AND LEVESQUE (1985) 97–118.

QUIRK, R., AND GREENBAUM, S. (1973) *A concise grammar of contemporary English.* New York: Harcourt Brace Jovanovich.

QUIRK, R.; GREENBAUM, S.; LEECH, G.; AND SVARTVIK, J. (1985) *A comprehensive grammar of the English language.* London: Longman.

RADFORD, A. (1988) *Transformational grammar.* Cambridge, England: Cambridge University Press.

RAPHAEL, B. (1968) SIR: a computer program for semantic information retrieval. In MINSKY (1968) 33-134.

RITCHIE, G. D.; BLACK, A. W.; RUSSELL, G. J.; AND PULMAN, S. G. (1992) *Computational morphology.* Cambridge, Massachusetts: MIT Press.

ROEPER, T. (1988) Grammatical principles of first language acquisition: theory and evidence. In NEWMEYER (1988), vol. 2, 35–52.

ROSENKRANTZ, D. J., AND LEWIS, P. M., II (1970) Deterministic left corner parsing. *Proceedings, Symposium on Switching and Automata Theory,* 139–152. IEEE Computer Society.

ROSS, J. R. (1967) *Constraints on variables in syntax.* Dissertation, Massachusetts Institute of Technology. Published as *Infinite Syntax,* Norwood, New Jersey: Ablex, 1985.

ROSS, P. (1989) *Advanced Prolog: techniques and examples.* Reading, Massachusetts: Addison-Wesley.

RUSSELL, B. (1905) On denoting. *Mind* 14:479–493. Reprinted in DAVISON, D., AND HARMAN, G., eds., *The logic of grammar,* 184–193, Encino, California: Dickenson, 1975.

SCHANK, R. C. (1975) *Conceptual information processing.* Amsterdam: North-Holland.

SCHANK, R. C., AND ABELSON, R. P. (1977) *Scripts, plans, goals, and understanding.* Hillsdale, New Jersey: Erlbaum.

SCHANK, R. C., AND RIESBECK, C. K., eds. (1981) *Inside computer understanding: five programs plus miniatures.* Hillsdale, New Jersey: Erlbaum.

SCOWEN, R., ed. (1992) *Prolog: part 1, general core, committee draft 1.0.* (ISO/IEC JTC1 SC22 WG17 N92.) Teddington, England: National Physical Laboratory (for International Organization for Standardization).

SELLS, P. (1985) *Lectures on contemporary syntactic theories.* (CSLI Lecture Notes, 3.) Stanford: Center for the Study of Language and Information.

SHANN, P. (1991) Experiments with GLR and chart parsing. In TOMITA, M., ed., *Generalized LR Parsing,* 17–34. Boston: Kluwer.

SHAPIRO, S. C., editor-in-chief (1987) *Encyclopedia of artificial intelligence.* 2 vols. New York: Wiley.

SHIEBER, S. M. (1984) Direct parsing of ID/LP grammars. *Linguistics and Philosophy* 7:135–154.

SHIEBER, S. M. (1986) Using restriction to extend parsing algorithms for complex-feature-based formalisms. In SHIEBER, S. M., ET AL., eds., *A compilation of papers on unification-based grammar formalisms* part II, 36–58. Report No. CSLI–86–48, Center for the Study of Language and Information, Stanford University.

SIMPKINS, N. K., AND HANCOX, P. (1990) Chart parsing in Prolog. *New Generation Computing* 8:113–138.

SKOLEM, T. (1920) Logisch-kombinatorische Untersuchungen über die Erfüllbarkeit oder Beweisbarkeit mathematischer Sätze nebst einem Theoreme über dichte Mengen. Reprinted in SKOLEM, T., *Selected works in logic,* 252–263. Oslo: Universitetsforlaget, 1970.

SLATOR, B. M., AND WILKS, Y. PREMO: parsing by conspicuous lexical consumption. In TOMITA (1991) 85–102.

SMITH, G. W. (1991) *Computers and human language.* Oxford: Oxford University Press.

SPENCER, A. (1991) *Morphological theory: an introduction to word structure in generative grammar.* Oxford: Blackwell.

SPENCER-SMITH, R. (1987) Semantics and discourse representation. *Mind and Language* 2.1:1-26.

SPROAT, R. (1992) *Morphology and computation.* Cambridge, Massachusetts: MIT Press.

STOCKWELL, R. P.; SCHACHTER, P.; AND PARTEE, B. H. (1973) *The major syntactic structures of English.* New York: Holt, Rinehart, and Winston.

TAMURA, N.; NUMAZAKI, H.; AND TANAKA, H. (1991) Table-driven bottom-up parser in Prolog. In FURUKAWA, K.; TANAKA, H.; AND FUJISAKI, T., eds., *Logic Programming '89* (Lecture Notes in Artificial Intelligence, 485), 144–162. Berlin: Springer.

THOUIN, B. (1982) The METEO system. In LAWSON, V., ED., *Practical experience of machine translation,* 39–44. Amsterdam: North-Holland.

TOMITA, M. (1986) *Efficient parsing for natural language: a fast algorithm for practical systems.* Boston: Kluwer.

TOMITA, M., ed. (1991) *Current issues in parsing technology.* Boston: Kluwer.

TROST, H. (1991) Recognition and generation of word forms for natural language understanding systems: integrating two-level morphology and feature unification. *Applied artificial intelligence* 5:411–457.

TURING, A. (1950) Computing machinery and intelligence. *Mind* 59:433–460.

VENDLER, Z. (1957) Verbs and times. *Philosophical review* 66:143–160. Reprinted in VENDLER, Z., *Linguistics in philosophy,* 97–121, Ithaca: Cornell University Press, 1967.

WALLACE, K., ED. (1988) *Morphology as a computational problem.* UCLA Occasional Papers #7: Working Papers in Morphology. Department of Linguistics, University of California, Los Angeles.

WALLACE, M. (1984) *Communicating with databases in natural language.* Chichester, England: Ellis Horwood.

WANNER, E., AND MARATSOS, M. (1978) An ATN approach to comprehension. In HALLE, M.; BRESNAN, J.; AND MILLER, G. A., eds., *Linguistic theory and psychological reality,* 119–161. Cambridge, Massachusetts: MIT Press.

WEBBER, B. L. (1983) So what can we talk about now? In BRADY, M., AND BERWICK, R. C., eds., *Computational models of discourse,* 331–371. Reprinted in GROSZ ET AL. (1986) 395–414.

WEIZENBAUM, J. (1966) ELIZA—a computer program for the study of natural language communication between man and machine. *Communications of the ACM* 9:36–45.

WEIZENBAUM, J. (1976) *Computer power and human reason.* San Francisco: W. H. Freeman.

WILKS, Y. (1975) An intelligent analyzer and understander of English. *Communications of the ACM* 18:264–274. Reprinted in GROSZ ET AL. (1986) 193–203.

WINOGRAD, T. (1983) *Language as a cognitive process,* vol. 1: *Syntax.* Reading, Massachusetts: Addison-Wesley.

WOODS, W. A. (1970) Transition network grammars for natural language analysis. *Communications of the ACM* 13:591–606. Reprinted in GROSZ ET AL. (1986) 71–87.

# Index